Business Guide

to the

World Trading System

Second edition

International Trade Centre

Commonwealth Secretariat

ABSTRACT FOR TRADE INFORMATION SERVICES

1999   07.03
                                         BUS

INTERNATIONAL TRADE CENTRE UNCTAD/WTO (ITC)
COMMONWEALTH SECRETARIAT (CS)
Business Guide to the World Trading System. Second edition
Geneva: ITC/CS, 1999. xxiv, 329 pp.

Trade agreements, WTO, trade liberalization. Updated version of *Business Guide to the Uruguay Round* 1995 ed., reviewing developments that have taken place between 1996 and 1999 – provides overall picture of the WTO system; explains role of WTO as a forum for negotiations and as an organization for settling trade disputes; presents rules applicable to trade in goods as embodied in GATT 1994 and its associate Agreements; reviews the main features of the General Agreement on Trade in Services and the related commitments of member countries; explains rules applicable to government procurement and State trading; describes the provisions of the Agreement on Trade-Related Aspects of Intellectual Property Rights; provides an overview of issues under discussion in the six trade-related subject areas added to the WTO work programme; chapters provide an analysis of the business implications of the issues covered.

English, French, Spanish

ITC, Palais des Nations, 1211 Geneva 10, Switzerland
CS, Marlborough House, London, United Kingdom

ITC/P33.E/TSS/HRDS/99-VII   ISBN 0-85092-621.1

Preface

As world trade becomes more and more global, the rules of the world trading system are being continuously refined. The international business community is increasingly experiencing the impact of this process. For a better participation in the world trading system, it is thus necessary, now more than ever before, to understand clearly the business implications of these rules. This is especially so in developing and transition economies.

Shortly after the establishment of the World Trade Organization in January 1995 and the coming into effect of the Uruguay Round Agreements, the International Trade Centre UNCTAD/WTO (ITC), jointly with the Commonwealth Secretariat, published a *Business Guide to the Uruguay Round*. The Guide explained the legal framework for international trade resulting from these Agreements in simple language, emphasizing the business implications of specific provisions and rules.

The Guide was very well received by the business community, trade negotiators and foreign trade officials alike. More than 17,000 copies in English, French and Spanish were distributed and the Guide has since been translated by partner organizations into Arabic, Chinese, Greek, Romanian, Russian and other languages. More than 150 seminars and information events on the multilateral trading system have been organized for the business community in developing countries and transition economies, using the Guide as a comprehensive reference tool.

This second edition of the Guide, now entitled *Business Guide to the World Trading System*, has been produced in response to requests and suggestions received from a variety of users of the earlier edition. While maintaining the overall approach, this Guide goes beyond the Uruguay Round Agreements. It contains updates to reflect many of the developments which have taken place between 1996 and mid-1999, and incorporates a new section touching upon the issues in six trade-related subject areas that have been included in the WTO work programme for study and analysis, viz. trade and environment, trade and investment, trade and competition policy, transparency in government procurement, trade facilitation, and electronic commerce. While certainly not exhaustive in terms of current and forthcoming areas for discussions in international trade forums, this section provides examples of issues that may need to be addressed in the days to come.

The *Business Guide to the World Trading System* is user friendly. It assumes no prior knowledge on the part of the readers of the WTO legal system or of its rules. However, while the rules are explained in a manner that is easy to understand, care has been taken to ensure that the Guide correctly reflects the legal situation. It has been produced in close collaboration with the World Trade Organization and has been reviewed and approved by the WTO Secretariat.

The Guide emphasizes aspects important to persons engaged in or concerned with foreign trade and is addressed primarily to:

❑ Business enterprises, particularly small and medium-sized enterprises;

❑ Industries, and associations of industry and trade;

❑ Teaching, training and research institutions directly or indirectly associated with foreign trade.

This Guide is one of the outputs of the technical cooperation activities of the Commonwealth Secretariat and ITC, and marks another step in the collaborative venture between the two organizations.

The Commonwealth Secretariat has 34 member Governments which are full Members of WTO and four member Governments which are observers in, and seeking membership of, WTO. Through an active programme to enable Commonwealth developing countries to gain maximum benefits from the new multilateral trading system, the Secretariat is providing assistance to these countries for their improved and effective participation in ongoing work and negotiations in WTO; it also gives support in accession negotiations to countries which have applied for membership. A number of technical assistance packages have been developed to assist Governments of developing countries which are struggling with the complexities of multilateral trading agreements.

The focus of ITC programmes in this area is providing support to the business community, i.e. enterprises, business associations and support agencies in developing and transition economies. The programmes facilitate understanding of the business implications of the evolving trading system, and assist in maximizing the benefits that can be derived from the new opportunities and in coping with the challenges the system represents. The ITC World Tr@de Net programme, in particular, channels information on the rapidly evolving and constantly changing trading system to the business community. ITC also supports local initiatives to provide advisory and training services on WTO-related issues to the business sector.

We have little doubt that the business community will find this publication exceedingly useful as we approach yet another phase of work and negotiations in WTO. It will assist them not only to better understand the world trading system but also to draw maximum benefit from it. We thank all those who have contributed to the preparation of this Guide.

Chief Emeka Anyaoku
Secretary General
Commonwealth Secretariat

J. Denis Bélisle
Executive Director
International Trade Centre

Acknowledgements

Vinod Rege, former Director of GATT and current Adviser on WTO issues to the Commonwealth Secretariat, wrote and prepared this Guide.

R. Badrinath, Director, Division of Trade Support Services, ITC, and Richard Gold, Director, Export and Industrial Development Division, Commonwealth Secretariat, provided overall strategic direction.

Sabine Meitzel, ITC Senior Trade Promotion Officer, coordinated the production of the manuscript. Angela Strachan, Chief Programme Officer, coordinated activities for the Commonwealth Secretariat.

Leni G. Sutcliffe edited the Guide and Carmelita Endaya handled the desktop publishing.

Jean-Maurice Léger, Director, and Maarten Smeets, Counsellor, Technical Co-operation Division, WTO, coordinated the review and approval of the Guide and provided valuable comments and suggestions.

Contents

PART ONE

THE WORLD TRADE ORGANIZATION: ITS ROLE AND FUNCTIONS

CHAPTER 1

WTO: Forum for negotiations, dispute settlement and trade policy reviews

PART TWO
INTERNATIONAL RULES GOVERNING TRADE IN GOODS (GATT 1994 AND ITS ASSOCIATE AGREEMENTS)

CHAPTER 2
Four main rules of GATT

CHAPTER 3

Valuation of goods for customs purposes   65

CHAPTER 4

Preshipment inspection   72

CHAPTER 5

Mandatory and voluntary product standards, and sanitary and phytosanitary regulations   82

CHAPTER 6
Import licensing procedures

CHAPTER 7
Rules applicable to exports

CHAPTER 12

Rules of origin

CHAPTER 13

Trade-related investment measures

CHAPTER 14

Agreement on Textiles and Clothing

Part Three

INTERNATIONAL RULES GOVERNING TRADE IN SERVICES 189

PART SIX
SUBJECTS ADDED TO THE WTO WORK PROGRAMME FOR STUDY AND ANALYSIS

CHAPTER 21
Trade and environment

CHAPTER 22

Trade and investment 273

CHAPTER 25

Trade facilitation 307

CHAPTER 26

Electronic commerce 313

Index 319

Boxes

Note

The following abbreviations are used:

ADP	(Agreement on) Anti-dumping Practices
ASEAN	Association of South-East Asian Nations
ATC	Agreement on Textiles and Clothing
BOP	Balance of payments
CRF	Clean Reports of Findings
CTE	Committee on Trade and Environment
DSB	Dispute Settlement Body
EC	European Communities
EFTA	European Free Trade Association
FAO	Food and Agriculture Organization of the United Nations
FDI	Foreign direct investment
FPEI	Foreign portfolio equity investment
GATS	General Agreement on Trade in Services
GATT	General Agreement on Tariffs and Trade
GNP	Gross national product
GSP	Generalized System of Preferences
HS	Harmonized System
ICC	International Chamber of Commerce
IEC	International Electrotechnical Commission
IFIA	International Federation of Inspection Agencies
ILP	Import Licensing Procedures
IMF	International Monetary Fund
IPRs	Intellectual property rights
ISO	International Organization for Standardization
ITA	Information Technology Agreement
ITC	International Trade Centre UNCTAD/WTO
ITU	International Telecommunication Union
LDCs	Least developed countries
MAI	Multilateral agreement on investment
M&As	Mergers and acquisitions
MEAs	Multilateral environmental agreements
MERCOSUR	Southern Common Market
MFA	Multi-Fibre Arrangement
MFN	Most favoured nation
MIA	Multilateral investment agreement
MRAs	Mutual recognition agreements
NAFTA	North American Free Trade Agreement
NGOs	Non-governmental organizations

OECD	Organisation for Economic Co-operation and Development
PPM	Process and production method
PSI	Preshipment inspection
R & D	Research and development
SCM	(Agreement on) Subsidies and Countervailing Measures
SMEs	Small and medium-sized enterprises
SPS	(Agreement on) Sanitary and Phytosanitary Measures
TBT	(Agreement on) Technical Barriers to Trade
TMB	Textiles Monitoring Body
TPRM	Trade Policy Review Mechanism
TRIMs	(Agreement on) Trade-Related Investment Measures
TRIPS	(Agreement on) Trade-Related Aspects of Intellectual Property Rights
UNCITRAL	United Nations Commission on International Trade Law
UNCTAD	United Nations Conference on Trade and Development
UNDP	United Nations Development Programme
UN/ECE	United Nations Economic Commission for Europe
VERs	Voluntary export restraints
WCO	World Customs Organization
WIPO	World Intellectual Property Organization
WPPS	Working Party on Professional Services
WTO	World Trade Organization

Introduction

The World Trade Organization (WTO) came into existence on 1 January 1995 as a result of the Uruguay Round of Trade Negotiations. It is responsible for overseeing the multilateral trading system which has gradually evolved over the last 50 years. WTO also provides a forum for continuing negotiations to liberalize the trade in goods and services through the removal of barriers and to develop rules in new trade-related subject areas. The WTO Agreements have a common dispute settlement mechanism through which Members enforce their rights and settle the differences that arise between them in the course of implementation.

The improved and strengthened rule-based system that has come into existence with the establishment of WTO is designed to promote the expansion of international trade. The system's primary goal is to provide liberal, secure and predictable access to foreign markets for the goods and service products of exporting enterprises. The system helps to ensure that enterprises can market their products internationally under conditions of competition that are equitable and without the disruptions caused by the sudden imposition of restrictions. The rules give industries and business enterprises certain rights *vis-à-vis* their own governments, and grant exporters in some cases the right to defend their interests in their export markets against the imposition of measures affecting their trade.

Almost all countries – whether developed, developing, least developed or transitional – are now pursuing market-oriented policies, opening up their industries to international competition. In some developing countries, virtually all industries, large and small, today depend on foreign trade either as exporters or as importers. They have therefore the same vital interest as their counterparts in developed countries in seeing that the uniform rules embodied in the WTO legal instruments are applied by all countries.

The ability of industries and business enterprises to benefit fully from this rule-based system in today's rapidly globalizing economy depends on their knowledge and understanding of the detailed rules. These rules are both voluminous and complex. The texts of the legal instruments run to over 400 pages. They are supplemented by more than 22,000 pages of national schedules which list the specific liberalization commitments assumed by WTO member countries. It is usually difficult for business persons not familiar with the system to understand its legal language.

The Guide

This *Business Guide to the World Trading System* seeks to explain the system. It begins with an overview, which gives the reader an overall picture of the WTO legal system and of the benefits that the business community can derive from improved knowledge and understanding of the system.

The overview should be useful to those who wish to have a general idea of the system but whose needs do not call for a detailed knowledge of its rules. For those who require a deeper understanding, the overview should make it easier to follow the detailed explanations given later in the Guide.

The Guide is divided into six main Parts:

❑ Part One explains the role of the WTO as a forum for negotiations and as an organization responsible for reducing trade friction among countries and for settling disputes between them.

❑ Part Two, consisting of 15 chapters, presents the rules applicable to trade in goods as embodied in GATT 1994 and its associate Agreements. It also describes the results of the negotiations in terms of the liberalization of the trade in goods.

❑ Part Three reviews the main features of the rules of the General Agreement on Trade in Services and of the commitments that countries have assumed to liberalize this trade.

❑ Part Four explains the rules applicable to government procurement and State trading.

❑ Part Five describes the provisions of the Agreement on Trade-Related Aspects of Intellectual Property Rights.

❑ Part Six looks at the new subject areas on which analytical work is being carried out to determine whether negotiations within WTO on the development of new rules to cover their trade-related aspects would be desirable.

Most of the 20 chapters in Parts One to Five begin with a short summary of the main rules and related issues. This is followed by a more detailed description of the rules applicable to the respective subject areas. To facilitate reference to the provisions of the WTO legal instruments, the numbers of the relevant Articles are set out in the margins. Most chapters end with an analysis of the business implications of the issues covered.

Chapters 21 to 26 in Part Six describe the differing views that are being expressed in the discussions that are currently taking place in six new subject areas.

References and up-to-date information

The WTO Web site (*http://www.wto.org*) provides a continually updated source of information on the rules of the world trading system, the problems and issues that have arisen in their implementation, and the development of WTO's work. Business enterprises can obtain from this Web site information on WTO laws, enquiry and information points, the specific liberalization commitments undertaken by individual countries, and WTO's ongoing work.

To complement the above information on the WTO legal framework, ITC has created a Web page focusing on the business implications of the world trading system under its main Web site (*http://www.intracen.org*). It contains information on ITC activities within its World Tr@de Net programme as well as reference and training materials on selected business issues of the trading system.

Overview

This overview introduces the reader to the rules of the WTO system, briefly explains the progress achieved in trade liberalization and refers to the new trade-related subject areas on which WTO is currently carrying out analytical work in order to determine whether it would be desirable to develop WTO rules in those areas. The overview is divided into five sections.

The first section briefly traces the evolution of the multilateral trading system since the adoption of GATT in 1948 to the establishment of WTO in 1995 and describes its importance in today's rapidly globalizing economy. The second section provides a résumé of the principles and rules embodied in the legal instruments that now constitute the WTO system. The third gives a short description of the trade liberalization commitments undertaken by various countries in the Uruguay Round and in the negotiations that have taken place since then. The fourth section focuses on the work undertaken during the period 1995 to l998, including the decisions taken at WTO's two Ministerial Conferences to add new subject areas to the WTO work programme for further study and the proposals that are under consideration for the possible launching of a comprehensive round of negotiations on a wide range of subjects. This is followed in the fifth section by an explanation of the implications for business of the WTO system. It stresses that governments negotiated the legal instruments and improvements in access to foreign markets primarily for the benefit of their industries, business enterprises and the trading community. The basic responsibility for taking advantage of the new trade opportunities that have been created as a result now falls on the business and trading communities. To assist them in converting these opportunities into business orders and in their overall efforts to develop trade, the legal system provides them with security of access and creates certain rights in their favour. Their ability, however, to derive full advantage from the system will greatly depend on their knowledge and understanding of its rules.

An illustrative listing of the benefits and rights which the various legal instruments confer on industry and the trading community is contained in annex I to this overview. An analytical summary of the provisions on the special and differential treatment of developing and least developed countries which have been incorporated in the various Agreements is provided in annex II.

The WTO system and the evolving global economy

The evolving multilateral trading system

The multilateral trading system can be broadly defined as the body of international rules by which countries are required to abide in their trade relations with one another. The basic aim of these rules is to encourage countries to pursue open and liberal trade policies. These rules are continuously evolving. The existing rules are being clarified and elaborated to meet the changing conditions of world trade; at the same time rules covering new subjects are being added to deal with problems and issues that are being encountered.

Establishment of GATT

The first major effort to adopt rules to govern international trade relations was made by countries in the years immediately after the Second World War. These efforts resulted in the adoption in 1948 of the General Agreement on Tariffs and Trade (or GATT, as it is commonly known). Its rules apply to international trade in goods. Over the years, the text of GATT has been modified to include new provisions, particularly to deal with the trade problems of developing countries. In addition a number of associate Agreements which elaborate on some of the GATT's main provisions were adopted.

The Uruguay Round of Trade Negotiations

The rules of GATT and its associate agreements were further revised and updated to meet changing conditions of world trade in the Uruguay Round of Trade Negotiations which were held from 1986 to 1994. The text of GATT, along with the decisions taken under it over the years and several Understandings developed during the Uruguay Round, has come to be known as GATT 1994. Separate Agreements have been adopted in such areas as agriculture, textiles, subsidies, anti-dumping, safeguards and other matters; together with GATT 1994, they constitute the elements of the Multilateral Agreements on Trade in Goods. The Uruguay Round also resulted in the adoption of new set of rules governing trade in services and the trade-related aspects of intellectual property rights.

One of its other achievements is the establishment of WTO. GATT, under whose auspices these negotiations were launched, has ceased to be a separate organization and has been subsumed into WTO.

The WTO system

The WTO system as it has emerged from the Uruguay Round now consists of the following main substantive Agreements:

❑ Multilateral Agreements on Trade in Goods including the General Agreement on Tariffs and Trade (GATT 1994) and its associate Agreements;

❑ General Agreement on Trade in Services (GATS);

❑ Agreement on Trade-Related Aspects of Intellectual Property Rights (TRIPS).

Box 1 lists the legal instruments that now form the WTO system.

The responsibility for overseeing the implementation of these Agreements rests with WTO. The organization also acts as a forum for negotiations among countries for the further liberalization of the trade in goods and service products. It provides a mechanism for settling trade disputes among member countries. Any member country which considers that its trade is adversely affected because of the failure of another country to comply with the rules can bring the matter to WTO for settlement, if it fails to find a satisfactory solution through bilateral consultations.

Decisions on all important matters falling under its competence are taken at the Ministerial Conference of member countries. The Conference must meet at least once every two years.

Box 1

The main legal instruments negotiated in the Uruguay Round

A. Marrakesh Agreement Establishing the World Trade Organization

B. Multilateral agreements

1. *Trade in goods*

   ☐ *General Agreement on Tariffs and Trade (GATT 1994)*
      Associate Agreements

      Agreement on Implementation of Article VII of GATT 1994 (Customs Valuation)

      Agreement on Preshipment Inspection (PSI)

      Agreement on Technical Barriers to Trade (TBT)

      Agreement on the Application of Sanitary and Phytosanitary Measures (SPS)

      Agreement on Import Licensing Procedures

      Agreement on Safeguards

      Agreement on Subsidies and Countervailing Measures (SCM)

      Agreement on Implementation of Article VI of GATT 1994 (Anti-dumping) (ADP)

      Agreement on Trade-Related Investment Measures (TRIMs)

      Agreement on Textiles and Clothing (ATC)

      Agreement on Agriculture

      Agreement on Rules of Origin

   ☐ *Understandings and Decisions*

      Understanding on Balance-of-Payments Provisions of GATT 1994

      Decision Regarding Cases where Customs Administrations Have Reasons to Doubt the Truth or Accuracy of the Declared Value (Decision on Shifting the Burden of Proof)

      Understanding on the Interpretation of Article XVII of GATT 1994 (State trading enterprises)

      Understanding on Rules and Procedures Governing the Settlement of Disputes

      Understanding on the Interpretation of Article II:1(b) of GATT 1994 (Binding of tariff concessions)

      Decision on Trade and Environment

      Trade Policy Review Mechanism

2. *Trade in services*
   ☐ *General Agreement on Trade in Services (GATS)*

3. *Intellectual property rights (IPRs)*
   ☐ *Agreement on Trade-Related Aspects of Intellectual Property Rights (TRIPS)*

C. Plurilateral trade agreements

   Agreement on Trade in Civil Aircraft
   Agreement on Government Procurement

WTO and the global economy

The pre-WTO system, which was embodied in GATT, was sometimes regarded as a rich man's club as it was felt that it was primarily of interest to affluent developed countries. At the time of the launching of the Uruguay Round of trade negotiations (1986), only a comparatively small number of developing countries were showing active interest in the work of GATT by having permanent missions in Geneva. The situation, however, changed dramatically after the Round was launched. By the time the Round was completed and GATT was transformed into the World Trade Organization, a much larger number of these countries had been engaged and were continuing to engage in negotiations and discussions. The majority of them have now established permanent missions in Geneva. In addition, following the collapse of Communism, a number of transitional economies began applying for membership. At present, 134[1] countries are members of the WTO. In addition, 30 developing countries and transition economies are negotiating for accession. These include countries like China, the Russian Federation and Ukraine, which have a significant impact on international trade.

What has led to the change in the attitude towards membership of the WTO and why are countries showing greater interest in the rule-based system that has emerged from the Uruguay Round? The reasons for these are many but three of them are worth noting.

The first is related to the pace at which the world economy is globalizing through international trade and the flow of foreign direct investment. The revolutionary changes which have taken place in transport and communications now make it possible even for small manufacturers in developing countries to look for markets for their products in countries thousands of miles away. The facility with which goods can be transported from one country to another is, as some observers have stated, making the world a 'global village'.

Second, this process of globalization which has increased the dependence of countries on international trade is further accelerated by the shift in economic and trade policies noticeable in most countries. The collapse of communism has led to the gradual adoption of market-oriented policies in most countries where production and international trade had been State controlled. These countries, which in the past traded primarily among themselves, are increasingly trading on a worldwide basis. Many developing countries have discarded import substitution policies and are now pursuing export-oriented policies, under which they seek to promote economic growth by exporting more and more of their products.

Third, these liberal and open trade policies and the measures countries are taking to encourage foreign direct investment have prompted multinationals to obtain their components and intermediate products from countries where costs are lower and to establish production facilities there. Thus, increasingly, the products available on the market today – whether they are consumer items like ready-made garments, or consumer durables like refrigerators and air-conditioners, or capital goods – result from production processes undertaken in more than one country. Concrete evidence of the globalization of the world economy and the increasing dependence of countries on foreign trade is given in a recent advertisement from a multinational producing electrical household goods which proudly proclaims that its products are made up of components from as many as five or six countries.

This increasing dependence on foreign trade, both as exporters and as importers of goods and service products, has made governments and business enterprises aware of the vital role which the multilateral trading system can play in safeguarding their trade interests. The rule-based system assures them that the

---

1   On 21 May 1999, the General Council approved Estonia's entry into WTO. It will become
     the 135th WTO member 30 days after it notifies the Secretariat that it has completed its
     national ratification proceedings.

access which their products enjoy in foreign markets will not be suddenly disrupted by governmental measures such as the raising of tariffs or the imposition of prohibitions or restrictions on imports. The predictable and secured access which the system provides to foreign markets enables business enterprises to plan and develop production for export without fear that the foreign market may be lost as a result of restrictive government actions. Furthermore, what is often not widely known is that the system also provides certain rights to business enterprises. While most of these rights are available to them *vis-à-vis* their own governments, a few can be used against foreign governments.

The framework of rights and obligations which the WTO system has created therefore plays a crucial role in the development of trade in the fast globalizing world economy. The ability of governments and business enterprises to benefit from the system depends greatly on their knowledge and understanding of the rules of the system, the advantages they provide and the challenges they pose.

Main features of the WTO Agreements

Multilateral Agreements on Trade in Goods

Objective and principles

The basic objective of GATT, which lays down multilateral rules for trade in goods, is to create a liberal and open trading system under which business enterprises from member countries can trade with one another under conditions of fair competition. Even though the detailed rules which GATT and its associate agreements (*see* box 1) prescribe may appear complex and their legal terminology often bewildering, they are based on a few simple principles and rules. In effect, the entire framework of GATT is based on four basic rules. (*See* chapter 2.)

Four basic rules

Protection to domestic industry through tariffs

Even though GATT aims at the progressive liberalization of trade, it recognizes that its member countries may have to protect domestic production against foreign competition. However, it requires countries to provide such protection through tariffs. The use of quantitative restrictions is prohibited, except in a limited number of situations.

Binding of tariffs

Countries are urged to reduce and, where possible, eliminate protection to domestic production by reducing tariffs and removing other barriers to trade in multilateral trade negotiations. The tariffs so reduced are bound against further increases by being listed in each country's national schedule. The schedules are an integral part of the GATT legal system.

Most-favoured-nation (MFN) treatment

This important rule of GATT lays down the principle of non-discrimination. The rule requires that tariffs and other regulations should be applied to imported or exported goods without discrimination among countries. Thus it is not open to a country to levy customs duties on imports from one country at a rate higher than it applies to imports from other countries. There are, however, some exceptions to the rule. Trade among members of regional trading arrangements, which is subject to preferential or duty-free rates, is one such exception. Another is provided by the Generalized System of Preferences. Under this system, developed countries apply preferential or duty-free rates to imports from developing countries, but apply MFN rates to imports from other countries.

National treatment rule

While the MFN rule prohibits countries from discriminating among goods originating in different countries, the national treatment rule prohibits them from discriminating between imported products and domestically produced like goods, both in the matter of the levy of internal taxes and in the application of internal regulations.

Thus, it is not open to a country, after a product has entered its market on payment of customs duties, to levy an internal tax [e.g. sales tax or value-added tax (VAT)] at rates higher than those payable on a product of national or domestic origin.

Rules of general application

The four basic rules described above are complemented by rules of general application governing goods entering the customs territory of an importing country. These include rules which countries must follow:

❑ In determining the dutiable value of imported goods where customs duties are collected on an *ad valorem* basis (*see* chapter 3);

❑ In applying mandatory product standards, and sanitary and phytosanitary regulations to imported products (*see* chapter 5);

❑ In issuing licences for imports (*see* chapter 6).

The detailed rules applicable in these and other areas are contained in the relevant associate Agreements. The main features of these rules are described in box 2.

Other rules

In addition to the rules of general application described above, the GATT multilateral system has rules governing:

❑ The grant of subsidies by governments;

❑ Measures which governments are ordinarily permitted to take if requested by industry; and

❑ Investment measures that could have adverse effects on trade.

Rules governing the use of subsidies

Governments grant subsidies for diverse policy objectives. Such subsidies could in practice distort conditions of competition in international trade. The basic aim of GATT rules, which have been further elaborated by the Agreement on Subsidies and Countervailing Measures (SCM), is to prohibit or restrict the use of subsidies that have trade-distorting effects.

The SCM Agreement divides subsidies granted by governments in the industrial sector into prohibited and permissible subsidies.

Prohibited subsidies include export subsidies and subsidies that aim at encouraging the use of domestic rather than imported goods. Prior to the Uruguay Round, the rule prohibiting the use of export subsidies was mandatory only for developed countries. It now applies in principle also to developing

> **Box 2**
>
> ***Summary of GATT rules applicable at the border***
>
> *Determination of dutiable customs values. [See chapter 3.] The Agreement on Customs Valuation protects the interests of importers by stipulating that value for customs purposes should be determined on the basis of the price paid or payable by the importer in the transaction that is being cleared by Customs. However, Customs can reject the declared value when it has reasonable doubts about the truth or accuracy of the declared value. In all such cases, it has to give importers an opportunity to justify their declared value. Where Customs is not satisfied with the justification, the Agreement sets out a hierarchy of five alternative yardsticks which may be applied.*
>
> *Application of mandatory standards. [See chapter 5.] Countries often require imported products to conform to the mandatory standards they have adopted to protect the health and safety of their people. The Agreement on Technical Barriers to Trade provides that such product standards should not be formulated and applied in a way as to cause unnecessary barriers to trade. Towards this end it calls on countries to use international standards where they exist and, where they do not, to base their mandatory standards on scientific information and evidence.*
>
> *Application of sanitary and phytosanitary regulations. [See chapter 5.] Such regulations are applied by countries to protect their plant, animal and human life from the spread of pests or diseases that may be brought into the country by contaminated fruits, vegetables, meat and other food products. The Agreement on the Application of Sanitary and Phytosanitary Measures requires countries not to apply such regulations in a way that would cause unreasonable barriers to trade, urges them to base their regulations on scientific principles, and encourages them to adopt international standards and guidelines wherever possible.*
>
> *Import licensing procedures. [See chapter 6.] The Agreement on Import Licensing Procedures sets out guidelines for licensing authorities to follow in issuing import licences with a view to ensuring that the procedures do not have additional trade restricting effects.*

countries. The latter have, however, a transitional period of eight years (i.e. up to 1 January 2003) to modify their subsidy practices. Developing countries with a per capita gross national product (GNP) of less than US$ 1,000 which have been listed in the Agreement and least developed countries are exempted from the rule prohibiting export subsidies. (*See* chapter 8.)

Permissible subsidies are further divided into two categories: actionable and non-actionable. When imports of products receiving actionable subsidies cause *adverse* trade effects, the affected importing countries can have recourse to remedial measures. Such remedial measures can take the form of countervailing duties when the subsidized imports cause injury to the domestic industry (see below). However, importing countries cannot levy countervailing duties on products that have benefited from the limited number of subsidies that are considered non-actionable.

Measures which governments of importing countries can take if requested by domestic industry

The rules further stipulate that certain types of measures, which could have restrictive effects on imports, can ordinarily be imposed by governments of importing countries only if the domestic industry which is affected by increased imports petitions that such actions should be taken. These measures include:

- ❏ Safeguard actions. (*See* chapter 9.)
- ❏ Levy of anti-dumping and countervailing duties. (*See* chapters 8 and 11.)

Safeguard actions

The Agreement on Safeguards permits importing countries to restrict imports of a product for a temporary period by either increasing tariffs or imposing quantitative restrictions. Such safeguard actions can be resorted to only when it has been established through properly conducted investigations that a sudden increase in imports (both absolute and relative to domestic production) has caused or threatens to cause serious injury to the domestic industry. Safeguard actions cannot be taken if only one or two companies producing a product similar to the imported product are affected. They are permitted solely when it is established that increased imports are causing serious injury to the producers accounting for a major proportion of the total domestic production of a product similar to the imported product. (*See* chapter 9.)

The primary purpose of providing such temporary increased protection is to give the affected industry time to adjust to the increased competition that it will have to face after the restrictions are removed. The Agreement ensures that such restrictions are applied only for temporary periods by stipulating a maximum period of eight years for the imposition of a safeguard measure on a particular product.

Even though the initiative for the commencement of investigations can be taken by governments themselves, in most countries the practice is to initiate such investigations only on the basis of a petition from the affected industry.

Anti-dumping and countervailing duties

It is also open to governments to levy compensatory duties on imported products where it is alleged that foreign suppliers are resorting to unfair trade practices. The rules deal with two types of unfair practices that can distort conditions of competition in international trade.

The first is dumping of goods in foreign markets. The Agreement on Anti-dumping Practices (ADP) lays down strict criteria for the determination of dumping. It stipulates that a product should be treated as being dumped where its export price is less than the price at which it is offered for sale in the domestic market of the exporting country.

The second is unfair competition, which could result when a foreign company is able to charge low export prices because it has been subsidized by the government.

The ADP Agreement authorizes countries to levy anti-dumping duties on products that are being dumped. Likewise, the Agreement on SCM permits countries to levy countervailing duties on imported products that have benefited from subsidies.

The levy of such duties is, however, subject to two important conditions. First, the duties cannot be levied simply on the grounds that the product is being dumped or subsidized. It is essential for the importing country to establish, through investigations carried out at national level, that increased imports are causing material injury to the domestic industry. Second, as noted earlier, governments can initiate such investigations if a petition is submitted by or on behalf of the domestic industry claiming that dumped or subsidized imports are causing material injury to producers accounting for at least 25% of total domestic production. It should be noted that the standard for determining injury to industry in safeguard actions is much higher than that required for determining injury for the levy of countervailing duties. For safeguard actions, it must be established that the injury to the industry is serious, while for anti-dumping and countervailing measures, a lower standard of proof of material injury is adequate. The difference is due to the fact that in the case of the former, the problems of the domestic industry in the importing country are caused by fair foreign competition; in the case of the latter the problems arise from the unfair trade practices of foreign suppliers. The two Agreements further lay down factors (such as fall in turnover or profits or decline in the labour force) which should be taken into account by the investigating authorities in determining whether industry is being injured by imports. (*See* chapter 11.)

Trade-related investment measures (TRIMs)

Countries often impose conditions on foreign investors to foster diversified industrialization. Where they affect trade, such conditions are known as trade-related investment measures.

The Agreement on TRIMs, which has been negotiated in the Uruguay Round, now prohibits countries from using five types of measures (such as local content and trade-balancing requirements) which are considered to be inconsistent with the GATT rule of national treatment and the rule which prohibits the application of quantitative restrictions to imported products. (*See* chapter 13.)

General Agreement on Trade in Services (GATS)

Four modes of international trade in services

Services cover economic activities ranging widely from banking, insurance and telecommunications to recreation, cultural and sporting services. WTO has identified over 150 service subsectors.

One of the main characteristics of services is that they are intangible and invisible; goods, by contrast, are tangible and visible. These differences also influence the modes in which international trade transactions take place. While international trade in goods involves the physical movement of goods from one country to another, only relatively few service transactions involve cross-border movements. For most service transactions, proximity between the service provider and the consumer is necessary. Such proximity can be obtained either by establishing a commercial presence in the importing country (e.g. opening a branch) or through the movement of natural persons for a temporary period (e.g. a lawyer or architect moving to another country). In the case of a few service activities, consumers may have to move to the country of importation (e.g. tourism, where tourists travel to another country). (*See* chapter 17.)

Trade in services is growing and currently accounts for over 20% of all international trade. The General Agreement on Trade in Services, which was negotiated in the Uruguay Round, has created a framework for bringing this trade under international discipline. Its provisions apply to all the modes in which international trade in services takes place, viz:

❑ Cross-border movement of service products;

❑ The establishment of a commercial presence in the country where the service is provided;

❑ Temporary movement of natural persons to another country to provide a service there; and

❑ The movement of consumers to the country of importation.

Main provisions of GATS

The Agreement consists of:

❑ A framework text which lays down a set of general principles that apply to measures affecting trade in services.

❑ Specific liberalization commitments that apply to the service industries and sub-industries listed in each country's schedule.

MFN and national treatment

These two basic principles, which apply to trade in goods, now also apply to trade in services. However, they have been modified to take into account the special characteristics of trade in services.

Thus the Agreement requires countries to apply MFN treatment by not discriminating between service products and service providers of different countries. However, it may be possible for a country to maintain for a transitional period of 10 years (i.e. up to 1 January 2005) measures that are not consistent with the MFN principle.

The national treatment principle visualizes that countries should not treat foreign service products and service providers less favourably than their own service products and service providers. The Agreement, however, does not as in the case of trade in goods, impose this as an obligation to be applied across the board in all service sectors but requires countries to indicate in their schedules of concessions the sectors in which, and the conditions subject to which, such treatment would be extended.

Transparency requirements

In order to ensure that foreign service providers are fully aware of the regulations which apply to trade in services, countries are required to publish all relevant laws and regulations. Each country is further required to establish an enquiry point from which other member countries can obtain information on laws and regulations in the service sector.

Developed countries are in addition required to establish contact points from which service providers in developing countries can obtain information on, *inter alia*, the availability of service technology and the commercial and technical aspects of the supply of services.

Increasing participation of developing countries

The Agreement recognizes that as service industries in developing countries are not fully developed, they may have to maintain higher levels of protection. It therefore provides that they should have the flexibility, when making liberalization commitments, to open fewer sectors to import competition and to impose on foreign suppliers wishing to invest or establish a branch or a subsidiary conditions that are necessary to secure transfer of technology or to achieve other developmental objectives.

Liberalization commitments

The specific liberalization commitments assumed by countries in the Uruguay Round are contained in each country's schedule of concessions. They indicate, on a sector-by-sector basis and for each of the four modes in which trade in services takes place, the conditions subject to which countries have agreed to improve market access and to extend national treatment by eliminating or reducing the treatment discriminating against foreign suppliers in comparison to domestic suppliers. Since the conclusion of the Uruguay Round, negotiations on further trade liberalization have been held in the sectors of telecommunications and financial services.

The Agreement further imposes on countries obligations, *inter alia*, not to apply restrictions on international transfers and payments (except when they are in balance-of-payments difficulties) in sectors where they have made specific liberalization commitments.

Agreement on Trade-Related Aspects of Intellectual Property Rights (TRIPS)

The nature of intellectual property

The Agreement on TRIPS forms with the Multilateral Agreements on Trade in Goods and GATS the tripod for the WTO legal system. The objects of intellectual property are the creations of the human mind. The rights of creators of innovative or artistic work are known as intellectual property rights. They include copyright (which protects the rights of authors of books and other artistic creations), patents (which protect the rights of inventors) and industrial designs (which protect rights to ornamental designs). They also cover trademarks and other signs that traders use to distinguish their products from those of others and thus build consumer loyalty and goodwill for their marks or brand names.

Background to the negotiations on TRIPS

The unauthorized use of intellectual property is an infringement of the right of the owner. The years before the Uruguay Round witnessed a considerable increase in the production of, and international trade in, counterfeit and pirated goods. This was largely due to the unsatisfactory enforcement of trademark and copyright laws in many countries. In addition, patented technology was being used by manufacturers without licensing from patent owners. The standards of protection as well as the periods for which rights were protected also varied widely from country to country. (*See* chapter 20.)

Main provisions of the Agreement

The Agreement on TRIPS complements agreements on the protection of intellectual property rights developed by the World Intellectual Property Organization (WIPO). In particular, it prescribes minimum standards and periods for which protection should be granted to different intellectual property rights. In doing so it takes on board the standards laid down in the WIPO Conventions and adds some more, particularly in the area of patents. Countries are further required not to discriminate among foreign nationals and between foreign and their own nationals in the acquisition, scope and maintenance of IPRs (extension of MFN and national treatment). An important feature of the TRIPS Agreement is that the standards of protection laid down in the WIPO Conventions have been made legally enforceable.

Categorization of WTO member countries

The WTO system envisages four groups of member countries: developed, developing, least developed and transitional economies. At the 1998 Geneva Ministerial Conference, mention was made for the first time of "certain small economies" within the overall group of developing countries.[2]

All countries identified as 'least developed' by the United Nations system are treated as least developed countries under the WTO system. There are at present 48 countries in this category. There is however no agreed and precise definition for identifying in which group the remaining countries fall. The determination of whether a country is 'developing' is made in accordance with the principle of 'self-election'. Countries which in the past had centrally

---

2   The Ministerial Declaration of the Geneva Conference states, *inter alia*, that "We remain deeply concerned over the marginalization of the least-developed countries and certain small economies and recognize the urgent need to address this issue which has been compounded by chronic foreign debt problem facing many of them."

planned economies (belonging mainly to Eastern and Central Europe and the former Soviet Union) and which are now taking steps to adopt systems based on a free market and democracy are treated as transitional economies. The remaining member countries are regarded as developed countries.

Single undertaking rule

The multilateral legal instruments which constitute the WTO system are treated as a single undertaking. All WTO member countries (whether they are developed, developing, least developed or transitional) are required to adopt national legislation and regulations to implement the rules prescribed by the Multilateral Agreements on Trade in Goods, viz. GATT 1994 and its associate Agreements, GATS and the Agreement on TRIPS. The obligation to abide by the discipline of the plurilateral Agreements, however, applies only to WTO member countries which choose to accede to these Agreements. (Box 1 lists the multilateral and plurilateral Agreements.)

Provisions for the special and differential treatment of developing and least developed countries

The multilateral Agreements recognize that developing, including least developed, countries may have difficulties in accepting all or some of the obligations which they impose and provide for the extension of special and differential treatment to these countries. These provisions can be broadly divided into three categories:

❑ Provisions requiring countries (developed and developing) to take measures facilitating the trade of developing and least developed countries.

❑ Flexibility available to developing and least developed countries in accepting the obligations which the WTO Agreements impose.

❑ Provision of technical assistance to developing and least developed countries to build their capacity for implementing the Agreements.

An analytical summary of these provisions is given in annex II.

Procedures for dispute settlement

The WTO system provides a mechanism for the settlement of disputes when a country finds that another country is in breach of the rules and efforts to find satisfactory solutions through bilateral consultations fail. Disputes brought to WTO are generally the result of the information provided by industries or their associations to their governments on the difficulties they are encountering in marketing their products in outside markets. (*See* chapter 1.)

Even though throughout the process of dispute settlement – bilateral consultations, examination by the dispute settlement panel and later by the Appellate Body – it is the governmental representatives who participate, they rely heavily on advice and support on a continuing basis from the industry and associations which have an interest in the subject matter under dispute. The ability of the governments to pursue a case effectively or to defend their interests in a case brought against them depends greatly on the assistance and support provided by the industry groups concerned.

Mechanism for trade policy review

In addition to providing a mechanism for settling disputes, WTO acts as a forum for the periodic review of the trade policies of member countries. The objectives of these reviews are twofold. First, they aim at finding out how far the countries are following the disciplines of, and the commitments made under, the multilateral Agreements (and, where applicable, under the plurilateral Agreements). By carrying out such reviews periodically, WTO acts as a watch-dog to ensure that its rules are carried out and thus contributes to the prevention of trade friction. The provisions establishing the review mechanism, however, clarify that it is not intended to serve as a basis for enforcing obligations; nor should such reviews be used for the settlement of disputes. The second equally important objective of these reviews is to provide greater transparency and understanding of the trade policies and practices of member countries. (*See* chapter 1.)

Liberalization measures taken by countries as a result of commitments assumed in the Uruguay Round

Improvements in market access

In addition to providing a legal framework for the conduct of international trade, the multilateral trading system provides a forum for continuous negotiations for the liberalization of trade. As a result of successive rounds of negotiations in the past 50 years, a significant reduction in tariffs and other barriers to trade has been obtained. The Uruguay Round took important steps towards this reduction in barriers.

The industrial sector

Reductions in tariffs

As a result of reductions made in earlier rounds, the average tariff levels in developed countries on industrial products had come down from around 40% in 1948 when GATT was established to about 7% at the end of the Tokyo Round. In the Uruguay Round, these countries agreed to cut their tariffs by a further 40%, generally in five equal annual instalments. However, the percentage of tariff reductions on some products of export interest to developing countries, such as textiles and clothing and leather and leather products, is much lower than the average. A number of developing countries and economies in transition have also agreed to reduce their tariffs by nearly two-thirds of the percentage achieved by developed countries. As a result, the weighted level of tariffs applicable to industrial products is expected to fall as follows (*see* chapter 16):

❑ 6.3% to 3.8% in developed countries;

❑ 15.3% to 12.3% in developing countries;

❑ 8.6% to 6% in the transitional economies.

As a general rule, the process of staged reductions is to be completed by 1 January 2000, when the final rates resulting from percentage cuts agreed in the Uruguay Round will become fully applicable. In some cases a longer staging has been provided for by member countries.

Agreement on Textiles and Clothing

Another important achievement of the Uruguay Round is the decision to phase out restrictions on imports of textiles and clothing. These restrictions were imposed by certain developed countries mainly on imports from selected developing countries under bilateral agreements negotiated under the Multi-Fibre Arrangement (MFA), which provided an exception to the GATT rules prohibiting the use of discriminatory quantitative restrictions. The Agreement on Textiles and Clothing (ATC), which replaces MFA, provides for the removal of restrictions on textiles in four phases over a period of 10 years. This phasing-out programme will end on 1 January 2005. From then on, the trade in textiles will be completely integrated into GATT 1994 and will be governed by its rules. (*See* chapter 14.)

Agreement on Agriculture

In the past, the rules of GATT on the agricultural sector were either less rigorous or were applied leniently. Some developed countries in particular protected their costly and inefficient production of temperate zone agricultural products (e.g. wheat and other grains, meat and dairy products) by imposing, in addition to high tariffs, quantitative restrictions and/or variable levies on imports. This level of protection often resulted in increased domestic production which, because of high prices, could not be disposed of in international markets without export subsidies. Such subsidized sales depressed international prices. They also took away from efficient producers their legitimate market shares. (*See* chapter 15.)

The reform programme adopted under the Agreement on Agriculture, negotiated in the Uruguay Round, aims at establishing a fair and market-oriented trading system in agriculture. The negotiations undertaken in pursuance of these rules have resulted in some progress in the liberalization of trade in these products.

All countries have agreed to replace quantitative restrictions and other non-tariff measures on agricultural products with tariffs. The new 'tariffied' rates (arrived at by adding the incidence of non-tariff measures to existing tariffs) as well as other tariffs are being reduced over a six-year period (10 years for developing countries) starting 1995 by a simple average of 36% for developed countries (24% for developing countries). No tariff reduction has to be made by LDCs. In addition, all countries have bound all tariffs applicable to agricultural products. In most cases, however, developing countries have given bindings at rates that are higher than their current applied or reduced rates. Member countries using subsidies have agreed to reduce both production and export subsidies by agreed percentages. (*See* chapter 15.)

Estimates of income and trade gains

For business enterprises deciding on marketing strategies, it is important to know what gains – in terms of income and trade – will flow from the liberalization of trade. As regards measures to remove tariffs and other barriers to trade in goods, WTO and other organizations have carried out a number of studies at the macroeconomic level to assess the impact of these measures on world income and trade. Broadly speaking the various estimates of the gains from the Uruguay Round concluded that, when fully implemented, the liberalization measures agreed by governments would boost world income by 1% per year or by US$ 200 billion to US$ 500 billion annually. Estimates of the increase in the volume of world trade varied according to the assumptions made in the studies, and ranged from 6% to 20% per annum. However, the studies cautioned that these gains would not be evenly shared by countries in different regions. The developed and some of the developing countries at higher stages of development would be the main beneficiaries. Countries in Africa and the least developed countries would benefit only marginally, if at all. (*See* chapter 16.)

Need for caution in interpreting macroeconomic studies

While macroeconomic studies provide guidelines that may be useful to the business community, their findings have to be used with caution, particularly in planning for the future and in day-to-day decision-making. There are now definite indications that these estimates, which were made either before or immediately after the conclusion of the Uruguay Round, will have to be revised downwards substantially for two main reasons.

First, it has now become clear that, in certain areas, countries have implemented their liberalization commitments in form rather than in substance. For instance, most of the studies had estimated that the bulk of the trade gains would occur from the liberalization of trade in textiles. The studies had not foreseen that the countries maintaining restrictions would use the flexibility available under the rules to remove only a very small number of restrictions during the first seven years of the 10-year transitional period, and that consequently the bulk of restrictions would be removed only by 1 January 2005, when the transitional period ends.

Second, the studies had assumed that the world economy would grow at a normal pace and that there would not be any backsliding in growth. These expectations have been belied. The Asian financial crisis which began in mid-1997 and Japan's poor economic performance in 1998 have led to a general decline in demand, particularly in Asian markets, and a fall in the prices of oil and other commodities.

Liberalization may also have a varying impact on enterprises in different countries. Take the case of textiles, on which restrictions are applied on a discriminatory basis by importing countries. Enterprises in country A whose exports had been restricted may find that they can benefit from the removal of restrictions in their main markets and therefore adopt production and export strategies to take advantage of the improved opportunities for trade. By contrast, enterprises in country B whose exports had not been so restricted will have to prepare themselves to cope with the increased competition that will follow the removal of restrictions on imports from country A.

Likewise, enterprises from countries benefiting from preferential tariff access in their major developed markets may find this access cut back by the MFN reductions resulting from commitments made in the Uruguay Round. The macroeconomic studies indicated that the reductions in preferential margins might not have any overall negative effects on the trade of preference-receiving countries. However, individual exporting enterprises may find that the loss of these margins could, in fact, have adverse trade effects. This could happen if the preferential margins were meaningful in actual trade, taking into account such factors as the prices charged by other suppliers in the importing market.

It is therefore important for business enterprises to supplement macroeconomic studies with reviews of the impact of tariff reductions and the removal of barriers in their target markets on the products they export. As the lack of financial and technical resources may hamper enterprises, particularly SMEs, from carrying out such reviews themselves, national research institutions will have to take the initiative in this regard. International organizations like the Commonwealth Secretariat and ITC could also assist by undertaking such studies for products in which a number of developing and least developed countries have an export interest.

Developments since the establishment of WTO

WTO, as noted earlier, provides a forum for the consideration of issues of concern in international trade, for continuing negotiations on the further liberalization of trade and on the development of rules in new subject areas that are considered by member countries to have an impact on international trade. A number of developments that have taken place in 1995-1998 are described below.

Trade problems of least developed countries

The alleviation of the trade problems of LDCs was one of the important issues to which WTO paid special attention during the 1995-1998 period. As noted earlier, the trade of LDCs was expected to benefit only marginally from the tariff reductions and the removal of barriers resulting from the Uruguay Round. This, combined with the steady deterioration in the prices of the commodities they export and their supply-side constraints to developing production for export, has contributed to their further marginalization in international trade. In order to find solutions to these problems, most developed countries have, in pursuance of the decisions taken at the High-Level Meeting on Integrated Initiatives for Least-Developed Countries' Trade Development, held in October 1997, improved their generalized systems of preferences to allow duty-free imports of products exported by LDCs. Steps to enhance imports from these countries on a preferential basis have also been taken by a few developing countries while others are considering the feasibility of introducing such schemes.

The High-Level Meeting also endorsed an integrated programme for trade-related assistance to LDCs. Under this programme, trade-related assistance is being provided on a coordinated basis by six agencies – ITC, WTO, UNCTAD, UNDP, IMF and the World Bank – on the basis of an assessment of needs by individual LDCs. The areas in which assistance is now being provided include compliance with WTO rules and obligations for the alleviation of supply-side constraints such as infrastructure, human and institutional capacity building, and the needs of the private sector. The programme visualizes the organization of trade-related round tables by individual LDCs; these will involve the participation of bilateral development partners, other multilateral agencies and regional organizations interested in financing or expanding the technical assistance programmes already drawn up.

Negotiations for the further liberalization of trade

Some steps for the further liberalization of the trade in both goods and services were taken during the period by member countries. Countries with trade interests in information technology products agreed, under the Ministerial Declaration on Trade in Information Technology Products (dated 13 December 1996, also known as the Information Technology Agreement or ITA), to eliminate tariffs on such products as computers, telecommunications equipment, semiconductors, semiconductor manufacturing equipment, software and scientific instruments. Likewise, countries having an export interest in pharmaceutical products have added 450 products to the list of products on which they had agreed in the Uruguay Round to eliminate tariffs. Even though these concessions were negotiated among a limited number of countries, the concessions are being extended on a most-favoured-nation (MFN) basis. (*See* chapter 16.)

In the area of services, negotiations were held in certain sectors where the progress achieved in the Uruguay Round was not considered satisfactory. These negotiations have resulted in the adoption of packages containing liberalization commitments (in addition to those exchanged in the Round) in two services sectors, viz. financial services and telecommunications. Some progress, though of a limited nature, was also made in the negotiations on the movement of natural persons. In the area of professional services, the negotiations have resulted in the development of disciplines on domestic regulations in the accountancy sector.

Built-in agenda for the commencement of new negotiations

Some Agreements have built-in provisions for the commencement of new rounds of negotiations. Thus, GATS provides that negotiations for further trade liberalization in all services sectors should begin on 1 January 2000. The provisions of the Agreement on Agriculture also call on member countries to commence before the end of 1999 negotiations in the agricultural sector, also with a view to securing the further liberalization of trade in this sector. Preparatory work for the launching of negotiations in these sectors is currently underway in the relevant WTO committees.

Some Agreements further provide for the review of all or some of their provisions. The reviews are to be conducted on the basis of experience with implementation with the objective of determining whether any modifications to these provisions are necessary.

Decisions at the Ministerial Conference

As noted earlier, the main responsibility for taking actions and decisions to ensure the fulfilment of the objectives for which WTO was established rests with the biennial Ministerial Conference. WTO has had two Ministerial Conferences since its establishment. The first was held in Singapore in December 1996, and the second in Geneva in December 1998. The third is to be held in Seattle in November-December 1999.

At the Singapore and Geneva Ministerial Conferences, after reviewing developments in international trade and the problems and issues that have arisen in the implementation of the various WTO Agreements, the Ministers decided to include in the WTO work programme for study and analysis six new subject areas which, in the view of the countries suggesting their inclusion, have an impact on the development of international trade. These are:

- ❑ Trade and environment;
- ❑ Trade and investment;
- ❑ Trade and competition policy;
- ❑ Trade facilitation;
- ❑ Transparency in government procurement; and
- ❑ Electronic commerce.

The study and analysis of trade-related issues, problems and solutions in these subject areas are being undertaken by working groups or other bodies that have been specifically established for the purpose. It is important to note that there is no commitment at this stage on the part of member countries on the desirability or otherwise of engaging in WTO negotiations on rule-making in these areas. (*See* chapters 21-26.)

Launching new negotiations

The Geneva Ministerial Conference authorized the General Council to draw up a programme for possible future work and negotiations in WTO taking into account, *inter alia*:

- ❑ The issues and problems that have arisen in the implementation of the WTO Agreement;

❑ The provisions in the Agreement's built-in agenda;

❑ The new subjects on which analytical work is currently going on; and

❑ Any other subjects that may be suggested by member countries for inclusion in the agenda for negotiations.

The General Council will examine whether any new negotiations should be restricted to agriculture and services, negotiations on which are called for by the WTO's built-in agenda, or whether they should cover a larger number of subject areas, as did the previous Rounds.

The General Council expects to complete its work on drawing up a work programme well in advance of the third Ministerial Conference (scheduled to be held in Seattle from 30 November to 3 December 1999, as mentioned earlier) so that appropriate decisions on launching negotiations can be taken at that Conference.

Benefits to the business community of the WTO system

What is the relevance of the WTO system to the decisions that industries and business enterprises make in their international trade activities? When considering this question, one must bear in mind that governments have negotiated improved market access to enable business enterprises to convert trade concessions into trade opportunities. The objective behind the rule-based system is to ensure that the markets remain open and that this access is not disrupted by sudden and arbitrary impositions of import restrictions.

Business communities in a number of developing countries, however, continue not to be entirely aware of the advantages of the WTO trading system. The main reason for this is the immense complexity of the system, which has so far prevented these communities from taking an interest in, and getting acquainted with, its rules. It is, for instance, not widely known that the legal system not only confers benefits on producing industries and business enterprises but also creates rights in their favour.

Benefits conferred on the business community

The benefits which the legal system confers on business enterprises and the advantages they can derive from it can be viewed from two different perspectives:

❑ From the perspective of enterprises as exporters of goods and services;

❑ From the viewpoint of enterprises as importers of raw materials, and other inputs and services required for export production.

Benefits to exporters of goods and services

Security of access

In trade in goods, almost all tariffs of developed countries and a high proportion of those of developing and transitional economies have been bound against further increases in WTO. Binding ensures that the improved market access resulting from the tariff reductions agreed and incorporated into each country's schedule of concessions will not be disrupted by sudden increases in rates of duties or the imposition of other restrictions by importing countries. In trade in services, countries have made binding commitments not to restrict access to service products and foreign service suppliers beyond the conditions and limitations specified in their national schedules.

The secured access to markets which bindings provide enables exporting industries to make investment and production plans under greater conditions of certainty.

Stability of access

The system also provides stability of access to export markets by requiring all countries to apply the uniform set of rules elaborated by the various Agreements. Thus countries are obliged to ensure that their rules for determining dutiable value for customs purposes, for inspecting products to ascertain conformity to mandatory standards, or for the issue of import licences, conform to the provisions of the relevant Agreements.

Benefits to importers of raw materials and other inputs

Enterprises often have to import raw materials, intermediate products and services for export production purposes. The basic rule requiring imports to be allowed in without further restrictions upon payment of duties, and the obligation to ensure that the other national regulations applied at the border conform to the uniform rules laid down by the Agreements facilitate importation. They give exporting industries some assurance that they can obtain their requirements without delay and at competitive costs. Furthermore, tariff bindings serve to assure importers that their importing costs will not be increased by the imposition of higher customs duties.

Rights conferred on the business community

In addition to conferring benefits, the legal system has created certain rights in favour of business enterprises. These rights can be divided into two categories. In the first category are the rights of domestic producers and importers *vis-à-vis* their own governments. In the second are the rights of exporting enterprises to defend their interests when authorities in importing countries contemplate action to curtail their exports.

Rights of domestic producers and importers

A number of Agreements require the legislation of member countries to provide certain rights to domestic producers and importers. Governments are obliged to enforce some of these rights under their legal systems. In regard to other rights, governments are merely asked to use their *best endeavours* to ensure that the parties concerned can benefit fully from them.

Enforceable rights include those provided for by the Agreement on Customs Valuation which oblige governments to legislate that importers have a right:

❑ To justify declared value, where Customs expresses doubts about the truth or accuracy of that value; and

❑ To require Customs to give them in writing its reasons for rejecting the declared value, so that they can appeal to higher authorities against the decision.

Rights requiring governments merely to use their best endeavours include those covered by provisions of the Agreement on Import Licensing which call for import licences to be issued within specified periods after receipt of application.

In this example, unless the national legislation provides otherwise, the importer has a right only to expect that the licence will be issued within the stipulated time.

The claim to such rights is often subject to conditions that the domestic industry or enterprise must fulfil. For instance, as noted earlier, an industry has a right to request its government to take safeguard actions or to levy anti-dumping or countervailing duties only if it is possible for the petitioning producing units to satisfy the investigating authorities that its request is supported by producers which account for a substantial proportion of total production. The investigating authorities are further required to ascertain whether the petitioner has such standing before commencing investigations.

Rights of exporting enterprises

An example of the rights which the Agreements create in favour of exporting enterprises is the right to give evidence during investigations in importing countries for the levy of anti-dumping or countervailing duties.

When the authorities in the importing countries fail to honour their rights, the exporting enterprises cannot approach them directly for redress. They must take the matter up with their own governments and leave it to the latter to pursue it on a bilateral basis with the government of the importing country and, if necessary, to raise it under WTO procedures for the settlement of differences and disputes.

Illustrative list of rights

Annex I presents an illustrative list of the benefits and rights which the various legal instruments confer on industry and the trading community. They are taken up in detail in the various chapters of this Guide.

Effective utilization of WTO dispute settlement procedures

Knowledge of the system will also enable the business and trading communities to help their governments to take full advantage of the WTO mechanism for the surveillance of the implementation of the Agreements and for the settlement of differences and disputes. Governments will be able to take up issues for discussion and solution in the appropriate committees only if the exporting enterprises bring marketing problems resulting from violation of the rules to their notice. Furthermore, governments can raise a complaint under the WTO dispute settlement procedures only if the affected industry first raises the complaint and provides the required information.

Influencing the future course of negotiations

The responsibility of producing and exporting enterprises, however, should not end with bringing to the notice of their governments the practical problems they are encountering. They and their national associations must exercise continuous vigilance and closely follow the ongoing work of WTO. It is important to note that negotiations do not cease with the adoption of Agreements. Further negotiations with important implications for trade are often held during the implementation stage, particularly during the reviews that are undertaken periodically to examine how the Agreements are operating and to determine whether any changes or modifications to their provisions are necessary. Feedback from the business community on the practical problems it has encountered (such as the technical regulations or sanitary and phytosanitary measures applied to imports by importing countries) would greatly assist governments in securing appropriate modifications to the Agreements.

In addition, analytical work on six new subject areas is currently being undertaken in WTO, with a view to finding out whether the elaboration of WTO rules in these areas would be appropriate. The views of the business communities on the desirability or otherwise of such rules and of how their interests and concerns can be taken into account if such rules are developed are of vital importance to governments in deciding on the policy approaches they should adopt in the related negotiations.

Business communities will be able to ensure that their interests and concerns are fully reflected by their governments only by closely following reviews of Agreements and negotiations on the adoption of rules in new subject areas. Among the difficulties these communities and other interest groups face in keeping abreast with developments in WTO work is the fact that WTO meetings are closed to the public; furthermore the documentation and reports on these meetings are restricted. Member countries have recently taken steps towards greater transparency by providing that documents should ordinarily be derestricted after a period of six months. The reports of the panels and of the Appellate Body in dispute settlement cases are derestricted at the time of their issue. All such documents are now available to the general public on the WTO Web site.

There is increasing recognition that non-governmental organizations (NGOs), representing different interests such as business, environment and development circles, consumers, trade unions and farmers, can play an important role in increasing public awareness of WTO activities, provided they are informed regularly and systematically on these activities. The WTO Secretariat has been seeking to improve its contacts with civil society by arranging periodic issue-specific symposia on subjects like trade and the environment, trade and development, and trade facilitation. NGOs are allowed to attend plenary sessions of the Ministerial Conferences, and are regularly briefed by the WTO Secretariat on the Conferences' working sessions. It is important to note in this context that one of the issues that will be addressed in the coming years is making WTO work more transparent by providing greater access to information on WTO activities.

Taking advantage of liberalization measures

In addition to assisting governments in developing the policy approaches they should adopt in discussions on the implementation of the rules of the Agreements and on negotiations on rule-making, the business community has primary responsibility for converting tariff reductions and liberalization commitments into opportunities for trade by adopting appropriate export promotion and development strategies. Detailed knowledge of the concessions obtained on goods and service products of actual and potential interest to the community would be necessary for evolving such strategies.

Summing up

It is important to note that trade does not expand automatically as a result of tariff reductions and the removal of trade barriers. This will happen only if business enterprises adopt appropriate export development strategies that take into account the impact of the liberalization measures on the products they export.

The implementation of current liberalization measures and those that may be agreed in the future creates both opportunities and challenges for the business community. The challenge comes from the increased competition in both domestic and foreign markets that follows the removal of tariffs and other barriers. The WTO system is expected to ensure that such increased competition remains fair and equitable. The legal system has also created in favour of the business community a number of rights. As has been said repeatedly, the community's ability to benefit from the system and these rights will depend on its knowledge and understanding of the system's detailed rules.

The chapters that follow elaborate on the points made in this overview, explain in detail the rules of the Agreements and the progress made in improving market access, and provide an outline of the main issues that are under discussion in the subject areas that have been added to the WTO work programme for study and analysis.

Annex I

Illustrative list of benefits arising from the WTO system

Binding of concessions and commitments

Business implication   Security of access to foreign markets

Rights of exporters   *Trade in goods*. Right to expect that the exported product will not be subject to customs duties that are higher than the bound rates or that the value of the binding will be reduced by the imposition of quantitative and other restrictions.

Trade in services. Right to expect that access of service products and of foreign service suppliers to a foreign market will not be made more restrictive than indicated by the terms and conditions given in the country's schedule of commitments.

Rights of importers   *Trade in goods*. Right to expect that imported raw materials and other inputs will not be subject to customs duties at rates higher than the bound rates.

Trade in services. Right to expect that the domestic service industries will be permitted to enter into joint ventures or other collaboration arrangements, if the conditions provided in the schedule of commitments are complied with.

(*See* chapter 2.)

Valuation of goods for customs purposes (Agreement on Customs Valuation)

Business implication   Assurance that the value declared by the importer will, as a rule, be accepted as a basis for determining the value of imported goods for customs purposes.

Rights of importers   Importers have a right:

❑ To expect that they will be consulted at all stages of the determination of values;

❑ To justify the declared value, where Customs expresses doubts about the truth or accuracy of the declared value or about the documents submitted;

❑ To require Customs to give in writing the reasons for rejecting the declared value, so that they can appeal to the higher authorities against the decision.

(*See* chapter 3.)

Use of preshipment inspection services (Agreement on Preshipment Inspection)

Business implications | By assisting governments in controlling such malpractices as the overvaluation and undervaluation of imported goods, PSI services help improve the trading environment. Experience has shown that these services speed up clearance of goods through Customs and reduce customs-related corruption.

Rights of exporters | Exporters to developing countries using mandatory PSI services have a right:

❑ To be informed of the procedures that PSI companies follow for physical inspection and price verification;

❑ To expect that any complaint they may have regarding the prices determined by the inspectors is considered sympathetically by designated higher officials in the PSI company; and

❑ To appeal to the Independent Review Entity when they are not satisfied with the decisions of the above-mentioned senior officials.

Benefits to importers | Importers benefit as:

❑ The utilization of PSI services speeds up customs clearance and in some cases reduces customs-related corruption,

❑ The physical inspection carried out by PSI companies prior to price verification provides an assurance that imported products will conform to the quality and other terms of the contract.

(*See* chapter 4.)

Import licensing procedures (Agreement on Import Licensing Procedures)

Business implication | Assures importers and foreign suppliers that for products for which import licences are required these licences will be issued expeditiously.

Rights of importers | Importers and foreign suppliers have a right to expect:

❑ That the procedures adopted for the issue of licences at the national level conform to the guidelines prescribed by the Agreement;

❑ That they will not be penalized unduly for clerical and other minor errors in the application;

❑ That the licences will be issued within the time periods prescribed by the Agreement.

(*See* chapter 6.)

Rules applicable to exports

Reimbursement of indirect taxes borne by exported products

Rights of exporters | Exporters have a right to expect that they will be:

❑ Either exempted from payment of, or reimbursed for, customs duties on inputs used in the manufacture of exported products,

❑ Reimbursed for all indirect taxes borne by the exported products.

Export duties | In addition, exporters have a right to expect that where governments levy export duties for revenue or other considerations, these will be applied at the same rates to exports to all destinations.

(*See* chapter 7.)

Anti-dumping and countervailing actions

Rights of exporters

❏ Right to expect that exporters alleged to be dumping or exporting subsidized products will be notified immediately after the investigations begin.

❏ Right to give evidence to defend their interests in such investigations.

❏ Right to expect that procedures will be terminated when preliminary investigations establish that the dumping margin/subsidy element is *de minimis* and imports are negligible.

Rights of domestic producers

Right to petition for the levy of anti-dumping or countervailing duties where dumped or subsidized imports are causing material injury to the domestic industry, provided the petition is supported by producers accounting for at least 25% of the industry's production.

(*See* chapter 11.)

WTO Agreements: provisions on special and differential treatment of developing countries – An analytical summary

General

The WTO Agreements contain provisions for the extension of special and differential (S&D) treatment to developing countries. Under these provisions, developing countries are given "more favourable" treatment than developed countries.

These provisions can be broadly divided into three categories:

❑ Provisions requiring countries to take measures to facilitate the trade of developing and least developed countries (LDCs);

❑ Flexibility available to developing and least developed countries in accepting the obligations imposed by the WTO Agreements;

❑ Provisions for technical assistance to developing and least developed countries in building their capacity to implement the Agreements.

An illustrative and selective description of the nature and content of the most important provisions in each of these categories is given below.

Provisions requiring countries to take S&D measures to facilitate the trade of developing countries

The S&D measures falling in this category include:

❑ Unilateral measures taken by developed countries to allow imports on a preferential basis from developing countries;

❑ Giving priority in trade negotiations to the reduction and elimination of MFN tariffs on products of interest to developing countries and LDCs;

❑ Extension of S&D treatment to developing and least developed countries in the application of

– Quota restrictions,

– Import licensing procedures, and

– Contingency protection measures, such as safeguard actions, and anti-dumping and countervailing measures.

Unilateral measures adopted by developed countries to allow imports on a preferential basis

Generalized System of Preferences (GSP)

Imports originating in developing and least developed countries are allowed entry, under GSP, on a duty-free or preferential duty basis. GSP covers almost all industrial products and selected agricultural products.

The legal basis for these preferential arrangements is provided by the Decision on Differential and More Favourable Treatment, Reciprocity and Fuller Participation of Developing Countries (adopted in 1979 and commonly known as the General Enabling Clause). However, GSP arrangements:

❑ Carry built-in restrictions like country quotas: imports up to quota limits are allowed on a preferential duty basis; imports exceeding quota limits are charged MFN duties.

❑ Deny preferential access to imports of certain products from countries which have become competitive (competitive need criteria).

❑ Deny preferential access to developing countries which have moved on to a higher stage of development or have failed to respect human rights. Countries reaching a certain per capita income level are said to have reached a higher stage of development.

More favourable treatment for LDCs

The General Enabling Clause provides that, under GSP, "special treatment" beyond that extended to developing countries may be given to LDCs. In pursuance of this, developed countries agreed at the October 1997 High-Level Meeting on Integrated Initiatives for Least-Developed Countries' Trade Development to allow imports of all products of interest to these countries on a duty-free preferential basis. Furthermore, the limitations built into GSP (e.g. quota limitations and competitive country criteria) are not generally applied to imports from LDCs.

Arrangements providing preferential access to a limited number of developing countries

These arrangements include:

❑ The Lomé Convention, under which the European Union allows imports from ACP countries on a preferential duty-free basis.

❑ The Caribbean Basin Initiative (CBI), under which imports from Caribbean countries are allowed into the United States on a duty-free preferential basis.

As there is no legal basis under WTO law for these arrangements, they are allowed to be implemented under waivers. The waiver period for the Lomé Convention, which expires on 1 January 2000, may be extended for a period of five years (i.e. up to 1 January 2005).

Priority in the reduction and elimination of tariffs in trade negotiations

Action by developed countries

Trade in goods

GATT's chapter on trade and development (Part IV) calls on developed countries to give high priority in trade negotiations to the reduction and, where possible, the elimination of MFN tariffs on products of interest to developing and least developed countries and to the removal of non-tariff measures affecting trade in such products.

The reduction of MFN tariffs, however, narrows the preferential margins available to beneficiary developing countries under preferential arrangements. The ground rules adopted in the GATT rounds of negotiations have recognized the need to consider, on a case-by-case basis, the possibility of excluding from MFN reductions tariffs on identified products in which developing countries enjoy a preferential advantage that is meaningful in trade terms.

Trade in services

The General Agreement on Trade in Services provides that developed countries should give priority in trade negotiations to liberalizing the service sectors and modes of supply of special export interest to developing countries.

Action by developing countries

The GATT's Part IV also encourages developing countries to take measures similar to those which developed countries are expected to take and to give priority to the removal of tariffs and other barriers to trade on products of interest to other developing countries.

Further, the General Enabling Clause permits developing countries to extend special and more favourable treatment to imports from LDCs under the regional or global preferential arrangements adopted by them for the expansion of trade among themselves on a regional and global basis.

Quantitative and other restrictions

The Uruguay Round has brought about the removal of a large number of quantitative restrictions in the agricultural and industrial sectors and the elimination of restrictive measures such as voluntary export restraints and variable levies. The only quantitative restrictions permitted now include the following:

❏ Restrictions imposed under the provisions of the Agreement on Textiles and Clothing.

❏ Restrictions imposed by countries in balance-of-payments difficulties, provided they are consistent with Articles XII and XVIII of GATT 1994 and with the Understanding on Balance-of-Payments Provisions of GATT 1994 (adopted in the Uruguay Round).

❏ Restrictions imposed in accordance with the other exception provisions of GATT 1994, particularly those provided by Article XX.

It should be noted that the Agreement on Textiles and Clothing provides that countries maintaining restrictions (mainly developed countries) should remove them in four stages over a period of 10 years ending on 1 January 2005. Furthermore, in order to provide increased access to the textile products that remain subject to restrictions during the transition period, the Agreement stipulates that a mandatory growth factor should be applied to existing rates of growth in bilateral quotas. These rules provide for the special and more favourable treatment of "small suppliers" and LDCs in regard to base quota levels, growth rates and flexibility requirements, among other matters.

Import licensing procedures

The Agreement on Import Licensing Procedures lays down principles and rules to ensure that the import licensing procedures adopted by countries (for the administration of quota restrictions and other purposes) do not create barriers to trade. These rules provide that special consideration should be given in the distribution of licences to imports from developing countries, particularly LDCs.

Contingency protection measures (safeguard actions, anti-dumping and countervailing measures)

Contingency protection measures are import restriction measures which countries are permitted to take in certain situations, provided specified conditions are met. The measures include:

❑ Safeguard actions to restrict imports where increased imports of a product are causing serious injury to domestic producers of like or competitive products.

❑ Levy of anti-dumping duties on dumped imports and countervailing duties on subsidized imports where such increased imports are causing injury to the domestic industry.

The rules provide for the extension of S&D treatment in the application of such measures. For instance:

❑ The Agreement on Safeguards provides that imports from a developing country should be exempt from safeguard measures if its share in the imports of the product concerned into the country taking the measure is less than 3%. This exemption does not apply if developing countries with individual shares in imports smaller than 3% collectively account for more than 7% of imports.

❑ The Agreement on Subsidies and Countervailing Measures requires the authorities to terminate investigations in the situations described below:

– In the case of a product originating from a developed country where the amount of subsidy is *de minimis* (i.e. less than 1%), or the volume of subsidized imports or injury to domestic industry is negligible.

– In the case of a product originating from a developing country when:

• The level of subsidies granted does not exceed 2% of the value calculated on a per unit basis;

• The subsidized imports are less than 4% of total imports into the importing country. However, the rules do not apply when developing countries with individual shares of less than 4% collectively account for more than 9% of total imports.

Provisions providing developing and least developed countries flexibility in accepting WTO obligations

These provisions can be broadly divided into the following groups:

❑ Flexibility in accepting binding obligations during trade negotiations;

❑ Flexibility for providing increased protection for temporary periods to encourage the development of new industries, and for taking restrictive measures when in balance-of-payments difficulties.

❑ Transition periods for accepting all or some of the obligations which the Agreements impose;

❑ Exemption of developing countries from certain specified obligations.

Flexibility in accepting binding obligations in trade negotiations

Trade in goods

According to GATT rules, negotiations on the reduction of tariffs and other barriers to trade should be conducted on a reciprocal and mutually advantageous basis. However, Part IV of GATT 1994 (which carries provisions on the promotion of economic development) provides that developing countries should not be required to make contributions in trade negotiations (in the form of tariff reductions and bindings) that are inconsistent with their trade, development and financial needs. The Part IV provisions are complemented by the General Enabling Clause which, *inter alia*, states that the capacity of countries to make contributions and negotiated concessions improves with the progressive development of their economies.

The rules thus visualize that the contributions which developing countries should be required to make should be related to their stage of development. This concept is often referred to as 'relative reciprocity'. During the Uruguay Round, developing countries thus reduced tariffs in both the industrial and agricultural sectors at percentage rates which were lower than those applied by developed countries.

The rule calling for across-the-board reductions in tariffs on a percentage basis was not applied to LDCs. In the industrial sector, these countries made a token reduction in tariffs on a very small number of products. In the agricultural sector they were not required to make any reductions.

Furthermore, developing and least developed countries could bind their tariffs at rates higher than their applied or reduced rates. Such ceiling bindings give them the flexibility to raise their tariffs to the higher bound rates, without infringing their GATT obligations, if they consider this necessary to provide increased protection to domestic industrial and agricultural production.

Trade in services

Article XIX of the General Agreement on Trade in Services gives developing countries the flexibility to open fewer sectors or to liberalize fewer types of transactions in trade negotiations, thus making explicit their right to take liberalization measures in line with their development situations. It also recognizes that offers of market access by developing countries may be subject to conditions aimed at strengthening their domestic services capacity and the transfer of technology on commercial terms. Article XIX further calls for special consideration to be given to LDCs.

Flexibility in providing increased protection for the development of new industries and in taking restrictive measures when in balance-of-payment difficulties

Protective measures for the development of new industries

Article XVIII:C of GATT 1994 permits developing countries to take trade restrictive measures (such as raising bound rates of duty or imposing quantitative restrictions) to promote the development of new industries or the further development of an established industry. However, such measures, which are inconsistent with the provisions of GATT, may be introduced only after approval by WTO member countries. GATT lays down procedures for consultations with countries whose trade interests may be adversely affected by the restrictive measures being contemplated.

Measures in balance-of-payment difficulties

The provisions permitting countries to take measures to restrict imports when they are in balance-of-payment difficulties are contained in Articles XII and XVIII of GATT. Article XII lays down the circumstances and conditions under which restrictions may be imposed by developed countries. Article XVIII applies to developing countries. It recognizes that, because of a number of factors (such as the failure of export earnings to grow while demand for imports is increasing), these countries may have to resort to trade restrictions to prevent a decline in its monetary reserves. It prescribes more flexible and less stringent criteria for the invocation of its provisions than those set out in Article XII.

Under Article XII, for instance, trade restrictive measures may be taken by a developed country when the threat of a serious decline in its monetary reserves is "imminent" or when their level is "very low". Under Article XVIII, a developing country may take restrictive actions when it considers that there is a threat of a serious decline in monetary reserves even though the threat may not be "imminent". Article XVIII further states that a developing country may take such actions if in its view its monetary reserves are "inadequate" to cover expected foreign exchange payments; by contrast, under Article XII such actions may be taken only if reserves are "very low".

Transition periods for accepting obligations

The multilateral Agreements constituting the WTO system are binding on all member countries. However, some of these Agreements recognize that it may not be possible for a number of developing countries and for LDCs to accept immediately all or some of the obligations they impose. These Agreements therefore provide for transition periods varying between 5 to 11 years to enable these countries to prepare themselves for accepting their obligations.

Here are some examples of the transition periods provided:

❏ Agreement on Customs Valuation: developing and least developed countries may delay the application of the Agreement by a period of five years, i.e. by 1 January 2000.

❏ Agreement on Trade-Related Aspects of Intellectual Property Rights: developing countries are expected to apply the provisions of the Agreement by 1 January 2000, and least developed countries by 1 January 2006.

The application of some obligations may be delayed, as illustrated below:

❏ Agreement on Customs Valuation: a developing country may request, over and above the five-year period of transition, an additional period of three years for the application of the provisions on the computed value methodology.

❏ Agreements on the Application of Sanitary and Phytosanitary Measures and Technical Barriers to Trade: these authorize their respective Committees to grant to a developing country time-limited exceptions, in whole or in part, from the obligations which the two Agreements impose.

Exemption of developing countries from specified obligations or additional flexibility in complying with obligations

Agreement on Subsidies and Countervailing Measures

An illustration of the exemption of developing countries from certain obligations is provided by the Agreement on Subsidies and Countervailing Measures. The Agreement's rule prohibiting member countries from using export subsidies does not apply to least developed countries and developing countries with per capita incomes of US$1,000 per annum or less. The latter countries are listed in the Agreement.

Agreement on Agriculture

An example of the additional flexibility given to developing countries in complying with obligations is provided by the Agreement on Agriculture. The Agreement prohibits countries which have not made reduction commitments from granting export subsidies for agricultural products. As most developing countries have not given such commitments, the prohibition applies to them. However, the Agreement does allow them to grant two types of subsidies:

❑ Subsidies to reduce the costs of marketing exports, including handling, upgrading and other processing costs, and the costs of international transport; and

❑ Internal transport charges on export shipments on terms more favourable than for domestic shipments.

The Agreement further requires countries to reduce domestic support (i.e. subsidies other than export subsidies) by an agreed percentage. In order to encourage agricultural and rural development, developing countries are permitted to exclude from the Aggregate Measurement of Support which is calculated for this purpose the following subsidies:

❑ Investment subsidies generally available to agriculture in a developing country;

❑ Input subsidies generally available to low-income or resource-poor producers;

❑ Subsidies to encourage diversification from narcotic crops.

Technical assistance to build capacity for implementing the Agreements

A number of WTO Agreements carry provisions calling on all member countries (developed, developing and transitional), the WTO Secretariat and other international organizations having competence in the areas covered by them to provide technical assistance to developing and least developed countries for developing the institutional and legal framework and capacities for implementing the Agreements.

PART ONE

The World Trade Organization: Its role and functions

CHAPTER 1

WTO: Forum for negotiations, dispute settlement and trade policy reviews

Summary

WTO is the umbrella organization responsible for the surveillance of the implementation of:

❑ *GATT and its associate agreements,*
❑ *GATS,*
❑ *Agreement on TRIPS, and*
❑ *WTO's other legal instruments.*

WTO provides a forum for continuous negotiations among its member countries for the further liberalization of the trade in goods and services and for discussions on other trade-related issues that may be selected for the development of rules and disciplines.

In addition, it carries out periodic reviews of the trade policies of individual member countries. It is also responsible for settling trade disputes among its member countries on the basis of the rules of its legal instruments.

By 31 May 1999, WTO had 134 members. In addition, 30 countries were negotiating for membership.[3]

WTO: Its objectives, functions and structure

Objectives and mandate

The WTO is the umbrella organization responsible for overseeing the implementation of all the multilateral and plurilateral Agreements that have been negotiated in the Uruguay Round and those that will be negotiated in the future. Its basic objectives are similar to those of GATT, which has been subsumed into WTO. These objectives have been expanded to give WTO a mandate to deal with trade in services. Furthermore, they clarify that, in promoting economic development through the expansion of trade, adequate attention has to be given to protecting and preserving the environment. (*See* box 3.)

Marrakesh Agreement
Establishing the World
Trade Organization (WTO
Agreement), Preamble

Functions

The Agreement establishing WTO provides that it should perform the following four functions:

---

3   On 21 May 1999, Estonia's application for membership was accepted by the General Council; it will become the WTO's 135th member 30 days after it notifies the Secretariat of the completion of its national ratification proceedings.

> ### Box 3
> ### Objectives of WTO
>
> *In its preamble, the Agreement Establishing the World Trade Organization reiterates the objectives of GATT. These are: raising standards of living and incomes, ensuring full employment, expanding production and trade, and allowing for the optimal use of the world's resources. The preamble extends these objectives:*
>
> ❑ *To trade in services.*
>
> ❑ *To the need to promote 'sustainable development' and to protect and preserve the environment in a manner consistent with various levels of national economic development.*
>
> ❑ *To the need for positive efforts to ensure that developing countries, and especially the least developed among them, secure a better share of the growth in international trade.*

WTO Agreement,
Article III:1

First, it shall facilitate the implementation, administration and operation of the Uruguay Round legal instruments and of any new agreements that may be negotiated in the future.

WTO Agreement,
Article III:2

Second, it shall provide a forum for further negotiations among member countries on matters covered by the Agreements, on new issues falling within its mandate, and on further liberalization of trade.

WTO Agreement,
Article III:3

Third, it shall be responsible for the settlement of differences and disputes among its member countries.

WTO Agreement,
Article III:4

Fourth, it shall be responsible for carrying out periodic reviews of the trade policies of its member countries.

Structure

WTO Agreement,
Article IV:1

The apex WTO body responsible for decision-making is the Ministerial Conference, which meets every two years. Since the establishment of WTO, two Ministerial Conferences have been held: the first in Singapore in December 1996 and the second in Geneva in May 1998. The third is to be held in Seattle from 30 November to 3 December 1999.

WTO Agreement,
Article IV:2

During the two years between meetings, the functions of the Conference are performed by the General Council.

WTO Agreement,
Article IV:3

The General Council meets as a Dispute Settlement Body when it considers complaints and takes necessary steps to settle disputes between member countries. It is also responsible for carrying out reviews of the trade policies of individual countries on the basis of the reports prepared by the WTO Secretariat.

The General Council is assisted in its work by the:

WTO Agreement,
Article IV:5

❑ Council for Trade in Goods, which oversees the implementation and operation of GATT 1994 and its associate Agreements;

❑ Council for Trade in Services, which oversees the implementation and operation of GATS; and

❑ Council for TRIPS which oversees the operation of the Agreement on TRIPS.

Annex I to this chapter contains a chart showing the organizational structure of WTO. It also indicates the various committees established by the WTO Agreement itself and the other committees that have been established for detailed work at the operational level under the various associate Agreements.

Decision-making process

WTO Agreement,
Article IX:1

The Agreement stipulates that WTO shall continue the GATT practice of decision-making by *consensus*. Consensus is deemed to have been reached when, at the time a decision is being taken, not a single member country voices opposition to its adoption.

When a consensus is not possible, the WTO Agreement provides for decision by majority vote, with each country having one vote.[4]

Despite these provisions, decisions on all important policy matters (like launching negotiations in areas not so far covered by the WTO legal instruments) are expected to continue to be taken by consensus. The rule of consensus prevents 'tyranny of the majority' particularly where a sizeable section of opinion strongly opposes the decision being taken.

There are, however, a few cases where special voting requirements are prescribed. These are listed in box 4.

Box 4

Special voting requirements

The Agreement lays down different voting requirements for decisions in the following cases:

❏ *The interpretation of the provisions of any of the agreements requires a three-fourths majority. [WTO Agreement, Article IX:2]*

❏ *Amendments generally require a two-thirds majority. However, amendments to:*

    – *The provisions in the WTO Agreement on amendments and decision-making, and*

    – *MFN provisions in GATT 1994, GATS and the TRIPS Agreement*

    will take effect only upon acceptance by all members. [WTO Agreement, Article X:1, 2]

❏ *Requests for a temporary waiver by any member country from its WTO obligations require a three-fourths majority. [WTO Agreement, Article IX:2]*

The WTO Secretariat

WTO Agreement,
Article VI:1

WTO is located at Geneva, Switzerland. It is headed by a Director-General, who is assisted by three Deputy Directors-General. They are appointed by the Director-General in consultation with member countries.

WTO Agreement,
Article VI:4

The WTO Secretariat has a staff of 500 of varying nationalities. In performing their duties, the Director-General and the WTO staff are expected not to "seek or accept any instructions from any government or any other authority external to the WTO" and thus maintain the international character of the Secretariat.

---

4   Unlike the International Monetary Fund (IMF) and other organizations, WTO does not have a *weighted voting* system, under which some countries have right to more votes than others.

Membership

WTO Agreement,
Article XI

WTO had 134 members as at 31 May 1999.

Final Act, §5; WTO
Agreement, Article XII;
Decision on the
Acceptance of and
Accession to the
Agreement Establishing
the WTO

Countries that are at present not members can become members of WTO by negotiating for accession. In such negotiations, they have to agree to take steps to bring their national legislation in conformity with the rules of the multilateral Agreements. In addition they have to make commitments to reduce tariffs and modify their regulations so as to provide improved access for foreign goods and services. These commitments are often referred to as the price of the 'entry ticket' entitling the acceding country to benefit on an MFN basis from all tariff reductions and other commitments undertaken by member countries in the past. Thirty countries are currently negotiating for accession.

Annex II lists members of WTO and the countries/areas that are seeking entry into it.

WTO as a forum for negotiations

Continuous negotiations

WTO Agreement,
Article III:2

WTO provides a forum for negotiations on a continuing basis on:

❑ The further liberalization of trade in both areas of goods and services, and

❑ The improvement of existing rules or the adoption of rules in new subject areas.

Built-in agenda for negotiations

The provisions for beginning or conducting negotiations to review all or some of the provisions of specific Agreements are often contained in the Agreements themselves. These provisions have come to be known as the 'built-in agenda' for negotiations.

GATS, Article XIX:1

Agreement on Agriculture,
Article 20

In accordance with the built-in agenda of GATS, negotiations to liberalize the trade in the telecommunications and financial sectors were held and completed after the conclusion of the Uruguay Round. GATS further provides that negotiations to liberalize trade in all services sectors should be held from 1 January 2000. In the area of trade in goods, the Agreement on Agriculture stipulates that negotiations to achieve a higher level of trade liberalization and to improve the agriculture reform programme adopted under its provisions should commence before the end of 1999.

Review of Agreements

In addition to provisions on launching negotiations by specific dates, some Agreements provide for a review of all or some of their provisions, with a view to examining, on the basis of experience gained in their implementation, whether any modifications or improvements in these provisions are necessary. Box 5 lists the Agreements that are under review and those due for review in the near future.

Addition of new subjects to the WTO work programme

Decisions to add new subject areas to the work programme of WTO, with a view to examining whether negotiations should be held on adopting rules in these areas, are taken at the biennial Ministerial Conferences. Box 6 lists the subjects that have been added to the WTO work programme as a result of the

---

Box 5

WTO legal instruments: schedule of ongoing and future reviews

Understanding on Rules and Procedures Governing the Settlement of Disputes: review ongoing

Agreement on TRIPS, Article 27:3(b) on the exclusion of plants, animals other than micro-organisms from patentability: review ongoing

Agreement on TRIPS: first biennial review provided for by Article 71:1 scheduled to begin on 1 January 2000.

Agreement on TRIMS: review provided for by Article 9 on the operation of the Agreement and to consider whether provisions on "investment policy and competition policy" should be included in the Agreement scheduled to begin on 1 January 2000.

Box 6

New subjects added to the WTO work programme as a result of decisions taken at WTO Ministerial Conferences

❑ *Trade and environment*

❑ *Trade and investment*

❑ *Trade and competition policy*

❑ *Trade facilitation*

❑ *Transparency in government procurement*

❑ *Electronic commerce*

WTO is currently carrying out analytical work to determine whether new rules should be adopted to deal with the trade-related aspects of these subject areas.

---

decisions taken at the Ministerial Conferences held at Marrakesh in 1995, Singapore in 1996 and Geneva in 1998. The study and analysis of the trade-related problems that arise in each of these areas are carried out on the basis of background documentation prepared by the Secretariat and submissions by delegations and do not involve any commitment on the part of member countries to engage in negotiations on rule-making. (This subject is taken up in greater detail in Part Six.)

Possible launching of a new round of trade negotiations

The WTO rules further visualize that Ministers may at their Conferences decide to launch a new round of negotiations on a wide range of subject areas.

At the 1998 Geneva Conference, the Ministers called on the General Council to prepare a programme for further work and negotiations, taking into account, *inter alia*:

❑ The problems that have arisen in the implementation of the Agreements;

❑ The provisions of the built-in agenda for the commencement of negotiations in certain subject areas; and

❑ The new subjects which are currently under study and analysis in WTO.

The programme is expected to pay special attention to the trade problems of developing countries, and particularly to the problems faced by least developed countries and certain small economies as a result of their increasing marginalization in world trade.

In drawing out such a work programme, the Council is expected to examine the desirability of launching by the beginning of 2000 a new round of negotiations – now being referred to as the 'millennium round' – embracing a wide range of subjects. The decisions on these matters are expected to be taken at the third Ministerial Conference to be held in November-December 1999.

WTO system for the settlement of disputes

For a multilateral trading system to function properly and without friction, it is not enough to have an agreed set of rules. The rules have to be supplemented by other rules giving countries the right of redress when infringements occur and for settling their differences and disputes. The establishment of a strong multilateral dispute settlement mechanism which removes some of the weaknesses of the earlier GATT system is thus one of the most critical achievements of the Uruguay Round talks.

Dispute Settlement Body

WTO Agreement, Articles III:3, IV:3; Understanding on Rules and Procedures Governing the Settlement of Disputes (DSU)

The WTO Agreement provides a common system of rules and procedures applicable to disputes arising under any of its legal instruments. The main responsibility for administering these rules and procedures lies with the General Council, which as noted in earlier, acts as the Dispute Settlement Body (DSB).

Importance of consultations and conciliation

DSU, Article 4

DSU, Article 5

One of the important principles which these procedures lay down is that a dispute should be brought to DSB by the government of a member country for settlement only after efforts to settle it through consultations on a bilateral basis have failed. The procedures also provide that, in order to reach mutually acceptable solutions, the two parties may request the WTO Director-General or any other person to use his or her good offices to conciliate and mediate between them.

DSU, Article5:4

DSU, Article 6.1

Only when consultations or efforts at conciliation have not produced the desired results within 60 days may the complaining party request DSB formally to commence the dispute settlement mechanism by establishing a *panel* to examine the complaint. In order to expedite the settlement of disputes and to ensure that the establishment of a panel is not delayed by the country against whom a complaint is made, the procedures require DSB to establish the panel, when requested by the complaining country, unless there is a consensus against the establishment of such a panel.

DSU, Article 8

DSU, Article 8:5

Panels

A panel normally consists of three persons, unless parties to the dispute agree that it should have five persons. The names of the persons to be appointed to the panel are proposed by the WTO Secretariat from the list maintained by it of governmental and non-governmental experts. The persons in the list are well-qualified senior officials of member countries, members of their delegations to WTO, senior officials who have worked in the Secretariat, and persons who have taught international trade law or policy.

DSU, Article 12:8

DSU, Article 11

The membership of the panels is usually settled in consultation with the parties to the dispute. The panels are generally required to submit to DSB within a period of six to nine months reports containing their recommendations after making an objective assessment of the facts of the case and of the conformity of the measures complained about with the relevant provisions of the legal instruments.[5]

DSU, Article 17

Appellate Body

The establishment of the Appellate Body as a kind of court of appeal is a new addition to the dispute settlement system. The Body consists of seven persons of recognized authority, with expertise in law, international trade and the subjects covered by the various Agreements. They must not be affiliated to any

DSU, Article 17:2
DSU, Article 17:5

government. Of the seven, only three persons are called to serve in any one case. The appeal can be made by any of the parties to the dispute. The report of the Appellate Body, which will be confined to issues of law in the panel report and the legal interpretations developed by it, has to be submitted to DSB within a period of 60 to 90 days.

Consideration of reports by DSB

DSU, Article 20

The report of the panel or of the Appellate Body, where one of the parties has appealed against the panel's report, is submitted to DSB for adoption and appropriate recommendations and rulings. In order to ensure prompt settlement of disputes, it is provided that the period "from the date of the establishment of the panel by the DSB" and the date "when it considers the panel or appellate report" should not exceed nine months when the panel report is not appealed and 12 months when it is appealed.

DSU, Article 21

Implementation of the reports

According to the procedures, the reports of the panels are to be implemented by the parties in the three ways described below.

DSU, Article 21.1

Compliance

DSU, Article 20

DSU, Article 21:3

First, the procedures emphasize that the party in breach of obligations must promptly comply with the recommendations of the panel or Appellate Body. If it is not possible for the party to implement the recommendations immediately, DSB may on request grant it a reasonable period for implementation.

DSU, Article 22

Provision of compensation

Second, where the party in breach does not comply within a reasonable period, the party that has invoked the dispute settlement procedure may request compensation. Alternatively, the party in breach of the obligations may itself offer to pay compensation.

Authorization of retaliatory action

DSU, Article 22:2-9

Third, where the party in breach fails to comply and adequate compensation where requested is not provided, the aggrieved party may request DSB to authorize it to take retaliatory action by suspending concessions or other obligations under the Agreements. This means that, where the party is for instance in breach of its obligations under GATT or under one of its associate Agreements, the aggrieved party may be authorized by DSB to raise tariffs on products which it imports from the party in breach; the trade in such products should be approximately equal to that affected by the measures complained about.

---

5   The procedures recognize that the parties may in certain cases by mutual consent agree to refer the dispute to arbitration. However, they provide that, in such cases, the award shall be binding on the parties and that it should be reported to DSB.

DSU, Article 22:3

The rules provide that such retaliatory actions shall be authorized by DSB as far as possible in the same sectors of GATT, GATS or the Agreement on TRIPS in which the panel or appellate body has found violation. However, where DSB considers that this is not possible, it can authorize retaliation under other sectors of the same Agreement. Only in rare cases and as a last resort can DSB authorize retaliation across Agreements, i.e. imposition of higher tariffs on goods for breach of an obligation under GATS or the Agreement on TRIPS.

DSU, Article 2

The provision of compensation and authorization by DSB of retaliatory measures are, however, temporary measures. The ultimate solution is for the country which is in breach of the obligation to implement the recommendations. The rules require DSB to keep such cases under review to secure their full implementation.

How the dispute settlement mechanism works in practice

An ambassador from a country which had a case before the Dispute Settlement Body explained in reply to a question from a journalist how his government decided to bring the matter to WTO:

> The petrochemical industry brought the problem to our notice and furnished us with the information on the restrictive import licensing procedure which the importing country had introduced. We requested our commercial representative to check the facts and obtain more detailed information on regulations. When we were satisfied on the basis of the information provided by the affected industry and the report received from our commercial representative that there was a violation of the rules by the importing country, we decided to invoke the dispute settlement procedures by requesting the importing country for bilateral consultations. When we found that these bilateral consultations were not resulting in solutions, we decided to request the Dispute Settlement Body for the appointment of a panel.

Almost all, if not all, disputes brought to WTO are the result of the information provided by industries or their associations to their governments on the difficulties they are encountering in marketing their products in foreign markets. The government invokes dispute settlement procedures when it agrees with the industry's assessment that the country where the difficulties are being encountered is in breach of the WTO rules.

The first step the government has to take when it decides to invoke dispute settlement procedures is to enter into bilateral consultations with the country considered in breach of its obligations. Only when these bilateral efforts at reaching mutually satisfactory solutions fail may the complaining country request WTO to appoint a panel to examine both the facts of the case and its legal issues.

It is important to note that a large number of problems raised by governments under dispute settlement procedures are settled in bilateral consultations. These consultations fail to provide solutions only in a much smaller number of cases, where the country against which the complaint is made does not agree with the view of the complaining country that it has breached the rules; it is these cases that are brought to WTO for settlement by panels.

Even though the participants in the entire process of dispute settlement – bilateral consultations, examination by the panel and later by the Appellate Body – are government representatives, they rely heavily on advice and support on a continuing basis from the industry and the associations with an interest in the subject matter under dispute. The ability of governments to pursue its case or to defend the industry's interests in a case brought against it depends greatly on the assistance and support provided by the industry groups concerned.

As regards the facts of the case, the government representatives have to depend on information from industry, which has first-hand information on problems encountered. In addition, the government representatives participating in the work of the panels or the Appellate Body often find useful the behind-the-scene advice provided by industry on legal issues.

The summaries of two recently settled disputes provided in box 7 illustrate the type of cases that are brought to WTO for settlement.

Box 7

Summary of issues of fact and law in two cases settled under WTO dispute settlement procedures

United States – Measure Affecting Imports of Woven Wool Shirts and Blouses, complaint by India (WT/DS33)

WTO rules

The Agreement on Textiles and Clothing (ATC) requires countries maintaining discriminatory restrictions on imports of textiles and clothing to remove them gradually over a period of 10 years ending on 1 January 2005. Even though the aim of the Agreement is to facilitate the removal of restrictions, it permits importing countries to take "transitional safeguard measures" to restrict imports, where imports of certain categories of textile products are causing or threatening to cause "serious damage or actual threat thereof" to the domestic industry producing the like product. Article 6 of Agreement sets out the economic factors (e.g. changes in output, productivity, utilization of capacity, inventories, market share, exports, wages, employment, domestic prices, profits and investment) that must be taken into account in determining whether the increased imports are causing injury. It further provides that such safeguard measures should not be imposed if the serious damage or actual threat thereof is caused by "such other factors as technological changes or changes in consumer preferences".

Facts of the case

The United States imposed a transitional safeguard measure restricting imports of woollen shirts and blouses from India on 18 April 1995. Prior to imposing this measure, the United States and India held consultations on the former's claim that imports of woollen shirts and blouses were causing serious damage to its domestic industry. As the consultations did not bring about a satisfactory solution, India brought the case to WTO for settlement.

Findings of the Panel

The Panel, after examining the facts, found that the United States, in determining whether or not increased imports were causing injury to its domestic industry, had not examined all the economic variables listed in Article 6 of ATC which countries are required to take into account in determining a causal link between injury, the domestic industry and increased imports. It had also failed to examine, as required by the Article, whether the damage to the industry was not the result of changes in consumer preferences or technological changes.

The Panel therefore concluded that in imposing the temporary safeguard measure, the United States was in breach of its obligations under ATC. The United States implemented the Panel's decision by withdrawing the transitional safeguard measure.

Japan – Taxes on Alcoholic Beverages, complaints by the European Communities (WT/DS8), Canada (WT/DS10) and the United States (WT/DS11)

WTO rules

According to the national treatment principle of GATT 1994 internal taxes and other charges should not be used to provide domestic industries a higher level of

↵

➡

protection than that extended by tariffs. Levying taxes and charges on an imported product, after it has entered the importing market on payment of customs duties, at rates which are higher than that imposed on the like domestic product is a violation of this principle. Article III:2 of GATT 1994 provides that imported products should not be subject to internal taxes and charges that are "in excess of those applied directly or indirectly to like domestic products".

Facts of the case

The dispute arose from the Japanese Liquor Tax Law which imposed a tax on imported alcoholic beverages like vodka, rum and gin (white spirits) and whisky and brandy (brown spirits) which was higher than the tax on Japan's domestically produced liquor shochu. The United States, Canada and the European Communities, which considered the law to be in violation of the provisions of GATT Article III:2, held individual bilateral consultations with Japan. The failure to reach satisfactory solutions in these bilateral consultations resulted in the establishment of the Panel.

Findings of the Panel and the Appellate Body

The Panel determined that white spirits such as vodka and brown spirits such as whisky which were being imported and the shochu which was being produced domestically in Japan were "like products" taking into account their physical characteristics and end uses. It also held that the alcoholic strengths of the beverages did not preclude the finding of likeness because alcoholic beverages were often drunk in diluted form and vodka and shochu were classified in the Japanese tariffs under the same heading.

Since the imported white and brown spirits and the domestically produced shochu were like products, the imposition of taxes at a higher rate on the imported products than was imposed on the domestic product under the Japanese Liquor Tax Law constituted a breach of Japan's obligations under the first sentence of GATT Article III:2.

The Panel also found that in terms of the provisions of Article III, the imported products concerned (vodka, rum, gin, brandy, whisky and liquors) were "directly competitive and substitutable" for shochu. In arriving at this finding, it relied on the study submitted by the complaining countries which demonstrated that there was a high degree of price elasticity between shochu and five brown spirits and three white spirits. The Panel further found that as under the Japanese Liquor Tax Law, directly competitive and substitutable imported products (white and brown spirits) and domestic produce (shochu) were not "similarly taxed" and the tax favoured domestic products, additional protection was being afforded to such products. The Panel therefore concluded that Japan had also violated its obligations under second sentence of Article III:2 by maintaining such a system.

Japan appealed against the ruling of the Panel. The Appellate Body endorsed the main findings of the Panel described above. The findings and the rulings of the Appellate Body were implemented by the Japanese Government by making the necessary changes in the relevant legislation.

Trade Policy Review Mechanism (TPRM)

WTO Agreement, Article III

TPRM, A

In addition to providing a mechanism for settling disputes, WTO acts as a forum for the periodic review of the trade policies of member countries. The objectives of these reviews are twofold. First, they aim at finding out how far countries are following the disciplines of, and the commitments made under, the multilateral Agreements (and, where applicable, under the plurilateral Agreements). By carrying out such reviews periodically, WTO acts as a watchdog to ensure that its rules are carried out and thus contributes to the

TPRM, B

prevention of trade friction. The provisions establishing the review mechanism, however, clarify that it is not intended to serve as a basis for enforcing obligations; nor should such reviews be used for the settlement of disputes. The second equally important objective of these reviews is to provide greater transparency and understanding of the trade policies and practices of member countries.

TPRM,C:ii

Periodicity of reviews

The frequency with which such reviews are carried out depends on the share of the individual member countries in world trade. The top four are examined every two years: at the moment these are the European Communities (counted as one), the United States, Japan and Canada.

The next 16 are reviewed every four years, and the rest every six, except that longer intervals may be fixed for least developed countries.

TPRM, C:v

The basis for the review is provided by:

❑ A full report prepared by the Member whose trade policy is being reviewed; and

❑ The report prepared by the Secretariat on its own responsibility, taking into account the information provided by the Member and other information, including that obtained during visits to the country concerned.

TPRM, C:i

TPRM, C:vi

The reviews are carried out by the General Council, which for the purpose of such reviews acts as Trade Policy Review Body. The country report and the reports prepared by the Secretariat, together with the minutes on the discussions, are published promptly after the review.

WTO-related consultations

Mechanism for consultations between governments and the private sector

Governments do not act in isolation. In most developed countries and a large number of developing countries, formal institutional mechanisms have been established for consultations with industries and their associations, chambers of commerce and other trade associations on issues discussed in WTO. In these consultations, governments seek to obtain the views of the business community on:

❑ The policy approaches they should adopt on the specific issues under negotiation;

❑ The stand they should take on proposals made for the inclusion of new subjects in the agenda for negotiations.

The mechanism also provides an opportunity for industries and businesses to raise any problems they may be confronting in their target export markets because of the measures taken by governments of importing countries.

In developing countries where such a mechanism for consultations does not exist, it will be necessary to develop it. In countries where it does, it may be necessary to improve it to ensure that different business interests are adequately represented and able to bring to the notice of their governments the problems they encounter abroad.

Influence of associations of industries

In addition to participating in consultations arranged by governments, industries and trade enterprises in developed countries make known their concerns and views on subjects under negotiation in WTO by holding discussions under the auspices of chambers of commerce or federations of industries. Furthermore, pressure groups try to ensure that their sectoral interests are adequately taken into account by their governments when specific issues are discussed at the international level. The reports on these discussions are widely publicized to influence public opinion in favour of the group's views. The reports are also used to lobby members of national legislatures to ensure that governments ultimately adopt policy approaches to negotiations in WTO which adequately reflect their views and concerns.

For instance, the basic groundwork on a number of subjects in the agenda for the Uruguay Round negotiations was carried out by associations of industries and trade. The detailed studies prepared by national and international federations of industries on the implications of the trade in counterfeit goods were to influence governments of developed countries to press for the inclusion of this item in the agenda, ultimately leading to the Agreement on TRIPS. Again, the genesis of the Agreement on TRIMs can be traced to the studies prepared by organizations of industries and other research institutes on the adverse implications for trade of the local content and export performance requirements imposed on foreign investors. Many of the proposals for improved rules in the Agreement on Anti-dumping Practices originated from the problems and concerns industries brought to the attention of their governments.

The Information Technology Agreement (ITA), which was adopted at the Ministerial Conference in Singapore in December 1996, was the result of pressures placed by exporting industries on their governments. In fact, most of the new subjects in the WTO work programme, such as trade facilitation and electronic commerce, were suggested by governments on the basis of the recommendations made by industries, business associations and other interest groups that there was a need for the development of new rules in these areas.

The interest taken by associations of industries does not end with suggesting subjects for inclusion in negotiations. In most cases they follow the negotiations closely, and make their views known to their governments when they consider that proposals for new rules would not be to their benefit. In the Uruguay Round, for instance, the final outcome of the negotiations on textiles was greatly influenced by the pressures exerted by textile lobbies on the governments of the importing developed countries. It is well known that the Uruguay Round negotiations were held in abeyance for over two years because of the pressures brought to bear on the governments of some countries by agricultural lobbies, which considered that they would be adversely affected by the liberalization proposals under discussion.

Trade and industry associations must therefore continue to follow WTO's ongoing work on the implementation of the rules of the various Agreements and the work at the analytical level that is being done in new subject areas.

To enable trade and industry associations and NGOs to take an active interest in the work of WTO, the Secretariat has been taking a number of steps to add greater transparency to its work. The working documents prepared by the Secretariat and reports on meetings, previously treated as restricted documents available only to governments, are now derestricted within a period of six months. Further, in certain subject areas, like trade and environment, the Secretariat has been arranging briefing meetings for NGOs and other private-sector organizations on developments in discussions in WTO.

In most developing countries, however, chambers of commerce and trade associations have so far not shown an active interest in the discussions in international organizations like WTO. This was partly due to the fact that, until a few years ago, a number of these countries were pursuing import substitution policies. Consequently they focused attention mainly on domestic policy issues. With the shift to policies promoting export-oriented growth, these associations are becoming increasingly conscious of their members' need to become familiar with the WTO legal system and of their own need to pay more active attention to WTO's ongoing work. Many of them require assistance in improving their understanding of the system's substantive and procedural rules. International organizations could assist such associations by holding for the benefit of their members:

❑ General seminars on the WTO legal system, and

❑ Workshops on rules in specific areas, such as mandatory standards and sanitary and phytosanitary regulations, customs valuation, subsidies, countervailing and anti-dumping measures, and intellectual property rights.

Effective utilization of the legal and trade information available in WTO

One of the other less publicized advantages to the business person of the WTO system arises from the increasing availability at the WTO Secretariat of information on national legislation and rules in the foreign trade sector. Almost all WTO Agreements require member countries to notify the WTO Secretariat of national legislation, rules and regulations in the subject areas covered by them.

In addition, valuable information on products is available in the country reports prepared under the Trade Policy Review Mechanism. This information should be useful to enterprises exporting or considering the export of specific products. By studying the report on consultations with a particular country, it may be possible for an exporter to obtain information on the tariffs, mandatory standards and other regulations that are applicable to specific products or product groups in his or her target market. Although these reports are published, they are rarely mentioned in the national business journals of developing countries.

The WTO Web site (http://www.wto.org) has become a rich and valuable source of information on all aspects of the WTO system.

Summing up

To sum up, the ability of business persons to benefit from the improved institutional framework that has resulted from the Uruguay Round will depend greatly on:

❑ Their knowledge of the trade rules and of the rights which these give as well as the obligations they impose.

❑ Their knowledge of the new opportunities for trade that have been created by the liberalization commitments undertaken by countries during the negotiations.

❑ Their initiative in bringing to the notice of their governments their problems in selling to international markets so that their governments can raise the issues in appropriate WTO forums and, if necessary, invoke WTO dispute settlement procedures.

Chapters 2 - 20 of this Guide explain the rules of the system, the new opportunities that have been created as well as the challenges which business enterprises may encounter in both domestic and foreign markets as a result of trade liberalization.

Annex I
WTO structure

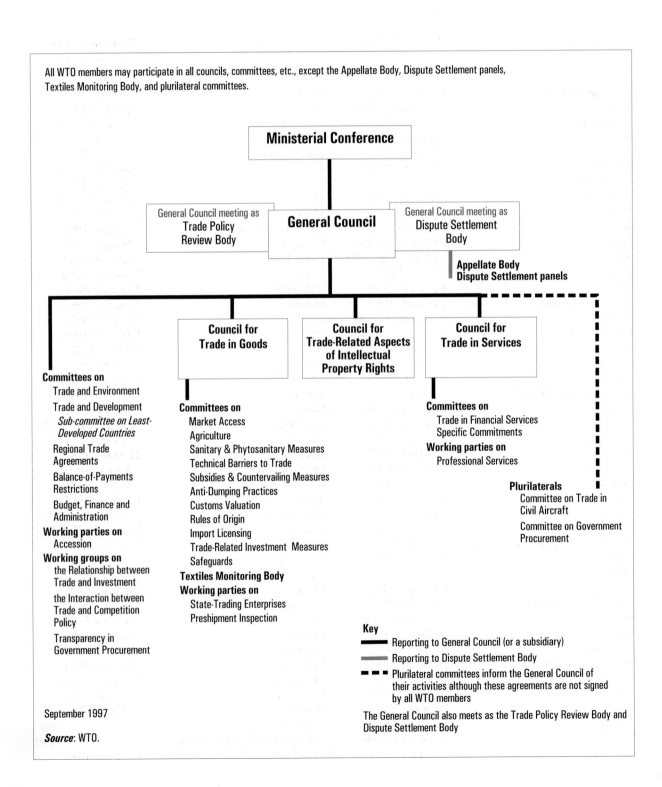

All WTO members may participate in all councils, committees, etc., except the Appellate Body, Dispute Settlement panels, Textiles Monitoring Body, and plurilateral committees.

Ministerial Conference

General Council meeting as
**Trade Policy
Review Body**

General Council

General Council meeting as
**Dispute Settlement
Body**

**Appellate Body
Dispute Settlement panels**

**Council for
Trade in Goods**

**Council for
Trade-Related Aspects
of Intellectual
Property Rights**

**Council for
Trade in Services**

Committees on
Trade and Environment
Trade and Development
*Sub-committee on Least-
Developed Countries*
Regional Trade
Agreements
Balance-of-Payments
Restrictions
Budget, Finance and
Administration
Working parties on
Accession
Working groups on
the Relationship between
Trade and Investment
the Interaction between
Trade and Competition
Policy
Transparency in
Government Procurement

Committees on
Market Access
Agriculture
Sanitary & Phytosanitary Measures
Technical Barriers to Trade
Subsidies & Countervailing Measures
Anti-Dumping Practices
Customs Valuation
Rules of Origin
Import Licensing
Trade-Related Investment Measures
Safeguards
Textiles Monitoring Body
Working parties on
State-Trading Enterprises
Preshipment Inspection

Committees on
Trade in Financial Services
Specific Commitments
Working parties on
Professional Services

Plurilaterals
Committee on Trade in
Civil Aircraft
Committee on Government
Procurement

Key
— Reporting to General Council (or a subsidiary)
— Reporting to Dispute Settlement Body
- - - Plurilateral committees inform the General Council of
their activities although these agreements are not signed
by all WTO members

The General Council also meets as the Trade Policy Review Body and
Dispute Settlement Body

September 1997

Source: WTO.

Annex II

WTO membership

(As of 31 May 1999, with dates of membership in WTO)

Government	Entry into force Membership	Government	Entry into force Membership
Antigua and Barbuda	1 January 1995	Ghana	1 January 1995
Angola	1 December 1996	Greece	1 January 1995
Argentina	1 January 1995	Grenada	22 February 1996
Australia	1 January 1995	Guatemala	21 July 1995
Austria	1 January 1995	Guinea Bissau	31 May 1995
Bahrain	1 January 1995	Guinea	25 October 1995
Bangladesh	1 January 1995	Guyana	1 January 1995
Barbados	1 January 1995	Haiti	30 January 1996
Belgium	1 January 1995	Honduras	1 January 1995
Belize	1 January 1995	Hong Kong, China	1 January 1995
Benin	22 February 1996	Hungary	1 January 1995
Bolivia	13 September 1995	Iceland	1 January 1995
Botswana	31 May 1995	India	1 January 1995
Brazil	1 January 1995	Indonesia	1 January 1995
Brunei Darussalam	1 January 1995	Ireland	1 January 1995
Bulgaria	1 December 1996	Israel	21 April 1995
Burkina Faso	3 June 1995	Italy	1 January 1995
Burundi	23 July 1995	Jamaica	9 March 1995
Cameroon	13 December 1995	Japan	1 January 1995
Canada	1 January 1995	Kenya	1 January 1995
Central African Republic	31 May 1995	Korea	1 January 1995
Chad	19 October 1996	Kuwait	1 January 1995
Chile	1 January 1995	Kyrgyzstan	20 December 1998
Colombia	30 April 1995	Latvia	10 February 1999
Congo	27 March 1997	Lesotho	31 May 1995
Costa Rica	1 January 1995	Liechtenstein	1 September 1995
Côte d'Ivoire	1 January 1995	Luxembourg	1 January 1995
Cuba	20 April 1995	Macau	1 January 1995
Cyprus	30 July 1995	Madagascar	17 November 1995
Czech Republic	1 January 1995	Malawi	31 May 1995
Democratic Republic of the Congo	1 January 1997	Malaysia	1 January 1995
Denmark	1 January 1995	Maldives	31 May 1995
Djibouti	31 May 1995	Mali	31 May 1995
Dominica	1 January 1995	Malta	1 January 1995
Dominican Republic	9 March 1995	Mauritania	31 May 1995
Ecuador	21 January 1996	Mauritius	1 January 1995
Egypt	30 June 1995	Mexico	1 January 1995
El Salvador	7 May 1995	Mongolia	29 January 1997
European Communities	1 January 1995	Morocco	1 January 1995
Fiji	14 January 1996	Mozambique	26 August 1995
Finland	1 January 1995	Myanmar	1 January 1995
France	1 January 1995	Namibia	1 January 1995
Gabon	1 January 1995	Netherlands - For the Kingdom in Europe and for the Netherlands Antilles	1 January 1995
Gambia	23 October 1996		
Germany	1 January 1995		

Government	Entry into force Membership	Government	Entry into force Membership
New Zealand	1 January 1995	Slovenia	30 July 1995
Nicaragua	3 September 1995	Solomon Islands	26 July 1996
Niger	13 December 1996	South Africa	1 January 1995
Nigeria	1 January 1995	Spain	1 January 1995
Norway	1 January 1995	Sri Lanka	1 January 1995
Pakistan	1 January 1995	Suriname	1 January 1995
Panama	6 September 1997	Swaziland	1 January 1995
Papua New Guinea	9 June 1996	Sweden	1 January 1995
Paraguay	1 January 1995	Switzerland	1 July 1995
Peru	1 January 1995	Tanzania, United Rep. of	1 January 1995
Philippines	1 January 1995	Thailand	1 January 1995
Poland	1 July 1995	Togo	31 May 1995
Portugal	1 January 1995	Trinidad and Tobago	1 March 1995
Qatar	13 January 1996	Tunisia	29 March 1995
Romania	1 January 1995	Turkey	26 March 1995
Rwanda	22 May 1996	Uganda	1 January 1995
Saint Kitts and Nevis	21 February 1996	United Arab Emirates	10 April 1996
Saint Lucia	1 January 1995	United Kingdom	1 January 1995
Saint Vincent & the Grenadines	1 January 1995	United States	1 January 1995
Senegal	1 January 1995	Uruguay	1 January 1995
Sierra Leone	23 July 1995	Venezuela	1 January 1995
Singapore	1 January 1995	Zambia	1 January 1995
Slovak Republic	1 January 1995	Zimbabwe	3 March 1995

Observer Governments

Albania	Ethiopia	Oman
Algeria	Former Yugoslav Republic of	Russian Federation
Andorra	Macedonia	Samoa
Armenia	Georgia	Saudi Arabia
Azerbaijan	Holy See (Vatican)	Seychelles
Belarus	Jordan	Sudan
Bhutan	Kazakhstan	Taiwan Province (China)
Cambodia	Lao People's Democratic Republic	Tonga
Cape Verde	Lebanon	Ukraine
China	Lithuania	Uzbekistan
Croatia	Moldova	Vanuatu
Estonia*	Nepal	Viet Nam

Note:

All observer countries have applied to join WTO except the Holy See (Vatican) and, for the time being, Ethiopia, Cape Verde, Bhutan and Yemen. Estonia's application for membership was approved by the General Council in May 1997.

International organization observers in the General Council (observers in other councils and committees differ):
    United Nations
    United Nations Conference on Trade and Development (UNCTAD)
    International Monetary Fund (IMF)
    World Bank
    Food and Agriculture Organization of the United Nations (FAO)
    World Intellectual Property Organization (WIPO)
    Organisation for Economic Co-operation and Development (OECD)

Source: WTO.

PART TWO

International rules governing trade in goods (GATT 1994 and its associate Agreements)

CHAPTER 2

Four main rules of GATT

The entire edifice of GATT's open and liberal multilateral trading system is built on four basic and simple rules.

The first rule, while recognizing that it is important for member countries to follow open and liberal trade policies, permits them to protect domestic production from foreign competition, provided that such protection is extended only through tariffs and is kept at low levels. To this end, it prohibits countries from using quantitative restrictions, except in specified cases. The rule against the use of quantitative restrictions has been strengthened in the Uruguay Round.

The second rule provides for the reduction and elimination of tariffs and other barriers to trade through multilateral negotiations. The tariffs so reduced are listed on a tariff-line basis in each country's schedule of concessions. The rates given in these schedules are known as bound rates. Countries are under an obligation not to increase tariffs above the bound rates shown in their schedules.

The third rule requires countries to conduct their trade without discriminating among countries from which goods are imported or to which goods are exported. This rule is embodied in the most-favoured-nation (MFN) principle. An important exception to this rule is permitted in the case of regional preferential arrangements.

The fourth rule is known as the national treatment rule. It requires countries not to impose on an imported product, after it has entered their domestic markets on paying customs duties at the border, internal taxes such as sales or value-added tax at rates higher than those levied on a similar domestic product.

GATT 1994, Preamble

The objective of the multilateral system for trade in goods created by GATT is to provide industries and business enterprises from different countries a secure, stable and predictable environment in which they can trade with one another under conditions of fair and equitable competition. This open and liberal trading system is expected to promote through increased trade, greater investment, production and employment and thus facilitate the economic development of all countries.

First rule: protecting the domestic industry by tariffs only

The legal system which GATT has created to attain the above objective is complex, but it is based on a few basic and simple rules

While GATT stands for liberal trade, it recognizes that countries may wish to protect their industries from foreign competition. It urges them to keep such protection at reasonably low levels and to provide it through tariffs. The principle of protection by tariffs is reinforced by provisions prohibiting member countries from using quantitative restrictions on imports. The rule, however, is subject to specified exceptions. An important exception permits countries that are in balance-of-payments (BOP) difficulties to restrict imports in order to safeguard their external financial position. This exception provides greater flexibility to developing countries than is available to developed countries to use quantitative restrictions on imports if these restrictions are necessary to forestall a serious decline in their monetary reserves.

GATT 1994, Article XI

GATT 1994, Article XII

Non-observation of the rule against quantitative restrictions

Agricultural sector

In the past, a number of countries did not abide by the GATT rule on protection by tariffs alone. In the agricultural sector for instance, a number of developed countries maintained quantitative restrictions which went far beyond those warranted by the exceptions provided in GATT. In addition to these restrictions, some of these countries, particularly those belonging to the European Union, applied variable levies instead of fixed tariffs to imports of temperate zone agricultural products such as wheat and other grains, meat and dairy products. The primary purpose of those levies was to ensure a reasonable income to farmers and to maintain a certain parity between the income earned by them and that earned by industrial workers. The levies payable were determined periodically and were generally equal to the difference between the landed import price and the guaranteed reference domestic price.

The variable levies thus resulted in domestic production being fully insulated from foreign competition, as the levies completely offset the competitive price advantages of foreign suppliers.

Trade in textiles and clothing

In the industrial sector, most developed countries did not apply the rule against the use of quantitative restrictions to trade in textiles, a sector of particular interest to developing countries. There was one significant difference between the restrictions applied in the agricultural sector and those applied to textiles. With some notable exceptions, the restrictions maintained in the agricultural sector were outside the scope of GATT rules. In the case of textiles, the restrictions were authorized under the provisions of the Multi-Fibre Arrangement (MFA), negotiated under GATT auspices. MFA permitted countries to derogate from their basic obligation and to impose restrictions on imports of textiles and textile products, provided the conditions it laid down were met.

Developing countries

A number of developing countries applied, in addition to high tariffs, quantitative restrictions on imports in both the agricultural and industrial sectors. Such use of restrictions was, however, in most cases justifiable from the legal point of view, under the exceptions to the GATT rules which permit countries in balance-of-payments difficulties to impose quantitative restrictions on imports.[6]

GATT 1994, Articles XII and XVIII:B

---

6   Countries are considered to be in balance-of-payments difficulties when their external earnings from trade in goods and services and the flow of investment and loans are far from adequate for their external payments liabilities, and when monetary reserves for meeting immediate liabilities are declining. GATT rules provide developing countries in balance-of-payments difficulties a greater flexibility to use quantitative restrictions on imports.

Reinforcement of the discipline against the use of quantitative restrictions

Tariffication in the agricultural sector

The WTO legal system has brought about a considerable change in the use of quantitative restrictions and other non-tariff measures affecting imports. In the agricultural sector for instance, in accordance with the provisions of the Agreement on Agriculture, WTO member countries have abolished quantitative restrictions and their systems of variable levies, replacing these with tariffs. The new tariff rates have been determined by tariffication, i.e. calculating the incidence of quantitative restrictions and other measures on the price of the imported products and adding it to the then-prevailing tariffs. After tariffication, countries may henceforth protect their domestic agricultural production only by means of tariffs. (*See* chapter 15.)

Phased removal of restrictions on textiles and clothing

In the area of textiles and clothing, the Agreement on Textiles and Clothing (ATC) requires member countries maintaining restrictions to phase them out gradually in four stages, so as to abolish them completely by 1 January 2005. (*See* chapter 14.)

Developing countries in balance-of-payments difficulties are urged to use price-based measures

Understanding on
BOP Provisions of GATT
1994: 2, 3

In addition, the Understanding on Balance-of-Payments Provisions of GATT 1994 strongly urges member countries not to use quantitative restrictions to safeguard their balance-of-payments (BOP) situations. It requires countries, whether developed or developing, to prefer in such situations price-based measures (such as import surcharges and import deposit requirements) to quantitative restrictions as their impact on the price of imported products is transparent and measurable. Quantitative restrictions can be resorted to only when, because of a critical BOP situation, it is perceived that price-based measures cannot arrest a further sharp deterioration in the external payments position.

The WTO legal system has thus, by strengthening the rules against the use of quantitative restrictions, further reinforced the basic GATT rule that protection to domestic production should be given primarily through tariffs.

Second rule: tariffs should be reduced and bound against further increases

Reductions in tariffs

GATT 1994, Preamble;
Article XXVIII bis

The second important rule of GATT is that tariffs and other measures that countries maintain to protect their domestic production should be reduced and, where possible, eliminated through negotiations among member countries and that the tariffs so reduced should be bound against further increases.

Binding against further increases

GATT 1994, Article II:1(b);
Understanding on the
Interpretation of Article
II:1(b)

The concept of binding needs some explanation. The rates of tariffs agreed in the negotiations as well as the other commitments assumed by countries are listed in schedules of concessions. Each WTO member country has a separate schedule and is under an obligation not to impose tariffs or other duties or charges which "are in excess of those set forth" in its schedule. It is also obliged not to take measures such as the imposition of quantitative restrictions which would reduce the value of the tariff concessions. The rates of tariffs listed in the schedule are known as bound rates of tariffs (*see* box 8).

Box 8

Binding of tariffs

It is not open to a country to increase the rates of tariffs above the bound rate indicated in its schedule of concessions. The schedule, inter alia, lists on a product-by-product basis the pre-negotiation tariff rate on a product and the rate of tariff at which the country has agreed "in the negotiations to bind the tariff rate". In trade negotiations, a country could agree:

❑ *To bind its existing positive rate (e.g. 10%) or zero rate; or*
❑ *To reduce the rate, for example from 10% to 5%, and to bind the reduced rate.*

It is also possible for a country to bind its tariffs at a ceiling rate which is higher than the rate resulting from the tariff reductions agreed in the negotiations. Thus a country which has agreed to reduce a tariff from 10% to 5% may indicate that, while it will apply the reduced rate to imports, the bound rate of the tariff will be 8%. In that case, the country is free to raise its tariffs to 8% at any time without infringing any of its GATT obligations.

The Uruguay Round has brought about substantial progress in the binding of tariffs of all countries. All countries – developed, developing and transitional economies – have bound their tariffs in the agricultural sector. In the industrial sector over 98% of imports into developed and transitional economies will be entering under bound rates of tariffs.

In the case of imports into developing countries, the proportion of imports entering under bound rates is around 73%. A number of developing countries have, however, given ceiling bindings in certain instances. Such ceiling bindings take the form of a commitment not to raise the tariff:

❑ *Over the ceiling rates shown for each product;*
❑ *Over the ceiling rate applicable to a particular sector;*
❑ *Over the ceiling rate applicable across the board to all products.*

It is possible for a country which has bound its tariffs to secure release from the binding and to raise the tariff above the bound rate. It does this by entering into renegotiations with the countries with which it had initially negotiated the concession as well as with the principal supplying countries of the product concerned and which therefore benefit from the concession. In such negotiations, the country requesting release is expected to make compensatory tariff concessions on other products in which the countries with which it is negotiating have a trade interest.

Principle governing the exchange of concessions in negotiations

What is the principle by which countries agree in trade negotiations to reduce tariffs, to bind them against further increases and to remove other barriers to trade? The basic principle governing the exchange of such concessions is the principle of reciprocity and mutual advantage. A country requesting improved access to the market of other countries, through tariff reductions or the removal of other barriers such as quantitative restrictions, must be ready to make concessions in tariffs and other areas that those countries consider to be advantageous and of reciprocal or equivalent value to the concessions they are making.

GATT 1994, Part IV
(Trade and Development),
Article XXXVI:8; Tokyo
Round Decision on
Differential and More
Favourable Treatment,
Reciprocity and Fuller
Participation of Developing
Countries, § 5,6 and 7

The rule of full reciprocity does not, however, apply to negotiations between developed and developing countries. Developing countries are required to make concessions in the form of tariff reductions on the basis of relative reciprocity, which takes into account the fact that, because of their lower level of economic development and their trade and financial needs, they may not be able to make concessions on the same basis as developed countries. The rule, however, recognizes that developing countries are not all at the same level of development; some of them have reached higher stages of growth while others are at various stages of development. Forty-eight of them are least developed countries.

The developing countries that have reached higher stages of development are required to make larger contributions and concessions in the form of tariff reductions and bindings than those at lower rungs of economic growth. This concept is also known as 'graduation', since it visualizes that as a developing country develops, it will graduate to a higher status and ultimately may be able to make tariff concessions and accept disciplines in other areas on the same basis as developed countries.

Greater contributions from developing countries in the Uruguay Round

Because of the rule of relative reciprocity only a few developing countries made tariff concessions in the Tokyo Round and earlier rounds of negotiations. Furthermore, those that made concessions did so on only a few products. This situation changed considerably in the Uruguay Round, and almost all developing countries have agreed to make concessions by reducing tariffs on a percentage basis. However, in accordance with the principle of relative reciprocity, these concessions have been made at a lower percentage than that applicable to developed countries.

During the Uruguay Round, two factors were responsible for the greater willingness of developing countries to make concessions and to accept through negotiations higher obligations. First, a significant number of these countries had made considerable progress in their economic development. The second factor, closely related to the first, was the dramatic shift which had taken place in the trade policies of almost all developing countries. Previously, when they had followed import substitution policies, built high tariff walls and insulated domestic production from foreign competition, it was difficult for them to offer concessions in the form of tariff reductions.

These countries are now following policies promoting export growth and are reducing tariffs and eliminating the plethora of licensing and other systems they had maintained to restrict imports. These open and liberal trade policies enabled them in the Uruguay Round not only to take credit for their unilateral tariff reductions by binding them but also to improve their bargaining position in negotiations with their developed country partners.

Third rule: trade according to the most-favoured-nation clause

GATT 1994, Article I

The third basic GATT rule, which provides that trade must not be discriminatory, is embodied in the famous most-favoured-nation clause. In simple terms, the principle means that if a member country grants to another country any tariff or other benefit to any product, it must immediately and unconditionally extend it to the like products of other countries. Thus if country A agrees, in trade negotiations with country B, to reduce custom duties on imports of tea from 10% to 5%, the reduced rate must be extended to all WTO member countries. The obligation to extend such MFN treatment applies not only to imports but also to exports. Thus, if a country levies duties on exports of a product to one destination, it must apply it at the same rate to exports to all destinations.

GATT 1994, Article I:1

Moreover, the obligation to provide MFN treatment is not confined to tariffs. It also applies to:

❑ Charges of any kind imposed in connection with importation and exportation;

❑ The method of levying tariffs and such charges;

❑ Rules and formalities in connection with importation and exportation;

❑ Internal taxes and charges on imported goods, and laws, regulations and requirements affecting their sales;

GATT 1994, Article XIII

❑ The administration of quantitative restrictions (e.g. by allocating quotas among supplying countries on a non-discriminatory basis) where such restrictions are permitted under the exceptions provisions.

The principle thus implies that, by agreeing to give MFN treatment, member countries undertake not to discriminate among countries and not to treat a country less favourably than another in all matters connected with foreign trade in goods.

Exceptions to the MFN rule

GATT 1994, Article XXIV

The GATT rules, however, recognize that tariffs and other barriers to trade can be reduced on a preferential basis by countries under regional arrangements. The lower or duty-free rates applicable to trade among members of regional arrangements need not be extended to other countries. Regional preferential arrangements thus constitute an important exception to the MFN rule. In order to protect the trade interests of non-member countries, GATT lays down strict conditions for forming such arrangements. These conditions, *inter alia*, provide that:

GATT 1994, Article XXIV:8

❑ Member countries of regional arrangements must remove tariffs and other barriers to trade affecting substantially all trade among themselves, and

❑ The arrangement should not result in the imposition of new barriers to trade with other countries.

GATT 1994, Article XXIV:8

Such arrangements may take the form of customs unions or free-trade areas. In both instances, trade among member States takes place on a duty-free basis while trade with other countries continues to be subject to MFN tariff rates. In the case of customs unions, tariffs of member countries are harmonized and are uniformly applied to imports from outside countries. In free-trade areas, member countries continue to use, without harmonization, the tariffs set out in their individual national schedules.

There are now over 100 regional preferential arrangements in force. As box 9 shows, the emphasis on promoting trade on a regional basis by strengthening and deepening tariff and other concessions exchanged under regional preferential arrangements has increased in recent years. As a result, regional trade is steadily on the rise and a growing proportion of world trade is taking place on a regional basis.

Such preferential arrangements provide advantages to industries marketing their products in other countries in the region. At the same time, they may put industries in countries outside the region, which have to pay customs duties on an MFN basis, in a position of competitive disadvantage. One of the major challenges which WTO member countries have to face in the coming years is

Box 9

Regional trade groupings: recent developments

During the past few years, the steady march towards the further strengthening of regional trade agreements has continued on all continents.

Africa

In Africa, the southern cone is moving towards closer integration within a free trade area through the Southern African Development Community (SADC). Within the group, member States of the Southern African Customs Union (SACU) are renegotiating their customs union relationships.

In other parts of Africa, there is also a revival of regional integration. For example, in West Africa, the new Economic and Monetary Union (WAEMU; in French UEMOA) plans to bring into effect a common external tariff, a joint Commission and many of the elements of the European system (a common currency in the shape of the CFA franc already exists). Members of the East African Cooperation (Kenya, Uganda and the United Republic of Tanzania) have continued their renewed movement towards eventual economic and monetary union, with a common currency.

The Common Market for Eastern and Southern Africa (COMESA), with 20 member States, remains the largest regional entity in Africa; its objective is to establish a customs union and a common external tariff.

Its members are: Angola, Burundi, Comoros, Djibouti, Eritrea, Ethiopia, Kenya, Lesotho, Madagascar, Malawi, Mauritius, Mozambique, Namibia, Rwanda, Seychelles, Somalia, Sudan, Swaziland, United Republic of Tanzania, Uganda, Zaire, Zambia and Zimbabwe.

The Americas

In the Americas, the establishment of the North American Free Trade Agreement (NAFTA) by the United States, Canada and Mexico has provided a new stimulus for the establishment of a free trade area for all countries in North and South America. In April 1998, 34 countries in the region signed an agreement to establish the Free Trade Area of the Americas (FTAA) by the year 2005. A number of agreements setting up regional or subregional groupings are expected to be fully implemented by that date.

One regional grouping is MERCOSUR (the Southern Common Market), which aims to establish a common market for its members Argentina, Brazil, Paraguay and Uruguay (Bolivia and Chile are associate members). Now a customs union, MERCOSUR has signed agreements with the Andean Community (to initiate a full free trade agreement by 2000) and with the Central American Common Market (to begin a tariff reduction programme leading to a free trade agreement). It has free trade agreements with Bolivia and Chile.

The Andean Community (consisting of Bolivia, Colombia, Ecuador, Peru and Venezuela) has agreed to establish a common market by the year 2005, and has signed a framework agreement with Panama aiming at the latter's full integration into the Community.

Asia

In Asia, the Association of South-East Asian Nations (or ASEAN, comprising Brunei Darussalam, Indonesia, Lao People's Democratic Republic, Malaysia, Myanmar, the Philippines, Singapore, Thailand and Viet Nam) is vigorously pursuing its efforts to establish a free trade area by further reducing tariffs and other barriers to intraregional trade.

The countries belonging to the Bangkok Agreement (Bangladesh, Bhutan, India, Maldives Nepal, Pakistan and Sri Lanka) are also seeking to promote intraregional trade though political difficulties have so far prevented significant progress from being made.

➥

> ➥
>
> *In Central Asia, Kazakhstan, Kyrgyzstan, Tajikistan, Turkmenistan and Uzbekistan have joined hands with the Islamic Republic of Iran, Pakistan and Turkey to develop closer trade links.*
>
> *The abolition of tariffs and other barriers to trade are also being sought by countries belonging to the Asia-Pacific Economic Cooperation forum (APEC). Its members are: Australia, Brunei Darussalam, Canada, Chile, China, Hong Kong, Indonesia, Japan, Malaysia, Mexico, New Zealand, Peru, Papua New Guinea, the Philippines, Republic of Korea, the Russian Federation, Singapore, Taiwan Province (China), Thailand, the United States and Viet Nam.*
>
> **Europe**
>
> *In Europe, close economic integration has been achieved among 15 countries following the establishment of the European Union. Negotiations are underway on the admission into the Union of Cyprus, the Czech Republic, Hungary, Poland and Slovenia. The European Union also maintains a customs union with Turkey and is negotiating a 'new generation' of agreements on free trade areas with its trading partners in the Mediterranean region. Its current members are: Austria, Belgium, Denmark, Finland, France, Germany, Iceland, Ireland, Italy, Luxembourg, the Netherlands, Portugal, Spain, Sweden and the United Kingdom.*
>
> *It is thus clear that both the economic and political impetus to conclude regional trade agreements, which already cover a high proportion of world trade, will intensify in the coming years.*
>
> **Source**: *WTO, Annual Report 1998. vol. 1, Special Topic: Globalization and Trade.*

how to ensure complementarity between efforts to develop regional trade and attempts to further liberalize trade at the multilateral level.

In addition to these arrangements, developed countries have introduced one-way free-trade arrangements under which imports from either all or a limited number of developing countries enter their markets duty free. These arrangements are non-reciprocal as the developing countries benefiting from preferential access do not extend any preferential treatment to imports from developed countries. Examples of such one-way preferential arrangements are:

GATT 1994;Tokyo Round Decision on Differential and More Favourable Treatment, Reciprocity and Fuller Participation of Developing Countries, § 2(a)

❑ The Generalized System of Preferences (GSP) under which developed countries allow imports from all developing countries of all industrial products, and of selected agricultural products on a preferential and duty-free basis;

❑ The Lomé Convention under which Member States of the European Union allow imports from a number of developing and least developed countries in Africa, the Caribbean, and Asia and the Pacific (i.e. the ACP countries) to enter on a duty-free basis;

❑ The Caribbean Basin Initiative, under which the United States allows imports from Caribbean countries on a duty-free basis.

The legal basis for the extension of preferential treatment by developed countries to imports from all developing countries under GSP is provided by the Decision on Differential and More Favourable Treatment, Reciprocity and Fuller Participation of Developing Countries. The Decision was adopted under GATT in 1979 and is commonly known as the General Enabling Clause. There is no definitive legal basis available under the provisions of GATT 1994 for preferential arrangements like the Lomé Convention and the Caribbean Basin Arrangement, which allow preferential or duty-free access only to the limited number of developing countries with which the developed countries extending preferential treatment have historical or other ties. These arrangements are currently allowed under 'waivers' granted to the preference-giving developed countries from their obligation to extend MFN treatment.

From the legal point of view, these limited preferential arrangements lead to discriminatory treatment of imports from developing countries which do not benefit from the preferences. There are therefore pressures on the preference-giving developed countries to modify them and bring them in conformity with GATT rules.

The current Lomé Convention (Lomé IV) will expire in February 2000. The indications are that the European Union may be able to get a waiver to continue the arrangement in more or less its existing form for an additional period of five years, i.e. up to 2005. Negotiations are now taking place between the European Union and the beneficiary ACP countries on how the Convention can be modified to make it consistent with the provisions of GATT 1994 and the General Enabling Clause.

The waiver granted to the United States to implement the Caribbean Basin Initiative expires at the end of 2005.

Fourth rule: national treatment

GATT 1994, Article III

The MFN principle, as has been noted, requires Members not to discriminate among countries. The national treatment principle, which complements the MFN principle, requires that an imported product which has crossed the border after payment of customs duties and other charges should not receive treatment that is less favourable than that extended to the like product produced domestically. In other words, the principle requires member countries to treat imported products on the same footing as similar domestically produced goods. Thus it is not open to a country to levy on an imported product, after it has entered the country on payment of customs duties at the border, internal taxes (such as a sales tax) at rates that are higher than those applied to comparable domestic products. Likewise, regulations affecting the sale and purchase of products in the domestic market cannot be applied more rigorously to imported products.

Business implications

The new framework of rules covering agricultural products and textiles which the Uruguay Round has developed will help ensure that GATT's basic rules – against the use of quantitative restrictions and requiring that protection to domestic production is given only through tariffs – are followed in practice by all countries. Exporting enterprises prefer tariffs to quantitative restrictions for many reasons. Tariffs are transparent and their incidence on price is predictable. The use of quantitative restrictions imposes a certain uncertainty on trade, as administering authorities have the power to adjust the sizes of quotas from time to time. Finally, as the operation of quota restrictions requires licensing, enterprises can export only if their foreign buyers are able to obtain a licence.

The Uruguay Round has also resulted in significant progress in tariff binding by all countries. The assurance that, because of the binding, the lower rates agreed in the negotiations will not be raised by countries to which exports are being made encourages enterprises to invest in manufacturing plants, equipment and distribution networks and to take other measures to develop trade. Furthermore, the bindings give enterprises a guarantee that the tariffs that are payable on the raw materials and inputs which they have to import for use in export production will not be increased by their own governments.

Lastly, the national treatment rule assures exporting enterprises that once their products have entered the importing market after payment of customs duties and other charges payable at the border, they will not be required to pay internal taxes at rates that are higher than those payable on products of domestic origin. The national treatment rule applies not only to internal taxes, but also to the rules governing mandatory standards for products and those applicable to the sale and distribution of goods. As governments are increasingly imposing taxes and adopting product regulations for the protection of the environment and for the health and safety of consumers, the rule that such taxes and regulations should be applied to domestic and imported products on a non-discriminatory basis is of vital importance to exporting enterprises.

CHAPTER 3

Valuation of goods for customs purposes

Summary

When customs duties are levied on an ad valorem basis (e.g. 10 % of the value of imported goods), the actual incidence of duty depends on how Customs determines dutiable value. The Agreement on Customs Valuation requires Customs to determine the value on the basis of the price paid or payable by the importer in the transaction that is being valued. As a result of a Decision adopted in the Uruguay Round, Customs can reject transaction values when it has reasons to doubt the truth or accuracy of the value declared by importers or of the documents submitted by them. In order to protect the interests of importers in such situations, Customs is required to provide them with an opportunity to justify their price. Where Customs is not satisfied with the justifications given, it is obliged to give to these importers in writing its reasons for not accepting the transaction value they have declared.

When the transaction value is not accepted by Customs, the Agreement lays down five methods for establishing value. In determining value on the basis of these methods, Customs is required to consult the importers and take their views into account.

A number of developing countries currently use valuation systems based on the Brussels Definition of Value, developed by the World Customs Organization (WCO). These countries will have to modify their systems to bring them in conformity with the rules of the Agreement on Customs Valuation within the transitional period of five years (i.e. up to 1 January 2000) that has been accorded to developing countries for changing over to the system established by the Agreement.

Types of customs duties

Customs duties are levied on an *ad valorem* basis (e.g. 20% of the value of the imported product) or as specific duties (e.g. $2 per kilogram or per litre). Combined or mixed duties containing both *ad valorem* and specific rates are also levied (10% of the value + $2 per kilogram) on some products.

With a few exceptions, most countries levy *ad valorem* duties. Governments prefer to levy such duties for three broad reasons. First, it is easier for the authorities to estimate collectable revenue from *ad valorem* duties, which are assessed on the basis of value, than revenue from specific duties, which are levied on the basis of volume or weight. Second, *ad valorem* duties are more equitable than specific duties as their incidence is lower on cheaper products and higher on more expensive goods. For instance, a specific duty of $2 per litre would have an incidence of 50% on a bottle of wine costing $4, and 10% on a higher-priced wine costing $20 a bottle. An *ad valorem* duty of 10% would have an incidence of $0.20 on the cheaper bottle and $2 on the more expensive bottle. Third, in international negotiations for reductions in tariffs it is far easier to compare the level of tariffs and negotiate reductions if the duties are *ad valorem*.

However, the incidence of *ad valorem* duties depends to a large extent on the methods used to determine dutiable value. Thus, if Customs determines the dutiable value at $1,000, an *ad valorem* duty of 10% will result in a duty of $100. If, on the other hand, it determines value at $1,200, the importer will have to pay an import duty of $120 for the same goods. The benefits to the trade arising from tariff bindings could fall considerably if Customs uses prices other than invoice prices for determining values for customs purposes. The rules that are applied for the valuation of goods are therefore of crucial importance in ensuring that the incidence of duties as perceived by the importer is not higher than that indicated by the nominal rates shown in the importing country's tariff schedules.

Rules of the Agreement on Customs Valuation

Agreement on Customs
Valuation, Preamble

The detailed WTO rules on the valuation of goods for customs purposes are contained in the Agreement on Customs Valuation (full title: Agreement on Implementation of Article VII of GATT 1994). The Agreement's valuation system is based on simple and equitable criteria that take commercial practices into account. By requiring all member countries to harmonize their national legislation on the basis of the Agreement's rules, it seeks to ensure uniformity in the application of the rules so that importers can assess with certainty in advance the amounts of duties payable on imports.

The main standard: transaction value

Agreement on Customs
Valuation, Article 1:1

Agreement on Customs
Valuation, Article 8:1

The basic rule of the Agreement is that the value for customs purposes should be based on the price actually paid or payable when sold for export to the country of importation (e.g. the invoice price), adjusted, where appropriate, to include certain payments made by buyers such as the costs of packing and containers, assists, royalties and license fees (*see* box 10). The rules exclude buying commissions and special discounts obtained by sole agents and sole concessionaires from being taken into account in arriving at dutiable value.

The Tokyo Round Agreement strictly limited the discretion available to Customs to reject transaction value to the small number of cases listed in box 11. This was a matter of concern to numerous developing countries. They considered that the rule unduly inhibited the ability of their customs administrations to deal with the traders' practice of undervaluing imported goods in order to reduce incidence on duties. This was one reason for the reluctance of a large number of developing countries to accede to the Agreement in the pre-WTO period.

Decision on Shifting the
Burden of Proof, §1

The Decision Regarding Cases where Customs Administrations Have Reasons to Doubt the Truth or Accuracy of the Declared Value (also known as the Decision on Shifting the Burden of Proof), adopted as a result of the initiative taken by developing countries during the Uruguay Round, corrects this lacuna. The Tokyo Round Agreement placed the burden of proof on Customs if it rejected the transaction value declared by the importer. The Uruguay Round decision shifts the burden of proof on to the importers when Customs, on the basis of the information on prices and other data available to it, "has reason to doubt the truth or accuracy of the particulars or of documents produced in support" of declarations made by the importers.

Box 10

Determining customs value: permitted adjustments to the price paid for goods

(Agreement on Customs Valuation, Article 8)

In order to arrive at the transaction value, Article 8 of the Agreement on Customs Valuation provides that payments made for the following elements can be added to the price actually paid or payable (i.e. the invoice price) by the importer for the imported goods:

❏ *Commissions and brokerage, except buying commissions;*

❏ *Costs of, and charges for, packing and containers;*

❏ *Assists, i.e. goods (materials, components, tools, dies, etc.) or services (designs, plans, etc.) supplied free or at reduced cost by the buyer for use in the production of the imported goods;*

❏ *Royalties and license fees;*

❏ *Subsequent proceeds of any sale accruing to the seller as a result of the resale or use of imported goods;*

❏ *The cost of transport, insurance and related charges to the place of importation, if the country bases its valuation on CIF prices.*

The Article further clarifies that no additions other than for the elements mentioned above shall be made to the price paid or payable in order to arrive at the transaction value. The Article, in addition, enumerates charges or costs that should not be added to customs value, if they can be distinguished from the price actually paid or payable. These are:

❏ *Freight after importation into the customs territory of the importing country;*

❏ *Cost of construction, erection, assembly, maintenance or technical assistance occurring after importation;*

❏ *Duties and taxes of the importing country.*

Box 11

Instances when customs can reject the transaction value declared by the importer

1. When there is no sale.

2. When there are restrictions on the disposition or use of the goods by the buyer. The transaction value need not be accepted if the sales contract imposes some restrictions on the use or disposition of goods except where:

    – *The restriction is imposed by law (e.g. packaging requirements);*

    – *The restrictions limit the geographical area in which the goods may be sold (e.g. distribution contract which limits sales to European countries);*

    – *The restrictions do not affect the value of goods (e.g. the new model imported should not be sold before a particular date).*

3. When the sale or price is subject to some conditions for which the value cannot be determined (e.g. the seller establishes the price of the imported goods on condition that the buyer also buys other goods in specified quantities).

4. When part of the proceeds of any subsequent resale by the buyer accrues to the seller.

5. Where the buyer and seller are related and if the price is influenced by the relationship.

In order to ensure that the transaction value is rejected by Customs in such cases on an objective basis, the Agreement on Customs Valuation stipulates that national legislation should provide certain rights to importers. First, where Customs expresses doubts as to the truth or accuracy of a declared value, importers should have a right to provide an explanation, including documents or other evidence to prove that the value declared by them reflects the correct value of the imported goods. Second, where Customs is not satisfied with the explanations given, importers should have a right to ask Customs to communicate to them in writing its reasons for doubting the truth or accuracy of the declared value. This provision is intended to safeguard the interests of importers, by giving them the right to appeal against the decision to higher authorities and, if necessary, to a tribunal or other independent body, within the customs administration.

Agreement on Customs Valuation, Article 2(a)

The rule that transaction values declared by importers should be used for valuation of goods applies not only to arms-length transactions but also to transactions between related parties. In the latter transactions, which generally take place among transnational corporations and their subsidiaries or affiliates, prices are charged on the basis of transfer pricing which may not always reflect the correct or true value of the imported goods. Even in such cases, the Agreement requires Customs to enter into consultations with the importer, in order to ascertain the type of relationship, the circumstances surrounding the transaction and whether the relationship has influenced the price. If Customs after such examination finds that the relationship has not influenced the declared prices, the transaction value is to be determined on the basis of those prices.

Agreement on Customs Valuation, Article 2(b)

Further, in order to ensure that in practice the transaction value is not rejected simply on the grounds that the parties are related, the Agreement gives importers the right to demand that the value should be accepted when they demonstrate that the value approximates the test values arrived at on the basis of:

❏ Customs value determined in past import transactions occurring at about the same time between unrelated buyers and sellers of identical or similar goods, or

❏ Deductive or computed values calculated for identical or similar goods (see below).

Five other standards

Agreement on Customs Valuation, Annex I: General Note

How should Customs determine dutiable value when it decides to reject the transaction value declared by the importer? In order to protect the interests of importers and to ensure that the value in such cases is determined on a fair and neutral basis, the Agreement limits the discretion available to Customs to using the five standards it lays down. The Agreement further insists that these standards should be used in the sequence in which they appear in the text, and only if Customs finds that the first standard cannot be used should the value be determined on the basis of the succeeding standards.

The standards, presented in the sequence in which they are to be used, are discussed below.

Agreement on Customs Valuation, Article 2

The transaction value of identical goods

Where value cannot be determined on the basis of the transaction value, it should be established by using an already determined transaction value for identical goods.

Agreement on Customs Valuation, Article 3

The transaction value of similar goods

Where it is not possible to determine value on the basis of the above method, it should be determined on the basis of the transaction value of similar goods.

Under both these methods, the transactions selected must relate to imported goods that were sold for export to the country of importation and at about the same time as the goods being exported.

Box 12 describes the rules to be followed in determining whether the goods that are used for determining dutiable value are identical or similar to imported goods.

Box 12

Rules for determining whether goods are identical or similar
(Agreement on Customs Valuation, Article 15:2)

Whether the goods are identical or similar to those in the transaction to be valued is determined by taking into account the characteristics described below.

Goods are identical if they:	**Goods are similar if they:**
Are the same in all respects including physical characteristics, quality and reputation.	*Closely resemble the goods being valued in terms of components, materials and characteristics;*
	Are capable of performing the same functions and are commercially interchangeable with the goods being valued.

In addition, in order to be treated as identical or similar, the goods must have been produced:

> *– in the same country*
> *– and by the same producer*

as the goods being valued.

Where, however, import transactions involving identical or similar goods produced by the same producer in the country of production of the goods being valued do not exist, goods produced by a different producer in the same country must be taken into account.

Deductive value

The next two methods are the deductive method and the computed value method.

Agreement on Customs Valuation, Article 5

Deductive value is determined on the basis of the unit sales price in the domestic market of the imported goods being valued or of identical or similar goods after making deductions for such elements as profits, customs duties and taxes, transport and insurance, and other expenses incurred in the country of importation.

Agreement on Customs Valuation, Article 6

Computed value

The computed value is determined by adding to the cost of producing the goods being valued "an amount for profit and general expenses equal to that usually reflected in sales of goods of the same class or kind as the goods being valued which are made by producers in the country of exportation for export to the country of importation."

Agreement on Customs Valuation, Article 7

Fall-back method

Where customs value cannot be determined by any of the four methods described above, it can be determined by using any of the previous methods in a flexible manner, provided that the criteria employed are consistent with Article VII of the General Agreement. The value so fixed should not, however, be based on the following factors, among others:

❑ The price of goods for export to a third country market,

❑ Minimum customs values,

❑ Arbitrary or fictitious values.

Agreement on Customs Valuation, Article 6; Note to Article 6

As a general rule, the Agreement visualizes that where a transaction value is not accepted, the value should be determined by using the above standards on the basis of the information available within the country of importation. However, it recognizes that in order to determine a computed value, it may be necessary to examine the costs of producing the goods being valued and other information which has to be obtained from outside the country of importation. The Agreement therefore suggests, in order to ensure that the importer is not subjected to unnecessary burdens, that the computed value standard should be used only when buyer and seller are related and the producer is prepared to provide to the customs authorities in the importing country the necessary cost data and facilities for their subsequent verification.

Developing countries and the Agreement

Prior to 1 January 1995, only 11 countries were applying the Agreement's valuation system. When the Agreement was being negotiated, it was recognized that the majority of developing countries (which based their valuation systems on the Brussels Definition of Value[7], a definition entirely different from that followed by the Agreement) would need some time to adopt the legislative and institutional framework and train the officials required for its implementation.

Agreement on Customs Valuation, Article 20:1

The Agreement therefore gave a delay period of five years to developing countries which considered that an immediate change to the new system would be difficult for them.

A number of developing countries have now become members of the Agreement. However, about 50 countries (including some LDCs) have invoked the provisions on the delay period. This period will expire for all countries by early or mid 2000. In order to facilitate adoption of the system by the target date, the WTO and WCO Secretariats have stepped up their technical assistance in training officials in the methods of the Agreement.

A request to extend the delay period of five years may be made to the Committee on Customs Valuation, which has been established under the Agreement. The developing country making the request must demonstrate the difficulties it is encountering in adopting the system. Any extension must be approved by the Committee.

Business implications

The basic aim of the Agreement is to protect the interests of honest traders by requiring that Customs should accept for determining dutiable value the price actually paid by the importer in a particular transaction. This applies to both arms-length and related-party transactions. The Agreement recognizes that the prices obtained by different importers for the same products may vary. The mere fact that the price obtained by a particular importer is lower than that at which other importers have imported the product cannot be used as a ground

---

7   A system developed by the Customs Co-operation Council, now the World Customs Organization (WCO).

for rejecting the transaction value. Customs can reject the transaction value in such situations only if it has reasons to doubt the truth or accuracy of the declared price of the imported goods. Even in such cases, it has to give importers an opportunity to justify their price and if this justification is not accepted, to give them in writing the reasons for rejecting the transaction value and for determining the dutiable value by using other methods. Furthermore, by providing importers the right to be consulted throughout all stages of the determination of value, the Agreement ensures that the discretion available to Customs for scrutinizing declared value is used objectively.

In addition to the right of importers to be consulted at all stages of the determination of dutiable value, the Agreement requires national legislation on the valuation of goods to provide the following rights to importers:

Agreement on Customs Valuation, Article 13

❑ The right to withdraw imported goods from Customs, when there is likely to be a delay in the determination of customs value, provided they leave a sufficient guarantee in the form of a surety or deposit to cover the payment of customs duties for which goods may be liable.

Agreement on Customs Valuation, Article 10

❑ The right to expect that any information of a confidential nature that is made available to Customs shall be treated as confidential.

Agreement on Customs Valuation, Article 11

❑ The right to appeal, without fear of penalty, to an independent body within the customs administration and to a judicial authority against decisions taken by Customs.

CHAPTER 4

Preshipment inspection

Summary

Since about the second half of the twentieth century importers have used the services of independent inspection companies to certify the quality and quantity of products they want to import. These inspections, which are conducted in most cases prior to shipment and in the country of exportation, assure the importer that the goods conform to the technical specifications and the quality standards laid down in the contract and that the quantities exported are accurate. The services of such inspection companies are utilized not only by private business firms, but also by State-owned enterprises and government departments. In fact, the regulations in many countries require goods procured by government departments to be inspected and certified for quality and quantity by independent and competent inspection companies.

Since the mid-1960s, the governments of some developing countries have also been using the services of preshipment inspection (PSI) companies to inspect goods to be imported and to verify their prices, prior to shipment and in the exporting countries. Their basic purpose in doing so is to bring under control the under- or over-invoicing of imported goods and other unfair or improper practices. Today, over 30 countries in Africa, Asia and Latin America use these services:

❑ *To carry out physical inspection of the goods to be imported in order to ensure that they conform to the terms of the contract;*

❑ *To verify their prices; and*

❑ *To ensure that they are classified by the exporter under the correct tariff classification of the importing country.*

The physical inspection of goods is an integral part of the procedures adopted by PSI companies to ensure that the prices indicated by the exporter in the invoice reflect the true value of the goods and that there is no under- or over-invoicing. Such inspections assure importers that the goods they have ordered meet contractual specifications and quality standards, thereby reducing possibilities for dispute after the goods arrive at destination. These inspections also prevent the import of products that are considered harmful to health and therefore cannot be sold (e.g. banned chemicals and pharmaceutical products, substandard food products) in the exporting countries.

In most PSI-using countries, physical inspection and price verification of almost all goods prior to exportation is obligatory for imports to be permitted. In one country, the system is voluntary and importers using PSI services are entitled to have their goods cleared through Customs without further scrutiny of the value recommended by the companies concerned.

Almost all PSI-using countries exempt goods valued below a specified threshold from preshipment inspection.

Objectives for using PSI services

Contracts for mandatory preshipment inspections can be grouped into two broad categories according to the purpose for which the services of PSI companies are employed. In the terminology used by PSI companies, these are *foreign exchange contracts (forex)* and *customs contracts*. The first is usually employed to designate contracts whose basic objective (and that of the government requiring them) is to prevent the flight of capital through over-invoicing. The second is used for contracts undertaken when the governments' main aim is to prevent slippage of customs revenue as a result of undervaluation or deliberate misclassification by traders of goods to be imported under low-duty headings.

Until about a few years ago, the predominant government objective was to prevent the overvaluation of imports. Traders tend to overvalue imports when the import trade and foreign exchange transactions are subject to restrictions. As a result of the steps which developing countries have taken to liberalize their trade and foreign exchange regimes, traders do not generally have at present any incentive to overvalue imported goods. The result has been that, as box 13 shows, the majority of the PSI contracts are now customs contracts; their main aim is to detect the undervaluation of imported goods, with a view to ensuring that revenue due is fully collected and to controlling customs-related corruption.

While PSI services are mainly used for the preshipment inspection of imports, a few governments also utilize them to control the flight of capital through the undervaluation of exports.

There are currently five PSI companies providing preshipment inspection services on a worldwide or a regional basis. The largest among them is the Société générale de surveillance (SGS) of Geneva. It has over 130 affiliated companies, with a presence in more than 140 countries and a staff of over 30,000. The other four companies are BIVAC International of Paris, COTECNA of Geneva, Inchape Testing Services International (ITSI) of London, and the Inspectorate of the United States. They are all members of the Preshipment Inspection Committee of the International Federation of Inspection Agencies (IFIA). There are indications that other companies providing either the same or more or less similar services may enter the market in the near future.

Background to the negotiations on the PSI Agreement

The extension of PSI services to the mandatory verification of the prices agreed between importer and exporter was viewed with concern by business and industry, especially in some developed countries. They were particularly worried by the fact that they were asked to revise their prices downward when the PSI companies found contractual prices to be overvalued. They argued that the criteria used by PSI companies for price comparison was not always known to the exporters. The lack of transparency not only created uncertainty about the acceptability of prices negotiated with buyers but also put exporters in a disadvantageous position, as there were no procedures for appealing to independent bodies against the decisions of PSI companies. The delays in carrying out physical inspections and price verifications also delayed shipment, adding to the exporters' costs.

Agreement on PSI,
Article 1

The Agreement on Preshipment Inspection, negotiated in the Uruguay Round, attempts to strike a balance between the concerns expressed by exporting enterprises in developed countries and the need to safeguard the essential interests of developing countries that consider PSI services useful. It clarifies

---

Box 13

Countries/areas using PSI services

Country/area	Type of PSI contract
Argentina	Customs
Bangladesh	Customs
Benin	Customs/Forex
Bolivia	Forex
Burkina Faso	Customs/Forex
Burundi	Forex
Cameroon	Customs/Forex
Central African Republic	Customs/Forex
Colombia	Customs
Comoros	Customs/Forex
Côte d'Ivoire	Customs
Democratic Republic of the Congo	Customs
Ecuador	Customs
Ghana	Customs/Forex
Guinea	Customs/Forex
Iran, Islamic Republic of	Quality/Quantity
Kenya	Customs
Liberia	Customs
Madagascar	Customs/Forex
Malawi	Customs/Forex
Mali	Customs
Mauritania	Customs/Forex
Mexico	Customs
Mozambique	Customs/Forex
Niger	Customs/Forex
Nigeria	Customs/Forex
Paraguay	Customs
Peru	Customs
Philippines	Customs
Rwanda	Customs/Forex
Senegal	Customs/Forex
Sierra Leone	Customs/Forex
Togo	Customs
Uganda	Customs
United Republic of Tanzania	Customs/Forex
Uzbekistan	Forex
Zanzibar	Forex

that its provisions apply only to preshipment activities carried out in exporting countries that are "contracted or mandated by the government". The term 'preshipment inspection' is defined as "all activities relating to the verification of the quality, the quantity, the price, including currency exchange rate and financial terms and/or the customs classification of goods to be exported".

Main provisions of the Agreement

Agreement on PSI,
Preamble

The Agreement further recognizes that a number of developing countries use PSI services, and allows their use "for as long as and in so far as" they are "necessary to verify the quality, quantity or price of imported goods". The basic aim of the Agreement is to lay down a set of principles and rules which countries using PSI services and exporting countries have to follow in order to ensure that their activities do not cause barriers to trade.

Obligations of PSI-using countries

The obligations which the Agreement imposes on countries using PSI services aim at ensuring the reduction or elimination of the practical problems encountered by exporters as a result of delays by PSI companies in carrying out physical inspections and price verifications, the lack of transparency in the procedures they follow, and the treatment of confidential information. Towards this end, the Agreement contains provisions covering, *inter alia*:

❏ Extension of MFN and national treatment,

❏ Protection of confidential business information,

❏ Avoidance of unreasonable delays, and

❏ The use of specific guidelines for conducting price verification.

Box 14 describes the main features of the obligations which the Agreement imposes on PSI-using countries.

Box 14

Main obligations of PSI-using countries

Non-discrimination. *Procedures and criteria should be applied on an equal basis to all exporters. There should be uniform performance of inspection by all inspectors. [Agreement on Preshipment Inspection, Article 2.1]*

National treatment. *Countries using PSI services should not apply national regulations in a manner that will result in less favourable treatment of the goods being inspected in comparison to the like domestic product. [Agreement on Preshipment Inspection, Article 2.2]*

Inspection site. *Physical inspection should be carried out in the exporting country and, only if this is not feasible, in the country of manufacture. [Agreement on Preshipment Inspection, Article 2.3]*

Standards. *Quality and quantity inspections should be conducted according to the standards agreed between buyer and seller or, in their absence, international standards. [Agreement on Preshipment Inspection, Article 2.4]*

Transparency. *Transparency should be ensured by providing exporters with information, inter alia, on the laws and regulations of user countries on PSI activities, and the procedures and criteria used for inspection. [Agreement on Preshipment Inspection, Article 2.5 to 2.8]*

Protection of confidential information. *Confidential information should not be divulged to third parties. [Agreement on Preshipment Inspection, Article 2.5 to 2.13]*

Delays. *Unreasonable delays should be avoided. [Agreement on Preshipment Inspection, Article 2.15 to 19]*

Price verification. *See box 15.*

Guidelines for conducting price verification

The Agreement stipulates that in order to determine whether the export price reflects the correct value of the goods, PSI companies could compare this price with the prices of identical or similar goods offered for export from the same country of exportation

  – to the country of importation, or

  – to other markets.

However, where for price comparison purposes the prices charged for export to countries other than the country of importation are used, the economic and other factors that influence the prices charged to different countries should be taken into account. In other words, the rules recognize that firms often charge varying prices for different markets, taking into account demand and growth potential as well as factors such as per capita income and standards of living in these markets. An exporting firm may thus charge higher prices for its exports of, say, shirts to Europe than it does for exports to Africa. The Agreement stipulates that when third-country prices are used for price-comparison purposes, the factors responsible for variations in the prices charged to importers in different countries should be taken into account and PSI companies should not "arbitrarily impose the lowest price upon the shipment". In addition, it states that PSI companies should make appropriate allowances for certain "applicable adjusting factors" in regard to the export price of the goods being inspected and the prices of identical or similar goods being used for price comparison. (*See* box 15 for details.)

Box 15

Agreement on Preshipment Inspection: Provisions on price verification

(the text of Article 2:20)

User Members shall ensure that, in order to prevent over- and under-invoicing and fraud, preshipment inspection entities conduct price verification according to the following guidelines:

(a) preshipment inspection entities shall only reject a contract price agreed between an exporter and an importer if they can demonstrate that their findings of an unsatisfactory price are based on a verification process which is in conformity with the criteria set out in subparagraphs (b) through (e);

(b) the preshipment inspection entity shall base its price comparison for the verification of the export price on the price(s) of identical or similar goods offered for export from the same country of exportation at or about the same time, under competitive and comparable conditions of sale, in conformity with customary commercial practices and net of any applicable standard discounts. Such comparison shall be based on the following:

    (i)   only prices providing a valid basis of comparison shall be used, taking into account the relevant economic factors pertaining to the country of importation and a country or countries used for price comparison;

    (ii)   the preshipment inspection entity shall not rely upon the price of goods offered for export to different countries of importation to arbitrarily impose the lowest price upon the shipment;

    (iii)   the preshipment inspection entity shall take into account the specific elements listed in subparagraph (c);

    (iv)   at any stage in the process described above, the preshipment inspection entity shall provide the exporter with an opportunity to explain the price;

(c)   when conducting price verification, preshipment inspection entities shall make appropriate allowances for the terms of the sales contract and generally applicable adjusting factors pertaining to the transaction; these factors shall include but not be limited to the commercial level and quantity of the sale, delivery periods and conditions, price escalation clauses, quality specifications, special design features, special shipping or packing specifications, order size, spot sales, seasonal influences, licence or other intellectual property fees, and services rendered as part of the contract if these are not customarily invoiced separately; they shall also include certain elements relating to the exporter's price, such as the contractual relationship between the exporter and importer;

➥

> *(d) the verification of transportation charges shall relate only to the agreed price of the mode of transport in the country of exportation as indicated in the sales contract;*
>
> *(e) the following shall not be used for price verification purposes:*
>
> > *(i) the selling price in the country of importation of goods produced in such country;*
> >
> > *(ii) the price of goods for export from a country other than the country of exportation;*
> >
> > *(iii) the cost of production;*
> >
> > *(iv) arbitrary or fictitious prices or values.*

Differing rules on the verification of prices in the Agreement on PSI and on the valuation of goods in the Agreement on Customs Valuation

The main differences in the provisions of the two Agreements

Since one of the main aims of governments in using PSI services is to prevent the loss of customs revenue from undervaluation of goods, the question arises of how Customs should use the prices recommended by PSI companies in determining value for customs purposes. The issue is of importance since under the Brussels Definition of Value, the system current in all PSI-using countries, customs authorities have considerable flexibility to use the prices recommended by the PSI companies in determining customs value. However, these countries are obliged to change to the system prescribed by the Agreement on Customs Valuation when the delay period available to developing countries for its implementation expires on 1 January 2000.

The stricter disciplines which the Agreement on Customs Valuation imposes considerably restrains the rights of Customs to use the price recommendations of PSI companies. Moreover, the Agreement prohibits countries from using prices charged by the same exporters to their third markets as a basis for valuation. By contrast, the PSI Agreement permits them to use such prices but, as noted earlier, lays down certain guidelines which they must take into account in recommending prices. (*See* box 15.) Taking this situation into account, the Agreement on Customs Valuation clarifies the role of Customs by stating that the obligations of user member countries "with respect to the services of preshipment inspection entities (in connection with customs valuation) shall be the obligations which they have accepted" under the Agreement on Customs Valuation.

Practical implications of the differences

The aim of the above clarification is to ensure that customs administrations in countries having recourse to PSI services use the prices recommended by them only as test values or advisory opinions when checking the truth or accuracy of the importer's declared value. Customs could use such recommended prices as test values even when the recommended prices are arrived at on the basis of the prices charged by exporters to third-country markets.

Customs however cannot automatically determine dutiable value for levying customs duties on the basis of prices recommended by a PSI company. An examination has to be carried out in each case. If on the basis of the examination and a comparison of the price declared by the importer and the one recommended by the PSI company, it finds that the latter reflects the correct price and the importer does not contest it, the value can be determined on the basis of that price. In all such cases, it will be necessary to ensure that in arriving at the recommended price, the PSI company has followed the rules on adjustments for various elements (e.g. buying commissions and sole agency commissions) laid down by the Agreement on Customs Valuation.

There will always be a few importers who will contest the PSI-recommended prices that are acceptable to Customs, and maintain that the prices they have declared reflect the true value of goods. Such importers have a right to expect Customs to give them the opportunity to produce documentary and other evidence to justify their declared price. If, after examining the evidence, Customs still maintains that the price declared by the importer involves either under- or over-valuation, it cannot under the provisions of the Agreement on Customs Valuation determine value on the basis of the PSI-recommended price.[8] It will have to determine it by using the methods laid down in the Agreement for the determination of value when the transaction value declared by the importer is not acceptable. These methods, *inter alia*, provide for the determination of the value of imported goods on the basis of the value determined in earlier transactions involving identical or similar goods. When the value cannot be determined under these methods, it has to be determined on the basis of price of the imported goods in the domestic market of the importing country (deductive value) or on the basis of cost of production (computed value).

Obligations of exporting countries

So far the discussion has centred on the obligation which the Agreement on PSI imposes on countries using PSI services with a view to ensuring that practices followed and actions taken by PSI companies do not cause barriers to trade. The Agreement also imposes certain obligations on countries which export to PSI-using countries. These are designated in the Agreement as 'exporting countries'. The main obligations which the Agreement imposes on these countries are summarized below:

Agreement on PSI,
Article 3:1

❑ *Non-discrimination*. Laws and regulations that may have been adopted to govern the operation of PSI services should be applied on a non-discriminatory basis.

Agreement on PSI,
Article 3:2

❑ *Transparency*. All such laws and regulations should be published.

As noted earlier, the Agreement visualizes the use of preshipment inspection by developing countries only on the short term. For the long term, the objective of these countries should be to reduce reliance on the use of PSI services to detect customs malpractices and fraud by gradually developing the technical capacities of their customs administrations to deal with such practices. To assist PSI-using countries in building up such capacities, the Agreement calls on exporting countries to provide them with technical assistance, with a view to gradually reducing their reliance on PSI services for verifying prices.

Agreement on PSI,
Article 3:3.

---

8   This applies even when the PSI company has arrived at the price by adhering to the rules of the Agreement on Customs Valuation.

Consideration of complaints and settlement of disputes

Agreement on PSI,
Article 2:21; Article 4

One of the major criticisms made by exporters of PSI activities was the absence of an institutional mechanism for considering complaints on arbitrary or wrong decisions. To facilitate the consideration of such grievances, the Agreement establishes a three-tier mechanism.

First, the Agreement calls on PSI entities to designate officials to whom exporters can appeal against the decisions of PSI entities.

Second, it establishes an independent review entity (IE) to which both exporters and PSI entities can submit grievances. The IE is constituted jointly by WTO, the International Chamber of Commerce (ICC, which represents the interests of exporters), and the International Federation of Inspection Agencies (IFIA, which represents the interests of PSI companies). WTO is responsible for the administration of the IE.

Third, the Agreement recognizes the right of the governments of countries using PSI services and of the exporting countries to invoke WTO dispute settlement procedures, if they consider that the rules of the Agreement are not being adhered to.

A complaint can be submitted to the IE by an exporting enterprise or by a PSI company. Once a complaint is filed, the IE is expected to appoint, with the agreement of the parties to the complaint, either a single trade expert or a three-member panel. Where a panel is constituted, one member is nominated by ICC, the second by IFIA and the third, who should be a trade expert and who will act as chairman, by the IE itself. The panel is required to make a decision, by a majority vote, within eight working days from the filing of the dispute. Both parties to the dispute are required to make financial deposits to cover expenditures incurred by the panel.

These procedures have, however, not been so far invoked either by exporters or by PSI companies.

Review of the provisions of the Agreement

Agreement on PSI,
Article 6

Recommendations adopted to clarify the rules of the Agreement

The Agreement provides that its provisions should be reviewed at the end of the second year of its operation. To carry out such a review the General Council has appointed a Working Party on Preshipment Inspection.

The work done by the Party has resulted in the adoption of recommendations clarifying and improving the provisions in the Agreement. These are set out below.[9]

❑ *Responsibility for determining dutiable value should rest with Customs.* Price verification by PSI entities for customs purposes should be limited to providing technical advice to facilitate the determination of customs value by the user Member. In this regard, the ultimate responsibility for customs valuation and revenue collection should rest with user Members. All activities of PSI entities should be monitored by user Members who should be encouraged to reflect this in national legislation or administrative regulations.

---

9   Source: "Report of the Working Party on Preshipment Inspection to the General Council", 2 December 1997 (WTO document G/L/214).

❑ *Making publicly available price verification criteria.* A user Member should be required to:

  – Make publicly available a single set of price verification criteria, and
  – Inform exporters and importers of the applicable valuation methodology.

The price verification criteria should include the customs valuation methodology, as specified in user Members' national legislation or administrative regulations, used when providing technical advice on customs valuation. In this regard, user Members should encourage PSI entities to utilize electronic means for purposes of providing the required information to exporters and importers.

User Members should ensure that requests for information do not go beyond that required by the provisions of the Agreement on Preshipment Inspection. Reciprocally, exporter members should inform user Members when they become aware that the PSI entities' requests for information go beyond these Articles.

❑ *Site for inspection.* User Members should ensure that PSI entities are encouraged to establish local focal points in countries where they do not have physical, on-site representation.

❑ *Use of electronic means of communication.* The establishment of Web sites by IFIA and by PSI entities with on-line services would enhance the efficiency of PSI operations in such areas as procedures, methods, inspection criteria, responses to enquiries, and dissemination of other usable, essential information by importers and exporters. In addition to providing hard copies, PSI entities should be encouraged to communicate Clean Reports of Findings (CRFs) to importers and exporters through electronic means.

❑ *Avoidance of delays.* User Members should ensure that PSI entities issue CRFs to importers and exporters immediately on receipt of the final documents and completion of inspection. In no case should the issue of a CRF exceed five working days after an inspection. If a CRF has not been issued, the user Member should ensure that the PSI entity puts out a detailed written explanation specifying the reasons for non-issuance.

❑ *Protection of confidential information.* User Members should ensure that contracts with PSI entities or national implementing legislation or administrative regulations specify procedures to be undertaken by such entities to limit the confidential business information they seek from exporters to that provided for under the Agreement and to ensure that any such information obtained by PSI entities is not used for any other purpose than PSI activities for the user Members. Any breach of the rule of confidentiality by the PSI entity is an action that may be brought against the PSI entity in the appropriate judicial or administrative forum of the user Member.

❑ *Fee structures.* User Members should ensure that contracts with PSI entities or national implementing legislation or administrative regulations provide for fee structures that do not create incentives for potential conflicts of interest in any way that may be inconsistent with the objectives of the Agreement. Additionally, contracts with PSI entities or national implementing legislation or administrative regulations should specify that PSI entities should not inspect transactions involving products in which a PSI entity or its related company may have a commercial interest.

❑ *Consideration of complaints from exporters.* Members should ensure that the PSI entity, when responding to a dispute on price verification, provides a detailed written explanation within 10 days of receipt of the complaint, setting forth the basis of its opinion of value by reference to the specific applicable elements of the price verification criteria.

❑ *Use of a model contract*. Members must ensure that contracts are in conformity with the provisions of the PSI Agreement and are encouraged to consider following wherever possible the model contract that has been developed by the Working Party.

❑ *Selectivity and risk assessment*. Members should examine incorporating the principles of selectivity and risk assessment in their contracts.

❑ *PSI auditing*. Members considering having their PSI programmes audited should be guided by the principles that have been developed by the Working Party or ensure that, when alternative criteria are used, the principles of the PSI Agreement are respected.

❑ *Technical assistance*. Developed countries must ensure that developing countries receive the necessary technical assistance for domestic capacity building in order that the transition from PSI can be made.

Future monitoring

Future monitoring of the Agreement on PSI will be undertaken initially by the Committee on Customs Valuation, where PSI will be a standing agenda item.

Business implications

It is important to note that the Agreement provides that countries using the services of PSI companies for verification of prices should do so only for temporary periods of time. The long-term objective should be gradually to reduce their dependence on the use of these services, by developing the capacities of their customs officials to detect cases of undervaluation and other customs malpractices.

The clarifications of the rules of the PSI Agreement described above seek to reduce further, if not completely eliminate, the difficulties enterprises experience in exporting to countries using PSI services. In addition, the Agreement has created a mechanism for the consideration of complaints. This will enable exporters who believe that their prices have been revised arbitrarily by the verifying inspector to complain to a designated senior official of the inspecting company and, if they are not satisfied, to bring the matter up for consideration by the independent review entity, which has been established under the Agreement.

Governments of PSI-using countries benefit from the increased customs revenue resulting from the detection of undervaluation and from the decline in the flight of capital through overvaluation. The employment of PSI services also brings indirect benefits to business enterprises. First, it speeds up the clearance of goods. Second, the use of PSI services lowers the level of customs-related corruption, thereby reducing demands for under-the-table payments for imported goods to be cleared. As has been said, one of the objectives of governments using PSI services is to bring customs-related corruption under control. Third, when verifying prices, PSI companies carry out physical inspections of goods to be imported in order to ensure that they conform to the conditions stipulated in contracts between importers and exporters in regard to quality and quantity. Except therefore in cases of low-value imports, which are not inspected, importers obtain an assurance that the goods they will receive will be in conformity with the terms of their contracts. However, as PSI companies enter into contracts with governments, importers have no right of recourse to these companies if they (the importers) ultimately find that the imported goods do not, in fact, meet the terms of their contracts.

CHAPTER 5

Mandatory and voluntary product standards, and sanitary and phytosanitary regulations

Summary

Countries often require imported products to conform to the mandatory standards they have adopted for the protection of the health and safety of their people or for the preservation of their environment.

The Agreement on Technical Barriers to Trade (TBT) provides that such mandatory product standards should not be so applied by countries as to cause unnecessary obstacles to international trade. Furthermore, they should be based on scientific information and evidence.

From the viewpoint of the Agreement, mandatory product standards do not create unnecessary barriers to trade if they are based on internationally agreed standards. Where for geographical, climatic and other reasons, it is not possible for member countries to base their mandatory regulations on international regulations, they are obliged to publish these regulations in draft form to give producers in other countries an opportunity to comment on them. The Agreement also obliges member countries to take such comments into consideration when the standards are finalized, thus ensuring that the characteristics of products produced in, and exported by, other countries are taken into adequate account.

Voluntary standards, with which compliance is not mandatory, may also pose problems in international trade if they differ widely from country to country. The Code of Good Practice for the Preparation, Adoption and Application of Standards, an integral part of the Agreement on TBT, therefore urges countries to use their best endeavours to require national standardizing bodies to use the same principles and rules in preparing and applying voluntary standards as are laid down for mandatory standards.

Countries also require the compliance of imported agricultural products with their national sanitary and phytosanitary regulations. The primary aim of these regulations is to protect human, animal or plant life or health from pests and diseases that may be brought in by imported agricultural products. The rules which the Agreement on the Application of Sanitary and Phytosanitary Measures (SPS) lay down are similar to those applicable to mandatory product standards. There are, however, some important differences.

The Agreement on TBT requires mandatory product standards to be applied on a non-discriminatory basis to imported products. Sanitary and phytosanitary regulations, particularly those which aim at preventing animal- or plant-borne diseases from entering a country, can, however, be related to "the level of prevalence of specific diseases or pests" and can be more rigorously applied to imports from countries where such diseases or pests are prevalent. The Agreement on SPS further permits countries to take measures to restrict imports on a provisional basis, as a precautionary step, where there is imminent risk of the spread of diseases but the "scientific evidence is insufficient".

The role of standards

In general

Standards permeate all business activities and even the day-to-day life of the man on the street. They play an important role in the manufacturing and service industries and in the sale of their products in national and international markets.

One of the characteristics of modern manufacturing is that manufacturing enterprises do not themselves produce all the parts and components they need, but buy these from ancillary industries, often situated in far-off countries. The standardization of parts and components gives enterprises a wider choice of lower-cost supplies. It also enables them to maintain inventories at comparatively low levels and gives them the flexibility to use substitute components on the assembly line. Standards thus help industries to cut costs and improve productive efficiency.

Standards are indispensable for the international marketing of products as they convey consistent and understandable information to the buyer. A foreign buyer who knows the standard to which a product is produced has an insight into its specifications and is able to assess its quality. Standards thus help reduce disputes over specifications and the quality of goods (and services) exported and imported.

Standards are also used by governments to promote its social goals. Government agencies at the national, State and local levels lay down thousands of regulatory standards to protect the health and ensure the safety of the population, and to conserve the environment. Such regulations cover both product characteristics and the materials and processes used in producing them. Compliance with standards imposed by government regulations is obligatory.

In practice, the distinction between voluntary and mandatory standards may often become blurred. For instance, from the perspective of suppliers, procurement specifications set by major manufacturers are mandatory for doing business, as are government procurement standards.

In promoting trade

While standards facilitate international trade transactions by enabling foreign buyers to assess the specifications and the quality of products offered for sale, they can become barriers to trade if they differ widely from country to country. Buyers are generally reluctant to purchase goods that are based on standards that differ from those of their own countries. Manufacturers wishing to carry out manufacturing operations in other countries may therefore have to adjust their production processes to those countries' specifications. This increases tooling costs and prevents producers from taking advantage of economies of scale. Likewise, where regulatory authorities require product testing in the importing country in order to ascertain compliance with that country's health or safety regulations, foreign suppliers may find themselves at a disadvantage if their products are subjected to stricter tests or higher fees than those required for domestic products.

The solution to these problems lies in harmonizing standards at the international level and in developing guidelines for determining conformity to standards. Work in these two areas in all sectors of industry and technology is being carried out by international standardization organizations.

International rules governing standards

In addition to collecting customs duties on imported goods, countries require that such goods should conform to the mandatory quality, health and safety standards applicable to like products produced domestically. Imported agricultural products have to conform, in addition, to the sanitary and phytosanitary regulations adopted to prevent them from bringing into the importing country pests and diseases not prevalent in that country.

The number of technical regulations laying down mandatory standards is steadily increasing in most countries. The trend is the response of governmental regulatory authorities to growing public demand that products marketed should meet minimum quality and safety standards, and not have any adverse impact on the health of the consuming public and on the environment. The same considerations often impel regulatory authorities to set and apply stricter sanitary and phytosanitary regulations. Box 16 contains an illustrative list of products to which countries apply mandatory safety or health regulations and the agricultural products subject to sanitary and phytosanitary regulations in most countries.

Box 16

Illustrative list of import products subject to technical, sanitary and phytosanitary regulations

Products subject to technical regulations

❏ *Machinery and equipment*

  Boilers
  Electricity-driven construction and assembly tools
  Metal and wood-working equipment
  Medical equipment
  Food-processing equipment

❏ *Consumer articles*

  Pharmaceuticals
  Cosmetics
  Synthetic detergents
  Household electric appliances
  Video and TV sets
  Cinematographic and photographic equipment

  Automobiles
  Toys
  Certain food products

❏ *Raw materials and agricultural inputs*

  Fertilizers
  Insecticides
  Hazardous chemicals

Products subject to sanitary and phytosanitary measures

  Fresh fruits and vegetables
  Fruit juices and other food preparations
  Meat and meat products
  Dairy products
  Processed food products

Though such regulations are adopted by countries to attain legitimate policy objectives, they could in practice be used to provide disguised protection to domestic products.

International rules on the application of mandatory standards (which are also called technical regulations) are contained in the Agreement on Technical Barriers to Trade (TBT). The Agreement on the Application of Sanitary and Phytosanitary Measures (SPS) lays down rules for applying SPS measures. The basic aim of the detailed rules and guidelines of the two Agreements is to ensure that technical, sanitary and phytosanitary regulations are not formulated and applied by countries so as to create unnecessary obstacles to trade.

Agreement on Technical Barriers to Trade

Definitions

Technical regulations and standards

International rules applicable to product standards used in the trade in goods and the procedures used for assessing conformity with such standards are contained in the Agreement on TBT. The Agreement uses the term 'technical regulation' to cover standards with which compliance is mandatory. The term 'standard' is used to cover standards used on a voluntary basis.

*Agreement on TBT,
Annex 1*

Both terms cover:

❑ Product characteristics including those relating to quality;

❑ Process and production methods (PPMs) that have an effect on product characteristics;

❑ Terminology and symbols; and

❑ Packaging and labelling requirements as they apply to the product.

*Agreement on TBT,
Annex 1*

The rules of the Agreement apply to process and production methods only if these methods have an effect on the quality or other characteristics of the product. Other processes and production methods are not covered by the provisions of the Agreement on TBT. (*See* box 17.)

Box 17

Distinction between product standards and PPM standards

Product standards define product characteristics, or the product's quality, design or performance. They need to be distinguished from standards for process and production methods (PPMs, as they are commonly called) which specify norms relating to how goods should be produced. PPM standards apply before and during the production stage, i.e. before the product is placed on the market.

The provisions of the Agreement on TBT apply primarily to product standards. They do not cover PPM standards, except when the production process or method used has an effect on product quality.

Assume that country A prohibits imports of pharmaceuticals from country B. Its grounds are that country B has failed to meet its requirements for proper manufacturing practices and plant cleanliness, thereby affecting product quality. In this case the PPM standard is covered by the TBT Agreement and country A can justify its action if it can establish that its production and processing requirements have an impact on product quality.

Now assume that country A prohibits imports of steel on the grounds that pollution standards at the steel plant in country B are much lower than those enforced by country A. In this case, no environmental damage is done to the importing country; country A's process standard would therefore not be covered by the Agreement and its prohibition on imports would not be justifiable.

Conformity assessment

The usefulness of standards in facilitating international trade depends greatly on how far the buyer has confidence in the manufacturer's statement that the product meets a particular standard. For most of the products entering international trade, buyers generally rely on the manufacturer's declaration that the product meets the standard. There are, however, two circumstances in which such declarations by themselves are not adequate. First, in certain cases manufacturers purchasing parts, components and materials may choose to get a neutral third party to certify that they meet the specifications of standards. Second, in relation to products that are regulated, the regulators often require that, before the domestically produced or imported products are offered for sale, there is positive assurance from a recognized institution or a laboratory that the products meet the safety, health or environmental requirements which the regulations prescribe.

Agreement on TBT, Annex 1:3

The Agreement on TBT defines conformity assessment procedures as "any procedure used, directly or indirectly, to determine that relevant requirements in technical regulations or standards are fulfilled." The assessment of conformity to standards by using a neutral third party takes the following forms:

❑ Testing of products;

❑ Certification of products after inspection;

❑ Assessment of quality management systems; and

❑ Accreditation procedures.

Testing of products

The first form of conformity assessment is product testing, generally carried out by independent testing laboratories. The International Organization for Standardization (ISO) defines a test, in the context of conformity assessment, as "a technical operation that consists of the determination of one or more characteristics of a given product, process or service according to a specified procedure".[10] Testing services thus include a broad spectrum of technical activities. Materials, parts and completed products may be tested for their physical properties, such as strength and durability; physical dimensions, electrical characteristics, including interference with other devices, acoustic properties; chemical composition; presence of toxic contaminants; and a multitude of other features.

Certification of products after inspection

The second form of conformity assessment is certification. Again, ISO defines certification as a "procedure by which a third party gives written assurance that a product, process or service conforms to specified requirements".[11]

Certification is distinguished from testing by two key features:

❑ First, certification always measures a product (or process or service) against one or more specific standards, whether voluntary or mandatory. Testing, by contrast, does not necessarily measure against a particular standard.

❑ Second, certification results in a formal statement of conformity – a certificate – that can be used by the manufacturer to show compliance with regulations and purchasing specifications, and to enhance the product's marketability.

Most certification bodies are private, profit-making testing laboratories. In addition to providing testing services, many of these laboratories take the additional step of certifying the product as meeting a particular standard and license the manufacturer to use their certification mark on the product or its packaging. The mark, however, is the property of the certifier and is covered by the national trade mark act.

---

10   ISO/IEC, *Conformity Assessment*, 3rd ed. (Geneva, 1995).
11   *Ibid.*

Quality management systems

The third form of conformity assurance is assessment by a third party of the producer's quality management system. While testing and certification aim at evaluating the quality of the products themselves, the assessment of the quality assurance system by a third party aims at assuring the purchaser that the manufacturer has in place a viable and effective system that is capable of producing products of consistent quality with little or no variation. It is a production management tool for controlling and monitoring variables in the manufacturing process that lead to product defects.

The best known quality assurance system is the ISO 9000 series of standards. Developed by ISO, the system emphasizes that the maintenance of consistent product quality is possible only if it is acknowledged as an important management responsibility. It further lays down the documentation procedures and records that a company should maintain in order to demonstrate to, and assure, its clients and purchasers that adequate attention is being paid to the maintenance of the quality system. ISO 9000 also provides guidelines for training, the statistical monitoring of results and continuous improvement.

Registration or certification of an enterprise to ISO 9000 is granted after an assessment is made by an independent third party that the system in place meets all the requirements. Subsequent periodic audits are made to ensure that the company continues to operate in accordance with the system.

Purchasing companies all over the world are increasingly giving preference to suppliers registered to ISO 9000 for their raw materials, parts and components. Regulations in many countries oblige government purchasing agencies to obtain their requirements from such companies.

Accreditation procedures

Supplying industries as well as their clients are likely to have confidence in conformity assurance systems if the competence of the testing laboratory, product certifier or quality assurance registrar is accredited by an independent technical body. The procedure by which such independent technical entities evaluate and formally acknowledge the competence of the above-mentioned first-layer conformity assessment bodies is known as 'accreditation'. Accreditors are generally professional bodies or associations of industries in the private sector. In a number of countries, however, the right to accredit is granted through legislation to a national standardization body or to a separate body acting jointly with it.

General principles and rules of the Agreement on TBT

Encouragement of the use of international standards, guidelines and recommendations

The basic aim of the Agreement is to ensure that:

- Technical regulations and standards including packaging, marking and labelling requirements, and
- Procedures used for assessing conformity with such regulations, requirements and standards

are not formulated and applied so as to create unnecessary barriers to trade. The Agreement assumes that this aim can be attained if countries use, wherever appropriate and possible, international standards in formulating their technical regulations or in developing voluntary national standards. Likewise, it calls on

Agreement on TBT, Article 2:4

member countries to use guidelines and recommendations developed by international standardization organizations as a basis for their conformity assessment procedures.

Agreement on TBT,
Article 2:5

Agreement on TBT,
Article 2:6

To provide an incentive to countries to use international standards, the Agreement provides that where international standards or guidelines or a conformity assessment system has been used as a basis for a technical regulation, it shall be presumed that they do not create unnecessary obstacles to trade. It further urges member countries to participate in the work of international standardization organizations, so that international standards are available for products for which they wish to adopt technical regulations or develop voluntary standards. Countries are also urged to participate in the activities of such organizations in order to develop international guides and recommendations that can be used in developing national conformity assessment procedures.

The Agreement, however, does not specify the international organizations whose standards may be used in adopting technical regulations. The main organizations developing international standards applicable to industrial products are the following:

- ❑ International Organization for Standardization (ISO);
- ❑ International Electrotechnical Commission (IEC);
- ❑ International Telecommunication Union (ITU); and
- ❑ Codex Alimentarius Commission.

Circumstances permitting deviations from international standards and guidelines

Agreement on TBT,
Article 2:4

Where international standards or guidelines are considered ineffective or inappropriate for the achievement of national objectives (for instance, because of fundamental climatic or geographical factors, or fundamental technological problems) or where international standards do not exist, countries are free to develop their own national standards. Likewise, a country may adopt a conformity assessment system which is not based on internationally accepted guidelines or recommendations if it considers that the technical content of these guidelines is not suitable for the achievement of the specific objective of the proposed national system. However, in all cases where such proposed

Agreement on TBT,
Article 2:9

measures are expected to have a significant effect on trade, the Agreement imposes an obligation on the countries, *inter alia*, to:

- ❑ Publish in draft form the proposed technical regulations, standards and the conformity assessment systems;

- ❑ Give reasonable opportunity to other interested parties to comment on these drafts; and

- ❑ Take into account these comments in finalizing the drafts.

Specific rules

Technical regulations and standards

In order to ensure that technical regulations which impose mandatory standards as well as voluntary standards do not create unnecessary barriers to trade, the Agreement further lays down certain principles and rules. These call on regulatory agencies to ensure that technical regulations and standards:

Agreement on TBT,
Article 2:1

- ❑ Are applied so as not to discriminate among imported products by origin (MFN principle);

<table>
<tr><td>

Agreement on TBT,
Article 2:1

</td><td>

❑ Do not extend to imported products treatment that is less favourable than that extended to domestically produced products (national treatment principle);

❑ Are, where relevant, based on scientific and technical information; and

</td></tr>
<tr><td>

Agreement on TBT,
Article 2:2

</td><td>

❑ Are not formulated or applied in a manner as to cause "unnecessary obstacles to international trade".

</td></tr>
</table>

The Agreement lays down specific guidelines for regulatory authorities in formulating technical regulations, in order to ensure that these regulations do not create unnecessary obstacles to trade (*see* box 18).

Box 18

Guidelines for determining whether technical regulations have the effect of creating unnecessary obstacles to trade

The Agreement on TBT provides that technical regulations which lay down product standards as well as packaging, marking and labelling requirements should not ordinarily be considered as causing unnecessary obstacles to trade if:

❑ *They are adopted to achieve legitimate objectives;*

❑ *They are based on international standards; and*

❑ *Where international standards are considered inappropriate or do not exist, the technical regulations are applied so that they*

   – *are not more restrictive than necessary to fulfill the above legitimate objectives, and*

   – *take into account the risks non-fulfilment (of these objectives) would create.*

The legitimate objectives for which countries can adopt technical regulations include:

❑ *National security requirements;*

❑ *The prevention of deceptive practices;*

❑ *Protection of human, animal or plant life or health, or the environment.*

In the light of these provisions, whether a technical regulation that is not based on international standards can be considered an unnecessary obstacle to trade would depend firstly on the objectives for which it has been adopted. If it has been adopted to attain one of the above-mentioned legitimate objectives, the next questions to be examined are whether the regulation is more trade restrictive than is necessary for the achievement of the objective, and whether, if a less trade restrictive measure were adopted, there were risks of non-fulfilment of the objective. In assessing the risks of non-fulfilment, the elements to be considered are:

❑ *Available scientific and technical regulations;*

❑ *Related processing technology; or*

❑ *The intended end use of a product.*

Conformity assessment procedures

<table>
<tr><td>

Agreement on TBT,
Article 5

</td><td>

The Agreement provides that systems adopted for assessing conformity to technical regulations should not be formulated or applied so as to create barriers to trade. Towards this end, it stipulates that:

❑ Conformity assessment procedures should not be prepared, adopted and applied to imported products under conditions that are less favourable than those applied to products of national origin;

❑ Foreign suppliers should be provided, on request, information on the processing period and the documentation required for assessing the conformity of the products they want to export;

</td></tr>
</table>

❑ Any fees charged to foreign suppliers should be equitable in relation to fees charged to products of national origin;

❑ The siting of facilities and the selection of samples for testing should not cause inconvenience to foreign suppliers; and

❑ The conformity assessment procedures should provide for a review of complaints on the operation of the procedures.

Agreement on TBT, Article 6

Arrangements for the mutual recognition of conformity assessment procedures

Product testing and inspection by regulatory authorities in importing countries in order to establish conformity with regulations could cause practical problems to foreign suppliers, even if the authorities follow the principles and rules described above. Foreign suppliers shoulder the costs of sending samples to importing countries and often need to employ agents who can expedite testing and inspection. Moreover, where the technical regulations require manufacturing facilities to be inspected by authorized inspectors of the importing country, in order to obtain confirmation, for instance, that good manufacturing standards are being followed, the foreign suppliers have to shoulder the inspectors' travel expenses.

To reduce such disadvantages for foreign suppliers, the Agreement urges member countries to accept, where possible, the results of conformity assessment tests carried out in exporting countries. It further suggests that countries should show willingness to accept the certificates issued by regulatory authorities in exporting countries, even when the procedures "differ from their own" provided they are satisfied that these are "equivalent" to their own procedures. The Agreement, however, recognizes that it will be possible for an importing country to accept the procedures of the exporting country as equivalent only where it has confidence in the "adequate and enduring technical competence" of the regulatory authority of the exporting country and therefore in the "continued reliability of their conformity assessment results". To facilitate acceptance by importing countries of conformity assessment certificates, the Agreement further encourages arrangements for the "mutual recognition" of member countries' conformity assessment procedures.

Code of Good Practice for voluntary standardization

As noted earlier, many of the standards used by industries are voluntary standards. These are often formulated by national standardizing bodies in the various member countries. Voluntary standards can create problems in international trade if they vary widely from country to country. The Agreement

Agreement on TBT, Article 4; Annex 3

has therefore developed a *Code of Good Practice for the Preparation, Adoption and Application of Standards* with which national standardizing bodies are expected to abide in preparing, adopting and applying standards. The Code requires national standardizing bodies to follow principles and rules that are similar to those specified for mandatory standards. Thus the Code urges member countries:

❑ To use international standards as a basis for their national standards,

❑ To participate fully, within the limits of their resources, in the preparation of international standards for products for which they propose to adopt national standards.

Furthermore, in order to acquaint foreign producers with the work on standardization being undertaken by national bodies in different countries, it

Code of Good Practice, J

requires these bodies to publish their work programme "at least once every six months", giving information on the standards they are preparing and the standards they have adopted in the preceding period. At the time of publication, the national bodies are also required to notify the ISO/IEC Information Centre of the name of the publication and how and where it can be obtained.

The Code requires standardizing bodies to allow a period of at least 60 days for the submission of comments on draft standards by interested parties in outside countries. The comments are usually forwarded through national standardizing bodies. The Code calls on the standardizing body formulating the standards to take these comments into account when finalizing the standard.

Agreement on the Application of Sanitary and Phytosanitary Measures

So far, the discussion has focused on technical regulations, standards and systems adopted for conformity assessment. The international rules in these areas, which are contained in the Agreement on TBT, apply to both industrial and agricultural products. Imported agricultural products may in certain cases have to conform not only to technical regulations but also to the importing country's sanitary and phytosanitary measures.

Definition of sanitary and phytosanitary regulations

What are sanitary and phytosanitary measures? And how do they differ from technical regulations? These measures are adopted by countries to protect:

Agreement on SPS, Annex A

❑ Human or animal life from food-borne risks which arise from the use of additives, contaminants, toxins or disease-causing organisms (and thus ensure food safety);

❑ Human health from animal or plant-carried diseases; and

❑ Animals and plants from pests and diseases.

The term 'sanitary regulations' is used to cover types of regulations whose basic objective is to ensure food safety, or to prevent animal-borne diseases from entering a country. Where the objective of the regulations is to ensure that imported plant varieties do not bring into a country plant-borne diseases, they are referred to as 'phytosanitary regulations'.

Difference between technical regulations and SPS measures

The basic difference between technical regulations and sanitary and phytosanitary measures arises from the objectives for which they are adopted. In the case of SPS measures, the aim is limited and specific – to protect human, animal and plant life or health by ensuring food safety and preventing animal and plant-borne diseases from entering a country. Technical regulations, on the other hand, are imposed for a variety of policy objectives. They include, as noted earlier, national security requirements, prevention of deceptive practices and protection of the environment. They may be adopted to protect human health or safety, or animal or plant life for objectives other that those for which health and sanitary measures are implemented (*see* box 19 for illustrations).

Approach of the SPS Agreement

The rules governing the use of sanitary and phytosanitary measures are contained in the Agreement on the Application of Sanitary and Phytosanitary Measures. Like the TBT Agreement, the SPS Agreement requires countries:

Box 19
Distinction between technical regulations and sanitary and phytosanitary measures: Some examples

Whether a particular regulation to protect the health and life of a country's human and animal population or of its plants and fauna is a technical regulation or a sanitary or phytosanitary measure depends on the objectives for which it has been adopted. The distinction is important, as the rules of the Agreement on TBT would apply if the regulation is treated as a technical regulation, and those of the Agreement on SPS, if it is treated as a sanitary and phytosanitary measure. While the provisions of the two Agreements are similar in most respects, they have some significant differences.

Broadly speaking, a measure would be considered a sanitary and phytosanitary measure where its objective is to protect:

❑ *Human life from the risks arising from additives, toxins, and plant- and animal-borne diseases;*

❑ *Animal life from the risks arising from additives, toxins, pests, diseases, disease-causing organisms;*

❑ *Plant life from the risks arising from pests, diseases, disease-causing organisms; and*

❑ *A country from the risks arising from damages caused by the entry, establishment or spread of pests.*

Regulations adopted for other purposes, in order to protect human, animal and plant life, would be treated as technical regulations.

The examples that follow illustrate how the objective of a measure determines whether it is a technical regulation (TR), or a sanitary and phytosanitary measure (SPS) and whether it therefore falls under the Agreement on TBT or the Agreement on SPS.

Controlling Agreement	Description of measure
Regulation on pesticides	
SPS	*If the measure relates to residues in food or in animal feed, and the objective is to protect human or animal health.*
TBT	*If the measure relates to the quality or efficacy of the product, or to a health risk to handlers.*
Establishment of labelling requirements for foods	
SPS	*If the measure is related to food safety.*
TBT	*If the regulation concerns such matters as the size of the typeface used on the label, the presentation of information on contents, grade, etc.*
Regulation on containers for the shipment of grains	
SPS	*If the regulation is on fumigation or other treatment of these containers, i.e. disinfection in order to prevent the spread of disease.*
TBT	*If the regulation relates to the size or structure of the containers.*

Source: WTO documents.

Agreement on SPS, Preamble

❑ To base their SPS measures on international standards, guidelines or recommendations developed by the:

  – Codex Alimentarius Commission;

  – International Office of Epizootics;

> – Relevant international and regional organizations operating within the framework of the International Plant Protection Convention; or
>
> – Any other international organization that may be designated by the WTO Committee on SPS.

Agreement on SPS, Article 3:4

❑ To play a full part in the activities of above-mentioned international organizations, in order to promote the harmonization of SPS measures on an international basis.

Agreement on SPS, Annex B: 5

❑ To provide an opportunity to interested parties in other countries to comment on draft standards when they are not based on international standards, or where they deviate from such standards, or where there are no international standards.

Agreement on SPS, Article 4

❑ To accept the SPS measures of exporting countries as equivalent if they achieve the same level of SPS protection and to enter into, where possible, arrangements for the mutual recognition of the equivalence of specified sanitary or phytosanitary measures.

Main differences between the SPS and the TBT Agreements

The rules of the SPS Agreement differ from those of the TBT Agreement in four important respects.

The first relates to the importance attached to scientific evidence in formulating regulations. In the case of sanitary and phytosanitary measures, the obligation to base them on scientific evidence is unequivocal. The Agreement prescribes that such measures must be "based on scientific principles" and must not be "maintained without sufficient scientific evidence". The TBT Agreement on the other hand recognizes that the use of scientific evidence would depend on the objectives for which the technical regulations are adopted. Regulations adopted for the purposes of protecting health and safety would have to be based on scientific evidence; these considerations may not be relevant where the objective of the regulation is protection against deceptive practices or where it is adopted for national security reasons.

Agreement on SPS, Article 2:2

Second, the TBT Agreement requires that technical regulations which prescribe product standards should be applied on an MFN basis to imports from all sources. Sanitary and phytosanitary regulations, particularly those which aim at preventing animal- or plant-borne diseases from entering a country, may be more or less demanding depending on "the level of prevalence of specific diseases or pests" in the country or in a region of that country.

Against this background, the Agreement on SPS requires countries:

Agreement on SPS, Article 6:1

❑ To "ensure that their sanitary and phytosanitary measures are adapted to the sanitary and phytosanitary characteristics of the area – whether all of a country, part of a country, or all or parts of several countries – from which the product originated and to which the product is destined." Such characteristics should be determined, *inter alia*, on the basis of the level of prevalence of specific diseases or pests; and

Agreement on SPS, Article 2:3

❑ Not to apply them as to cause arbitrary or unjustifiable discrimination among countries or regions where similar conditions prevail or as to constitute a disguised restriction on international trade.

It should be noted, however, that flexibility to deviate from the MFN principle is permitted only for SPS measures that aim at preventing the entry of plant- or animal-borne pests and diseases into a country. SPS measures aiming at ensuring food safety (e.g. regulations on additives, contamination, or permitted residue levels) would ordinarily have to be applied on an MFN basis.

Third, the Agreements differ in regard to the conditions under which it may be possible for countries to deviate from international standards. Many of these differences arise because of the varying objectives for which technical regulations and SPS measures are adopted.

Agreement on TBT,
Article 2.4

Agreement on SPS,
Article 3:3; Article 5

The TBT Agreement, for instance, specifies the conditions under which countries may deviate from international standards. The Agreement states that, where an international standard exists, a country may adopt a national standard which is different or higher than the international standard if it is considered necessary, for "fundamental climatic or geographical factors or fundamental technological problems". The SPS Agreement, on the other hand, gives countries the unrestrained right to introduce sanitary and phytosanitary measures which result in a higher level of "protection than would be achieved by measures based on the relevant international standards, guidelines or recommendations" if:

❑ There is a scientific justification, or

❑ Where a country determines on the basis of an assessment of risks that a higher level of sanitary and phytosanitary protection would be appropriate.

In order to ensure that decisions to adopt higher standards than those stipulated by international standards are taken objectively, the Agreement provides guidelines for assessing risks to human, animal or plant life or health. These are listed in box 20.

Box 20

Guidelines for assessing risks and determining an appropriate level of sanitary and phytosanitary protection
(Agreement on SPS, Article 5)

The Agreement calls on countries to ensure that the level of sanitary and phytosanitary protection which they consider appropriate should be determined on the basis of an assessment of risks to human, animal or plant life or health arising from the entry of the imported product. In assessing such risks, the following elements should be taken into account:

❑ *Scientific evidence;*

❑ *Methods of production, processing (and control) used in the exporting country;*

❑ *Prevalence of specific diseases or pests, and the existence of pest- or disease-free areas in the exporting country;*

❑ *Ecological and environmental conditions (in both the exporting and the importing country adopting the SPS measure);*

❑ *Facilities for sanitary, quarantine and other treatment (in the country adopting the measures).*

Where the sanitary and phytosanitary measures are intended to protect animal or plant life or health, the assessment of risks should take into account, in addition to the above elements, the following economic factors:

❑ *The potential damage in terms of loss of production or sales in the event of the entry, establishment or spread of a pest or disease;*

❑ *The likely costs of controlling or eradicating the pests or diseases if they were to spread; and*

❑ *The relative cost effectiveness of alternative approaches to limiting risks.*

The Agreement emphasizes that, in adopting sanitary and phytosanitary measures, countries should keep in mind the need to ensure that these measures are not more trade restrictive than is required to achieve the desired level of protection, taking into account both the technical and economic factors mentioned above.

In carrying out such risk assessments, countries are urged to use the risk assessment techniques developed by the relevant international organizations. In a dispute brought to WTO for settlement (on European Community measures concerning meat and meat products – hormones, WT/DS26), the Appellate Body observed that the Agreement's provisions on risk assessment should not be interpreted to imply that a country planning to ban or restrict imports on the basis of sanitary and phytosanitary measures must itself carry out a risk assessment. The country could rely on the risk assessment carried out by other countries or by international organizations.

Agreement on SPS, Article 5.7

Fourth, the SPS Agreement permits countries to adopt SPS measures on a provisional basis as a precautionary measure when there is immediate risk of the spread of diseases but the scientific evidence is insufficient. The TBT Agreement does not contain any such provision.

Other provisions common to the SPS and TBT Agreements

Level of obligations

Technical regulations, sanitary and phytosanitary measures, standards and conformity assessment systems are prepared not only by bodies controlled by central governments but also at local government level. In countries with federal governments, an increasing number of measures are being promulgated by State governments. In most countries, voluntary standards are prepared and adopted by professional bodies or by autonomous national standardizing bodies.

The Agreements on TBT and SPS impose binding obligations on member countries to require the bodies controlled by them to abide by the discipline of the Agreements. However, as central governments are not allowed by their national constitutions to assume binding obligations on behalf of local or State governments or autonomous standardization bodies, the Agreements call on central governments to take such reasonable measures as may be available to them to ensure that State governments and local bodies follow the discipline of the Agreements.

Special and differential treatment of developing countries

The two Agreements contain provisions for the extension of special and differential treatment to developing countries. Under these provisions, developing countries could have delayed the application of the SPS Agreement, with the exception of its transparency provisions, by two years. This period has already expired. The transitional period for the application of the Agreement by least developed countries is five years, which expires on 1 January 2001. Both Agreements further provide that in order to facilitate compliance with their provisions, the relevant Agreement Committees could, at the request of a developing or a least developed country, grant time-limited exceptions from all or some of the obligations which they impose. No member country has, however, requested such an exception to be made.

The two Agreements also contain provisions calling on the WTO Secretariat and member countries to provide technical assistance to developing and least developed countries to assist them, *inter alia*, in developing the legal and institutional framework required for the application of technical regulations and SPS measures.

Enquiry points

Agreement on TBT, Article
10:3; Agreement on SPS,
Annex B:3

One of the main problems enterprises from developing countries face in promoting exports is the lack of information on the standards and health and sanitary measures applicable to their products in target markets. To help enterprises obtain such information, the two Agreements require each member country to establish *enquiry points* from which information can be obtained by the governments of other countries and by interested business firms on:

❑ Technical regulations and voluntary standards adopted or proposed to be adopted;

❑ Conformity assessment procedures adopted or proposed to be adopted;

❑ Sanitary and phytosanitary measures adopted or proposed to be adopted;

❑ Control and inspection procedures, production and quarantine treatment, pesticide tolerance treatment and food additive approval procedures;

❑ Risk assessment procedures developed for the determination of the appropriate level of sanitary and phytosanitary protection.

The services provided by these enquiry points are being increasingly used by business firms as well as by civil society (consumer associations and other interest groups) to obtain information on the technical regulations and sanitary and phytosanitary measures of other countries.

The annex to this chapter lists the enquiry points established in accordance with the Agreements on TBT and SPS.

Business implications and experience of the operation of the Agreements

Reviews of the Agreements

The two Agreements provide for periodic reviews of their operation. A triennial review of the Agreement on TBT was conducted by the Committee on Technical Barriers to Trade in 1997; the review of the Agreement on SPS was carried out by the Committee on Sanitary and Phytosanitary Measures in 1998. The Committees considered that on the whole the Agreements had worked well and no major changes in their provisions were necessary.

Participation in international standardization activities

Both Agreements encourage countries to participate in the work of international organizations developing international standards for the products for which they propose to adopt standards or regulations.

The participation of developing countries in international standardization activities is on the whole marginal. Apart from a few of the more advanced countries, developing countries are not able to participate actively in the meetings of the technical committees because of financial constraints. And even if they are able to attend meetings, their participation is often not effective, as it is not supported by the background research needed for the submission of technical papers.

In this context, it is relevant to note that, because of the budgetary difficulties through which even governments of developed countries are going through, the responsibility for undertaking and financing research for participating in international standardization activities is falling on industries. Against this background, the business community in all countries must take an active interest in promoting research and technical work to improve the participation of their countries in international standardization activities covering their main export products.

Making full use of rights to comment on draft standards and regulations

The two Agreements visualize that one way of ensuring that the standards and the technical and SPS measures introduced by member countries do not become barriers to trade is to give both domestic and foreign producers an opportunity to comment on their drafts. The obligation to take such comments into account goes a long way towards guaranteeing that the concerns of foreign producers and suppliers about the possible adverse effects of proposed measures are taken into consideration when these measures are finalized.

In practice, however, the right to comment may not be of any real value to foreign producers if they do not know in time that work on preparing and adopting a standard or regulation is underway. The two Agreements have therefore adopted procedures for ensuring greater transparency in the work being done in the areas covered.

In particular the Agreements stipulate that in addition to publishing notices in the relevant technical journals, member countries should notify the WTO Secretariat of the products that are covered by technical or SPS regulations and the objectives and rationale for these regulations. Under the existing procedures, these notifications are immediately sent by the Secretariat to the national governments. It is the responsibility of the governments to pass on the notifications to the industry associations and professional technical bodies concerned, so that, if they judge it necessary, they can obtain copies of the draft regulations and comment on them.

Agreement on TBT: Code of Good Practice, J

The procedure for voluntary standards, prepared by national standardizing bodies, is, though somewhat different, based on similar principles. In order to acquaint foreign producers with the standardization work of these bodies, the Code of Good Practice embodied in the TBT Agreement requires these bodies to publish their work programme "at least once every six months", giving information on standards that are under preparation and those that have been adopted in the preceding period. The national bodies are also required to notify the ISO/IEC Information Centre of the name of the publication containing this information and where it can be obtained. Foreign industries and their associations can take advantage of the right to comment on draft standards which the TBT Agreement has created in their favour only by exercising continuous vigilance on the work being carried out by national standardizing bodies in their target export markets and examining the information they publish on draft standards.

Quality management systems: ISO 9000

A related issue that is becoming of increasing importance in international trade relations is the insistence of manufacturing industries on buying components, parts and other intermediate products from enterprises which operate viable quality management systems. As noted earlier, the Agreement on TBT encourages countries to adopt for this purpose internationally agreed quality management systems like ISO 9000.

The increasing preference for suppliers implementing quality management systems has resulted in a spectacular rise in the number of companies registered to ISO 9000 worldwide. Many of these companies are in Europe. However, the trend is also noticeable in the United States among companies which want to retain their European markets.

There is growing awareness among manufacturing and service companies in the developing world of the important role which quality management systems play in marketing their products. Practical difficulties however prevent companies in a large number of developing countries from taking advantage of ISO 9000. Many countries have no local certifying firms which can provide guidance on introducing the system, assess and register companies to ISO 9000 and carry out the periodic audits needed. Most countries have yet to develop the legal framework and the institutions required for the accreditation of certifying firms. As mentioned earlier, accreditation establishes and attests to the technical competence of institutions to register (certify) companies to ISO 9000. From the point of view of purchasing companies, a certificate of ISO registration is of no better value than a manufacturer's own declaration unless it is issued by an accredited registration or certification body.

Registration to ISO 9000 involves expenditure on fees to the registering firm and the costs of administering the system. Costs are higher when the services of foreign certifying bodies acceptable to buyers abroad have to be used in the absence of accredited local institutions. The system also calls for documentation of actions taken on essential elements of the ISO 9000 system.

For small and medium-sized enterprises, the adoption of the ISO 9000 system, even though necessary from the point of view of improving confidence in their products, therefore presents a dilemma. In SMEs where staff literacy levels are low the paper work required is particularly burdensome. However, many SMEs may find themselves compelled to seek ISO 9000 registration, especially if they intend to produce intermediate products for further processing or to undertake final processing under subcontracts from foreign companies.

It is important to note that quality management systems like ISO 9000 are not intended to evaluate the quality of the products themselves. Registration only supports the manufacturer's claim that it has a system capable of delivering a product of consistent quality. The quality consciousness which the introduction of the system creates, however, results in greater attention to enhancing product quality, for instance by improving its design and performance.

Opportunities provided by the Agreements for settling differences through bilateral consultations

The opportunity for bilateral consultations, which the Agreements on TBT and SPS Agreements provide prior to the invocation of dispute settlement procedures, has created new possibilities for settling problems which exporters encounter as a result of the application of technical, sanitary and phytosanitary regulations. Experience has shown that many of these problems are of a practical nature, relating to the administration of inspection, quarantine or other regulations, and do not raise questions of scientific justification or of acceptable levels of risk.

As box 21 shows, it has been possible for exporting countries to find satisfactory solutions to some of these problems by holding discussions on a bilateral basis. Solutions to other disputes were found by raising the disputed issues under the WTO dispute settlement procedures.

It is necessary for the business community to take advantage of this opportunity by bringing to the notice of their government the practical problems they may be encountering as a result of the application of technical, sanitary and phytosanitary regulations in their target markets.

Box 21
Examples of disputes settled under the WTO mechanism

Disputes settled through bilateral consultations

- *European Communities – Maximum level for certain contaminants (aflatoxins) in foodstuffs*

A number of countries (United States, Argentina, Australia, Brazil, the Gambia, India, Indonesia, Malaysia, the Philippines, Senegal and Thailand) had in their submissions to the Committee on Sanitary and Phytosanitary Measures expressed concern at the possible restrictive effects which the proposed EU regulations providing for maximum levels of aflatoxins could have on their exports of groundnuts, other nuts, milk and other products. They pointed out that the proposal to set more stringent levels for aflatoxins than the standards currently fixed internationally was not founded on a proper risk assessment undertaken on the basis of scientific evidence. Consequently, while the adoption of the measures would not result in a significant reduction in health risks for EU consumers, it provided a potential threat to their exports.

Even though the European Community maintained that there was no consensus at the international level on maximum levels of aflatoxins in food products and that, in proposing the new levels, it had taken into account the recommendations of scientific committees, it agreed to revise the levels proposed in the draft regulations for most of the food products concerned in the light of the views expressed in the country submissions.

- *Republic of Korea – restrictions on imports of poultry*

Thailand had pointed out that the "criteria of zero tolerance for listeria" which might be included in the proposed amendments to the Korean Food Code would adversely affect its exports of frozen chicken. Taking into account the points made and the concerns expressed by Thailand, the authorities of the Republic of Korea decided to insist on zero tolerance criteria for listeria only for meat for direct consumption and excluded meat for further processing and cooking from the application of the criteria.

- *United Republic of Tanzania – European Community ban on imports of fish from the United Republic of Tanzania, Kenya, Uganda and Mozambique*

The United Republic Tanzania complained that the European Community had banned imports of fresh, frozen and processed fish products from the country as well as from Kenya, Uganda and Mozambique, alleging health concerns. The European Community maintained that the ban was considered necessary as there was a risk of the transmission of cholera through foodstuffs containing fresh water. It however agreed to withdraw the ban, following the consultations which were held with competent authorities in the exporting countries, as it was satisfied that the necessary guarantees were in place.

Disputes settled on the basis of findings of Panels and the Appellate Body

- *European Communities - Measures concerning meat and meat products (hormones)*

The Appellate Body, which endorsed the findings of the Panel established to consider a complaint by the United States against the EC's ban on imports of hormone-treated meat, held that the ban was not justifiable, as the international standard relating to such meat recognized that consumption of the meat was not harmful to health. In the situation, it would have been possible for EC to adopt measures which were more stringent than the international standard, only if it was able to justify its need on scientific grounds on the basis of a risk assessment undertaken by it. However, EC had not carried out such a risk assessment.

→

> *After the announcement of the decision, EC decided to carry out a risk assessment to justify the ban on scientific grounds. There was, however, disagreement between the parties to the dispute on the "reasonable period of time" for the implementation of the rulings on the case which included the obligation to carry out a risk assessment. An arbitrator was then appointed in accordance with the procedures. The arbitrator determined that the "reasonable period of time for the European Communities to implement the recommendations and rulings of the Dispute Settlement Body ... is 15 months ... from 13 February 1998."*
>
> *As EC was not able to take implementation measures within the 15-month period, the General Council has authorized the United States to impose sanctions. These take the form of increased customs duties on imports of selected products from EC member countries totalling US$ 116.8 million annually – equal to the trade which the United States is assessed to have lost as a result of the ban. The measures taken by the United States will be reviewed after EC has been able to complete the risk assessment.*
>
> * *Australia – Measures affecting the importation of salmon*
>
> *The Appellate Body agreed with the findings of the Panel established to consider the complaint of Canada against Australian measures prohibiting the importation of fresh, chilled and frozen salmon from Canada that the prohibition was not based on scientific evidence and was maintained without risk assessment.*

Mutual recognition agreements

The other issue of some concern to traders in developing countries is the increasing resort being made by developed countries to negotiations on agreements for the mutual recognition of:

❑ Testing methods, and

❑ Conformity assessment certificates.

The bilateral agreements stipulating that an importing country should allow imports of products which conform to its technical regulation or SPS measures may take two forms.

An importing country may under a bilateral agreement agree to allow imports of products such as meat, fruits, vegetables and other horticultural products on the basis of certificates issued by regulatory authorities in the exporting country. A number of developing countries have entered into such bilateral agreements with their main trading partners, both developed and developing countries.

The above one-way agreements, under which an importing country in effect agrees to treat as equivalent the conformity assessment procedures of the exporting country, need to be distinguished from mutual recognition agreements or MRAs. Under the latter agreements, the parties agree to treat as equivalent one another's testing methods and conformity assessment procedures. These agreements are negotiated on a bilateral or plurilateral basis.

Negotiations on MRAs are difficult and take a long time to complete as parties want to ensure through visits and consultations that the procedures adopted for testing and inspection by the participating countries are indeed equivalent and that the officers responsible for ascertaining conformity have the necessary technical competence.

Most MRAs have been negotiated among developed countries. The United States and the European Union have, for instance, recently concluded negotiations on two such agreements. The first covers industrial products and areas like telecommunications equipment, electromagnetic compatibility, electrical safety, recreational crafts, pharmaceutical and manufacturing practices, and medical devices. The second covers agricultural products like red meat, dairy products, eggs, fish products and pet food. Under the agreements, both parties have agreed to rely on the certificates issued in the country of export and not to inspect the products again on importation. The agreements are expected considerably to reduce the importers' delivery time and save exporters billions of dollars in inspection fees in the importing country.

While MRAs facilitate trade among participating countries, they put exports (of the products covered) from other countries at a disadvantage. This is because their products continue to be subjected to inspection and other requirements in the countries that are parties to the agreements. If MRAs result in the establishment of exclusive arrangements among a few countries, they may impede the development of multilateral trade instead of expanding it.

National enquiry points

AGREEMENT ON TECHNICAL BARRIERS TO TRADE

ARGENTINA
Director Ing. Silvio Peist
Dirección Nacional de Comercio Exterior
Avda. Julio A. Roca 651, Piso 4E, Sector 1
1322 Buenos Aires
Tel: +(54 11) 4349 40 39, +(54 11) 4349 40 51
Fax: +(54 11) 4349 40 38
E-mail: speist@secind.mecon.ar

AUSTRALIA
The Director
WTO Enquiry Point
WTO Industrials & Market Access Unit
Trade Negotiations and Organisations Division
Department of Foreign Affairs and Trade
Canberra
A.C.T. 2600
Tel: +(61 2) 6261 24 00
Fax: +(61 2) 6261 35 14
E-mail: TBT. Enquiry@DFAT.gov.au

AUSTRIA
(a) Technical regulations:
Bundesministerium für wirtschaftliche Angelegenheiten
(Federal Ministry for Economic Affairs)
Abteilung II/11 (Unit II/11)
Stubenring 1
A-1011 Wien
Tel: +(43 1) 711 00/Ext. 5452
Fax: +(43 1) 715 96 51/718 05 08
Telex: (047) 111780 regeb a, (047) 111145 regeb a
E-mail/Internet: Gabriela.Habermayer@bmwa.bmwa.ada.at

(b) Non-governmental standards:
Österreichisches Normungsinstitut - ON
(Austrian Standards Institute)
Heinestrasse 38
P.O. Box 130
A-1021- Wien
Tel: +(43 1) 213 00/Ext. 613
Fax: +(43 1) 213 00 650
Telex: (047) 115 960 norm a
E-mail/Internet: IRO@TBXA.telecom.at
E-mail/Geonet: TBXA:IRO

BAHRAIN
Directorate of Standards and Metrology
Ministry of Commerce
P.O. Box 5479
Manama

BARBADOS
Barbados National Standards Institution

"Flodden"
Culloden Road
St Michael
Tel: +(246) 426 38 70
Fax: +(246) 436 14 95

BELGIUM
CIBELNOR
Centre d'information belge sur les normes et les règlements techniques
(Belgian Information Centre on Standards and Technical Regulations)
Secrétariat: Institut Belge de Normalisation (IBN)
(Belgian Standards Institute)
Avenue de la Brabançonne, 29
B-1000 Bruxelles
Tel: +(32 2) 738 01 11
Fax: +(32 2) 733 42 64
Telex: 23877 BENOR B

BELIZE
The Financial Secretary
Ministry of Finance
Belmopan

BENIN
Ministry of Trade and Tourism
P.O.B 2037 Cotonou
Tel: +(229) 31 52 67, +(229) 31 54 02
Fax: +(229) 31 52 58

BOLIVIA
(a) Technical regulations and conformity assessment procedures:
Viceministerio de Industria y Comercio Interno
Av. Camacho 1488
Casilla No. 4430
La Paz
Tel: +(591 2) 37 20 46
Fax: +(591 2) 31 72 62

(b) Technical standards:
Instituto Boliviano de Normalización y Calidad
(IBNORCA)
Av. Camacho 1488
Casilla No. 5034
La Paz
Tel: +(591 2) 31 72 62, +(591 2) 31 01 85
Fax: +(591 2) 31 72 62

BOTSWANA
Botswana Bureau of Standards
Private Bag BO 48
Gaborone

Tel: +(267) 351 420
Fax: +(267) 308 194
E-mail: bobs.standard@info.bw

BRAZIL
Centro de Informação e Difusão Tecnológica (CIDIT)
Instituto Nacional de Metrologia, Normalizacão e
Qualidade Industrial - INMETRO
Rua Santa Alexandrina, 416 - Rio Comprido
20261-232 Rio de Janeiro (RJ)
Tel: +(55 21) 293 06 16
Fax: +(55 21) 502 04 15
E-mail: asbtcponto@inmetro.gov.br

BULGARIA
Committee for Standardization and Metrology
21, 6th September Street
1000 Sofia
Tel: +(359 2) 803 513
Fax: +(359 2) 801 402
Telex: 22 570 dks bg
Contact person: Violetta Veleva

CANADA
Standards Information Service
Standards Council of Canada
45 O'Connor Street
Suite 1200
Ottawa
Ontario K1P 6N7
Tel: +(1 613) 238 32 22
Fax: +(1 613) 995 45 64
E-mail: info@scc.ca

CHILE
Dirección de Relaciones Económicas Internacionales
Ministerio de Relaciones Exteriores
(Directorate-General for International Economic Relations,
Ministry of External Relations)
Alameda Bernardo O'Higgins 1315, 2º piso
Santiago
Tel: +(56 2) 696 00 43
Fax: +(56 2) 696 06 39
Telex: 240836 PROCH CL, 340120 PROCH CK

COLOMBIA
Ministerio de Desarrollo Económico
División de Normalización y Calidad
Dirección: Carrera 13 No. 28-01. Piso 8
Santafé de Bogotá
Tel: +(57 1) 338 06 41
Fax: +(57 1) 245 72 56

COSTA RICA
Dirección General de Normas y Unidades de Medida
Ministerio de Economía, Industria y Comercio
Apartado Postal 1736-2050
San Pedro de Montes de Oca
Tel/Fax: +(506) 283 51 33

CUBA
Oficina Nacional de Normalización
Director de Relaciones Internacionales
Calle E No. 261 entre 11 y 13
La Habana
Tel: +(53 7) 30 00 22, +(53 7) 30 08 25/35
Fax: +(53 7) 33 80 48
Telex: +(53 7) 51 22 45
Contact person: Sr. Javier Acosta Alemany

CYPRUS
Permanent Secretary
Ministry of Commerce, Industry and Tourism
CY 1421 Nicosia
Tel: +(357 2) 30 80 41, +(357 2) 30 80 46-49
Fax: +(357 2) 37 51 20
Telex: 22 83 Mincomind CY

CZECH REPUBLIC
Czech Office for Standards, Metrology and Testing
(COSMT)
WTO Enquiry Point
Biskupský dvur 5
110 02 Praha 1
Tel: +(42 2) 218 02 170
Fax: +(42 2) 232 45 64
Contact person: Ms. Klara Dvorackova

DENMARK
Dansk Standard
(Danish Standards Association)
Kollegievej 6
DK-2920 Charlottenland
Tel: +(45) 39 96 61 01
Fax: +(45) 39 96 61 02
E-mail: Dansk.Standard@ds.dk

DOMINICAN REPUBLIC
(a) Agricultural products:
Ministry of Agriculture (Secretaría de Estado de
Agricultura)
Km. 6½ Autopista Duarte
Urbanización Los Jardines del Norte
Santo Domingo, D.N.
Tel: +(1 809) 547 38 88
Fax: +(1 809) 227 12 68
Contact person: Mr. Luis Toral C. (Secretario de Estado de
Agricultura)

(b) Industrial products:
Dirección General de Normas y Sistemas
(DIGENOR)
Secretaría de Estado de Industria y Comercio
Edif. de Oficinas Gubernamentales Juan Pablo Duarte,
piso 11
Ave. México, esq. Leopoldo Navarro
Santo Domingo, D.N.
Tel: +(1 809) 686 22 05
Fax: +(1 809) 688 38 43
Contact person: Mr. Luis Mejía

(c) Pharmaceutical products and food additives:
Secretaría de Estado de Salud Pública y Asistencia Social
(SESPAS)
Av. San Cristóbal, Esq. Tiradentes
Santo Domingo, D.N.
Tel: +(1 898) 541 84 03, +(1 898) 541 31 21
Fax: +(1 809) 547 28 43
Contact person: Mr. Victoriano García Santos (Secretario
de Estado de Salud Pública y Asistencia Social)

ECUADOR
Ingeniero Felipe Urresta
Director General del Instituto Ecuatoriano de
Normalización, INEN
Baquerizo Moreno E8-29 (454) y Almagro
Quito
Casilla Postale: 17-01-3999
Tel: +(593 2) 501 885 (to 891)

Fax: +(593 2) 567 815, +(593 2) 222 223
E-mail: inen1@inen.gov.ec
Internet: http//:www.ecua.net.ec/inen/

EGYPT
Egyptian Organization for Standardization
2 Latin America Street
Garden City
Cairo
Tel: +(20 2) 354 07 71, +(20 2) 354 97 20
Fax: +(20 2) 355 78 41
Telex: 93296 EOS UN
E-mail: moi@idso.gov.eg

EL SALVADOR
Ministerio de Economía
Dirección de Política Comercial
División de Normas Técnicas
Centro de Gobierno, Plan Maestro Edificio c-2
Alameda Juan Pablo II y Calle Guadalupe
San Salvador, El Salvador, C.A.
Tel: +(503) 281 11 22, +(503) 281 11 55
Fax: +(503) 221 47 71

EUROPEAN COMMUNITY
EC TBT Enquiry Point
DG III - B/4
Rue de la Science, 15 - 1/61
1049 Brussels
Belgium
Tel: +(32 2) 295 57 38, +(32 2) 295 87 49
Fax: +(32 2) 299 57 25, +(32 2) 296 08 51
E-mail: sabine.lecrenier@dg3.cec.be
There will no longer be a separate enquiry point for
agricultural products.

FINLAND
Suomen Standardisoimisliitto SFS
(Finnish Standards Association SFS)
P.O. Box 116
FIN-00241 Helsinki
Tel: +(358 0) 149 93 31
Fax: +(358 0) 146 49 14

FIJI
Department of Fair Trading and Consumer Affairs
Ministry of Commerce, Industry and Public Enterprises
P.O. Box 2112
Suva
Tel: +(679) 305 411
Fax: +(679) 302 617

FRANCE
Centre d'information sur les normes et règlements
techniques (CINORTECH)
(Information Centre on Standards and Technical
Regulations)
Association française de normalisation (AFNOR)
(French Standard Association)
Tour Europe Cedex 07
F-92049 Paris La Défense
Tel: +(33 1) 42 91 56 69
Fax: +(33 1) 42 91 56 56
Telex: 611974 AFNOR F
(address care of CINORTECH)
Contact person: Mme Martine Vaquier
"The Centre is fully operational. CINORTECH can
provide all information on AFNOR standards and on
technical regulations and certification systems."

GERMANY
Deutches Informationszentrum für technische Regeln (DITR)
(German Information Centre for Technical Regulations)
Postfach 11 07
Burggrafenstr. 6
D-10787 Berlin
Tel: +(49 30) 26 01 26 00
Fax: +(49 30) 26 28 125

The DITR is being established by DIN, the German
Standards Institute, in cooperation with the Federal
Government. This body is the central point to which to
address all questions concerning technical rules in the
Federal Republic of Germany.

The Centre provides information about all technical rules
(including standards, technical regulations and certification
systems) valid in the Federal Republic of Germany,
irrespective of whether the technical rules have been issued
by federal or local authorities or by non-governmental
bodies. At present the computer-aided DITR databank
comprises information about 36,000 technical rules either in
force or in the draft stage.

GHANA
The Director
Ghana Standards Board
P.O. Box 245
Accra
Tel: +(233 21) 776 171
Fax: +(233 21) 776 092

GREECE
Hellenic Organization for Standardization (ELOT)
Information Center
313 Acharnon Street
GR 11145 Athens
Tel: +(30 1) 201 98.90
Fax: +(30 1) 202 07.76
Tlx: 21 96.21 ELOT GR
E-mail: eem@elot.gr

HONDURAS
(a) Enquiry point for all notifications:
Secretaría de Industria y Comercio
(Ministry of Industry and Trade)
Dirección General de Integración
Económica y Política Comercial
Edificio Larach, Piso No. 10
Tegucigalpa
Tel: +(504) 222 60 55, +(504) 222 18 19
Fax: +(504) 238 13 36

*(b) Technical regulations, standards and conformity assessment
procedures:*
Secretaría de Industria y Comercio
(Ministry of Industry and Trade)
Dirección General de Protección al Consumidor
Departamento de Normalización y Metrología
Edificio Larach y Cia Piso No. 8
Tegucigalpa
Tel: +(504) 222 70 48
Fax: +(504) 238 13 36
E-mail: rosorio@sieca.org.gt

(c) Pharmaceutical products:
Secretaría de Salud
Departamento de Farmacia
Edificio Vigil 3era Planta

Tegucigalpa
Tel: +(504) 238 62 88
Fax: +(504) 237 53 43

(d) Food products:
Secretaría de Salud
Departamento Control de Alimentos
Paseo Monumento a la Paz, Edificio CEESCO
1er Piso Barrio Morazán
Tel: +(504) 232 11 39
Fax: +(504) 232 27 13

HONG KONG, CHINA
Industry Department
36th Floor, Immigration Tower
7 Gloucester Road, Wan Chai
Hong Kong
Tel: +(852) 2829 4824
(Assistant Director-General, Quality Services Division)
Fax: +(852) 2824 1302
Telex: 50151 INDHK HX
E-mail: psib@id.gcn.gov.hk

HUNGARY
Magyar Szabvanyugyi Testulet
(Hungarian Standards Institute)
25 Ulloi ut
H-1091 Budapest
Tel: +(36 1) 218 30 11
Fax: +(36 1) 218 51 25

ICELAND
Ministry for Foreign Affairs and External Trade
External Trade Department
Raudararstig 25
150 Reykjavík
Tel: +(354) 560 99 30
Fax: +(354) 562 48 78
Contact person: Mr. Sverrir Júlíusson

INDIA
Bureau of Indian Standards
Manak Bhavan
Bahadur Shah Zafar Marg 9
New Delhi 110 002
Tel: +(91 11) 323 09 10
Fax: +(91 11) 323 40 62
Telex: (031)-65870 - Answer Back 'BIS/IN'

INDONESIA
Badan Standardisasi Nasional (BSN)
(National Standardization Agency)
Sasana Widya Sarwono Lt 5
Jalan Gatot Subroto No. 10
Jakarta 12710
Tel: +(62 21) 520 65 74, +(62 21) 522 16 86
Fax: +(62 21) 520 65 74
E-mail: pustan@rad.net.id

IRELAND
(a) Technical regulations and certification systems:
EU/WTO Division
Department of Tourism and Trade
Kildare Street
Dublin 2
Tel: +(353 1) 662 14 44
Fax: +(353 1) 676 61 54

(b) Standards:
Standards Development

National Standards Authority of Ireland
Glasnevin
Dublin 9
Tel: +(353 1) 807 38 00
Fax: +(353 1) 807 38 38
Telex: 45301

ISRAEL
The Standards Institution of Israel
42 Chaim Levanon Street
Tel-Aviv 69977
Tel: +(972 3) 646 51 54
Fax: +(972 3) 641 96 83 (Director-General)
         +(972 3) 641 27 62 (Inf. Center,
         WTO Enquiry   Point)

ITALY
(a) WTO notifications:
MICA DGPI
Ministero Industria, Commercio e Artigianato
Divisione XIX
Via Molise 19
I-00187 Roma
Tel: +(39 6) 470 526 69
Fax: +(39 6) 478 877 48
E-mail: Min.Ind.Isp.Tecnico@agora.stm.it

(b) Technical regulations:
Consiglio Nazionale delle Ricerche (CNR)
Ufficio Trasferimento, Innovazione, Brevetti, Normativa
Tecnica (Stibnot)
Via Tiburtina 770
I-00159 Roma
Tel: +(39 6) 40 758 26
Fax: +(39 6) 49 932 440
E-mail: Utinob@IRMRETI.CED.RM.CNR.IT

(c) Standards of all sectors, except electronics which can be requested to CEI:
Ente Nazionale Italiano di Unificazione (UNI)
Via Battistotti Sassi 11-b
I-20153 Milano
Tel: +(39 2) 70 02 41
Fax: +(39 2) 70 10 61 06
E-mail: Presidenza@UNI.UNICEI.IT

(d) Electronics standards:
Comitato Elettrotecnico Italiano (CEI)
Viale Monza 259
I-20126 Milano
Tel: +(39 2) 25 77 31
Fax: +(39 2) 25 77 32 01
E-mail: Camagni@CEIUNI.IT

JAMAICA
Jamaica Bureau of Standards
6 Winchester Road
P.O. Box 113
Kingston 10
Tel: +(1 809) 926 3140-6, +(1 809) 968 2063-71
Fax: +(1 809) 929 47 36
Telex: 2291 STANBUR JA
This government agency has responsibility for standards development and standards implementation as follows:
- laboratory testing;
- product and systems certification;
- technical information;
- training;
- energy efficiency evaluation;

- metrology;
- ISO 9000 certification; and
- laboratory accreditation.

JAPAN

(a) Standards Information Service

Standards Information Service at MOFA mainly handles
enquiries in the fields of drugs, cosmetics, medical devices,
foodstuffs, food additives, telecommunications facilities,
motor vehicles, ships, aircraft and railway.

First International Organization Division
Economic Affairs Bureau
Ministry of Foreign Affairs
2-2-1 Kasumigaseki, Chiyoda-ku
Tokyo
Tel: +(81 3) 35 80 33 11
Fax: +(81 3) 35 03 31 36
Telex: C. J22350 A. GAIMU A-B J22350

(b) Standards Information Service

Standards Information Service at JETRO mainly handles
enquiries in the fields of electric equipment, gas appliances,
measurement scales, foodstuffs, food additives, etc. Those
enquiries concerning JIS on medical devices, motor
vehicles, ships, aircraft and railway equipment are handled
by JETRO.

Information Service Department
Japan External Trade Organizations (JETRO)
2-2-5 Toranomon, Minato-Ku
Tokyo
Tel: +(81 3) 35 82 62 70
Fax: +(81 3) 35 89 41 79
Telex: C. J24378 A. JETRO A-B J24378

In relation to the services of these two bodies, a Standards
Agreement Office has been established in the Ministry of
Foreign Affairs (MOFA). Enquiries can be made in a WTO
language.

KENYA

The Managing Director
Kenya Bureau of Standards
P.O. Box 54974
Nairobi
Tel: +(254 2) 50 22 10-9
Fax: +(254 2) 50 32 93
Tlx: 252 52 "VIWANGO"
E-mail: KEBS@ARGO GN.APC.ORG

KOREA, REPUBLIC OF

(a) Industrial products:

Korean National Institute of Technology and Quality
(KNITQ)
International Cooperation and Metrology Division
2 Choongang-dong, Kwachon
Kyunggi-do, 427-010
Tel: +(822 2) 507 43 69
Fax: +(822 2) 503 79 77
E-mail: int_coop@mail.nitq.go.kr

(b) Agricultural products:

Ministry of Agriculture, Forestry and Fisheries (MAFF)
Bilateral Cooperation Division
1 Choongang-dong, Kwachon
Kyunggi-do 427-760
Tel: +(82 2) 503 72 94
Fax: +(82 2) 507 20 95
E-mail: bcd@maf.go.kr

(c) Fishery products:

Ministry of Maritime Affairs and Fisheries
Trade Promotion Division
826-14 Yoksam-dong, Kangnam-gu
Seoul, 135-080
Tel: +(82 2) 567 27 29
Fax: +(82 2) 556 78 17

(d) Health, sanitation and cosmetic products:

Ministry of Health and Welfare (MOHW)
International Cooperation Division
2 Choongang-dong, Kwachon
Kyunggi-do 427-760
Tel: +(82 2) 503 75 24
Fax: +(82 2) 504 64 18
E-mail: invuiou1@chollian.net

LATVIA

World Trade Organization Information Division
Department of Quality Management and Structure
Development
Ministry of Economy
55 Brivibas Street
Riga LV-1519
Tel: +(371) 701 31 97, +(371) 701 32 36
Fax: +(371) 728 08 82

LIECHTENSTEIN

Office for foreign Affairs
Heiligkreuz 14
9490 Vaduz
Liechtenstein

LUXEMBOURG

Inspection du travail et des mines (ITM)
Rue Zithe 26
Boîte postale 27
L - 2010 Luxembourg
Tel: +(352) 478 61 50
Fax: +(352) 491 447

MACAU

Macau Government Economic Services
1-3 Rua do Dr. Pedro José Lobo
Edificio "Luso Internacional" 25th floor
Macau
Fax: +(853) 59 03 10

MALAYSIA

Standard and Industrial Research Institute of Malaysia
(SIRIM)
Persiaran Dato' Menteri
Section 2
P.O. Box 7035
40911 Shah Alam
Selangor Darul Ehsan
Tel: +(60 3) 559 26 01, +(60 3) 559 16 30
Fax: +(60 3) 550 80 95
Telex: SIRIM MA 38672

MALAWI

Malawi Bureau of Standards
P.O. Box 946
Blantyre
Tel: +(265) 670 488
Fax: +(265) 670 756
Telex: 44325 "MSD" MI

MALI

Direction nationale des industries

Rue Famalo Coulibaly
BP 278
Bamako
Tel: +(223) 22 57 56, +(223) 22 06 63
Fax: +(223) 22 61 37

MALTA
Malta Standards Authority (MSA)
Department of Industry
Kukkanja Street
St. Venera CMR02
Tel: +(356) 446 250
Fax: +(356) 446 257

MAURITIUS
Mauritius Standards Bureau
Moka
Tel: +(230) 433 36 48
Fax: +(230) 433 50 51, +(230) 433 51 50

MEXICO
Lic. Carmen Quintanilla Madero
Dirección General de Normas
Av. Puente de Tecamachalco No. 6, 3º piso
Col. Lomas de Tecamachalco
C.P. 53950
Naucalpan, Mexico
Tel: +(52 5) 729 94 80
Fax: +(52 5) 729 94 84
E-mail: cidgn@secofi.gob.mx, cqm@secofi.gob.mx

MONGOLIA
Mongolian National Centre for Standardization and
Metrology
Peace Street 46 A
Ulaanbaatar 51
Mongolia
Tel: +(976 1) 358 349
Fax: +(976 1) 358 032

MOROCCO
Ministry of Trade, Industry and Handicrafts
Standardization and Quality Promotion Division
Moroccan Industrial Standardization Service (SMINA)
Administrative District Rabat-Chellah
Tel: +(212) 7 76 63 17, +(212) 7 76 66 98
Fax: +(212) 7 76 62 96

MOZAMBIQUE
Instituto Nacional de Normalização e Qualidade
Av. 25 de Setembro, 1179 2º andar
Maputo
P.O. Box 2983 Maputo
Tel: +(258 1) 42 14 09, +(258 1) 42 14 98
Fax: +(258 1) 42 45 85
Telex: 6-933 INNOQ MO

MYANMAR
Director General
Directorate of Trade
Ministry of Commerce
228-240 Strand Road
Yangon
Tel: +(95 1) 286 442, +(95 1) 283 235
Fax: +(95 1) 289 578

NAMIBIA
Namibia Standards Information and Quality Office
(NSIQO)

Private Bag 13340
Windhoek
Tel: +(264) 61 283 7111
Fax: +(264) 61 220 227

NETHERLANDS
(a) Enquiry point for Article 10, paragraph 1.1:
Ministry of Finance
Central Licensing Office for Imports and Exports
Tax and Customs Administration
Section EEC/WTO- Notifications
P.O. Box 30003
9700 RD Groningen
Tel: +(31 50) 52 39 178, +(31 50) 52 39 275
Fax: +(31 50) 52 39 219
E-mail: cdiuor@noord.bart.nl

The CDIU is responsible for the implementation of
regulations in the field of international trade and also for
information on technical regulations, including
notifications.

(b) Enquiry point for Article 10, paragraph 1.2:
Nederlands Normalisatie Instituut (NNI)
(Netherlands Standardization Institute)
P.O. Box 5059
NL 2600 GB Delft
Tel: +(31 15) 69 02 55
Fax: +(31 15) 69 01 30

(c) Enquiry point for Article 10, paragraph 1.3:
Raad voor Accreditatie
(Council for Accreditation)
P.O. Box 2768
NL-3500 GT Utrecht
Tel: +(31 34) 28 94 500
Fax: +(31 34) 23 94 539

NEW ZEALAND
Standards New Zealand
Standards House
155 The Terrace
Private Bag 2439
Wellington
Tel: +(64 4) 498 59 90
Fax: +(64 4) 498 59 9

NIGER
Ministère du commerce et de l'industrie
BP 480
Niamey
Tel: +(227) 72 34 67, +(227) 73 29 74
Fax: +(227) 73 21 50

NIGERIA
The Director-General
Standards Organization of Nigeria
Federal Secretariat
9th floor, Phase 1
Ikoyi, Lagos
Tel: +(234 1) 68 26 15
Fax: +(234 1) 68 18 20

NORWAY
Norges Standardiseringsforbund
(Norwegian Standards Association)
P.O. Box 7020 Homansbyen
(Hegdehaugsveien 31)
N-0306 Oslo 3

Tel: +(47) 22 04 92 00
Fax: +(47) 22 04 92 11
Telex   19050 nsf n

PAKISTAN

(a) Standardization and certification undertaken by the Pakistan Standards Institution:
Pakistan Standards Institution
39 Garden Road
Saddar, Karachi 74400
Tel: +(92 21) 77 29 527
Fax: +(92 21) 77 28 124

(b) Technical regulations relating to food and health safety:
Ministry of Health, Social Welfare and Population Planning
Government of Pakistan
Secretariat Block 'C', Islamabad
Tel: +(92 51) 820 930
Fax: +(92 51) 829 703

PAPUA NEW GUINEA
Director General
National Institute of Standards and Industrial Technology (NISIT)
P.O. Box 3042
Boroko
National Capital District
Port Moresby
Tel: +(675) 323 18 52
Fax: +(675) 325 87

PERU
Comisión de Reglamentos Técnicos y Comerciales
Instituto de Defensa de la Competencia y de la Propiedad Intelectual
Calle La Prosa No. 138
Lima 41, Perú
Tel: +(51 1) 224 07 88
Fax: +(51 1) 224 03 48, +(51 1) 224 0347
E-mail: cnmamel@indecopi.gob.pe

PHILIPPINES
Bureau of Product Standards
Department of Trade and Industry
3/F Trade and Industry Bldg.
361 Sen. Gil J. Puyat Avenue
Metro Manila, Makati City 1200
Postal Address: P.O. Box 3228 MCPO
Tel: +(63 2) 890 49 65
Fax: +(63 2) 890 49 26, +(63 2) 890 51 30
E-mail: dtibpsrp@mnl.sequel.net

POLAND
Polski Komitet Normalizacyjny (PKN)
(Polish Committee for Standardization)
WTO/TBT National Enquiry Point
P.O. Box 411
ul. Elektoralna 2
PL-00-950 Warsaw
Tel: +(48 22) 620 02 41 ext. 651,
          +(48 22) 624 71 22
Fax: +(48 22) 624 71 22
E-mail: polknor@atos.warman.com.pl
Contact person: Mr. Marek Zarnoch

PORTUGAL
Instituto Português da Qualidade
(Portuguese Institute for Quality)
Rua C à Avenida dos Três Vales

P-2825 Monte da Caparica
Tel: +(351 1) 294 81 00
Fax: +(351 1) 294 82 23, +(351 1) 294 81 01
          +(351 1) 294 82 22
E-mail: PINCDCP@IPQM.IPQ.GTWMS.MAILPAC.PT

ROMANIA
Romanian Standards Institute
13 Jean Louis Calderon Street
Sector 2
Bucharest
Tel: +(40 1) 211 32 96
Fax: +(40 1) 210 08 33
Telex: (065) 11 312 ins r

SAINT LUCIA
St Lucia Bureau of Standards
Government Buildings
Block B, 4th Floor
John Compton Highway
Castries
Tel: +(1 758) 453 00 49
Fax: +(1 758) 453 73 47

SINGAPORE
(a) Standardization and certification undertaken by the Singapore Productivity and Standards Board:
Singapore Productivity and Standards Board
1 Science Park Drive
PSB Building
Singapore 118221
Tel: +(65) 778 77 77
Fax: +(65) 776 12 80

(b) Technical regulations relating to specific electrical fittings and accessories:
Public Utilities Board
111 Somerset Road
15-01
Singapore 238164
Tel: +(65) 235 88 88
Fax: +(65) 731 30 20

(c) Technical regulations relating to processed food:
Food Control Department
Ministry of the Environment
Environment Building
40 Scotts Road
Singapore 228231
Tel: +(65) 732 90 15
Fax: +(65) 731 98 44

(d) Technical regulations relating to fish, meat, fruits and vegetables:
Primary Production Department
National Development Building
5 Maxwell Road
Singapore 169110
Tel: +(65) 222 12 11
Fax: +(65) 220 60 68
Telex: RS 28851 PPD

SLOVAK REPUBLIC
Slovenský ústav technickej normalizácie
WTO Enquiry Point
Karloveská cesta 63
842 45 Bratislava
Visiting address:
Stefanovicova 3

814 39 Bratislava
Tel: +(421 7) 397 886
Fax: +(421 7) 397 886

SLOVENIA
Standards and Metrology Institute of the Republic of
Slovenia (SMIS)
WTO TBT Enquiry Point
Kotnikova 6
SI-1000 Ljubljana
Tel: +(386 61) 178 3041
Fax: +(386 61) 178 3196
E-mail: smis@usm.mzt.si

SOUTH AFRICA
Standards Information Centre
South African Bureau of Standards
Private Bag X191
0001 Pretoria
Tel: +(27 12) 428 7911
Fax: +(27 12) 344 1568
E-mail: info@sabs.co.za

SPAIN
(a) Ministerio de Comercio y Turismo
Dirección General de Comercio Exterior
(Subdirección General de Control, Inspección y
Normalización del Comercio Exterior)
Paseo de la Castellana, 162, 6a planta
28046 Madrid
Tel: +(34 1) 349 37 70, +(34 1) 349 37 64
         +(34 1) 349 37 54
Fax: +(34 1) 349 37 40, +(34 1) 349 37 77

(b) Spanish national standards:
Asociación Española de Normalización y de Certificación
(AENOR)
Calle Fernández de la Hoz, 52
28010 Madrid
Tel: +(34 1) 310 48 51
Fax: +(34 1) 310 49 76

SRI LANKA
Director of Commerce
Department of Commerce
"Rakshana Mandiraya"
21 Vauxhall Street
Colombo 2
Tel: +(94 1) 29 733, +(94 1) 43 61 14
Fax: +(94 1) 43 02 33
Telex: 21908 COMMERCE

SWAZILAND
Quality Assurance Unit
Ministry of Enterprise and Employment
P.O. Box 451
Mbabane
Tel: +(268) 432 01
Fax: +(268) 447 11

SWEDEN
(a) Enquiry point for Article 10.1:
Kommerskollegium
(National Board of Trade)
WTO-TBT Enquiry Point
Box 6803
S-113 86 Stockholm
Tel: +(46 8) 690 48 00
Fax: +(46 8) 690 48 40

(b) Enquiry point for Article 10.2:
SIS Service AB
WTO-TBT Enquiry Point
Box 6455
S-10382 Stockholm
Tel: +(46 8) 610 30 00
Fax: +(46 8) 307 757

SWITZERLAND
Swiss Association for Standardization
SNV
Mühlebachstrasse 54
CH-8008 Zürich
Tel: +(41 1) 254 54 54
Fax: +(41 1) 254 54 74
E-mail: switec@snv.ch
The SNV has been established as the Enquiry Point by the
Federal Office of External Economic Affairs.

TANZANIA, UNITED REPUBLIC OF
The Principal Secretary
Ministry of Industries and Trade
P.O. Box 9503
Dar Es Salaam
Tel: +(255 51) 117 222-5
Fax: +(255 51) 46919
Telex: 41689

The Director
Tanzania Bureau of Standards
P.O. Box 9524
Dar Es Salaam
Tel: +(255 51) 450 298
Fax: +(255 51) 450 983
Telex: 41667 TBS TZ

THAILAND
Thai Industrial Standards Institute (TISI)
Ministry of Industry
Rama VI Street
Bangkok 10400
Tel: +(66 2) 202 34 01, +(66 2) 202 35 08
         +(66 2) 202 35 12
Fax: +(66 2) 247 87 34, +(66 2) 202 34 02
E-mail: stdinfo@tisi.go.th

TRINIDAD AND TOBAGO
The Director
Trinidad and Tobago Bureau of Standards (TTBS)
P.O. Box 467
Port of Spain
Tel: +(868) 662 88 27, +(868) 662 44 81/2
Fax: +(868) 663 43 35
E-mail: ttbs@opus.co.tt

TUNISIA
(a) Standards:
Institut national de la normalisation et de la propriété
industrielle (INNORPI)
(National Standardization and Industrial Property
Institute)
Contact point: Mr. Ali Ben Gaied
Cité El Khadhra par Rue Alain Savary
1003 Tunis-Belvédère
B.P. 23
1012 Tunis
Tel: +(216 1) 78 59 22
Fax: +(216 1) 78 15 63

For information on: standards; standardization and certification systems; industrial property; quality; relations with foreign standardization and certification bodies.

For services in the areas of: quality promotion; certification; Industrial property; other services include sale of standards and draft standards, access to domestic and foreign databases, consultation of Tunisian and foreign standards.

(b) Seeds and plants:
Ministry of Agriculture
Directorate-General of Agricultural Production
Seeds and Plants Monitoring and Certification Division
30 rue Alain Savary
1002 Tunis-Belvédère
Tel/Fax: +(216 1) 80 04 19
Contact point: Mr. Aissa Bouziri
For information on: Standards for seeds and plants

Documents available: Analysis reports and texts of regulations and standards

(c) Technical regulations on Telecoms:
Ministry of Communications
Contact point: Mr. Ridha Guellouz
3 bis, rue d'Angleterre
1000 Tunis
Tel: +(216 1) 33 34 36
Fax: +(216 1) 33 26 85

Documents available on: Regulations and technical subjects

(d) Pesticides and disinfectants for domestic use:
Ministry of Public Health
Directorate of Environmental Health and Environmental Protection
5 rue Chaabane El B' houri
1002 Tunis
Tel: +(216 1) 79 17 15
Fax: +(216 1) 79 09 73
Contact point: Mr. Shlaheddine CHENITI

For information on: Regulatory and organizational aspects relating to pesticides for domestic use and disinfectants.

Documents available on: Approval and attribution procedures relating to pesticides for domestic use and disinfectants.

(e) Pharmaceuticals, medical accessories and special diet foods:
Ministry of Public Health
Directorate of Pharmacy and Medicaments
31 rue Khartoum
1002 Tunis
Tel: +(216 1) 79 68 24
Fax: +(216 1) 79 78 16
Contact point: Professor Amor TOUMI

For information on: Regulatory and organizational aspects relating to:
- Human medicaments;
- Veterinary medicaments;
- Serums and vaccines;
- Pharmaceutical accessories;
- Cosmetics.

Documents available on: Legislation and approval and attribution procedures for the above-mentioned products.

(f) Technical regulations in other areas:
Ministry of Trade
Directorate-General of Competition and Internal Trade
6, rue Venezuela

1002 Tunis-Belvédère
Tel: +(216 1) 78 08 15
Fax: +(216 1) 78 18 47
For information on: Any technical regulations not covered above

TURKEY
(a) Enquiry point for Article 10.1:
Prime Ministry
Undersecretariat for Foreign Trade
General Directorate for Standardization for Foreign Trade
06510 Emek-Ankara
Tel: +(90 312) 212 58 96, +(90 312) 212 87 17
Fax: +(90 312) 212 87 68
E-mail: gokali@foreigntrade.gov.tr

(b) Enquiry point for Article 10.1.2:
Turkish Standards Institution
Necatibey Cad. No: 112 Bakanhklar
06100 Ankara
Tel: +(90 312) 418 01 15
Fax: +(90 312) 418 01 16
E-mail: biedb@tse.org.tr

UGANDA
Uganda National Bureau of Standards (UNBS)
Plot M 217, Nakawa Industrial Area
P.O. Box 6329
Kampala
Tel: +(256 41) 22 23 69, +(256 41) 22 23 67

UNITED KINGDOM
(a) Enquiry point of Article 10.1:
WTO Section
Department of Trade and Industry
Room 360
Kingsgate House
66-74 Victoria Street
London SW1E 6SW
Tel: +(44 171) 2 15 45 11
Fax: +(44 171) 2 15 45 12

(b) Enquiry point of Article 10.3:
BSI Information Centre
389 Chiswick High Road
London W4 4AL
Tel: +(44 181) 996 71 11
Fax: +(44 181) 996 70 48

UNITED STATES
National Center for Standards and Certification Information
National Institute of Standards and Technology
Bldg. 820, Room 164
Gaithersburg, MD 20899
Tel: +(1 301) 975 40 40
Fax: +(1 301) 926 15 59
E-mail: ncsci@nist.gov

The United States' enquiry point, in the National Institute of Standards and Technology, maintains a reference collection of standards, specifications, test methods, codes and recommended practices. This reference material includes United States' government agencies regulations, and standards of United States private standards-developing organizations and foreign national and international standardizing bodies. The enquiry point responds to all enquiries for information concerning federal, state and private regulations, standards, and conformity assessment procedures.

URUGUAY
Dirección General para Asuntos Económicos
Internacionales
Ministerio de Relaciones Exteriores
Colonia 1206
Montevideo
Tel: +(598 2) 902 06 18
Fax: +(598 2) 901 74 13

Dirección General de Comercio del Ministerio de
Economía y Finanzas
Servicio de Información Comercial
Colonia 1206 - PB
C.P. 11.100
Montevideo
Tel: +(598 2) 900 26 22
Fax: +(598 2) 902 82 06
E-mail: coensic@tips.org.uv

ZAMBIA
(a) Zambia Bureau of Standards
The Director
Box 50259
ZA 15101
Ridgeway
Lusaka
Tel/Fax: +(260 1) 227 171
Telex: 40555 zabs
E-mail: zabs@zamnet.zm

(b) Permanent Secretary/Attention of Director of Trade
Ministry of Commerce, Trade and Industry
P.O. Box 31968
Lusaka
Tel: +(260 1) 228 301/9
Fax: +(260 1) 226 673

(c) Zoo - Sanitary (Animal/animal material)
Senior Veterinary Officer
Department of Animal Production and Health

Mulungushi House
P.O. Box 50060
Lusaka
Tel: +(260 1) 250 274, +(260 1) 252 608
Fax: +(260 1) 236 283

(d) Phytosanitary service (Plant material)
Mount Makulu Research Station
P/B 7
Chilanga
Tel: +(260 1) 278 655, +(260 1) 278 242
Fax: +(260 1) 230 62 22

ZIMBABWE
(a) Standards, technical regulations and certification schemes:
The Director General
Standards Association of Zimbabwe
P.O. Box 2259
Northend Close, Northridge Park
Borrowdale
Harare
Tel: +(263 4) 882 017-19, +(263 4) 885 511/2
Fax: +(263 4) 882 020

(b) Agricultural products:
The Permanent Secretary
Ministry of Agriculture
1 Borrowdale Road
P/Bag 7701
Causeway
Harare
Tel: +(263 4) 708 061
Fax: +(263 4) 734 646

(c) Food and health safety:
Ministry of Health and Child Welfare
P.O. Box CY 1122
Causeway
Harare
Tel: +(263 4) 730 011
Fax: +(263 4) 729 154

AGREEMENT ON THE APPLICATION OF SANITARY AND PHYTOSANITARY MEASURES

ANTIGUA AND BARBUDA
Permanent Secretary
Ministry of Trade
P.O. Box 1550
Redcliffe Street
St. John's
Tel: +(809) 462 16 26/28, 462 15 42
Fax: +(809) 462 16 25

ARGENTINA
Secretaría de Agricultura, Ganadería, Pesca y Alimentación
Dirección Nacional de Mercados Agroalimentarios
Paseo Colón 922, Oficina 40
1063 Buenos Aires
Tel: +(541) 349 22 42/349 22 43
Fax: +(541) 349 22 44

AUSTRALIA
Policy and International Division
Australian Quarantine and Inspection Service
GPO Box 858
Canberra ACT 2601
Tel: +(612) 6272 4146

Fax: +(612) 6272 3678
E-mail/Internet: sps.contact@aqis.gov.au
Web site: http://www.aqis.gov.au

BANGLADESH
Mr. Ghulam Rahman
Joint Secretary
Ministry of Commerce
Government of the People's Republic of Bangladesh
Bangladesh Secretariat
Dhaka
Tel: +(8802) 83 46 65
Fax: +(8802) 86 57 41

BELIZE
The Permanent Secretary
Ministry of Agriculture
Belmopan
Tel: +(5018) 22 330
Fax: +(5018) 22 409

BOLIVIA
Dirección Nacional de Producción y Protección Agrícola
Av. Camacho No. 1471, Piso 5

La Paz
Tel: +(5912) 37 42 68/37 42 70 interno 126
Fax: +(5912) 35 75 35

BOTSWANA
The Permanent Secretary
Ministry of Agriculture
Private bag 003
Gaborone
Tel: +(267) 35 05 00/35 06 03
Fax: +(267) 35 60 27

BRAZIL
Secretaria de Defesa Agropecuária (SDA)
Ministério da Agricultura e da Reforma Agrária (MAARA)
Esplanada dos Ministérios
Bloco 'B', Anexo 'B', sala 406
Brasilia - DF - 70.170
Tel: +(5561) 218 23 14/218 23 15
Fax: +(5561) 224 39 95
E-mail/Internet: cenagri@ibict.br

BRUNEI DARUSSALAM
International Relations and Trade and Development
Division
Ministry of Industry and Primary Resources
Tel: +(6732) 38 28 22
Fax: +(6732) 38 28 46/38 38 11

BULGARIA
Phytosanitary Measures:
Mr. Stefan Uzunov, *Responsible for WTO SPS Enquiries*
National Service for Plant Protection, Quarantine and
Agrochemistry
Ministry of Agriculture, Forests and Land Reform
55, "Hristo Botev" Blvd.
1040-Sofia
Tel: +(3592) 981 2734/981 0106
Fax: +(3592) 980 8082
E-mail/Internet: nsrzka@alpha.acad.bg

Sanitary Measures:
Dr. Svetla Tchamova, *Responsible for WTO SPS Enquiries*
National Veterinary Service
15-A, "Pencho Slaveikov" Blvd.
1606-Sofia
Tel: +(3592) 525 298
Fax: +(3592) 522 925

Food Safety Measures:
Dr. Snejana Altankova, *Responsible for WTO SPS Enquiries*
Ministry of Health
5, "Sveta Nedelya" Square
1000-Sofia
Tel: +(3592) 875 234
Fax: +(3592) 883 413

BURKINA FASO
Direction de la Protection des Végétaux et du
Conditionnement (DPVC)
BP 5362 Ouagadougou
Tel: +(226) 30 13 47/30 11 61
Fax: +(226) 30 11 61

CANADA
WTO/NAFTA Enquiry Point
Standards Council of Canada
1200-45 O'Connor Street
Ottawa, Ontario
K1P 6N7

Tel: +(1613) 238 32 22
Fax: +(1613) 569 03 78
E-mail/Internet: info@scc.ca

CHILE
Servicio Agrícola y Ganadero (SAG)
Avenida Bulnes 140
Santiago
Tel: +(562) 672 36 35/698 22 44/698 25 41
Fax: +(562) 671 74 19
E-mail/Internet: rrii@sag.minagri.gob.cl

CHINA
(Observer)
Administration of Animal and Plant Quarantine of the
People's Republic of China (PRC)
12 Yi Nong Zhan Guan Beilu
Chaoyang District
Beijing 100026
Tel: +(8610) 64 19 40 40/64 19 40 31
Fax: +(8610) 65 02 52 73

COLOMBIA
Ministerio de Desarrollo Económico
División de Normalización y Calidad
Carrera 13 No. 28-01 Piso 8
Santafé de Bogota
Tel: +(571) 338 06 41
Fax: +(571) 245 72 56

COSTA RICA
Ministerio de Agricultura y Ganadería
Dirección de Servicios de Protección Fitosanitaria
Dirección de Salud Animal
Centro de Información Fitosanitaria y Zoosanitaria para el
Comercio
Apartado 10094-1000
San José
Tel: +(506) 260 61 90/260 08 45/260 82 91
Fax: +(506) 260 83 01
E-mail/Internet: protagro@sol.racsa.co.cr

CÔTE D'IVOIRE
Côte d'Ivoire Normalisation (CODINORM)
Immeuble le Général – 5ème étage
Angle Botreau Roussel
Rue du Commerce
01 BP 1872 Abidjan 01
Tel: +(225) 21 55 12/22 83 29
Fax: +(225) 21 25 60

CUBA
Plant health:
Sr. Jorge Opies Díaz
Director
Calle 110 Esquina 5ta. B y eta. F, Playa
Habana
Tel: +(537) 29 61 89/22 25 16
Fax: +(537) 33 50 86

Veterinary medicine:
Dr. Emerio Serrano Ramírez
Director
Calle 12 No. 355 entre 15 y 17 Playa
Habana
Tel: +(537) 30 66 15/30 35 35/37 07 77/30 34 47
Fax: +(537) 33 50 86

CYPRUS
Permanent Secretary

Ministry of Agriculture, Natural Resources and
Environment
1412 Nicosia
Tel: +(357-2) 30 22 47
Fax: +(357-2) 78 11 56

CZECH REPUBLIC
Ing. Miluška Vrlová
Director
Department of International Trade Cooperation - 4010
Ministry of Agriculture of the Czech Republic
Tišnov 17
117 05 Praha 1
Tel: +(4202) 218 124 48
Fax: +(4202) 248 106 52
E-mail/Internet: kantorova@mze.cz

DJIBOUTI
Ministère du commerce et de l'industrie
Service du contrôle de la qualité et des normes
Djibouti
Tel: +(253) 35 25 40
Fax: +(253) 35 49 09
E-mail/Internet: commerce@internet.dji

DOMINICA
Permanent Secretary
Ministry of Agriculture and the Environment
Government Headquarters
Kennedy Avenue
Roseau
Tel: +(767) 448 2401 Ext 3282
Fax: +(767) 448 7999

DOMINICAN REPUBLIC
Zoosanitary analyses:
Atención: Dr. Rafael Jáquez
- *Departamento de Sanidad Animal*
- *Departamento de Recursos Pesqueros*

Sanitary control of fruits and vegetables:
Atención: Dr. Pedro Jorge
- *Departamento de Sanidad Vegetal*
Secretaría de Estado de Agricultura
Dirección General de Ganadería
Urbanización Jardines del Norte
Santo Domingo
Tel: +(1809) 547 38 88
Fax: +(1809) 227 12 68

Drugs and food additives:
Atención: Lusitania Acosta
División de Drogas y Farmacias
Secretaría de Salud Pública y Asistencia Social (SESPAS)
Ave. San Cristóbal, esq. Tiradentes
Santo Domingo, D.N.
Tel: +(1809) 541 84 03/541 31 21
Fax: +(1809) 547 28 43

ECUADOR
Servicio Ecuatoriano de Sanidad Agropecuaria (SESA)
Ministerio de Agricultura y Ganadería
Avenida Eloy Alfaro y Av. Amazonas
Edificio MAG noveno piso
Quito
Tel: +(5932) 56 72 32/54 33 19
Fax: +(5932) 22 84 48
E-mail/Internet: http://www.iica.saninet.net

EGYPT
Ministry of Agriculture
Department of Economic Affairs
7 Nady El-Said St.
Dokki
Tel: +(202) 337 48 73
Fax: +(202) 337 48 73
E-mail/Internet: capi@idsc.gov.eg

EL SALVADOR
Ministerio de Agricultura y Ganadería
Dirección de Sanidad Vegetal y Animal (DGSVA)
Cantón El Matazano de Soyapango
San Salvador
Tel: +(503) 227 39 24
Fax: +(503) 227 25 94

ESTONIA
(Observer)
Sanitary measures:
Mr. Toivo Nõvandi
Ministry of Agriculture
Lai 39/41
Tallinn EE0100
Tel: +(372) 6256 142
Fax: +(372) 6313 600

Mr. Ago Pärtel
State Veterinary Department
Väike Paala 3
Tallinn EE0014
Tel: +(372) 6380 079
Fax: +(372) 638 0210

Phytosanitary measures:
Mr. Toomas Kevvai
Ministry of Agriculture
Lai 39/41
Tallinn EE0100
Tel: +(372) 6256 139
Fax: +(372) 6313 200

Mr. Ülo Saamere
Estonian State Plant Quarantine Inspection
Lai 11
Tallinn EE0001
Tel: +(372) 6411 620
Fax: +(372) 6411 618

EUROPEAN UNION
Mr. Marco Castellina
86 rue de la Loi
Office 7/8
1049 Brussels
Tel: +(322) 295 81 82
Fax: +(322) 296 27 92
E-mail/Internet: marco.castellina@dg6.cec.be

Member State Contact Points:

AUSTRIA
Bundesministerium für wirtschaftliche Angelenheiten
(Federal Ministry for Economic Affairs)
Abteilung II/11 (Division II/11)
Stubenring 1
A-1011 Wien
Tel: +(431) 711 00/ext. 5452
Fax: +(431) 715 96 51
E-mail/Internet:gabriela.habermayer@bmwa.bmwa.ada.at

BELGIUM
Institut belge de normalisation (IBN)
(Belgian Standards Institute)
Avenue de la Brabançonne 29
B-1040 Bruxelles
Tel: +(322) 734 92 05
Fax: +(322) 733 42 64

DENMARK
Landsbrugs - og Fiskeriministeriets (Ministry of
Agriculture and Fisheries)
Holbergsgade 2
1057 Copenhagen K
Tel: +(45) 33 92 33 01
Fax: +(45) 33 14 50 42
E-mail/Internet: 1fm@lfm.dk OR era@lfm.dk

FINLAND
Eha Rantanen
Finnish Standards Association (SFS)
P.O. Box 116
00241 Helsinki
Tel: +(358 9) 149 34 37
Fax: +(358 9) 146 49 14
E-mail/Internet: eha.rantanen@sfs.fi
Web site: http://www.sfs.fi

FRANCE
Monsieur le Chef de la Mission de coordination
sanitaire internationale
Direction générale de l'alimentation
Ministère de l'agricuture et de la pêche
251 rue de Vaugirard
75732 Paris Cedex 15
Tel: +(33) 1 49 55 81 20 or 49 55 84 86
Fax: +(33) 1 49 55 83 14 or 49 55 44 62
E-mail/Internet: mcsi@wanadoo.fr **or**
alain.dehove@agriculture.gouv.fr

GERMANY
Bundesministerium für Ernährung, Landwirtschaft und
Forsten
Referat 716
Postfach 14 02 70
53107 Bonn
Tel: +(49228) 529 37 97
Fax: +(49228) 529 44 10
E-mail/Internet: tka3472@bml.bund400.de
Attention: Mr. Peter Witt (tel: (49228) 529 37 97) or
Ms Christine Rabenschlag (tel: 529 34 72)

GREECE
Ministry of Agriculture
Directorate of Agricultural Policy and Documentation
Division of EU, International Relations and Trade
Policy
5 Acharnon Street
Athens 10176
Tel: +(301) 529 1461
Fax: +(301) 524 8584

IRELAND
Mr. Ray McGlynn
EU Trade Division
Department of Agriculture, Food and Forestry
Agriculture House, Kildare Street
Dublin 2
Tel: +(353 1) 607 2000
Fax: +(353 1) 661 4515

ITALY
Ministero della Sanità
Dipartimento degli Alimenti, Nutrizione e della Sanità
Publica Veterinaria
Ufficio III: Rapporti Internazionali
Director: Dr. Piergiuseppe Facelli
Piazzale Marconi 25
00144 EUR Roma
Tel: +(3906) 59 94 36 13
Fax: +(3906) 59 94 35 55
E-mail/Internet: danspv@IZS.IT

LUXEMBOURG
Ministère de l'agriculture, de la viticulture et du
développement rural
SPS - Point de contact
L-2913 Luxembourg
Tel: +(352) 478 25 27
Fax: +(352) 46 40 27

NETHERLANDS
Ministry of Economic Affairs
Central Service Imports and Exports
Section EEC/WTO-Notifications
P.O. Box 30003
9700 RD Groningen
Tel: +(3150) 523 91 11
Fax: +(3150) 526 06 98

PORTUGAL
Prof. Doutor Francisco Cordovil
Gabinete de Planeamento e Política Agro-Alimentar
Rua Padre António Vieira 1
1099-073 Lisboa

SPAIN
Dirección General de Comercio Exterior
(Subdirección General de Control, Inspección y
Normalización del Comercio Exterior)
Punto de Informacion del Comité de Medidas
Sanitarias y Fitosanitarias/SPS
Paseo de la Castellana 162 - planta 6a
28046 Madrid
Tel: +(341) 349 37 64
Fax: +(341) 349 37 40

SWEDEN
Kommerskollegium (National Board of Trade)
WTO-SPS Enquiry Point
Box 6803
11386 Stockholm
Tel: +(468) 690 48 00
Fax: +(468) 30 67 59
E-mail/Internet: sps@kommers.se

UNITED KINGDOM
Ms H. C. Blake
Ministry of Agriculture, Fisheries and Food
Trade Policy and Tropical Foods Division, Branch A
10 Whitehall Place (East Block)
London SW1A 2HH
Tel: +(44171) 270 82 38
Fax: +(44171) 270 84 15
E-mail/Internet: h.blake@tptf.maff.gov.uk

FIJI
The Permanent Secretary for Agriculture, Fisheries, Forests
and ALTA
Private Mail Bag
Raiwaqa

Suva
Tel: +(679) 38 42 33
Fax: +(679) 38 50 48

GABON
M. Eyi Metou Martin
Inspection générale de l'agriculture
Ministère de l'agriculture, de l'élevage et du
développement rural
B.P. 189
Libreville
Tel: +(241) 76 38 36
Fax: +(241) 72 82 75

GEORGIA
Coordinator: Levan Chiteishvili
Ministry of Agriculture and Food
Room 328, 41 Kostava Street
Tbilisi
Tel: +(995 32) 33 48 37
Fax: +(995 32) 33 48 37
E-mail/Internet: sps_levan@access.sanet.ge

GHANA
The Director
Plant Protection & Regulatory Services
Ministry of Food & Agriculture
P.O. Box M.37
Accra
Tel: +(23321) 66 58 84
Fax: +(23321) 66 82 45

GRENADA
Mr. Paul Graham
Agricultural Officer
Pest Management Unit
Botanical Gardens
St Georges's
Tel: +(1 473) 440 00 19
Fax: +(1 473) 440 88 66
E-mail/Internet: PMU@Caribsurf.com

GUATEMALA
Dirección Técnica de Sanidad Vegetal
Dependencia de la Dirección General de Servicios
Agrícolas - DIGESA
7a. Avenida 3-87 Zona 13
Guatemala
Tel: +(5022) 72 04 93

Dirección Técnica de Sanidad Animal
Dependencia de la Dirección General de Servicios
Pecuarios - DIGESEPE
Bárcenas, Carretera a Amatitlan, km. 22.5
Guatemala
Tel: +(5022) 31 20 12/31 20 18

GUYANA
Food safety standards and policy:
Director
Government Analyst Food and Drugs Department
Ministry of Health
Mudlot, Kingston
P.O. Box 1019
Georgetown
Tel: +(592 2) 56 482
Fax: +(592 2) 54 259

Plant protection and livestock health:
Chief Crops and Livestock Officer

Ministry of Agriculture
Regent and Vlissengen Roads
Georgetown
Tel: +(592 2) 56 281
Fax: +(592 2) 56 281

HONDURAS
Secretaría de Agricultura
Unidad de Planeamiento y Evaluación de Gestión (UPEG)
Boulevard Miraflores, Av. La Fao
Tegucigalpa, M.D.C.
Tel: +(504) 239 01 15
Fax: +(504) 231 00 51

HONG KONG, CHINA
Trade Department
The Government of the Hong Kong
Special Administrative Region
17/F, Trade Department Tower
700 Nathan Road
Hong Kong
Tel: +(852) 2398 5398
Fax: +(852) 2789 2491

HUNGARY
Ministry of Agriculture
Department for International and Economic Affairs
Kossuth Lajos tér 11
1055 Budapest
Tel: +(361) 131 35 78
Fax: +(361) 132 67 96

ICELAND
Ministry of Agriculture
Mr. Halldór Runólfsson
Chief Veterinary Officer
Sölvhólsgata 7
150 Reykjavík
Tel: +(354) 560 97 50/560 97 75 (direct)
Fax: +(354) 552 11 60
E-mail/Internet: halldor.runolfsson@lan.stjr.is

INDIA
The Joint Secretary
Plant Protection Division
Ministry of Agriculture (Department of Agriculture &
Cooperation)
Krishi Bhavan, Rafi Marg
New Delhi - 110001
Tel: +(9111) 338 37 44
Fax: +(9111) 338 82 57

INDONESIA
Centre for Agricultural Quarantine (Enquiry Point)
Jalan Pemuda nE 64, Kav. 16-17
Jakarta
Tel: +(6221) 489 48 77/489 20 20
Fax: +(6221) 489 48 77
E-mail/Internet: caqsps@indo.net.id

ISRAEL
Mr. Eldad Landshut
Director
Plant Protection and Inspection Services
Ministry of Agriculture and Rural Development
P.O. Box 78
Beit Dagan 50250
Tel: +(972 3) 968 1500
Fax: +(972 3) 968 1507
E-mail/Internet: ppis@netvision.net.il

Prof. A. Shimshony
Director
Veterinary Services & Animal Health
Ministry of Agriculture and Rural Development
P.O. Box 12
Beit Dagan 50250
Tel: +(9723) 968 16 06/12
Fax: +(9723) 968 16 41
E-mail/Internet: vsahshim@netvision.net.il

JAMAICA
Chief Plant Quarantine/Produce Inspector
Ministry of Agriculture
Hope Gardens
Kingston 6
Tel: +(1809) 927 35 14
Fax: +(1809) 927 17 01/927 19 04

JAPAN
Standards Information Service
First International Organizations Division
Economic Affairs Bureau
Ministry of Foreign Affairs
2-2-1 Kasumigaseki, Chiyoda-ku
Tokyo
Tel: +(813) 3580 3311
Fax: +(813) 3503 3136

KENYA
Human Health:
The Director of Medical Services
P.O. Box 30016
Nairobi
Tel: +(2542) 71 70 77
Fax: +(2542) 71 52 39

Plant Health:
The Director of Agriculture
P.O. Box 30028
Nairobi
Tel: +(2542) 71 88 70
Fax: +(2542) 72 57 74

Animal Health:
The Director of Veterinary Services
P.O. Box Kabete
Nairobi
Tel: +(2542) 63 22 31
Fax: +(2542) 63 12 73

KOREA, REPUBLIC OF
Animal or plant health or zoonoses (excluding aquatic animals):
Bilateral Cooperation Division
Ministry of Agriculture and Forestry (MAF)
1, Choongang-dong, Kwachon
Kyunggi-do, 427-760
Tel: +(822) 503 72 94
Fax: +(822) 507 20 95
E-mail/Internet: bcd@maf.go.kr

Food safety relating to food additives, veterinary drug and pesticide residues, contaminants, methods of analysis and sampling, and codes and guidelines of hygienic practice:
Food and Drug Industry Division
Ministry of Health and Welfare (MOHW)
1, Choongang-dong, Kwachon
Kyunggi-do, 427-760
Tel: +(822) 503 75 45
Fax: +(822) 503 75 46
E-mail/Internet: foodkor@chollian.net

Aquatic animal health and sanitation:
Trade Promotion Division
Fisheries Policy Bureau
Ministry of Maritime Affairs and Fisheries
826-14 Yoksam-dong, Kangnam-gu
Seoul 135-080
Tel: +(822) 567 27 29
Fax: +(822) 566 78 17

KYRGYZSTAN
Information Centre of the State Inspectorate on Standardization and Metrology (Kyrgyzstandard)

LATVIA
WTO Information Division
Department of Quality Management and Structure Development
Ministry of Economy
55 Brivibas Street
Riga LV-1519
Tel: +(371) 7 01 31 97/7 01 32 36
Fax: +(371) 7 28 08 82

LIECHTENSTEIN
Office for Foreign Affairs
Heiligkreuz 14
9490 Vaduz
Tel: +(4175) 236 60 52
Fax: +(4175) 236 60 59

MACAU
"Leal Senado"
Avenida Almeida Ribeiro
Edificio Leal Senado
Tel: +(853) 38 73 33/38 39 93
Fax: +(853) 34 18 90

MALAWI
Animal health:
The Director
Department of Animal Health
P.O. Box 2096
Lilongwe
Tel: +(265) 74 39 94/74 43 90
Fax: +(265) 74 39 94

Plant protection:
Head of Plant Protection Services
Ministry of Agriculture
Bvumbwe Research Station
P.O. Box 5748
Limbe
Tel: +(265) 47 15 03
Fax: +(265) 47 13 23

Food safety including testing and analysing of additives and contaminants:
The Director General
Malawi Bureau of Standards
P.O. Box 946
Blantyre
Tel: +(265) 67 04 88
Fax: +(265) 67 07 56

MALAYSIA
Secretary General
Ministry of Agriculture
Macro and Strategic Planning Division
Wisma Tani
Jalan Sultan Salahuddin

50624 Kuala Lumpur
Tel: +(603) 298 69 68
Fax: +(603) 291 56 42
Web site: http://agrolink.moa.my/

Animals and animal products:
Director-General
Department of Veterinary Services
9th floor, Wisma Chase Perdana
Off Jalan Semantan, Bukit Damansara
50630 Kuala Lumpur
Tel: +(603) 254 00 77
Fax: +(603) 254 00 92
E-mail/Internet: krishnan@jph.gov.my
Web site: http://agrolink.moa.my/jph/

MALTA
The Permanent Secretary
Ministry of Food, Agriculture and Fisheries
Barriera Wharf
Valletta
Tel: +(356) 22 52 36
Fax: +(356) 23 12 94

MAURITIUS
Mr M. Chinappen
Ag. Principal Research and Development Officer
Plant Pathology Division
Ministry of Agriculture, Fisheries and Cooperatives
Réduit
Tel: +(230) 464 48 72
Fax: +(230) 464 87 49
E-mail/Internet: plpath@intnet.mu

MEXICO
Centro de Información de la Dirección General de Normas
SECOFI
Avenida Puente de Tecamachalco n° 6
Col. Lomas de Tecamachalco
Naucalpan, 53950 Edo. de México
Tel: +(525) 729 94 85
Fax: +(525) 729 94 84

MONGOLIA
Mr Khorloobaatar (responsible for WTO SPS enquiries)
State Agricultural Inspection Agency
Peace Avenue 16
Ulaanbaatar 49
Tel: +(976 1) 45 47 42
Fax: +(976 1) 45 47 42

MOROCCO
Sanitary measures:
Ministère de l'agriculture et de la mise en valeur agricole
Direction de l'élevage
Quartier Administratif
Chellah-Rabat
Tel: +(2127) 76 50 77/76 51 47
Fax: +(2127) 76 44 04

Phytosanitary measures:
Ministère de l'agriculture et de la mise en valeur agricole
Direction de la protection des végétaux, des contrôles
techniques et de la répression des fraudes
Avenue de la Victoire - B.P. 1308
Rabat
Tel: +(2127) 77 10 78
Fax: +(2127) 77 25 53

MYANMAR
Directorate of Investment and Company Administration
(DICA)
Ministry of National Planning and Economic Development
653-691 Merchant Street
Yangon
Tel: +(951) 822 07/720 52/752 29
Fax: +(951) 821 01

NAMIBIA
Phytosanitary issues:
Mr. G.B. Rhodes
Division Law Enforcement
Directorate of Extension and Engineering
Private Bag 13184
Ministry of Agriculture, Water & Rural Development
Windhoek
Tel: +(264 61) 202 21 35/208 71 11
Fax: +(264 61) 23 56 72
E-mail/Internet: agrlaw@iafrica.com.na

Zoosanitary issues:
Dr. Schmidt-Dummont
Directorate of Veterinary Services
Private Bag 13184
Ministry of Agriculture, Water & Rural Development
Windhoek
Tel: +(264 61) 208 75 05
Fax: +(264 61) 208 77 79
E-mail/Internet: smithg@gov.na

NEW ZEALAND
Andrew Matheson
Regulatory Authority
Ministry of Agriculture and Forestry
ASB Bank House, 101 The Terrace
P.O. Box 2526
Wellington
Tel: +(64) 4 474 41 00
Fax: +(64) 4 474 41 33
E-mail/Internet: sps@maf.govt.nz

NICARAGUA
Ing. Danilo Cortés
Dirección General de Sanidad Vegetal y Animal
Ministerio de Agricultura y Ganadería
Kilometro 8 1/2, Carretera a Masaya
Managua
Tel: +(5052) 783 412
Fax: +(5052) 785 864

NORWAY
Ministry of Agriculture
Att: WTO-SPS
Post Office Box 8007 Dep.
0030 Oslo
Tel: +(47) 22 24 92 69
Fax: +(47) 22 24 95 56
E-mail/Internet: firmapost@ld.dep telemax.no

PAKISTAN
Dr. Muhammad Shafi
First Plant Protection Advisor
Jinnah Avenue
Malir Halt
Karachi
Tel: +(9221) 457 73 82/48 20 11
Fax: +(9221) 457 43 73

PANAMA
Ministry of Agricultural Development:
Dirección Nacional de Salud Animal
Río Tapia Tocumen
Panamá
Apartado postal: 5390 Zona 5, Panamá
Tel: +(507) 266 18 12
Fax: +(507) 266 29 43/220 79 81

Dirección Nacional de Sanidad Vegetal
Río Tapia Tocumen
Panamá
Apartado postal: 5390 Zona 5, Panamá
Tel/Fax: +(507) 220 79 79/220 07 33

Dirección Ejecutiva de Cuarentena Agropecuaria
Alto de Curundu River Road
Edificio 576
Panamá
Apartado postal: 5390 Zona 5, Panamá
Tel: +(507) 232 53 40
Fax: +(507) 232 59 06

Ministry of Health:
División de Control de Alimentos y Vigilancia Veterinaria
Edificio 265 Ancón
Panamá
Apartado postal: 2048 Panamá, 1 Panamá
Tel: +(507) 262 19 02/212 03 97
Fax: +(507) 262 02 77/262 66 21

División de Farmacia y Drogas
Edificio 265 Ancón
Panamá
Apartado postal: 2048 Panamá, 1 Panamá
Tel: +(507) 262 60 25
Fax: +(507) 212 05 62

PAPUA NEW GUINEA
Director-General
Multilateral Operations
Department of Foreign Affairs and Trade
P.O. Box 422
Waigani
Tel: +(675) 27 13 20
Fax: +(675) 25 44 67

PARAGUAY
For information on plant health:
Ministerio de Agricultura y Ganadería
Dirección de Defensa Vegetal
Ayolas y Benjamin Constant
Edificio Mercurio, 6° Piso
Asunción
Tel: +(59521) 44 03 07/44 52 01/49 37 64
Fax: +(59521) 44 03 07

For information on animal health:
Ministerio de Agricultura y Ganadería
Subsecretaría de Estado de Ganadería
Alberdi no. 611 y General Díaz
Asunción
Tel: +(59521) 44 94 04/44 13 94/44 06 32
Fax: +(59521) 44 72 50

Servicio Nacional de Salud Animal (SENACSA)
Ruta Mcal. Estigarribia, Km 10 y 1/2
San Lorenzo
Tel: +(59521) 50 57 27/50 13 74/50 78 62
Fax: +(59521) 50 78 63

PERU
In the field of human health:
National Health Institute (INS)
Head: Dr. Carlos Carrillo
Tizón y Bueno 268, Jesús María
Lima 21
Tel: +(51-1) 463 38 33/460 0310/460
           0316/ 471 3254
Fax: +(51-1) 463 9617

Functions: To promote, plan, implement and evaluate research on health and the development of appropriate technologies in the field of contagious disease control, environmental sanitation and nutrition; as well as the production, registration and quality control of reagents, diagnostic inputs, medicinal products and organic health foods. It administers the public laboratories of national standing and supports those of regional standing. It also prepares standards within its area of jurisdiction and proposes policies and standards, within its area of jurisdiction, to the Higher Directorate of the Ministry of Health, for implementation at national level.

In the field of agrarian health:
National Agrarian Health Service (SENASA)
Head: Dr. Elsa Corbonell Torres
Psje Francisco de Zela s/n, piso 10
Lima 21
Fax: +(51-1) 433 8048/433 7802

Functions: To develop and promote private sector participation in the implementation of plans and programmes for the prevention, control and eradication of pests and diseases which have a significant socio-economic impact on agricultural activity. At the same time, it is the body responsible for the sanitary protection of national agriculture. It has the task of proposing standards of national and regional scope to the Minister of Agriculture, in connection with monitoring, inspection, registration, control, supervision and sanitary assessment activities in the agricultural field. It also establishes sanitary rules for the import, export, marketing and internal transit of animals, plants and agricultural products and inputs.

PHILIPPINES
Policy Analysis Service
Department of Agriculture
Elliptical Road, Diliman
Quezon City
Tel: (632) 920 40 84/929 82 47
Fax: (632) 928 08 50
E-mail/Internet: policy@skyinet.net

POLAND
Ministry of Agriculture and Food Economy
Departament Rynku i Gield
ul. Wspólna 30
00-930 Warszawa
Tel: +(4822) 623-22-66, 621 57 54
Fax: +(4822) 623 21 05

QATAR
The Ministry of Public Health
P.O Box 42
Doha
Tel: +(974) 41 71 11
Fax: +(974) 42 95 65

ROMANIA
National Sanitary - Veterinary Agency

Ministry of Agriculture and Food
B-dul Carol I, no. 24, sector 3
70033 Bucharest
Tel: +(401) 615 78 75/614 40 20
Fax: +(401) 312 49 67

SAINT LUCIA

Ministry of Agriculture, Lands, Fisheries and Forestry
Manoel Street
Castries
Tel: +(758) 452 25 26
Fax: +(758) 453 63 14

SENEGAL

Ministère du commerce, de l'artisanat et de
l'industrialisation
Direction du commerce extérieur
Rue Passage Le Blanc
Angle Emile Zola, Thiaroye
Dakar
Tel: +(221) 21 57 25
Fax: +(221) 22 09 32

SINGAPORE

Director of Primary Production
Primary Production Department
5 Maxwell Road #03-00
National Development Building
Singapore (0106)
Tel: +(65) 325 76 90
Fax: +(65) 220 60 68
E-mail/Internet: PPD_Email@PPD.gov.sg

Area of competence:

(a) Food safety relating to food additives, veterinary drug and pesticide residues, contaminants methods of analysis and sampling, and codes and guidelines of hygienic practice concerning international movements of meat and meat products (including canned meat), fish and fishery products, vegetables and fruits;

(b) Animal, health and zoonoses, the standards and guidelines and recommendations developed under the auspices of the International Office of Epizootics (OIE) especially concerning the international movements of animals and birds, and their products including bones and bone meal, hides and skins, hoofs, horns, hoof meal, horn meal, offal and any other product of animal origin; semen, fodder, litter, dung or any animals or birds; veterinary biologics for use on animals or birds; and simple and compounded feedstuffs for animal consumption;

(c) Plant health including phytosanitary certifications;

(d) Fish health including certifications for ornamental fish and fishery products;

(e) International movements and certifications of endangered species of fauna and flora under agreements of the Convention on International Trade in Endangered Species (CITES).

SLOVAK REPUBLIC

Slovak Institute for Standardization
Information Centre WTO
Karloveská 63
84245 Bratislava
Tel: +(421) 39 78 86
Fax: +(421 39 78 86

SLOVENIA

The Ministry of Agriculture and Forestry
Attn: Ms. Katarina Groznik
Parmova 33
1000 Ljubljana
Tel: +(386 61) 322 197/323 643
Fax: +(386 61) 313 631

SOUTH AFRICA

The Director: Marketing
Department of Agriculture
Private Bag X791
Pretoria 0001
Tel: +(2712) 319 65 18
Fax: +(2712) 326 34 54

SRI LANKA

Director
Department of Animal Productions and Health
Getambe
Peradeniya
Tel: +(948) 884 62/63
Fax: +(948) 881 95

SWAZILAND

Mr. N.M. Nkambule
Principal Secretary
Ministry of Agriculture and Cooperatives
P.O. Box 162
Mbabane
Tel: +(268) 404 63 61/404 27 46
Fax: +(268) 404 47 00

SWITZERLAND

Association suisse de normalisation (SNV)
Mühlebachstrasse 54
CH-8008 Zurich
Tel: +(411) 254 54 54
Fax: +(411) 254 54 74
In its capacity as enquiry point, the SNV works under mandate of the Federal Office of External Economic Affairs.

TAIWAN PROVINCE (CHINA)

Bureau of Animal and Plant Health Inspection and Quarantine
Council of Agriculture, Executive Yuan
9F, 51 Sec.2, Chung Ching South Road
Taipei, Taiwan 100
Tel: +(886) 2 2343 1401
Fax: +(886) 2 2343 1400

TANZANIA, UNITED REPUBLIC OF

The Director
Tanzania Bureau of Standards
PO Box 9524
Dar es Salaam
Tel: +(255) 51 450 298
Fax: +(255) 51 450 983

THAILAND

Thai Industrial Standards Institute (TISI)
Ministry of Industry
Rama VI Street, Bangkok 10400
Tel: +(662) 202 34 01/202 35 07/202 35 10
Fax: +(662) 247 87 41

TRINIDAD AND TOBAGO

Mr. Winston Rudder
Permanent Secretary
Ministry of Agriculture, Land and Marine Resources

St. Clair Circle
Port of Spain
Tel: +(809) 622 12 21
Fax: +(809) 622 42 46

TUNISIA
Animal health, zoonoses and plant safety:
Ministère de l'agriculture
30 rue Alain Savary
1002 Tunis
Tel: +(2161) 78 56 33
Fax: +(2161) 79 94 57

Food safety:
Ministère du Commerce
(Direction générale de la concurrence et du commerce intérieur)
6 rue Venezuela
1002 Tunis
Tel: +(2161) 78 77 02
Fax: +(2161) 78 18 47

TURKEY
Mr. Yusuf Salcan
Tarim ve Köyisleri Bakanligi
Koruma ve Kontrol Genel Müdürlügü
Akay Cad. No. 3
Ankara
Tel: +(90312) 418 14 68
Fax: +(90312) 418 80 05$

UGANDA
Uganda National Bureau of Standards
Plot M217, Nakawa Industrial Area
P.O. Box 6329
Kampala
Tel: +(25641) 222 369/222 367

UNITED STATES
USDA/FAS/FSTSD
Attn: Carolyn F. Wilson
Stop 1027
Room 5545, South Agriculture Building
1400 Independence Avenue, SW
Washington, D.C. 20250

Tel: +(202) 720 22 39
Fax: +(202) 690 06 77
Email/Internet: wilsonc@fas.usda.gov

URUGUAY
Ministerio de Relaciones Exteriores
Dirección General de Asuntos Económicos
Avenida 18 de Julio 1205
Montevideo
Tel: +(5982) 92 06 18
Fax: +(5982) 92 13 27/92 42 90

VENEZUELA
Food safety:
Ministerio de Sanidad y Asistencia Social
Dirección de Higiene de los Alimentos
Centro Simón Bolívar, Edificio Sur
3er. piso, Oficina 313
Caracas
Tel: +(582) 482 06 57
Fax: +(582) 482 06 57

Animal health and plant protection:
Ministerio de Agricultura y Cría
Servicio Autónomo de Sanidad Agropecuaria (SASA)
Parque Central, Torre Este, Piso 12
Caracas 1010
Tel: +(582) 509 05 05/509 03 79
Fax: +(582) 509 06 57

ZAMBIA
Mr. F. Siame
Permanent Secretary
Ministry of Commerce, Trade and Industry
Lusaka
Tel: +(2601) 22 14 75
Fax: +(2601) 22 66 73

ZIMBABWE
Secretary for Agriculture
Ministry of Agriculture
P/Bag 7701
Causeway Harare
Tel: +(2634) 706 081
Fax: +(2634) 734 646

CHAPTER 6

Import licensing procedures

Summary

National import licensing procedures can adversely affect the flow of imports, particularly if these procedures are not transparent or if they unnecessarily delay the issue of licences. The Agreement on Import Licensing Procedures divides licences into two categories: automatic and non-automatic. Automatic licences should be issued within a maximum period of 10 working days after the receipt of applications. Non-automatic licences, which are generally used to administer quantitative restrictions, must be granted within a maximum period of 30 days from receipt of application where licences are issued on a first-come first-served basis and 60 days if all applications are considered simultaneously.

The Agreement further lays down certain principles and rules to ensure that the flow of international trade is not impeded by the inappropriate use of import licensing procedures and that procedures are administered fairly and equitably.

Agreement on Import
Licensing Procedures (ILP),
Preamble

GATT's basic approach is that, in order to facilitate trade, the formalities and documentation requirements for importation and exportation should be kept to a minimum. However, GATT recognizes that countries often, for various reasons, require importers to obtain import licences. Such licensing systems may be adopted to administer quantitative restrictions in the limited number of situations permitting member countries to use such restrictions. Alternatively, they may be used for the surveillance of trade statistics or the prices of certain goods.

Agreement on ILP,
Article 1.1
Agreement on ILP,
Articles 2 and 3

The Agreement on Import Licensing Procedures lays down rules for adopting and implementing national procedures for issuing import licences. It defines 'import licensing' as "administrative procedures ... requiring the submission of an application ... to the relevant administrative body as a prior condition for importation ... of goods." It divides licensing systems into two categories: automatic and non-automatic.

Under automatic systems, the authorities issue licences automatically without using any discretionary powers. Non-automatic licensing systems administer quota restrictions and other measures, and the authorities use their discretion in granting licences. The Agreement lays down general rules applicable to both systems and specific rules for each system. National licensing authorities must comply with these rules, the basic objective of which is to protect the interests of importers and foreign suppliers. The rules require national licensing authorities to ensure that licensing procedures:

❏ Are not more burdensome than absolutely necessary to administer the licensing system, taking into account the purpose for which they are adopted;

❑ Are transparent and predictable; and

❑ Protect importers and foreign suppliers from unnecessary delays and arbitrary actions.

Common rules

Agreement on ILP,
Article 1.4(a)

The Agreement obliges member countries to publish all information on import licensing procedures, so that importers, exporters and their governments are fully aware of:

❑ The eligibility of persons, firms and institutions to make applications;

❑ The administrative body responsible for the issue of licences; and

❑ The products subject to licensing.

Agreement on ILP,
Article 1.5 - 11

To protect the interests of importers and to facilitate speedy and prompt issue of licences, the Agreement further stipulates that:

❑ Application forms and procedures, including procedures for the renewal of licences, should be as simple as possible;

❑ Applications should not be refused for minor documentation errors which do not alter the basic data contained therein;

❑ Penalties imposed for such errors, except where fraudulent intent or gross negligence is involved, should not be more severe than required to serve as a warning;

❑ Licensed imports should not be refused for minor variations in value, quantity or weight from those designated in a licence, where such differences are consistent with commercial practice or are due to differences in value, weight and quantities arising as a result of shipping or bulk loading.

Automatic import licensing

Agreement on ILP,
Article 2

In systems where administrative authorities do not exercise any discretion and "licences are granted in all cases", the Agreement requires approval or licence to be granted immediately, on receipt of the application, and in any case "within a maximum period of 10 working days".

Non-automatic import licensing

Agreement on ILP,
Article 3

Non-automatic licensing systems are used, as noted earlier, where the government's primary purpose is to restrict imports. Governments may do this by publicly announcing the quota or quantitative limits applicable to restricted goods.

Where import licensing is utilized for the administration of quotas, the Agreement requires the publication of the overall amount of the quota (quantity and/or value), its opening and closing dates, so that all interested parties – importers, exporters and foreign producers and their governments – are fully aware of them. Further, where a quota is allocated among supplying countries, the country granting the quota is not only required to publish information on the shares allotted to each country, but must also specifically inform the governments of all interested supplying countries of the distribution of shares.

The Agreement requires import licences to be issued within 30 days of the receipt of the application where the procedures provide that licences should be issued "on a first-come first-served basis". They must be issued within 60 days of the date of closing for the receipt of applications where these applications "are considered simultaneously".

The rules further aim at ensuring that, in the distribution of licences, consideration is given to the practical difficulties that importers might have encountered in utilizing the licences issued to them. As a principle, licences should be issued to those importers who have made the best possible use of past licences. At the same time, care should be taken to ensure that importers who have not been able to use their licences for legitimate reasons are not unduly penalized by denial of a licence or by unduly reducing the value or quantity authorized under the licence. Licensing authorities are further required to give special consideration in distributing licences to new importers, particularly to those who import from developing and least developed countries.

Business implications

By obliging national licensing authorities to follow its principles and rules, the Agreement seeks to protect the interests both of foreign suppliers wanting to export products subject to licensing and of producing industries interested in importing such products. It further requires countries to adopt licensing procedures which, *inter alia*, would give importers the right to expect that:

❑ Licences will be issued promptly within the prescribed periods, and

❑ They will not be penalized for minor documentation errors.

CHAPTER 7

Rules applicable to exports

Summary

GATT rules permit an export product to be relieved of all indirect taxes borne by it in the exporting country. The rules further allow countries to levy duties on exports if these are necessary to control exports or to achieve any other policy objective. As with imports, the rules prohibit export restrictions except in a few specified situations.

The Guide has so far described the GATT rules applicable predominantly to imported products. This chapter briefly discusses the rules on exports.

Export incentives providing for the reimbursement of indirect taxes

GATT 1994, Annex I, Ad Article XVI.
Agreement on SCM, Footnote to Article 1 and Annexes I to III

GATT rules permit countries to relieve a product to be exported of:

❑ Customs duties and other indirect taxes levied on inputs used and consumed in its manufacture;

❑ Indirect taxes on the exported product; and

❑ Indirect taxes on the production and distribution of the exported product.

Agreement on SCM, Annex I: footnote 58

The term 'indirect taxes' covers such taxes as "sales, excise, turnover, value added, franchise, stamp, transfer, inventory and equipment taxes". The Agreement on Subsidies and Countervailing Measures (SCM), which provides that foregoing by governments of the taxes that are due and payable constitutes an export subsidy, clarifies that:

> Exemption of an exported product from duties or indirect taxes borne by the like product when destined for domestic consumption, or the remission of such duties or taxes in amounts not in excess of those which have accrued, shall not be deemed to be a subsidy.

It is important to note the reasons for these rules. Under GATT's national treatment rule, a country may levy on an imported product, in addition to customs duties, all indirect taxes that it imposes on like products produced domestically, provided the duties are not levied at rates higher than those applied to domestic products. Unless therefore the exported product is either relieved or exempted from the indirect taxes payable in the exporting country, it becomes subject to double taxation – in both the exporting and importing country.

The rules, however, allow an exported product to be relieved of indirect taxes only. It may not be relieved of the direct taxes (such as income tax and taxes on profits) payable by producing enterprises. The SCM Agreement clarifies that "exemption, remission or deferral specifically related to exports, of direct taxes or social welfare charges paid or payable" by the producing enterprise constitute a prohibited export subsidy. The economic rationale for this rule arises from the assumption that the burden of indirect taxes is generally shifted to the product and is reflected in its price, while direct taxes are not so shifted, but are generally absorbed by the tax payer producer.

Almost all countries today have incentive schemes. These schemes make it possible for exporting enterprises to claim exemption from, or drawback of, customs duties paid on inputs used in the manufacture of export products and the reimbursement of indirect taxes borne by such products. Further, in order to ensure that exporting enterprises are not disadvantaged in selling in outside markets, countries rarely impose taxes on exports.

Rule governing export control measures

GATT rules, however, recognize that in certain situations countries may have to take measures to control exports. As with imports, countries are required in such situations to give preference to price-based measures. The rules thus permit countries to use export taxes but prohibit restrictions on exports unless they can be justified under one of the exceptions.

Export taxes

Revenue considerations have led some developing countries to levy export duties. Today, these countries are reducing their dependence on these duties because of their adverse effects on the export trade.

However, apart from revenue considerations, export duties may also be levied to attain certain other policy objectives. They may, for example, be temporarily imposed immediately after a devaluation if the lower export prices in foreign currency terms do not bring about the expected rise in exports while providing undue benefit to exporters.

Duties are levied by countries exporting primary commodities to improve their terms of trade. They may also be used to control exports in order to increase the availability of resources to the domestic processing industry or to control for environmental or ecological reasons further exploitation of the country's natural resources.

One of the major advantages of export duties over export restrictions is that they provide governments with additional revenue. Governments often use such revenue to assist the producers of the taxed commodities and products.

GATT 1994, Article I:1

The basic GATT rule requiring countries to extend MFN treatment applies to duties on both imports and exports. The MFN principle also applies to:

❑ The method of levying such duties, and

❑ All rules and formalities connected with exportation.

Export restrictions

The GATT provisions prohibiting restrictions on imports also apply to exports. There are, however, a few exceptions to this rule. Thus it is open to a country to restrict or prohibit exports, if this is necessary:

GATT 1994, Article XI:2(b)

❑ To implement standards or regulations on the classification, grading or marketing of commodities in international trade, and

❑ To prevent or relieve critical shortages of foodstuffs or other essential products.

In addition, the rules prevent countries from imposing restrictions:

❑ On raw materials in order to protect or promote a domestic fabricating industry,

❑ To avoid competition among exporters.

Business implications

It is important for the business person to note that GATT rules permit the reimbursement of customs duties paid on production inputs as well as the refund of the indirect taxes borne by exported products. As regards customs duties, the practice in most countries is either to exempt inputs imported for use in export production from payment of duties, or to permit exporters to claim a duty drawback after export. Most countries also have incentive schemes allowing exporters to claim the reimbursement of indirect taxes borne by the exported product. As relief from such taxes on products exported is granted by almost all countries, enterprises in countries that do not provide such a relief may find themselves at a disadvantage on foreign markets. It is necessary to ensure that the amount reimbursed does not exceed the actual incidence of the customs duties on inputs and of the indirect taxes on the exported product. Any payment in excess of the actual incidence would amount to an export subsidy.

As is explained in chapter 8, countries are prohibited from granting export subsidies. Developing countries have a transitional period of eight years (i.e. up to 1 January 2008) to phase out their existing export subsidy schemes. The rules do not permit these countries to grant during the transitional period subsidies on products that have not benefited from them earlier. Furthermore, the rules permit the refund only of indirect taxes borne by the exported product. Any exemption or payments to exporters to compensate for direct taxes payable on export earnings are not allowed.

GATT's basic approach that exported products should be relieved of all indirect taxes also implies that, where in special situations countries levy export duties, the need for maintaining them should be kept under continuous review. It is important for the business person to know that such duties, like import duties, can be applied by governments only on an MFN basis. It is not open to a country to levy a higher export duty on exports to one destination and lower or no duty on exports to other destinations.

CHAPTER 8

Rules governing subsidies on industrial products

Summary

The GATT rules on subsidies stipulated in Article XVI have been clarified and elaborated by the Agreement on Subsidies and Countervailing Measures (SCM) and the Agreement on Agriculture. Broadly speaking, the provisions of the Agreement on SCM apply to industrial products; those of the Agreement on Agriculture cover agricultural products.

The SCM Agreement recognizes that governments utilize subsidies to attain various policy objectives. However, it restrains the right of governments to grant subsidies that have significant trade-distorting effects. Its rules are complex.

The Agreement divides subsidies into prohibited and permissible subsidies. Prohibited subsidies include export subsidies. In the past, the rule against the use of export subsidies on industrial products applied only to developed countries; the Agreement extends this rule to developing countries. The latter countries have a transitional period of eight years within which to bring their subsidy practices into conformity with the rule. During this period, they cannot increase the level of their export subsidies. The rule against the use of export subsidies does not apply to least developed countries and to developing countries with per capita GNPs of less than US$ 1,000.

All subsidies that are not prohibited are permissible. The permissible subsidies are divided into two categories: subsidies that are actionable and those that are not actionable.

The Agreement provides two types of remedies where the subsidies granted by governments cause "adverse effects" to the trade interests of other countries.

Where such adverse effects take the form of material injury to a domestic industry in the importing country, the Agreement authorizes that country to levy countervailing duties to offset the subsidy. Such duties can be levied only if, after duly conducted investigations, the investigating authorities are satisfied that there is a causal link between subsidized imports and material injury to the industry concerned. Furthermore, such investigations can normally be initiated only on the basis of a petition from the affected industry alleging that such imports are causing it damage.

Alternatively, both in the case of serious prejudice to a domestic industry and in the case of other adverse effects, the importing country can bring the matter before the Dispute Settlement Body (DSB) to secure withdrawal or modification by the subsidizing country of the subsidies that are causing adverse effects.

Governments grant subsidies to attain various policy objectives. Thus, subsidies may be made available to promote the development of new industries; to encourage investment and the establishment of industries in a country's backward regions; to assist industries in export development; to improve the infrastructure for agricultural production and to ensure a reasonable income level for farmers.

The GATT rules governing the use of subsidies are complex, and they differ for industrial and for agricultural products. The main GATT provisions on subsidies are elaborated in the Agreement on Subsidies and Countervailing Measures (SCM), and in the Agreement on Agriculture. The provisions of the Agreement on SCM apply, with a few exceptions, to industrial products; those of the Agreement on Agriculture relate to agricultural products. The rules of the SCM Agreement are described in this chapter, those applicable to agriculture are discussed in chapter 15.

Definition of subsidies; aim of the Agreement on SCM

Under the SCM Agreement, an industry is deemed to have received a subsidy where a *benefit* is conferred on the industry as a result of:

Agreement on SCM, Article 1

❑ Direct transfer from the government of funds (e.g. grants, loans or equity infusion) or government guarantees of payment of loans;

❑ The government foregoing the revenue that should otherwise have been collected;

❑ The government providing goods or services, or purchasing goods.

The concept of *benefit* is essential to determining whether a measure represents a subsidy. Although the Agreement provides only limited guidance on this point, as a general rule it may be said that a government action that is not consistent with commercial considerations confers a benefit. Thus, a government infusion of equity on terms a private investor would not accept, a loan on terms more favourable than those offered by commercial banks, or the provision by a government of goods or services for less than the prevailing market price, is likely to confer a benefit and may therefore be a subsidy.

The aim of the Agreement is not to restrain unduly the right of governments to grant subsidies but to prohibit or discourage them from using subsidies that have adverse effects on the trade of other countries. Towards this end, it categorizes subsidies into those that are prohibited and those that are permissible.

Prohibited subsidies (red subsidies)

The following subsidies are prohibited:

Agreement on SCM, Article 3

❑ Export subsidies, i.e. subsidies that are contingent on export performance (see box 22 for an illustrative list),

❑ Subsidies that are contingent on the use of domestic over imported goods.

In the past the rule prohibiting the use of export subsidies on industrial products applied only to developed countries. The Agreement extends the application of the rule to developing countries. These countries (with some exceptions) may, however, gradually abolish the use of such subsidies over a transitional period of eight years expiring on 1 January 2003. They also have a transitional period of five years to eliminate subsidies that are contingent on the

> **Box 22**
>
> **Illustrative list of prohibited export subsidies**
>
> *The Agreement on SCM's illustrative list of prohibited export subsidies includes the following:*
>
> ❑ *Direct subsidies based on export performance;*
>
> ❑ *Currency retention schemes involving a bonus on exports;*
>
> ❑ *Provision of subsidized inputs for use in the production of exported goods;*
>
> ❑ *Exemption from direct taxes (e.g. tax on profits related to exports);*
>
> ❑ *Exemption from, or remission of, indirect taxes (e.g. VAT) on exported products in excess of those borne by these products when sold for domestic consumption;*
>
> ❑ *Remission or drawback of import charges (e.g. tariffs and other duties) in excess of those levied on inputs consumed in the production of exported goods;*
>
> ❑ *Export guarantee programmes at premium rates inadequate to cover the long-term costs of the programme;*
>
> ❑ *Export credits at rates below the government's cost of borrowing, where they are used to secure a material advantage in export credit terms.*

use of domestic over imported products. This period expires on 1 January 2000. Box 23 describes the provisions of the Agreement which extend special and differential treatment to developing countries in regard to the use of prohibited and permissible subsidies.

Permissible subsidies

Under the Agreement's rules, governments are in principle permitted to grant subsidies other than those described above, which are prohibited. However, the Agreement groups permissible subsidies into two categories: those that are actionable and those that are non-actionable. It has become common practice to compare the Agreement's categorization of subsidies to the traffic light. Prohibited subsidies are called red subsidies; those that are actionable, amber; and those that are non-actionable, green.

Permissible subsidies that are actionable (amber subsidies)

Broadly speaking the Agreement uses the concept of *specificity* to categorize subsidies that are actionable and those that are non-actionable. A subsidy is specific if it is limited to:

Agreement on SCM, Articles 2, 5

❑ An enterprise or group of enterprises;

❑ An industrial sector or group of industries; or

❑ A designated geographic region within the jurisdiction of the granting authority.

All specific subsidies (other than those identified in the section that follows) are actionable if they cause what the Agreement calls "adverse effects to the interests of other Members". Such adverse effects take the form of:

❑ Serious prejudice to the domestic industry;

❑ Injury to the domestic industry in the importing country;

❑ Nullification and impairment of the benefits of bound tariff rates.

Box 23

Flexibility available to developing countries in the use of subsidies
(Agreement on SCM, Article 27)

The Agreement on SCM recognizes that "subsidies may play an important role in economic development programmes of developing country Members." Because of this, it further acknowledges that these countries may not be able to abide immediately by the full discipline of the rules which it lays down. To allow for flexibility in the application of the rules, the Agreement provides for special and differential treatment of developing countries.

Export subsidies

As noted earlier, the rule prohibiting export subsidies will apply to developing countries only after a transitional period of eight years, i.e. by 1 January 2003. These countries are, however, urged to phase out such subsidies progressively within the eight-year period and are not allowed to increase the level of their export subsidization. The transitional period may, if requested by a developing country, be extended by another two years.

These countries are further required to phase out within a period of two years export subsidies for any product in which they have become export competitive. A country is considered to have reached export competitiveness in a product if it has attained a share in the world market of 3.25% for two consecutive years. A product for this purpose is defined as a section heading of the Harmonized System Nomenclature, developed by the World Customs Organization for the classification of tariffs and trade statistics.

The least developed and low-income developing countries, with per capita GNPs of less than US$ 1,000, are totally exempt from the rule prohibiting export subsidies.* If, however, they are found to have developed export competitiveness in any product, they are under an obligation to phase out the export subsidies granted to that product within eight years (compared with the two-year period given to other developing countries).

Export subsidies by developing country members remain actionable, however, both multilaterally and through countervailing duties.

Subsidies to promote the use of domestic goods

The rule prohibiting subsidies to promote the use of domestic over imported goods will be applicable to developing countries after a transitional period of five years (by 1 January 2000) and to least developed countries after eight years (by 1 January 2003).

Subsidies to encourage privatization

To encourage privatization, the Agreement provides that "direct forgiveness of debts, subsidies to cover social costs, in whatever form, including relinquishment of government revenue ..." by the government of a developing country shall be treated as non-actionable multilaterally, provided such subsidies are granted for a limited period and are in accordance with a privatization programme. They remain subject to countervailing measures, however.

---

* The low-income countries whose per capita GNPs are currently less than US$ 1,000 per annum are: Bolivia, Cameroon, Côte d'Ivoire, the Dominican Republic, Egypt, Ghana, Guatemala, Guyana, India, Indonesia, Kenya, Morocco, Nicaragua, Nigeria, Pakistan, the Philippines, Senegal, Sri Lanka and Zimbabwe. These countries will, however, be required to accept the obligation to prohibit the use of export subsidies when their per capita GNPs reach US$ 1,000.

One basis for actionability is the existence of *serious prejudice* to the interests of other countries. This course of action is likely to be invoked when the subsidized product is displacing the complainant's exports from the market of the subsidizing country or of a third country. Box 24 describes the criteria which the Agreement lays down for determining whether a subsidy granted by a country is causing serious prejudice to the interests of other Members.

> **Box 24**
> **Criteria for determining serious prejudice to the interest of another country**
> (SCM, Article 6)
>
> *The Agreement clarifies that serious prejudice to the interest of another country shall be presumed to have occurred, inter alia, where:*
>
> ❑ *Total ad valorem subsidization of a product exceeds 5%;*
>
> ❑ *Subsidies cover operating losses sustained by an industry;*
>
> ❑ *Subsidies other than one-time measures cover operating losses sustained by an enterprise; or*
>
> ❑ *There is direct forgiveness of debt by the government.*
>
> *In all other cases, in order to establish that serious prejudice has actually occurred, the complainant must demonstrate that the effect of the subsidy is:*
>
> ❑ *To displace or impede imports from another member country into the subsidizing country;*
>
> ❑ *To displace exports to a third country market;*
>
> ❑ *Significantly to undercut or suppress prices in the subsidizing market;*
>
> ❑ *An increase in the world market share of the subsidizing country over its average share in the previous three years for the product or commodity benefiting from subsidy.*

Material injury is another basis for actionability. In particular it is the basis under which an importing country can levy countervailing duties on subsidized imports that are causing injury to its domestic industry.

Subsidies that cause *nullification and impairment* of the benefits which the GATT system provides are also actionable. Such nullification and impairment of benefits could be deemed to have occurred when an exporting country finds that the value of the concession in the form of tariff binding it has obtained in trade negotiations by making a reciprocal concession has been greatly reduced because a domestic industry has lost market share to an industry in the importing country benefiting from subsidy.

Permissible subsidies that are non-actionable (green subsidies)

Agreement on SCM, Articles 2, 8

With a few exceptions, all permissible subsidies that are specific are actionable. Those which are not specific are non-actionable. Subsidy programmes providing subsidies on the basis of objective economic criteria and which are horizontal character and "do not favour certain enterprises over others" are not specific. They are therefore non-actionable. Thus the subsidies given by governments to small and medium-sized enterprises, identified on the basis of their size or number of employees, would ordinarily be non-actionable.

In addition, certain subsidies that are specific are non-actionable, provided the specific conditions governing their grant comply with the rules of the Agreement. These include subsidies:

❑ For research activities conducted by firms, provided certain conditions are met;

❑ To adapt existing production facilities to new environmental requirements, provided that the subsidy is a one-time non-recurring measure and is limited to 20% of the cost of adaptation; and

❑ To assist in the development of industries in disadvantaged regions, provided certain conditions are met.

Importing countries cannot levy countervailing duties on products benefiting from non-actionable subsidies.

Remedies available to affected industries and to their governments

What are the remedies available to industries and to governments of countries which consider that their interests are being damaged by subsidized imports?

Agreement on SCM, Articles 4, 7, 9

The Agreement provides for two types of remedies. First, a country which considers that either a prohibited subsidy is being used or that it is being adversely affected by the grant of a permissible subsidy, may raise the matter before the WTO Dispute Settlement Body (DSB) for redress. Where the adverse effects take the form of "material injury" to its domestic industry, the importing country may, instead of invoking dispute settlement procedures, levy countervailing duties on the imported subsidized products (see box 25). Such duties can however be levied only when investigations carried out at the national level and on the basis of a petition from the affected industry have established that the subsidized imports are causing injury to the domestic industry. Countervailing duties cannot be levied on products benefiting from non-actionable subsidies.

Box 25

Remedies available to importing countries under the Agreement on SCM

(Articles 4, 7 and 9)

Two types of remedies are available to an importing country which considers that the use of subsidies by other member countries is affecting its interests adversely. It may levy countervailing duties if, after investigations carried out in pursuance of a petition made by the affected industry, it is established that subsidized imports are causing the industry material injury. It may also bring the matter for redress before the Dispute Settlement Body (DSB).

Prohibited subsidies. *Any country which considers that another country is using a prohibited subsidy may, if bilateral consultations with that subsidizing country do not lead to its withdrawal, bring the matter before DSB.*

Actionable subsidies. *A country which finds that an actionable subsidy granted by another country has adversely affected its interests may refer the matter to DSB for settlement, if bilateral consultations fail to bring about a mutually agreed solution.*

Non-actionable subsidies. *Countervailing duties cannot be levied on products that have benefited from non-actionable subsidies. However, where a country "has reasons to believe" that the subsidy programmes have had "serious adverse effects" on its domestic industry as to cause damage which would be difficult to repair, it may request consultations with the country granting subsidies. If the consultations fail, it may request the Committee on Subsidies and Countervailing Measures (SC), which has been established under the Agreement, to determine whether such effects exist.*

In all the three cases mentioned above, if the subsidizing country fails to take appropriate steps to implement the recommendations made, the DSB/Committee on SC could authorize the affected country to take countermeasures that would affect the trade of the subsidizing country.

The Agreement on SCM lays down detailed rules and procedures for investigating authorities to follow in carrying out investigations and calculating the amount of countervailing duties that can be levied. Since the rules applicable to the levy of countervailing duties and to the use of anti-dumping measures are similar, and since in most countries the investigations for the levy of both these duties are carried out by the same investigating authorities, these rules are explained together in chapter 11.

Business implications

The rule against the use of export subsidies for industrial products, which in the past applied only to developed countries, is now also valid for developing countries. (The exceptions are least developed and developing countries with per capita GNPs of less than US$ 1,000.) These countries have a transitional period of eight years (to 1 January 2003) within which to withdraw their existing subsidy systems. During this period, they may not increase the level of their subsidies or grant subsidies to products not previously covered. Enterprises currently benefiting from export subsidies will therefore have to prepare themselves for the withdrawal of these subsidies by their governments by the end of the transitional period, if not earlier.

It should be noted that while the SCM Agreement permits developing countries to use export subsidies during the transitional period, these subsidies can be countervailed by importing countries even during that period if they cause injury to their domestic industries. This also applies to the developing countries that are exempt from the rule prohibiting the use of export subsidies. The maintenance of export subsidies on products that are considered import sensitive by importing countries (e.g. textiles, leather and leather products, etc.), albeit permitted under the Agreement, is therefore fraught with danger. It is thus important for governments to adopt trade and foreign exchange policies that will remove the bias against their countries' exports and reduce the need for export subsidies. It is also necessary for them to examine, in consultation and in cooperation with their exporting enterprises and their associations, whether assistance, where needed, can be provided in the form of permissible subsidies and preferably those that are not actionable by importing countries. In this context it is important to note that subsidies that are not specific to particular industries but are of general application are not countervailable by importing countries.

CHAPTER 9

Safeguard measures to restrict imports in emergency situations

Summary

The Agreement on Safeguards authorizes importing countries to restrict imports for temporary periods if, after investigations carried out by competent authorities, it is established that imports are taking place in such increased quantities (either absolute or in relation to domestic production) as to cause serious injury to the domestic industry that produces like or directly competitive products. It further provides that such measures, which could take the form of an increase in tariffs over bound rates or the imposition of quantitative restrictions, should normally be applied on an MFN basis to imports from all sources.

The investigations for the imposition of such measures can be initiated either by the government itself or on the basis of a petition from the affected industry. In practice, however, the investigations are generally initiated on the basis of petitions from the affected industry.

The Agreement lays down the criteria which investigating authorities must consider in determining whether increased imports are causing serious injury to the domestic industry. It also sets out basic procedural requirements for the conduct of investigations. One aim of the procedural requirements is to provide foreign suppliers and governments whose interests may be adversely affected by the proposed safeguard actions with an adequate opportunity to give evidence and to defend their interests.

The primary purpose of providing such temporary increased protection is to give the affected industry time to prepare itself for the increased competition that it will have to face after the restrictions are removed. The Agreement seeks to ensure that such restrictions are applied only for temporary periods by setting a maximum period of eight years for the application of a measure on a particular product. Developing countries can, however, impose them for a maximum period of 10 years.

To give industries time to adjust gradually to the increased competition resulting from reductions in tariffs and from the removal of other barriers to trade, the GATT practice has been to require that the cuts in tariffs agreed in multilateral trade negotiations should be implemented in stages over an agreed number of years. Thus tariff reductions on industrial products agreed in the Uruguay Round are to be made over five years in five equal instalments. Likewise, reductions in the agricultural sector as well as in domestic and export subsidies are to take place in stages over a period of six years. Developing countries have been given longer periods within which to implement reductions.

The GATT rules recognize that, despite the phased implementation of tariff reductions, certain industrial or agricultural sectors may face, in the short term, problems in adjusting to increased import competition. These problems may flow from their failure to rationalize production structures or to adopt the technological innovations necessary to raise productivity. To provide affected industries time to adjust to competition, Article XIX of GATT provides that where, as a result of tariff reductions, a country finds that a product is being imported "in such increased quantities and under such conditions as to cause or threaten serious injury to domestic producers", it can impose safeguard measures to restrict such imports for temporary periods.

GATT 1994, Article XIX:1(a)

Circumventing GATT rules through VERs

Largely because of the GATT requirement that safeguard measures should be applied on a non-discriminatory basis, in the past countries entered into voluntary export restraints (VERs) or orderly marketing arrangements (OMAs). Under these arrangements, exporting countries with rising exports were required by importing countries to restrain their exports to agreed limits. Though these arrangements were called "voluntary", in reality they were not always so. As the restraints were applied only to imports from certain countries, they were also inconsistent with the rule that restrictions on imports should be employed on a non-discriminatory basis.

The use of such grey area measures (called so because their consistency with GATT rules was in doubt) by some developed countries, notably the United States and members of the European Union, increased in the last three decades. The governments of these countries had also in some instances either encouraged or supported the initiatives taken by their industries to enter into voluntary export restraint arrangements with their counterparts in exporting countries. It is estimated that in 1995, when WTO came into existence, there were over 200 such bilateral or plurilateral arrangements. They covered products ranging from agricultural goods (like beef); simple merchandise (such as leather and rubber products, travel goods, pottery and chinaware); to sophisticated manufactures like television sets, motor cars and trucks.

Agreement on Safeguards

Commitment to abolish VERs

The main aim of the Uruguay Round negotiations in this area was to ensure that restrictive measures like VERs and other similar discriminatory measures are brought into conformity with GATT principles and rules. The Agreement on Safeguards (negotiated in the Round) did this by requiring countries to phase out the grey area measures which they were maintaining within a period of four years (i.e. by 1 January 1999)[12]. In addition, countries are committed "not to seek, take or maintain any voluntary export restraints, orderly marketing arrangements or any other similar measures on the export or import

---

12   Each member country can, however, maintain one such measure over an additional period of one year.

side". They are also required not to "encourage or support the adoption or maintenance" of inter-industry arrangements that are comparable to the governmental measures described above.

Serious injury standard

The Agreement further provides that safeguard measures should be applied only after it has been determined by the investigating authorities that:

Agreement on Safeguards, Article 2

❑ A product is being imported in increased quantities (absolute or relative to domestic production), and

❑ In such conditions as to cause or threaten to cause serious injury to producers of like or directly competitive products.

Agreement on Safeguards, Article 4:1

The term 'serious injury' is defined as the "significant overall impairment in the position of a domestic industry." It must be established that imports are causing such injury to the domestic industry, defined as the "producers as a whole of the like or directly competitive products" or those "whose collective output of the like or directly competitive products constitutes a major proportion of the total domestic production of those products." In other words, it is not permissible to take safeguard measures to restrict imports where only a few producers are finding it difficult to meet import competition.

Rules governing investigations

The Agreement requires each member country to designate authorities to be responsible for carrying out investigations and to publish the procedures it proposes to follow, so that these are known to the public.

The request for the initiation of such investigations can be made by the government itself or by an industry whose collective output constitutes a major portion of the total domestic production of the imported product. However, in practice, investigations are generally triggered by an application made by producers or on their behalf by an association of producers. Such applications typically claim that increased imports are causing the producers serious injury, leading for instance to loss of profits, reduction in production and under-utilization of capacity and/or requiring cuts in the labour force.

Agreement on Safeguards, Article 3

The investigating authorities must give public notice of investigations and arrange for public hearings or other appropriate means in which "importers, exporters and other interested parties could present evidence and their views." The authorities should also examine views and comments against the requested safeguard action and on whether the application of such a measure would be in the public interest.

Agreement on Safeguards, Article 4:2

The investigating authorities can authorize a safeguard action only after an evaluation of all relevant factors of an objective and quantifiable nature establishes that there is a "causal link between increased imports of the product concerned and serious injury or threat thereof" to the industry. Safeguard actions should not be authorized if the problems the industry is encountering arise from factors other than increased imports (e.g. decline in overall demand for the product). In order to provide transparency, the investigating authorities are further required to publish their reports and conclusions.

Application of safeguard measures

Agreement on Safeguards, Preamble

The Agreement emphasizes that, in taking safeguard measures, the aim of the governments should be to promote "structural adjustment" and to "enhance rather than limit competition in international markets". To this end it provides that such safeguard measures should be applied only for temporary periods to enable the affected industry to take steps to adjust itself to the increased competition that will follow the removal of those measures. Adjustment could take the form of the adoption of improved technology or the rationalization of production structures.

Agreement on Safeguards, Article 5

Furthermore, safeguard measures should be applied only "to the extent necessary to prevent or remedy serious injury and to facilitate adjustment" and on a "non-discriminatory basis to imports from all sources". The type of safeguard action to be taken – increase in the bound rate of tariffs or imposition of quantitative restrictions on imports – is decided by the investigating authorities. Where a quantitative restriction is used, quotas may be allocated among the main supplying countries. In such cases, individual shares are allocated in consultation with the supplying countries on the basis of their shares in imports during a previous representative period. In allocating shares on this basis, the interests of new suppliers should also be adequately taken into account.

The Agreement permits, in exceptional situations, member countries to depart from the non-discriminatory rule and to apply quota restrictions only to one or more countries when imports from these countries "have increased in disproportionate percentage in relation to the total increase of imports of the product concerned in the representative period". In order to ensure that such actions are taken only in exceptional situations, the Agreement stipulates that they should be taken after consultations with, and approval by, the Committee on Safeguards. The Committee has been established under the Agreement.

Compensation for the loss of trade

Agreement on Safeguards, Article 8

A member country proposing to apply safeguard measures is expected to offer adequate trade compensation to countries whose trade interests would be adversely affected by such measures.[13] If agreement on an adequate trade compensation cannot be reached by the country proposing to apply a safeguard measure and the affected exporting member countries, the exporting members may take retaliatory action.[14] However, the right to retaliatory action cannot be exercised for the first three years that the measure is in effect, where the safeguard measure has been taken in accordance with the provisions of the Agreement and as a result of an absolute increase in imports (and not relative to domestic production).

Special and differential treatment of developing countries

Agreement on Safeguards, Article 9

The Agreement provides for the special and differential treatment of developing countries in the application of safeguard measures. Imports from a developing country are exempt from safeguard measures if its share in the imports of the product concerned into the country taking the measure is less than 3%. This exemption does not apply if developing countries with individual shares in imports smaller than 3% collectively account for more than 9% of the imports.

Duration of safeguard measures

The other provisions of the Agreement are mainly directed towards ensuring that safeguard measures are applied for temporary periods. It is thus provided that:

---

13 The compensation is generally a concession, in the form of tariff reductions, from the country wishing to take safeguard actions to the countries whose trade is to be restricted, on other products of export interest to them.

14 Such retaliatory action is generally the suspension of a concession or other obligation to which the country applying the safeguard measure is entitled.

❑ Safeguard measures in force on 1 January 1995, when the Agreement went into effect, must be terminated after eight years or by 1 January 2000, whichever comes later.

Agreement on Safeguards,
Article 7

❑ The maximum initial period for the application of a safeguard measure is four years. This initial period may be extended up to a maximum of eight years (10 years for developing countries).

In order to assist affected industries in preparing themselves for the increased competition that will follow the ultimate lifting of safeguard measures, the Agreement requires any measure with a duration of more than one year to be progressively liberalized. There should also be mid-term reviews of measures with durations of over three years, to see whether they should be withdrawn or liberalized faster.

In addition, the Agreement prevents countries from circumventing the time limits on safeguard measures by prohibiting the reimposition of protection on the same product for a period equal to that of the original safeguard action. In no event can a measure be reapplied within an immediately following period of less than two years. However, temporary safeguards that have been imposed for six months or less may be reinstated after one year, as long as actions are not taken on the same product more than twice in a five-year period. Here again, developing countries are subject to less rigorous obligations and may reimpose actions on the same product after a period equal to half the duration of the previous measure (but not within a period of less than two years).

Business implications

The new and improved rules on safeguards reinforce the GATT rules providing for security of access. Importing countries are prohibited from requesting exporting countries to ask their enterprises to restrain their exports under VERs or similar arrangements. It is important to note that by providing further that governments should not encourage their industries to conclude such arrangements with industries in other countries, the Agreement has cautioned industries against entering into similar arrangements even on an informal basis.

As has been mentioned, almost all tariffs of developed countries and a high proportion of the tariffs of developing countries have been bound against further increases, thus restricting the right of countries to raise tariffs. Under the rules of the Agreement on Safeguards, importing countries will therefore be able to take measures to restrict imports only when investigations have established that increased imports are causing serious injury to their domestic industries. The rules further try to protect the interests of exporting enterprises by giving them the right to defend their interests during the investigations and to produce, if necessary, evidence to establish that the imposition of restrictions would not be in the interest of the consuming public in the importing country.

It is, however, important to note that these general rules on safeguard actions do not immediately apply to textile products. The Agreement on Textiles and Clothing, negotiated in the Uruguay Round, provides that the discriminatory restrictions currently applied to textile products by some importing countries should be phased out in four stages over a period of 10 years. During this phase-out period the Agreement permits countries to take safeguard actions to restrict imports on a discriminatory basis from those exporting country or countries, where as a result of "sharp and substantial increase in imports" from these countries, "serious damage" is caused to the domestic industry.

The trade in textiles will be governed by the rules of the Agreement on Safeguards on non-discriminatory application of safeguard measures only after 1 January 2005. On that date, the Agreement on Textiles and Clothing, after having been under implementation for 10 years, will cease to exist.

It is essential to look at these rules not only from the viewpoint of exporting enterprises but also from the perspective of enterprises which as a result of a sudden surge in imports are finding it difficult to compete with foreign suppliers in their domestic markets. These enterprises have the right to petition their governments to take safeguard actions to restrict imports. Such petitions cannot be made by a single firm or a few enterprises, but by producers whose "production constitutes a major proportion of total domestic production". In practice, such petitions or applications are often made on behalf of producers by the associations to which they belong. Petitions can be submitted only when it is possible to establish that there is a causal link between increased imports and the alleged serious injury to the industry. The ability of the affected industries to take advantage of these provisions will depend on how far they are able to build up the case for such temporary protection, taking into account the Agreement's strict conditions for the imposition of safeguard measures.

CHAPTER **10**

Safeguard actions for economic development purposes: special flexibility available to developing countries

Summary

GATT rules provide special flexibility to developing countries to take safeguard measures to restrict imports, for temporary periods, in order to promote the development of new or infant industries. However, GATT lays down strict conditions for the invocation of these rules. Furthermore, safeguard measures can ordinarily be introduced only with WTO approval.

GATT 1994, Article XVIII: Section C; Tokyo Round Declaration: Safeguard Action for Development Purposes

The GATT rules recognize that governments of developing countries, in pursuance of their programmes and policies of economic development, may find it necessary to provide assistance to new or infant industries or for the further development of existing industries and that such assistance may take the form of safeguard actions restricting imports for temporary periods. As the imposition of these restraints could adversely affect the interests of exporting countries, the rules lay down stringent conditions for their adoption.

Conditions for the invocation of safeguard provisions

A government wishing to provide higher protection through the imposition of restrictions is expected to notify the WTO Secretariat of the:

❑ Particular industry or industries, either existing or new, for the development of which such higher protection is necessary;

❑ The nature of the proposed restrictive measure (increase in tariffs that are bound against further increases, imposition of quantitative restrictions on imports or the introduction of a licensing system);

❑ The special difficulties that imports pose for the development of such industries; and

❑ Why measures other than import restrictions are not practicable.

The notification must be made before the measure is introduced. In exceptional cases, where delay in the introduction of the measure is expected to pose special difficulties to the industry concerned, the notification can be made immediately after the measure is imposed.

The introduction of safeguard measures or their continuation where notification is made after the measures have been introduced is ordinarily[15] possible if WTO member countries, after examining the reasons for it, approve it.

Business implications

In practice, the special flexibility available to developing countries under these provisions has rarely been invoked. One of the main reasons for this was that, until the conclusion of the Uruguay Round, the tariffs of nearly all developing countries were not bound against increases. This enabled them to protect developing infant industries, where necessary, by raising their tariffs.

In the Uruguay Round, as noted earlier, a large proportion of the tariffs of developing countries has been bound against further increases. Enterprises in developing countries which believe that they need more protection to develop new industries or further develop existing ones will therefore have to request their governments to invoke the provisions on "safeguard actions for development purposes". On their part, the governments will have to obtain approval from WTO prior to taking such measures (e.g. increase in bound rates of tariffs or imposition of quantitative restrictions).

As the adoption of such measures will be a derogation from the basic rules, WTO will grant such approval only if member countries are satisfied that, taking into account such factors as available natural resources and existing production and consumption trends, the higher level of protection will help the industry to become internationally competitive within a reasonable period. Furthermore, in granting such approval, WTO may impose strict conditions to ensure that the restrictions are maintained only for temporary periods and that steps are taken for their gradual withdrawal during these periods.

---

15   If the tariff on a product is bound against further increases, restrictive measures can be taken only with WTO's prior approval. Where, however, the duty is not bound, two courses are open to the developing country wishing to give higher protection. It may raise the rate of duty. As a rise in the rates of tariffs that are not bound is permissible under GATT rules, it can take such an action without invoking the provisions of GATT Article XVIII:C. Where, however, it proposes to give higher protection by imposing restrictions that are not permissible under GATT (such as the application of quantitative restrictions or a restrictive licensing system), it has to notify WTO and enter into consultations with other member countries in order to obtain approval of the proposed measure. While the Article provides that, in such cases, the developing country concerned could apply the measure even if the approval is not granted, in practice this is not possible. The reason is that the Article also gives other member countries the right to take retaliatory actions if they consider the measure to be adverse to their trade interests.

CHAPTER 11

Response to unfair trade practices: rules on the use of countervailing and anti-dumping duties

Summary

The GATT rules deal with two types of "unfair" trade practices which distort conditions of competition. First, the competition may be unfair if the exported goods benefit from subsidies. Second, the conditions of competition may be distorted if the exported goods are dumped in foreign markets.

In common parlance, it is usual to designate all low-cost imports as dumped imports. The Agreement on Anti-dumping Practices (ADP), however, lays down strict criteria for determining when "a product is to be considered as being dumped". In general, a product is considered dumped if the export price is less than the price charged for the like product in the exporting country.

The Agreements on Anti-dumping Practices and on Subsidies and Countervailing Measures (SCM) authorize countries to levy compensatory duties on imports of products that are benefiting from unfair trade practices. However, an importing country can levy countervailing duties on subsidized imports and anti-dumping duties on dumped imports only if it is established, on the basis of investigations carried out by it, that such imports are causing "material injury" to a domestic industry. Investigations for the imposition of such duties should ordinarily be initiated on the basis of a petition made by or on behalf of an industry, alleging that imports are causing it injury.

The two Agreements lay down similar criteria for determining injury. The procedures for carrying out investigations for the levy of anti-dumping and countervailing duties are likewise similar.

As noted in chapter 9, the rules permit countries to take safeguard actions restricting imports for temporary periods when, as a result of a sudden and sharp increase in imports, serious injury is caused to the domestic industry of the importing country. The increased imports covered by these particular rules are not attributable to unfair trade practices by foreign suppliers.

However, the GATT rules acknowledge that the rise in imports may indeed be due to the adoption of unfair trade practices by foreign suppliers. The rules therefore lay down the basis on which governments may levy compensatory duties on imports of products benefiting from such unfair practices. They deal with two forms of unfair trade practices which distort conditions of competition. First, the competition may become unfair if the exported goods benefit from specific subsidies. Second, the conditions of competition may be distorted if the producer dumps its goods in foreign markets.

The basic provisions of GATT 1994 on the use of subsidies have been elaborated by the Agreement on SCM. As noted earlier, the basic aim of these provisions is either to prohibit or to restrain the use of subsidies that cause adverse effects to the interests of other Members. However, where the use of permitted subsidies results in material injury to a domestic industry in an importing Member, the rules permit that importing Member to take remedial measures which could take the form of countervailing duties on subsidized imports. Likewise the Agreement on Anti-dumping Practices (full title: Agreement on Implementation of Article VI of the General Agreement on Tariffs and Trade 1994), which elaborates the basic GATT rules on dumping, authorizes Members to levy anti-dumping duties on dumped imports.

In general, a product is considered dumped if the export price is less than the price charged for the like product in the exporting country. Broadly speaking, a producing enterprise is able to charge higher prices on sales in the domestic market if, as a result of a high level of protection, foreign competition is absent or weak.

The rules of the Agreements on SCM and ADP do not *per se* condemn dumping or subsidization. They recognize that the lower prices of imported goods arising from dumping or subsidization could benefit industrial users and consumers in the importing countries. The two Agreements therefore lay down an important principle: that compensatory duties in the form of countervailing duties on subsidized imports and anti-dumping duties on dumped imports cannot be levied solely on the ground that a product has benefited from a subsidy or that it is being dumped. They can be levied only if it is established after an investigation, which must normally be initiated on the request of a domestic industry, that dumped or subsidized imports are causing "material injury" to that industry.

Similar principles apply when governments take safeguard measures to restrict imports in order to assist a domestic industry that is being injured by a sudden and sharp increase in imports. The standard of "injury" to the industry that must be established to justify safeguard actions is, however, much higher than that required for the levy of countervailing or anti-dumping duties. In the case of safeguard actions, injury to the industry must be "serious"; in the case of countervailing and anti-dumping duties, a lower standard of proof of material injury is adequate. The difference in standards is attributable to the fact that, in the first instance, the industry's problems do not arise from unfair competition, while in the second, these are due to the unfair trade practices of foreign producers.

This chapter discusses the following subjects:

❑ The concept of dumping as embodied in GATT law,

❑ The rules and procedures that countries must follow in levying anti-dumping and countervailing duties.

The rules that the Agreements on SCM and ADP lay down for the levy of these compensatory duties are similar. Furthermore, at the national level, the authorities responsible for investigating petitions for the levy of countervailing and of anti-dumping duties are the same in most cases.

Concept of dumping as embodied in GATT law

In common parlance, it is usual to designate all low-cost imports as dumped imports. The Agreement on Anti-dumping Practices, however, lays down strict criteria for determining when an imported product should be treated as being

Agreement on Anti-dumping Practices, Article 2:1

dumped. In particular it states that "a product is to be considered as being dumped", if its export price is less than the price at which a like product is sold for consumption in the exporting country. In other words, if on the basis of a comparison of the export price and the home consumption price in the exporting country it is found that the latter price is higher, the product could be treated as being dumped.

The Agreement, however, provides that the determination of dumping on the above basis may not be appropriate:

Agreement on Anti-dumping Practices, Article 2:2

❑ Where sales in the domestic market of the exporting country are not in the ordinary course of trade (e.g. sales below the cost of production), and

❑ Where the volume of sales in the domestic market is low.

In these cases, the Agreement permits dumping to be determined by comparing the export price with:

❑ A comparable price charged for the like product when exported to a third country, or

❑ A constructed value, calculated on the basis of the production costs of the imported product, plus general, selling and administrative costs, and profits.

Agreement on Anti-dumping Practices, Article 2:2, footnote 2

However, in order to ensure to the maximum extent possible that dumping is being determined on the basis of a comparison of the export price with the price for home consumption in the exporting country, the Agreement lays down the so-called *5% representative test*. The investigating authorities must use for price-comparison purposes prices charged to third country markets or use constructed values calculated on the basis of the cost of production if the value of sales in the domestic market of the exporting country constitutes less than 5% of the sales of the products to the importing country.

Rules and procedures for levying countervailing and anti-dumping duties

Main criteria for the levy of duties

Injury to domestic industry

The basic rule which the Agreements on ADP and SCM lay down is that anti-dumping and countervailing duties should be levied only where it has been established on the basis of investigations that:

❑ There has been a significant increase in dumped or subsidized imports, either in absolute terms or relative to production or consumption; and

Agreement on Anti-dumping Practices, Article 3; Agreement on Subsidies and Countervailing Measures, Article 15

❑ The prices of such imports have undercut those of the like domestic product, have depressed the price of the like product or have prevented that price from increasing; and

❑ As a result, injury is caused to the domestic industry or there is a threat of injury to the domestic industry of the importing country.

Causal link between dumped, subsidized imports and injury to the domestic industry

The two Agreements specify that, in determining whether dumped imports are causing injury to the domestic industry, "relevant economic factors having a bearing on the state of the industry" should be taken into account (see box 26

Box 26

Factors to be taken into account in determining material injury to domestic industry

(Agreement on Anti-dumping Practices, Article 3; Agreement on Subsidies and Countervailing Measures, Article 15)

The Agreements on SCM and ADP provide that the determination of whether subsidized or dumped imports are causing injury to a domestic industry should be made on the basis of all "relevant economic factors having a bearing on the state of the industry". Such factors include:

❑ *Actual or potential decline in output, sales, market share, profits, productivity, return on investments, or utilization of capacity;*

❑ *Effects on domestic prices;*

❑ *Actual or potential effects on cash flow, inventories, employment, wages, growth, ability to raise capital or investments.*

In the case of anti-dumping investigations, one of the other factors to be taken into account is the magnitude of the margin of dumping. Likewise in investigations for the levy of countervailing duties on imports of agricultural products, an additional factor to be taken into account is whether there has been an increased burden on government support programmes.

The two Agreements clarify that the above list of economic factors is illustrative and not exhaustive, and that "one or several of these factors necessarily give decisive guidance".

The Agreements further stipulate that the investigating authorities must also examine whether any factors other than subsidized or dumped imports are causing injury to domestic industry. Countervailing or anti-dumping duties should not be levied if the main factors responsible for the difficulties of the industry are factors other than subsidized or dumped imports. Such factors could include:

❑ *Contraction in demand or changes in the patterns of consumption;*

❑ *Trade restrictive practices of, and competition between, foreign and domestic producers;*

❑ *Developments in technology and export performance; and*

❑ *Productivity of the domestic industry.*

---

for a listing of these factors). Furthermore, for anti-dumping or countervailing duties to be levied, it must be clearly established that there is a causal link between dumped or subsidized imports and the injury to the industry.

Where the problems being encountered by the domestic industry are caused by such factors as "contractions in demand or changes in the pattern of consumption" and cannot be directly attributed to dumped or subsidized imports, anti-dumping or countervailing duties must not be levied. Furthermore, such duties must not be levied where increased imports are adversely affecting only a few producers. They can be levied solely when it has been established that the imports are posing problems to the producers "whose collective output of the product constitutes a major proportion of the total domestic production" of the industry.

Cumulation of imports

Agreement on Anti-dumping Practices, Article 3.3; Agreement on Subsidies and Countervailing Measures, Article 15.3

Normally when imports from several countries are subject to investigations, the assessment of whether such imports are causing injury to the domestic industry has to be made separately for each country. The Agreements, however, allow the investigating authorities in certain situations to assess the combined effects of all imports under investigation in determining injury. Such cumulation of imports is allowed only if:

❑ The dumping margin or the amount of subsidization of each individual country exceeds a *de minimis* level;

❑ The volume of imports from each country is not negligible; and

❑ Such cumulative assessment is appropriate in the light of conditions of competition between imported products and the conditions of competition between the imported products and like domestic products.

Standing of petitioners

It is important to note that the two Agreements stipulate that, save in exceptional situations,[16] anti-dumping or countervailing investigations shall be initiated only on the basis of a complaint made "by or on behalf" of the domestic industry.

Agreement on Anti-dumping Practices, Article 5.4; Agreement on Subsidies and Countervailing Measures, Article 11.4

Further, in order to ensure that applications for the levy of such duties are made only when a substantial number of producers are affected, the Agreements lay down two complementary criteria:

❑ First, the producers supporting the application must account for over 50% of the production of the producers who express an opinion either in support of, or against, the petition.[17]

❑ Second, the producers supporting the application should account for at least 25% of the industry's total production.

The investigating authorities are under an obligation to ascertain whether petitioners have such standing before initiating an investigation.

Procedural rules

Information to be provided in the application

The Agreements further stipulate the type of information (see box 27) that the petitioning industry must provide in its application in order to substantiate its claim that dumped or subsidized imports are causing it injury.

Agreement on Anti-dumping Practices, Article 5.5; Agreement on Subsidies and Countervailing Measures, Article 11.5

Agreement on Anti-dumping Practices, Article 12.1; Agreement on Subsidies and Countervailing Measures, Article 22.2

A large number of applications that are unsubstantiated or do not meet the criteria described above are in practice rejected by investigating authorities. As the mere submission of such applications often creates uncertainty in trade, the Agreements require the investigating authorities to avoid publicizing the submission of applications. However, after the decision is taken to initiate investigations, authorities are obliged to give public notice of the initiation of investigations giving, *inter alia*, the names of the exporting country or countries, the basis on which dumping or subsidization is alleged and a summary of the allegations on which the claim for injury is based.

Notification to governments

Agreement on Anti-dumping Practices, 6.1.3; Agreement on Subsidies and Countervailing Measures, 12.1.3

Agreement on Subsidies and Countervailing Measures, Article 13

In addition, the investigating authorities are required to notify the governments of exporting Members of the receipt of a properly documented complaint and before initiating anti-dumping or countervailing investigations. As soon as an investigation is initiated, the authorities must make available the full text of the written application to the governments of the exporting countries. Furthermore, the SCM Agreement imposes an obligation on the investigating country to enter into consultations with the government of the exporting

---

16 The government of an importing country can initiate action for the levy of anti-dumping and countervailing duties only in exceptional circumstances.

17 A section of the producers may not wish to express an opinion either for or against the petition. The share of such producers is to be excluded in arriving at the percentage.

> ***Box 27***
>
> ***Information to be provided in applications for the levy of anti-dumping or countervailing duties***
>
> *The application for the levy of anti-dumping and countervailing duties should contain the following information:*
>
> ❑ *The volume of the domestic production of the producers making the application;*
>
> ❑ *Description of the alleged dumped or subsidized product;*
>
> ❑ *The names of the exporting countries, each known exporter or foreign producer, and a list of the importers of the product;*
>
> ❑ *Information on dumping/subsidization:*
>
> – *In applications for anti-dumping action, such information should include prices at which the product is sold in the domestic market of the exporting country and information on export prices.*
>
> – *In applications for countervailing duties, such information should include evidence of the existence, amount and nature of the subsidy.*
>
> – *Information regarding injury and causality.*
>
> – *Information on the volume of dumped or subsidized imports.*
>
> – *Information on the adverse effects of such imports:*
>
>   • *On domestic prices, and*
>
>   • *On the domestic industry.*

country after the petition is accepted but before the investigations begin. Such consultations provide the government of the investigating country an opportunity to ascertain whether, taking into account the information presented in the application on the alleged injurious effects of subsidies on the industry, the exporting country is prepared to modify its subsidy practices so as to reach mutually acceptable solutions.

Right to give evidence

The rules of the two Agreements further aim at ensuring that, once investigations have begun, exporters and importers of the alleged dumped or subsidized products, the governments of the exporting countries, and other interested parties (e.g. trade or business associations of which the exporters or producers are members) have adequate opportunity to tender oral and written evidence to rebut the claim made by the petitioners and to defend their interests. Towards this end, the Agreements specifically provide that:

Agreement on Anti-dumping Practices, Article 6.1; Agreement on Subsidies and Countervailing Measures, Article 12.1

❑ The full text of the application should be made available to all known exporters alleged to be dumping or benefiting from subsidies and to the governments of the exporting countries concerned;

❑ The evidence presented by one party should be promptly made available to the other parties participating in the investigations; and

❑ Parties have a right to see all information (excluding confidential information) used by the investigating authorities during the investigations to help them in preparing their presentations.

Agreement on Anti-dumping Practices, Article 6.12; Agreement on Subsidies and Countervailing Measures, Article 12.10

In addition, the two Agreements provide that, in anti-dumping and countervailing investigations, industrial users and organizations of consumers of the products under investigation shall be given an opportunity to express their views on whether the case meets the statutory criteria for the levy of such duties (i.e. dumping or subsidization, injury and causality).

This provision can be used to safeguard the essential interests of users and consumers when the authorities consider that the levy of such duties could lead to an unjustified rise in prices.

Provision of information by exporters and the best information rule

Agreement on Anti-dumping
Practices, Article 6.1.1;
Agreement on Subsidies
and Countervailing
Measures, Article 12.1.1

While giving exporting enterprises the right to defend their interests during the investigations, the Agreements also oblige them to cooperate with investigating authorities and to provide the latter with any information they may request on production costs and other matters. In practice, investigating authorities require such information to be given on the basis of a questionnaire and within a period of not less than 30 days of the request for information. Where enterprises are not able to reply within that period, the Agreements call on investigating authorities to consider requests for extension with sympathy and to assist the enterprises, if requested, in providing the information in the format required. Where, however, producing enterprises refuse to cooperate or do not provide the information demanded within a reasonable period of time, the investigating authorities can take decisions on the basis of the best information available, i.e. information provided by the petitioning industry.

On-the-spot investigations

Agreement on Anti-dumping
Practices, Article 6.7 and
Annex I;
Agreement on Subsidies
and Countervailing
Measures, Article 12.6
and Annex VI

Investigating authorities often find it necessary to undertake on-the-spot investigations to verify the information provided by exporters or producing companies in response to the questionnaire or to collect additional information. The Agreements stipulate that such investigations can be carried out only with the agreement of the exporters or producers concerned and if the government of the exporting country does not object to the investigations. Sufficient advance notice of the intended visit should be given. The notice should indicate the type of the information needed so that the exporters/producers can prepare themselves to provide that information.

A refusal to permit an on-the-spot investigation could result in use by the authorities of the best information available.

Methodological rules

The methods used by the investigating authorities to calculate the per unit subsidy received by a product or the margin of dumping can greatly influence the level of countervailing or anti-dumping duties to be paid. The two Agreements therefore provide certain guidelines for the investigating authorities to follow in making these calculations.

Agreement on SCM

Agreement on Subsidies
and Countervailing
Measures, Article 14

The SCM Agreement provides that the national legislation or implementing regulations of member countries should specify the methods to be used by the investigating authorities in determining per unit subsidy. In addition, to ensure transparency, it imposes an obligation on the investigating authorities to explain in their decision how the per unit subsidization was arrived at by using the method specified in the legislation.

Agreement on ADP

Price comparison: general principles

Agreement on Anti-dumping
Practices, Article 2.4

As noted earlier, a product is considered dumped only if the foreign producer's export price is lower than the price charged for home consumption in the country of export. The margin of dumping is therefore determined primarily by comparing these two prices.

The ADP Agreement sets out guidelines to ensure a fair comparison between the home consumption price and the export price. In particular, it states that such comparison should be made "at the same level of trade, normally at the ex-factory level, and in respect of sales made at as nearly as possible the same time." Due allowance should also be made for "differences in conditions and terms of sale, taxation, levels of trade, quantities, physical characteristics" and other factors affecting price comparability.

In making a price comparison, the question often arises of what benchmark to use in determining the price for home consumption when the producer is selling in the home market at prices below average production costs or at a loss. A producer who over a long period has been selling a product at a loss in its domestic market would be able to dump it in foreign markets only by making use of its sales profits from other products (i.e. cross-product subsidization). A number of countries have in the past excluded such domestic sales in determining domestic consumption prices. In order to ensure uniformity in the practices adopted by investigating authorities for that purpose, the Agreement provides that sales in the home market below fully allocated production costs (including administrative and selling costs) may be disregarded only when:

Agreement on Anti-dumping Practices, Article 2.1.1 and footnotes 3, 4, 5

❏ Such sales are made over an extended period (normally one year);

❏ The average selling price in the home market is less than the weighted average unit cost; or

❏ The volume of sales below unit cost is more than 20% of the total; and

❏ The costs are not recovered over a reasonable period.

Averaging prices

Agreement on Anti-dumping Practices, Article 2.4.2

To arrive at the margin of dumping by comparing the exporter's domestic and export prices, investigating authorities often use a system of averaging, particularly when a large number of small transactions are involved. In order to ensure that, in such cases, prices are compared on an apple-to-apple basis, the Agreement requires that comparison should normally be based on:

❏ Either the weighted average of home consumption prices with the weighted average of the prices of all export transactions,

❏ Or the home market prices and export prices on a transaction-to-transaction basis.

The Agreement permits an exception to this general rule when export prices differ significantly among purchasers, regions or periods. In such instances, a weighted average home consumption price may be compared with the price of an individual export transaction.

Currency conversion

Agreement on Anti-dumping Practices, Article 2.4.1

Comparing the home consumption price with the export price normally involves the conversion of the latter into the exporting country's currency. Because of fluctuations, the rate used for currency conversion could greatly influence the margin of dumping. In order to ensure consistency in the methods used by investigating authorities, the ADP Agreement provides that the exchange rate prevalent on the date of sale should be used for conversion purposes. However, if the transaction is based on an exchange rate stated in a forward contract, that rate should be used.

Constructed value

The Agreement on ADP recognizes, as noted earlier, that where the volume of domestic sales is "low", the consumption price in the exporting country may not

Agreement on Anti-dumping
Practices, Articles 2.2, 2.3

provide a proper basis for price comparison. In such cases, the Agreement permits the investigating authorities to use, for price comparison purposes, a constructed value instead of the domestic consumption price. The constructed value is calculated on the basis of cost to the exporting industry of producing the product. Box 28 describes the guidelines which the Agreement on ADP lays down for calculating constructed values.

Box 28

Guidelines for calculating constructed values

(Agreement on Anti-dumping Practices, Articles 2.2 and 2.3)

When investigating authorities decide, for price comparison purposes, to replace the consumption price in the exporting country, with a constructed value calculated on the basis of the production costs of the exporting industry, the ADP Agreement lays down principles for arriving at such a value. In particular, it states that the costs should "normally be calculated on the basis of records kept by the exporter or producer under investigation, provided that such records are in accordance with the generally accepted accounting principles of the exporting country". The Agreement further provides that the amounts for administrative, sales and general costs and profits should be based on "actual data pertaining to production and sales in the ordinary course of trade of the like product by the exporter or producer under investigation." However, when it is not possible to determine such amounts on the above basis, the Agreement provides that they can be determined on the basis of:

❏ *Actual data from other exporters or producers of products in the same general category;*

❏ *The weighted average of the costs and profits of other exporters of the same product; and*

❏ *Any other reasonable method, as long as the amount does not exceed that of the exporters or producers of the same general category of product.*

De minimis rule

Very often during the course of preliminary investigations, the authorities are satisfied that it will not be possible for the petitioners to establish injury as the margin of dumping is small or import penetration is negligible. The ADP Agreement provides that the application should be immediately rejected and the investigation terminated if:

Agreement on Anti-dumping
Practices, Article 5.8

❏ The margin of dumping is *de minimis*, i.e. less than 2%, expressed as a percentage of the export price; or

❏ The volume of imports from a particular country is less than 3% of all imports of like products into the importing country. However, this rule does not apply when countries with individual shares of less than 3% collectively account for more than 7% of imports of the product under investigation; or

❏ The injury is negligible.

Agreement on Subsidies
and Countervailing
Measures, Article 11.9

Likewise, the SCM Agreement requires the authorities to terminate investigations in the situations described below.

❏ In the case of a product originating from a developed country, where:

– The amount of subsidy is *de minimis*, i.e. less than 1%, or

– The volume of subsidized imports or the injury is negligible.

Agreement on Subsidies
and Countervailing
Measures, Article 27.10

❑ In the case of a product originating from a developing country, when:

– The level of subsidies granted does not exceed 2% of the value calculated on a per unit basis,

– The subsidized imports are less than 4% of total imports of the importing country. However, the rule does not apply when developing countries with individual shares of less than 4% collectively account for more than 9% of total imports.

Lesser duty rule

Agreement on Anti-dumping
Practices, Article 9.1;
Agreement on Subsidies
and Countervailing
Measures, Article 19.2

In this context, it is also important to note that both the ADP and SCM Agreements emphasize that, after completion of the investigations, the governments should carefully consider whether additional duties should be levied even if "all requirements regarding their imposition are met".

They further encourage the use of the lesser duty rule. Under this approach even after it is established that dumped or subsidized imports are causing injury to the domestic industry, the decision on whether the amount of duty should be the full margin of dumping or the full amount of subsidy or less should be made by the appropriate governmental authorities and, if a lesser duty is adequate to remove the injury to the domestic industry, the lesser duty should be levied. This principle is followed by some countries which, after the investigations are completed, try to determine the injury margin and levy duty on the basis of that margin if it is lower than the dumping margin or the amount of subsidy.

Provisional measures

Agreement on Anti-dumping
Practices, Article 7;
Agreement on Subsidies
and Countervailing
Measures, Article 17

The two Agreements further authorize provisional measures – in the form of cash deposits or bonds – to be taken when the investigating authorities judge that such measures are "necessary to prevent injury being caused during the investigation." However, the Agreements stipulate that such provisional measures should be taken only after the investigating authorities have made a preliminary affirmative determination of dumping or subsidization and consequent injury to the domestic industry. If a definitive decision is made to levy duty and the duty is higher than the cash deposit or bond, the difference is not collected from the importer. The importer, however, has a right to claim for reimbursement of the difference when the definitive duty is lower than the cash deposit.

Price undertakings

Agreement on Anti-dumping
Practices, Article 8;
Agreement on Subsidies
and Countervailing
Measures, Article 18

Exporters can avoid anti-dumping or countervailing duties by undertaking to increase their export prices. However, to prevent exporters from being required to give such price undertakings even when their exports are not causing injury to the domestic industry of the importing country, the Agreements permit such price undertakings only after the investigating authorities have made a preliminary affirmative determination of injury to the domestic industry and of dumping or subsidization. They further stipulate that the decision to offer a price undertaking should be left to the exporter and that "no exporter shall be forced to enter into such undertakings." It is also possible that the authorities of the importing countries may consider the acceptance of undertakings impractical; this would be the case when the "number of actual or potential exporters is too great".

Disclosure prior to final determination

Agreement on Anti-dumping
Practices, Article 6.9;

The two Agreements stipulate that the investigations should be completed within a period of one year, and in no case more than 18 months after its

Agreement on Subsidies
and Countervailing
Measures, Article 12.8

initiation. Before making the final determination, the investigating authorities are required to "disclose" to the interested parties (e.g. exporters or producers under investigation, their governments, and importers) the essential facts on which the decision to apply the duty is made.

Determination of the amounts of subsidy and dumping margins

Agreement on Anti-dumping
Practices, Articles 6.10, 9.2;
Agreement on Subsidies
and Countervailing
Measures, Article 19.3

It is important to note that the Agreements visualize that as far as possible the amounts of countervailing and anti-dumping duties should be determined separately for each exporter or producer. The amounts of duties payable could therefore vary according to the element of subsidy in the price or dumping margin determined for each exporter. However, the investigating authorities may determine duties on the basis of statistically valid samples (or the largest volume of exports from the country in question) when the number of exporters or producers is so large as to make the calculation of individual subsidy elements or dumping margins impracticable. In making such a selection, the investigating authorities are urged to consult the exporters or producers concerned and to make the selection preferably with their consent. In addition, any exporter or producer not included in the sample has a right to request that the dumping margin should be fixed separately for it.

Sunset clause

Agreement on Anti-dumping
Practices, Article 11;
Agreement on Subsidies
and Countervailing
Measures, Article 21

The Agreements further require that the continued imposition of anti-dumping and countervailing measures (duties and price undertakings) should be kept under constant review. Such reviews should be conducted by the authorities on their own initiative or upon request by any interested party. If as a result of such a review the authorities conclude that the measures are no longer warranted, these measures should be terminated. In addition, the Agreements have a sunset clause, under which anti-dumping and countervailing measures automatically expire five years after their imposition, unless a review of the cases determines that, in the absence of such measures, dumping and injury will continue or recur. Reviews for this purpose must be initiated before the sunset date and should normally be concluded within one year.

Business implications

For business persons, knowledge of the complex rules on the levy of anti-dumping and countervailing duties is essential in their capacities as exporters and producers whose interests may be adversely affected by the unfair price practices of producers in other countries.

In recent years, there has been a steady increase in the number of petitions for anti-dumping and countervailing actions by both developed and developing countries (see box 29). Enterprises in many developing countries are finding that as their exports of manufactured products rise, there are increasing pressures from industries in the importing countries for the levy of such duties, on the grounds that the goods are being dumped or subsidized. Such duties may be levied on any imported product, including such products as textiles, which are of considerable importance in the trade of developing countries.

In the circumstances, it is becoming essential for enterprises to be familiar with the rules applicable in this area. An understanding of the rules could, for instance, enable an exporting enterprise to take precautionary steps to avoid

---

Box 29

Anti-dumping and countervailing actions taken by WTO members in 1997

Anti-dumping investigations

During the period 1 January - 31 December 1997, a total of 240 anti-dumping investigations were initiated by WTO member countries. The most active Members were the following:

Country/area	Number of investigations initiated
Australia	42
European Community	41
South Africa	23
United States	16
Argentina	15
Korea, Rep. of	15
Canada	14
India	13
Brazil	14
Malaysia	8
Mexico	6

In terms of the export products investigated during the year, the European Community had the largest number (59), followed by China (31), Taiwan Province, China (16), Republic of Korea (16), United States (15) and Japan (12).

At the end of 1997 there were 880 anti-dumping measures in force in various member countries. Of these 34% were maintained by the United States, 16% by the European Community, 10% by Canada and 9% by Mexico. Other countries accounted for less than 5% of the measures taken.

Countervailing actions

During the period 1 January to 31 December 1997, 16 investigations for the levy of countervailing duties were initiated by member countries.

At the end of 1997 there were a total of 87 countervailing actions in force in member countries.

---

anti-dumping actions in foreign markets where there are increasing pressures from industrial and other groups for such actions. While it may continue to charge export prices that are lower than its domestic prices in markets where it faces no threat, it should avoid doing so in markets where anti-dumping actions are possible. In such markets, anti-dumping duties can be avoided if the exporter does not allow the difference between its domestic price and export price to fall below a reasonable margin. As noted, if the margin is *de minimis* or less, investigating authorities are required to reject applications for the levy of duties. Investigating authorities also take into account the share of an exporting country in total imports of a product. It would be in the interest of the exporting enterprise not to allow its exports to rise to a market where it is apprehensive of a petition for anti-dumping action and, where possible, to diversify its trade to other markets.

When investigations begin, the Agreements give exporting enterprises (and the trade or business associations to which they belong) the right to defend their interests. The ADP Agreement obliges them to provide information on the cost of production and other matters on the basis of a questionnaire sent by the investigating authorities. It is essential for exporters to cooperate with these authorities and to give them the required information, the reason being that in anti-dumping cases the duty payable is fixed separately for each exporting enterprise on the basis of the margin between the price charged by it in its domestic market and its export price.

The Agreements also oblige the investigating authorities to notify the governments of the exporting countries of their decision to begin investigations. The governments have a right to tender evidence against the petition and to defend the interests of their exporters. As the legal and other costs of participating in investigations are substantial and are often beyond the resources of small and medium-sized enterprises, it is often necessary for them to rely on their governments to defend their interests.

The Agreements also seek to protect the interests of enterprises which find that they are being injured or hurt as a result of the unfair pricing practices of foreign suppliers. The affected enterprises have the right to petition their national investigating authorities for the levy of anti-dumping duties if the imports are being dumped and for the levy of countervailing duties if the imports are being subsidized. However, the Agreements lay down strict conditions for invoking that right. In particular, an application for the levy of duties can be made only if it has *standing*, i.e. the support of producers accounting for at least 25% of the total domestic production of the product alleged to be dumped or subsidized. In addition, the application must provide information establishing a causal link between increased dumped and subsidized imports and injury to the producers in the form of loss of production, domestic sales or loss of jobs.

As noted earlier, complaints of dumping or subsidized imports are also on the increase in most developing countries implementing liberalization measures. While many of these complaints are due to the inability of domestic industries, long accustomed to heavy levels of protection, to adjust to the changed competitive situation resulting from the removal of tariffs and other barriers, some complaints about unfair price practices of foreign suppliers are undoubtedly genuine. A better understanding of the Agreements will enable the affected producing enterprises to make appropriate use of their right to petition the authorities for the levy of anti-dumping or countervailing duties in such cases. The stringent conditions the Agreements lay down will ensure that such duties are levied only when the dumped or subsidized imports are established to be causing injury to the industry concerned.

CHAPTER 12

Rules of origin

Summary

Rules of origin are used by governments to determine the country in which imported goods should be treated as having been produced. The revolutionary changes that are taking place in communications and transport now enable manufacturing companies to obtain inputs for the production of final products in far-off countries where trained personnel are available and costs are lower. This trend towards sourcing inputs from different countries is further facilitated by steps being taken to remove tariffs and other barriers to trade.

Virtually all manufactured products available in markets today are produced in more than one country. This is so whether the products are consumer articles like textiles or cosmetics or the sophisticated machinery used in the manufacture of consumer goods. For instance, in the case of textile articles – say shirts or blouses – it is possible that the cotton or synthetic fibre used in their manufacture is produced in one country; the textile woven, dyed and printed in another country; and the cloth cut and stitched in yet another country.

Purposes for which rules are applied to determine country of origin

Why it is necessary for governments to determine the origin of imported goods? Such determination is necessary in three situations.

First, for imports under preferential arrangements, importing countries have to ensure that the lower or preferential rates are made available to products originating from preference-receiving countries. They therefore need evidence to show that the imported product has been, if not wholly produced, at least substantially transformed in a preference-receiving country.

Second, for imports under MFN tariff rates, the determination of origin is ordinarily not necessary as such duties are applied on a non-discriminatory basis to imports from all sources. However, where the measures applicable at the border take into account the country of origin, the determination of origin becomes necessary. These measures include the following:

❑ Collection of anti-dumping and countervailing duties;

❑ Administration of country-specific quota restrictions (e.g. those imposed under the provisions of the Agreement on Textiles and Clothing or under a country's safeguard measures);

❑ Administration of tariff quotas; and

❑ Application of marks of origin or labels to indicate the country of origin.

Third, the determination of origin is also necessary in the collection of trade statistics.

Main principles on which current national rules are based

The national systems currently in use to determine origin vary considerably. Moreover, within countries the rules may differ according to the purpose for which they are used (e.g. administering quantitative restrictions, collecting preferential duties, labelling to indicate origin). However, despite the wide variations in the systems adopted, broadly speaking they are based on two main principles.

The first is the principle of value added in manufacturing or further processing. Under systems based on this principle, a product would be considered to have been manufactured in the country where a specified percentage (e.g. 40%, 50%, 60%) of the product value has been added.

The second principle is the determination of origin on the basis of changes in tariff classification. WTO member countries are encouraged to use the Harmonized System Nomenclature (HS) developed by the World Customs Organization (WCO, the former Customs Co-operation Council) for both the collection of trade statistics and the imposition of customs duties. The System has 97 chapters, within each of which products are arranged according to the degree of processing, commencing with raw materials, through to semi-processed products and ending with finished products. By using this system of classification, a product is determined to have originated in the country where, as a result of processing, its tariff classification changes.

Problems posed by differences in the rules for determining origin

GATT does not contain specific rules for the determination of origin. This has given countries the flexibility to adopt their own rules and to apply them differently according to the purpose for which they are used (*see* above). Moreover, this flexibility has enabled countries to adopt rules of origin for protective purposes, for instance to deny access to quotas on the grounds that the import product cannot be considered to have originated in the country to which a quota is allotted.

To find solutions to these and the other problems that have arisen as a result of the absence of precise rules, the Agreement on Rules of Origin was negotiated in the Uruguay Round.

Agreement on Rules of Origin

Coverage and objectives

Agreement on Rules of
Origin, Article 1:1

The provisions of the Agreement apply to "laws, regulations and administrative determinations of general application applied by any Member to determine the country of origin of goods" imported on an MFN basis. It specifically states that its substantive provisions do not apply to imports made under preferential arrangements.

The basic objective of the Agreement is to require countries to adopt a uniform set of harmonized rules for determining the origin of goods imported on an MFN basis. Since it was expected that technical work on developing such rules would take time, the Agreement provides two sets of provisions.

The first set lays down the disciplines which countries are expected to follow during the transition period, i.e. until the entry into force of the new harmonized rules. The technical work on the harmonization of these rules is currently being done by the WCO Technical Committee under the guidance of the WTO Committee on Rules of Origin, which has been established under the Agreement. The second set of provisions is applicable after the transition period. It also lays down principles and guidelines for the technical work on the harmonization of rules of origin.

Rules applicable in the transition period

Agreement on Rules of
Origin, Article 2

In the transition period, it is open to a country to apply different standards according to the purpose or the objective for which the rules are applied. After the transition period, however, the harmonized standards elaborated on a product-by-product basis are to be applied uniformly, irrespective of the purpose for which they are used. In other words, it will not be open to a country to apply one set of standards for determining origin for the purpose of administering quantitative restrictions and another set for indicating origin through labelling.

The Agreement further lays down the principles (e.g. transparency, non-discrimination and provisions for review of administrative decision) which countries are expected to follow during the transition period. These are set out in box 30.

Rules applicable after the transition period

Agreement on Rules of
Origin, Article 3(b)

After the transition period, the rules provide that the origin of goods shall always be "the country where the last substantial transformation has been carried out". For this purpose, the WCO Technical Committee is required to elaborate for particular products or product sectors the change in tariff subheading or heading that must occur, through manufacturing or processing, for a country to claim origin. However, for products for which the "exclusive use" of a change in tariff subheading "does not allow for the expression of substantial transformation", the Committee is advised to provide supplementary criteria. Such criteria could include additional requirements relating to "ad valorem percentages and/or manufacturing or process operations".

Agreement on Rules of
Origin, Article 9:2(c)(iii)

Present state of play in the technical work on harmonization

The technical work on the harmonization of rules of origin was to have been completed by 1998. The highly complex nature of the work and the differences that have arisen among countries on specific criteria for determining origin in certain product groups have prevented the WCO Technical Committee from completing its work by the target date. The results of its work when completed will, after approval by the WTO Committee on Rules of Origin, be adopted by the WTO Ministerial Conference. They will then incorporated into the

---

Box 30

Disciplines during the transition period
(Agreement on Rules of Origin, Article 2)

During the transition period (i.e. until the entry into force of the new harmonized rules), Members are required to ensure that:

(a)   Rules of origin, including specifications for the substantial transformation test, are clearly defined.

(b)   Rules of origin are not used as a trade policy instrument.

(c)   Rules of origin do not themselves create restrictive, distorting or disruptive effects on international trade and do not require the fulfilment of conditions not related to the manufacture or processing of the product in question.

(d)   Rules of origin applied to imports and exports are not more stringent than those applied to determine whether a good is domestic, and do not discriminate between Members (the GATT MFN principle).

(e)   Rules of origin are administered in a consistent, uniform, impartial and reasonable manner.

(f)   Rules of origin are based on a positive standard. Negative standards are permissible either as part of a clarification of a positive standard or in individual cases where a positive determination or origin is not necessary.

(g)   Rules of origin are published promptly.

(h)   Upon request, assessments of origin are issued as soon as possible but no later than 150 days after such a request is submitted. Assessments are to be made publicly available; confidential information is not to be disclosed except if required in the context of judicial proceedings. Assessments of origin remain valid for three years provided the facts and conditions remain comparable, unless a decision contrary to an assessment is made in a review referred to in (j).

(i)   New rules of origin or modifications thereof do not apply retroactively.

(j)   Any administrative action in relation to the determination of origin is reviewable promptly by judicial, arbitral or administrative tribunals or procedures independent of the authority issuing the determination; such findings can modify or even reverse the determination.

(k)   Confidential information is not disclosed without the specific permission of the person providing such information, except to the extent that this may be required in the context of judicial proceedings.

Agreement on Rules of Origin as an annex. All member countries will be required to apply the harmonized criteria specified in the annex on an MFN basis from the date agreed for its entry into force.

It should be noted that in addition to the obligation to apply the harmonized criteria, member countries will have to abide by the principles relating to transparency, non-discrimination, administrative assessment and judicial review listed in box 30 [(d) to (k)].

Preferential rules of origin

Though the harmonized rules of origin being developed by WCO will not apply to imports obtained under regional preferential arrangements or under Generalized Systems of Preferences, the Agreement provides that countries should take into account the general principles listed in box 30 in applying and administering such rules of origin.

Business implications

The adoption of harmonized criteria for determining origin is expected to resolve many of the problems faced by exporters today, particularly those related to textiles, in utilizing quotas allotted specifically to their countries. Harmonization will also eliminate current differences in national rules for determining origin. This will reduce the administrative burden on exporting enterprises which today have to ensure that they meet the varying requirements imposed by different countries on products subject to quantitative or other restrictive measures.

CHAPTER 13

Trade-related investment measures

Summary

Governments often impose conditions on foreign investors to encourage investment in accordance with certain national priorities. Conditions that can affect trade are known as trade-related investment measures or TRIMs.

The Agreement on TRIMs, which was negotiated in the Uruguay Round, requires countries to phase out TRIMs that have been identified as being inconsistent with GATT rules. The phasing-out period for developed countries was two years from 1 January 1995. Developing countries have a transition period of five years, and least developed countries seven years.

When the Uruguay Round of negotiations was being launched, the United States proposed that there was a need to bring under discipline investment measures that distort trade. It also suggested that the negotiations should cover policy issues affecting the flow of foreign direct investment. In particular it suggested that it would be necessary to consider the feasibility of applying to foreign direct investment the GATT principles of national treatment (which would give foreign companies the same right as domestic companies to invest in, and to establish, local operations) and MFN treatment (which would prevent countries from discriminating amongst sources of investment).

While these proposals received some support from other developed countries, they were not looked on with favour by developing countries. Apart from holding that GATT's mandate did not permit it to negotiate on investment issues, these countries maintained that, if any such negotiations were to be held, they would have to include the problems posed to trade by transnational corporations resorting to transfer pricing, restrictive business methods and other practices. This reluctance of developing countries to allow discussions in GATT on investment issues ultimately resulted in negotiations taking place on a narrowly defined concept of trade-related investment measures.

What are TRIMs?

The measures adopted by governments to attract and regulate foreign investment include fiscal incentives, tax rebates and the provision of land and other services on preferential terms. In addition, governments impose conditions to encourage or compel the use of investment according to certain national priorities. Local content requirements, which require the investor to undertake to utilize a certain amount of local inputs in production, are an example of such conditions. Export performance requirements are another example; they compel the investor to undertake to export a certain proportion of its output. Such conditions, which can have adverse effects on trade, are known as trade-related investment measures or TRIMs. An illustrative list of TRIMs is presented in box 31.

Box 31

An illustrative list of TRIMs

Local content requirements (LCRs). *Impose the use of a certain amount of local inputs in production.*

Trade-balancing requirements. *Oblige imports to be equivalent to a certain proportion of exports.*

Foreign exchange balancing requirements. *Stipulate that the foreign exchange made available for imports should be a certain proportion of the value of foreign exchange brought in by the firm from exports and other sources.*

Exchange restrictions. *Restrict access to foreign exchange and hence restrict imports.*

Domestic sales requirements. *Require a company to sell a certain proportion of its output locally, which amounts to a restriction on exportation.*

Manufacturing requirements. *Require certain products to be manufactured locally.*

Export performance requirements (EPRs). *Stipulate that a certain proportion of production should be exported.*

Product mandating requirements. *Oblige an investor to supply certain markets with a designated product or products manufactured from a specified facility or operation.*

Manufacturing limitations. *Prevent companies from manufacturing certain products or product lines in the host country.*

Technology transfer requirements. *Require specified technologies to be transferred on non-commercial terms and/or specific levels and types of research and development (R & D) to be conducted locally.*

Licensing requirements. *Oblige the investor to license technologies similar or unrelated to those it uses in the home country to host country firms.*

Remittance restrictions. *Restrict the right of a foreign investor to repatriate returns from an investment.*

Local equity requirements. *Specify that a certain percentage of a firm's equity should be held by local investors.*

Trade-related investment measures have been used mainly, if not exclusively, by developing countries to promote development objectives. For instance, the growth of domestic ancillary industries has been sought through the imposition of local content requirements and export expansion through export performance requirements. In many cases, TRIMs are designed to deal with the restrictive business practices of transnational corporations and their anti-competition behaviour.

A recent survey shows that TRIMs tend to be concentrated in specific industries – automotive, chemical and petrochemical, and computer/informatics. Local content requirements are more predominant than export performance requirements in the automotive industry and are less so in the computer/informatics industry. In the chemical and petrochemical industries both local content and export performance requirements are prominent.[18]

---

18   Patrick Low and Arvind Subramanian, "TRIMs in the Uruguay Round: An Unfinished Business" (paper presented at the World Bank Conference on the Uruguay Round and Developing Economies, 26-27 January 1995).

Agreement on Trade-Related Investment Measures

Agreement on Trade- Related
Investment Measures
(TRIMs), Article 2

The TRIMs Agreement, which was negotiated in the Uruguay Round, prohibits countries from using five TRIMs from the list in box 31. These are considered inconsistent with GATT rules on national treatment and the rules against the use of quantitative restrictions.

TRIMs prohibited on the grounds that they extend more favourable treatment to domestic products in comparison to imports and thus infringe the national treatment principle include those that require:

❑ Purchase or use by an enterprise of products of domestic origin or from any domestic source (local content requirements), or

Agreement on TRIMs,
Article 2; Annex

❑ That an enterprise's purchase or use of imported products should be limited to an amount related to the volume or value of the local products it exports (trade-balancing requirements).

TRIMs considered inconsistent with the provisions of Article XI of GATT against the use of quantitative restrictions on imports and exports include those that:

❑ Restrict imports to an amount related to the quantity or value of the product exported (i.e. trade-balancing requirements constituting restrictions on imports);

❑ Restrict access to foreign exchange to an amount of foreign exchange attributable to the enterprise (i.e. exchange restrictions resulting in restrictions on imports);

❑ Specify exports in terms of the volume or value of local production (i.e. domestic sales requirements involving restrictions on exports).

The Agreement provides transition periods for the elimination of prohibited TRIMs. For developed countries, the period was two years from 1995 when the Agreement entered into force; this period has already expired. Developing countries have a transition period of up to five years (i.e. until 1 January 2000) and least developed countries up to seven years (until 1 January 2002). It should be noted, however, that these transition periods are available only for the prohibited TRIMs notified when the Agreement became operational.

Business implications

For the business person, it is important to note that the Agreement is limited in scope. It identifies only five TRIMs that are inconsistent with GATT and gives countries transition periods within which to remove them. It does not prevent countries from using at least some of the other TRIMs listed in box 31. For instance, countries are not prevented from imposing export performance requirements as a condition for investment. They are not prohibited from insisting that a certain percentage of equity should be held by local investors or that a foreign investor must bring in the most up-to-date technology or must conduct a specific level or type of R & D locally.

A number of developing countries today impose local content requirements. The abolition of these requirements may have an impact on ancillary industries that are benefiting from the protection they provide. However, most of these countries are reviewing the need for the continued maintenance of such measures in the light of the open trade policies they are now pursuing and the steps they are taking to attract foreign investment. For instance, Argentina, Brazil, India and Mexico had taken decisions to abolish local content requirements even before the conclusion of the Uruguay Round. The Agreement therefore only reinforces the trend towards the removal of TRIMs that are considered inconsistent with GATT.

The Agreement's limited coverage of TRIMs has led countries to provide that its operation should be reviewed within a period of five years of its coming into force (i.e. before 1 January 2000) and that the review should consider the desirability of complementing the Agreement with provisions on investment and competition policy.

In this context it is important to note that, in pursuance of decisions taken at the 1996 Singapore Ministerial Conference, analytical discussions are currently going on in WTO on the relationship of trade with investment on the one hand and with competition policy, particularly the anti-competition behaviour of business enterprises, on the other. (*See* chapters 22 and 23 for further details.) The results of these discussions will influence the positions countries may take in any discussions on the desirability of complementing the Agreement on TRIMs with provisions dealing with investment and competition policy.

CHAPTER 14

Agreement on Textiles and Clothing

Summary

The basic aim of the Agreement on Textiles and Clothing (ATC) is to secure the removal of restrictions currently applied by some developed countries to imports of textiles and clothing. To this end the Agreement sets out procedures for integrating the trade in textiles and clothing fully into the GATT system by requiring countries to remove the restrictions in four stages over a period of 10 years ending on 1 January 2005. The flexibility available under the integration procedures has, however, enabled countries to remove restrictions in the first two stages only on a limited number of products. The first major impact of the integration programme is therefore expected when the third-stage integration takes place (on 1 January 2002); the bulk of the restrictions will be withdrawn in the last phase, when the transition period ends and the Agreement expires.

The textile and clothing industries are important to a large number of developing countries. However, the world trade in textiles and clothing has been subject to an ever-increasing array of bilateral quota arrangements over the past three decades. The range of products covered by quotas expanded from cotton textiles under the Short-Term and Long-Term Arrangements of the 1960s and early 1970s to an ever-widening list of textile products fashioned from natural and man-made fibres under five extensions of the Multi-Fibre Arrangement (MFA) over the period 1974-1994.

At the end of 1994, when MFA was terminated, it had a membership of 39 countries. Eight of these were developed countries, informally designated as 'importers'; the remaining 31 developing country members were considered 'exporters'. MFA permitted exporting and importing countries to enter into bilateral arrangements requiring exporting countries to restrain their exports of certain categories of textiles and clothing. In entering such bilateral agreements, countries were expected to adhere strictly to MFA rules:

❑ For determining serious damage or a threat thereof;

❑ For setting restraint levels; and

❑ For including such provisions as annual growth rates, carry-over of unutilized quotas from the previous year and carry-forward of part of the current year's quota for use in the following year.

When the WTO Agreement on Textiles and Clothing, negotiated in the Uruguay Round, became operational on 1 January 1995, several importing Members [the United States, Canada, the European Union (15 countries) and Norway] had a total of 81 restraint agreements with WTO Members, comprising over a thousand individual quotas. In addition, there were 29 non-MFA agreements or unilateral measures imposing restrictions on imports of textiles.

Integrating trade in textiles into GATT

From the strictly legal point of view, the maintenance of these restrictions was not consistent with GATT rules. However, MFA (negotiated within the framework of GATT) provided a legal cover for derogation from GATT discipline. The basic aim of the Agreement on Textiles and Clothing, which carried over the quotas from MFA, is to integrate the trade in textiles and clothing into GATT rules and disciplines by requiring countries maintaining restrictions to eliminate them over a period of 10 years. After the expiry of the 10-year period, i.e. from 1 January 2005, it will not be possible for any member country to maintain restrictions on imports of textiles, unless it can justify them under the provisions of Article XIX of the GATT as interpreted by the WTO Agreement on Safeguards. In other words, an importing country can impose restrictions only when, after carrying out investigations, it can establish that increased imports are causing or threatening to cause its domestic textile industry serious injury. Furthermore, such restrictions will have to be applied to imports from all sources, and not on a discriminatory basis to imports from one or two countries as was the case with restrictions under MFA and is now under ATC.

Methodology for integration

Agreement on Textiles and Clothing, Article 1; Annex

The methodological base for integrating the textile and clothing trade into GATT rules is the list of textile products contained in the Annex to ATC. The list covers all textile products – yarns and fabrics, made-up textiles and clothing – whether or not they are subject to restrictions. The integration process is to be carried out in four stages. At each stage, products amounting to a certain minimum percentage of the volume of the country's imports in 1990 are to be included in the integration process, that is, moved from the purview of ATC to the purview of the general rules of WTO. These percentages are:

Agreement on Textiles and Clothing, Article 2:6

❏ 16% of the volume of a country's imports of the products on the list, on the date of entry into force of the Agreement (i.e. 1 January 1995);

Agreement on Textiles and Clothing, Article 2:8

❏ A further 17% at the end of the third year (i.e. 1 January 1998);

❏ A further 18% at the end of seven years (i.e. 1 January 2002); and

❏ The balance, up to 49%, at the end of the tenth year (i.e. 1 January 2005).

In deciding on which products to bring into the integration process, countries are under no obligation to limit themselves to products subject to restrictions. Indeed, countries have begun with the least sensitive items and included very few products under quota. The only constraint the Agreement places is that the integration list should have products from each of four segments, namely, tops and yarn, fabrics, made-up-textile products, and clothing.

Experience of implementation of the integration process

In the case of the United States and the European Union, the percentage of imports of products not covered by restrictions in 1990 (the base year to be used for integration) was around 34% and 37% respectively. For the other countries maintaining restrictions the percentage was much higher. Notionally therefore, it was possible for these major restraining countries to meet their obligations to integrate products in the first two stages without significantly removing restrictions.

In fact this is what has happened in the first two stages. The three major restraining Members, viz. the United States, the European Union and Canada, have been able to meet the required percentage levels of integration (16% in the first stage and 17% in the second) by integrating products involving a very small proportion of quota restrictions.

It is therefore expected that the first major impact of the integration programmes will be felt only when the third-stage integration takes place (on 1 January 2002), and that the bulk of the restrictions will be withdrawn only on 1 January 2005, when the transition process ends and ATC expires.

Accelerated enlargement of quotas

Agreement on Textiles and Clothing, Article 2:13-2:14

The Agreement, however, tries to provide improved and enlarged access for textile and clothing products that continue to be restricted during the transition period. It seeks this by requiring that rates for annual increases in quotas should be escalated at each stage in the transition process. Thus, if the annual growth rate for a quota (say, for shirts) is fixed under a bilateral agreement at 3%, it will have to be increased by:

❑ 16% per year in each of the first three years (i.e. 3% x 1.16 = 3.48%);

❑ 25% per year in each of the next four years (i.e. 3.48% x 1.25 = 4.35%); and

❑ 27% in each of the next three years (i.e. 4.35% x 1.27 = 5.52%).

This will raise the growth rate of 3% to 5.52% by the eighth year. If the size of a quota is 100 tons at the beginning of the transition period, it will more than double to around 204 tons in the tenth year.

Agreement on Textiles and Clothing, Article 2:18

ATC further provides that countries which are small suppliers (i.e. countries the restrictions on which were equivalent to 1.2% or less of the total volume of the importing country's restrictions) and least developed countries should be given "an advancement by one stage of the growth rates".

Implementation of the provisions

The countries maintaining restrictions have generally abided by the provisions on growth factors. However, the extent to which countries benefit from the application of accelerated growth rates depends on the initial growth rate provided under the bilateral agreements. In the majority of cases, this initial rate is 6%. In a few instances, it is as low as 1% or even less. Many of the quotas for which higher growth rates are provided are not being fully utilized; for such quotas, the application of accelerated growth rates will not result in any meaningful advantage for the exporting country.

Moreover, developing countries had expected the enlargement of quotas to complement the process of integrating textiles into GATT through the removal of restrictions. In their view, unless positive steps are also taken to remove these restrictions, the mere application of accelerated growth rates will not achieve the expected liberalization.

Integration of non-MFA restrictions

Agreement on Textiles and Clothing, Article 3

ATC also requires countries applying non-MFA quantitative restrictions which are not allowed under a GATT provision either to phase them out in a period of 10 years or to bring them into conformity with GATT. The programme for the gradual phasing out of such restrictions is to be prepared by the importing country and presented to the Textiles Monitoring Body (TMB), the body established under the Agreement to supervise its operation.

Transitional safeguard measures

Agreement on Textiles and Clothing, Article 6

It is interesting to note that even though the aim of the Agreement is to facilitate the removal of restrictions on textiles, it permits countries to take safeguard actions during the transition period under very strict rules. Such transitional safeguard actions can be taken only in respect of textile and clothing products that are not already subject to quotas and not integrated into GATT, and if the importing country determines that:

❑ The product is being imported in such increased quantities as to cause serious damage or actual threat thereof to the domestic industry producing the like product, and

❑ There is a causal link between such serious damage to the domestic industry and sharp and substantial increase in imports from the exporting country or countries whose exports are sought to be restrained.

The right to use transitional safeguard measures is available to all WTO members, i.e. not only to countries which in the past applied quantitative restrictions under MFA but also to other countries (including developing and least developed countries), subject to the strict conditions described below.

Agreement on Textiles and Clothing, Article 6:1

First, in order to be eligible to apply such measures, countries were required to notify to WTO their intention to retain the right to use these provisions within a specified period after ATC became operational. In accordance with these provisions, 55 countries notified their wish to retain the right, while 9 notified that they did not want to retain it.

Second, the countries which notified their intention to retain the right are under an obligation to integrate their trade in textiles into GATT in four stages, following the procedures applicable to countries imposing MFA restrictions.

Third, the country proposing to impose safeguard measures is required first to enter into consultations with the exporting country or countries concerned and to demonstrate the existence of a situation of serious damage or actual threat thereof.

Agreement on Textiles and Clothing, Article 6:8

The consultations may result in agreement that the situation does indeed call for restraint on the product in question, in which case the level of the restraint and its period of application are specifically provided for in ATC. Restrictions may also be imposed by the importing member even if the consultations are not successful. But in such cases, the matter has to be referred to the Textiles Monitoring Body for prompt examination and appropriate recommendations. Further, in order to ensure that even restrictions agreed in bilateral consultations are in strict conformity with the provisions of ATC, the Textiles Monitoring Body is required to determine whether the imposition of such restrictions is justifiable under ATC.

Experience of the application of ATC provisions

Agreement on Textiles and Clothing, Article 6:2

Transitional safeguard measures are, as noted earlier, permitted sparingly and only in exceptional situations, where the industry producing a specified category of products is suffering serious damage or actual threat thereof as a result of an increase in total imports. The provisions make it clear that such transitional actions should be taken only after it has been possible for the importing country to establish that there was a causal link between increased imports and damage to the industry. For this purpose, ATC lays down economic variables that must be examined to ascertain whether there was such a causal link. It further states, that where the alleged state of the industry was not due to an increase in imports, but was caused by such factors as "technological changes or changes in consumer preferences", no safeguard actions shall be taken.

Since the Agreement entered into force, these provisions have been invoked by three countries, viz. the United States, Brazil and Colombia. In the first six months of its operation (January-June 1995), the United States resorted to safeguard measures in 24 cases. The review process found that many of these actions were taken without strictly following the rules of the Agreement. In the two cases which were raised under dispute settlement procedures, the Panels observed that the United States had failed to examine all of the factors that should have been taken into account in determining whether increased imports were causing injury to the producers of a particular category of products.

From the second half of 1995, there has been a substantial slowdown in recourse to these provisions, with the United States using safeguard measures only four times from mid-1995 to end-1998. This may have resulted from the interaction of two factors. In its investigation of cases, the Textile Monitoring Board stressed that the rules on the invocation of these measures should be applied strictly. There is also greater awareness that unless such measures are taken on justifiable grounds, the exporting countries affected may invoke dispute settlement procedures.

Rules of origin

For the administration of quotas allocated by country or area, it is necessary to adopt rules of origin which determine to which country's quota imported products processed in different countries should be allocated. In the United States, prior to 1 July 1996, the origin was considered to be the country where substantial transformation of the product had taken place (in the case of clothing, this was generally where the cloth was cut). Since that date, the rules of origin have provided that the country where a textile or apparel product is wholly obtained or produced or assembled shall be its country of origin. However, 16 specified product categories are subject to a separate set of rules. Thus the origin of articles made from yarn, strips, twine, cordage, rope or cables is not the country where such articles are produced, but the country where the yarn, etc. is produced. Likewise, for the other product categories listed in box 32, the origin is the country where the fabric is produced.

Box 32

United States: product groups to which special rules of origin apply

Articles of yarn, strip, twine, etc. (HTS 5609)	*Household linen (HTS 6302)*
Labels, badges, emblems (HTS 5807)	*Curtains, etc. (HTS 6303)*
	Bedspreads and furnishings (HTS 6304)
Quilted products (HTS 5811)	*Sacks and bags for packing (HTS 6305)*
Baby diapers (HTS 6209.20.5040)	*Tarpaulins, tents, etc. (HTS 6306)*
Handkerchiefs (HTS 6213)	*Dust cloths, mops, etc. (HTS 6307.10)*
Shawls, scarves, etc. (HTS 6214)	*Pillow shells, banners and other items (HTS 6307.90)*
Blankets and traveling rugs (HTS 6301)	*Needlecraft sets (HTS 6308)*
	Pillows, cushions, etc. (HTS 9404.90)

HTS: Harmonized Tariff System

The new United States rules could adversely affect the trade of several exporting countries, especially with regard to the products listed in box 32. Many of these products, such as dyed and printed fabrics, quilted products, bed linen, handkerchiefs, scarves, dust cloths and mops, and pillow and quilt shells, are restricted items for a number of countries. Some developing countries import grey fabrics, for dyeing and printing, and then re-export the processed products. Under the new rules, the origin of those exports will be the country where the grey fabric was produced. Similarly, many countries import fabrics for conversion into household linen, draperies, or for embroidery. Once again, the origin of these products will be the country from where the fabric was imported.

Other difficulties are also expected to arise for exporting countries. For example, a country supplying base fabrics will find it difficult to accommodate in its quota the goods shipped by other countries and debited to it as origin. Obtaining a visa from a country of origin may also cause considerable administrative inconvenience for the exporting country/area.

Some of these problems may be resolved when, as a result of the work being undertaken in WTO in cooperation with WCO under the Agreement on Rules of Origin, harmonized rules are adopted for the determination of origin. At present, there is no binding multilateral agreement specifying rules for the determination of origin. (*See* chapter 12.)

Increasing use of anti-dumping actions

Another major problem is the increasing resort to anti-dumping and countervailing actions. Box 33 lists the countries currently applying anti-dumping duties on imports of one or more textile and clothing products and the countries whose exports are affected.

In some countries, these duties were applied to products whose imports were restricted by quotas; this resulted in providing double protection to domestic goods. Investigations were often initiated without adequate justification; some were terminated within a short period on the grounds of lack of evidence. Even though investigations may be terminated without imposing anti-dumping duties, they could induce importers to change their sources of supply and result in trade harassment. It is therefore necessary for investigating authorities to examine carefully requests from industries for anti-dumping actions and exercise restraint in initiating investigations, particularly where the products concerned are subject to quota restrictions.

Box 33

Anti-dumping duties on textiles and clothing

Members applying duties:

Argentina, Brazil, Canada, the European Community, Japan, Mexico, New Zealand, the Philippines, the Republic of Korea, South Africa, Turkey and the United States

Members affected:

Brazil, Egypt, Hong Kong (China), India, Indonesia, Japan, Malaysia, Pakistan, Portugal, the Republic of Korea, Romania, Thailand, Turkey and the United States

Business implications

Preparing for increased competition

In countries whose exports to certain developed countries are subject to quota restrictions, the textile industry is no doubt disappointed at the slow progress in the removal of these restrictions during the first two stages provided for by ATC. It is, however, necessary to recognize that as the remaining restrictions are removed during the third and fourth stages, exporters will face greatly increased competition in international markets. Further, the benefits of the removal of restrictions are not likely to be evenly distributed among exporting countries.

The competitive position of countries currently subject to quota restrictions will determine whether the removal of these restrictions will be advantageous to them. Those whose industries have sharpened their competitive edge by adopting up-to-date technology may benefit fully from this removal. Other exporting countries, particularly those that are not able to use up their full quotas, may draw only marginal benefits unless they immediately take steps to assist their industries to become more competitive. Countries not now subject to restrictions on import markets will also have to prepare themselves to meet increased competition from countries whose exports are currently restrained.

Textile industries in exporting countries will therefore have to use the remaining transition period to prepare themselves to meet heightened competition. They should modernize their technology, rationalize production methods, and carry out market research to identify the textile products in which they can compete effectively in international markets on the basis of quality and price.

Traditionally, many enterprises (particularly in some developing countries) have concentrated on markets in developed countries. In adopting programmes and strategies for export development in the post-ATC period, the vast potential that now exists for increased trade with other developing countries should also be adequately taken into account. A number of these countries have unilaterally reduced under the Uruguay Round the high tariffs that they previously applied to imports of textile products. The countries currently applying quantitative restrictions are removing them by stages under the ATC integration process. Demand for textile products in these countries will expand as they make further progress in economic development and as their per capita incomes rise.

CHAPTER 15

Agreement on Agriculture

Summary

The reform programme adopted under the Agreement on Agriculture negotiated in the Uruguay Round tries to bring under the discipline of GATT the trade in agriculture – a sector in which its rules were not always fully applied by all member countries.

Under the reform programme, countries which, in addition to tariffs, applied such measures as quantitative restrictions and variable levies were required to eliminate them by adding the tariff equivalents of the measures to the existing tariffs. Countries were further obliged to reduce the tariffs applicable to imports of agricultural products, including the rates resulting from tariffication, by agreed percentages. Developing countries were however permitted to reduce their tariffs at a percentage rate which was lower than that imposed on developed countries and over a longer time frame. Least developed countries were exempted from the obligation to reduce tariffs.

All countries – developed, developing and least developed – were further required to bind their tariffs against increases in the levels shown in their schedules of concessions. However, developing and least developed countries were given flexibility to give ceiling bindings at rates which were higher than their existing applied and reduced rates.

Under the reform programme, countries using subsidies agreed to reduce by specified percentages export subsidies and domestic support subsidies considered to be trade distorting.

The Agreement provides that negotiations for the further liberalization of trade and improvements in the rules adopted under the reform programme should be launched before the end of 1999.

Overview

Agreement on Agriculture, Preamble

The Agreement on Agriculture establishes a programme for the gradual reform of trade in agriculture. The programme aims at establishing "a fair and equitable market-oriented agricultural trading system" by requiring countries to adopt new disciplines governing both:

❑ The use of border measures to control imports,

❑ The use of export subsidies and other subsidies that governments grant to support the prices of agricultural products and assure a reasonable income to farmers.

In order to ensure that the benefits of the reform programme are shared equally among member countries, the Agreement provides that the commitments which countries are required to make, should take into account:

Agreement on Agriculture, Preamble

❏ Non-trade concerns, including food security;

❏ The need to protect the environment;

❏ The need to extend special and differential treatment to developing countries; and

❏ The possible negative effects which the implementation of the reform programme could have on least developed and net food-importing countries.

The provisions of the Agreement apply to products falling under Chapters 1 to 24 of the Harmonized System and a few other specified products. Its coverage thus includes both primary and processed agricultural products.

For practical reasons, agricultural products are sometimes divided into two groups, viz. tropical products and others. Though there is no agreed definition of tropical products, beverages like tea, coffee and cocoa; cotton and hard fibres like jute and sisal; fruits like bananas, mangoes and guavas; and other products that are almost predominantly produced in developing countries are treated as tropical products. In the years following the establishment of GATT, these products were subject to both high tariffs and internal taxes in most developed countries. As these products are of export interest predominantly to developing countries, priority was given in the past rounds of GATT negotiations to removing the barriers to trade in such products. As a result, even before the Uruguay Round, a large number of these products, in both raw and processed forms, were entering developed markets on a duty-free basis, at low rates on MFN terms or under preferential arrangements.

Most developed countries, however, continued to apply to imports of other agricultural products – like wheat and other grains, meat and meat products – both high levels of tariffs and non-tariff measures such as quantitative restrictions, discretionary licensing and variable levies. The governments' basic objective in providing protection to such products (which are often referred to as temperate zone products) was to guarantee domestic producers prices that were much higher than world prices, in order to assure them reasonable incomes. These policies, apart from reducing trade opportunities for competitive foreign producers, also put heavy burdens on the budgetary resources of governments. This was inevitable, as the high cost of production in excess of domestic requirements could be disposed of in international markets only through export subsidies.

Developing countries also protect their agricultural sector by imposing high tariffs and restrictions on imports.

Border measures

Tariffication

Agreement on Agriculture, Article 4 and footnote 1

The most important aspects of the Agreement on Agriculture are the new rules. These require the countries which applied non-tariff measures (such as quantitative restrictions, discretionary licensing and variable levies) to abolish them by calculating their tariff equivalents and adding these to the fixed tariffs. As a result, countries have established new rates of tariffs for products (mostly temperate zone) to which they previously applied non-tariff measures. The tariff equivalent of non-tariff measures was calculated on the basis of average world market prices for the product subject to non-tariff measures and its internal price in the importing country.

The obligation to tariffy quantitative restrictions was however not applicable to restrictions maintained by developing countries in balance-of-payments difficulties under the provisions of GATT 1994.

Current and minimum access commitments

Exporting countries were apprehensive that, for some products the imports of which were restricted by quantitative restrictions or variable levies, there was a danger that the tariffication process by itself would not have a significant liberalizing effect. The use of current and minimum access commitments was therefore adopted to complement the tariffication process. (*See* box 34 for details.)

Box 34

Agricultural products: current and minimum market access commitments

(Agreement on Agriculture, Article 5.2)

Current access commitments

A number of countries had special arrangements for imports of meat and other mainly temperate-zone products up to quota limits on either a duty-free or a preferential basis. In order to ensure that such imports are not affected by the application of higher rates resulting from tariffication, importing countries have given current access commitments by establishing tariff quotas to cover imports that were entering the market at lower duty rates. As a result of these commitments, imports up to quota levels are allowed at the lower existing rates. The higher rates ensuing from tariffication are applicable to imports over and above quota limits.

Minimum access commitments

For products for which little or no imports took place in the past because of the highly restrictive nature of the then-existing regime, countries were required to give minimum market access opportunity commitments. The commitments provide for the establishment of tariff quotas equal to 3% of domestic consumption in the base period 1986-1988 and rising to 5% by the end of 2000 for developed countries and 2004 for developing countries. Lower rates (specified in the national schedules but generally not greater than 32% of the bound tariffied rates) are applicable to imports up to the quota limits, while the higher rate resulting from tariffication apply to imports over quota limits. As a result of these minimum access commitments, countries will have to import modest amounts of their most restricted products. Products covered by minimum access commitments include meat, dairy products, and specified fresh vegetables and fruits.

Agreement on Agriculture, Article 5

Special safeguards

The Agreement responds to the concern of importing countries that the removal of quantitative restrictions may lead, despite the tariff equivalents, to sudden increases in imports, by permitting them to impose special safeguards on tariffied products.

The special safeguard provisions allow the imposition of an additional tariff when certain criteria are met. The criteria involve either a specified rapid surge in imports (volume trigger) or, on a shipment-by-shipment basis, a fall of the import price below a specified reference price (price trigger). In the case of the volume trigger, the higher duties apply only until the end of the year in question. For the price trigger, additional duties can be imposed only on the shipment concerned. The additional duties may be charged only on products to which tariffied rates apply and only if a reservation to invoke such safeguards is indicated against the product in the country's schedule of concessions.

Percentage reductions in tariffs

Countries agreed during the Uruguay Round to reduce tariffs (both the new tariffied rates and other tariffs) by fixed percentages. Developed and transition countries undertook to reduce tariffs by an average of 36% and developing countries by 24%. Such reductions are to be made by developed countries over a period of six years from 1 January 1995 and by developing countries in 10 years. The least developed countries, even though they have bound tariffs at higher ceiling rates, were not required to reduce them.

The rules further require that a tariff on an individual product must be reduced by at least 15% by developed countries and 10% by developing countries.

Binding of tariffs

One of the other features of the reform programme is that tariffs (including those resulting from tariffication) applicable to agricultural products have been bound by all countries (developed, developing, least developed and transition) against increases above the levels indicated in their schedules of concessions. This, in addition to the elimination of non-tariff measures through tariffication, is considered one of the major achievements of the reform programme: before its adoption, very few of the tariffs of both developed and developing countries had been bound.

Flexibility for developing countries: ceiling bindings

Developing and least developed countries were given the flexibility to bind their tariffs at ceiling rates, which could be higher than their applied rates or those resulting from reductions agreed in the negotiations. A number of these countries have taken advantage of this flexibility and have given a ceiling binding undertaking not to raise any tariffs applicable to agricultural products over an agreed level (say 60% or 80%). The applied rates in all these countries are significantly lower than their ceiling rates.

Export subsidies and governmental support measures

Apart from high levels of protection, distortions in the international trade in agricultural products are caused by subsidy practices, mainly in some developed countries. While over the years GATT had been able to develop rules for subsidies on industrial products, it had failed to bring under discipline subsidies granted by governments to the agricultural sector. The Agreement on Agriculture contains rules for subsidies on agricultural products.

Export subsidies

Export subsidies are considered the most trade distorting of the subsidies granted by governments. These are given to enable farmers to sell their products in international markets.

Rules applicable to industrial products

The rules on the use of export subsidies for agricultural products differ from those applicable to industrial products. GATT rules have, since early times, prohibited developed countries from using export subsidies on industrial products. The Agreement on SCM, revised in the Uruguay Round, extended this prohibition to the industrial products of developing countries. They have a transition period of up to eight years (up to 1 January 2003) to comply with this obligation. However, least developed countries and countries with per capita incomes of less than US$ 1,000 are currently exempt from this obligation. (*See* chapter 8.)

Rules applicable to agricultural products

Agreement on Agriculture, Article 9

In the agricultural sector, it was recognized that a number of countries relied on the use of subsidies to dispose of their surplus production in international markets. The Agreement on Agriculture requires countries to undertake commitments to reduce their use. Countries are permitted to use the six categories of subsidies listed in box 35, provided they agree to undertake commitments to reduce both the amounts of subsidies (expressed in terms of budgetary outlays) and the quantities of subsidized exports.

It should be noted that the countries that used such subsidies made extensive commitments during the negotiations. These commitments have been incorporated on a product-by-product basis in their WTO schedules of concessions.

Agreement on Agriculture, Article 10

These countries are under an obligation not to exceed the commitment levels shown in their schedules in respect of both budgetary outlays and volumes. They are also under an obligation not to extend the coverage of products for which subsidies can be granted beyond that specified in the schedule.

Table 1 in the annex to this chapter lists the export subsidy commitments undertaken by these countries and the products to which they apply.

Countries which have not given reduction commitments are prohibited from using export subsidies on agricultural products. However, the provisions on special and differential treatment permit developing countries to use two of the types of export subsidies listed in box 35. These are:

❑ Subsidies to reduce the cost of marketing exports of agricultural products, including upgrading and other processing costs, and the cost of international transport and freight,

❑ Internal transport and freight charges on export shipments on terms more favourable than domestic shipments.

Domestic support subsidies

Agreement on Agriculture, Article 1(a); Article 6

As regards domestic subsidies, the approach of the Agreement is to require countries to accept commitments to reduce trade distorting subsidies. For this purpose, it divides subsidies into three categories: green, blue and amber. Green and blue subsidies are permitted subsidies and to which reduction commitments do not apply. Amber subsidies are subsidies to which reduction commitments apply.

Green box subsidies

Agreement on Agriculture, Annex 2:1

All subsidies that have "no, or at most minimal, trade-distorting effects or effects on production" and do not have the "effect of providing price support to

> *Box 35*
> *Export subsidies subject to reduction commitments*
> (Agreement on Agriculture, Article 9.1)
>
> The Agreement on Agriculture establishes six basic categories of export subsidies that are to be reduced by member countries. These are:
>
> ❑ The provision of direct subsidies by governments that are contingent on export performance;
>
> ❑ The sale of non-commercial (publicly owned) stocks of agricultural products by governments at a price lower than the comparable price charged for the like products to buyers in the domestic market;
>
> ❑ Payments on the export of an agricultural product that are financed by virtue of government action whether or not a charge on the public account is involved, including payments financed from the proceeds of a levy imposed on the product concerned or on an agricultural product from which the export product is derived;
>
> ❑ The provision of subsidies to reduce the costs of marketing exports of agricultural products (other than widely available export promotion and advisory services), including handling, upgrading and other processing costs, and the cost of international transport and freight;*
>
> ❑ International transport and freight charges on export shipments on terms more favourable than for domestic shipments;* and
>
> ❑ Subsidies on agricultural products contingent upon their incorporation in exported products.
>
> * Developing countries are not required to undertake reduction commitments in respect of these export subsidy practices (Article 9.4).

producers" are considered green box subsidies and are exempt from reduction commitments. The Agreement does not unduly restrict the rights of governments to grant subsidies to improve the productivity and efficiency of agricultural production. Box 36 contains an illustrative list of green box subsidy practices.

Blue box subsidies

In addition to the practices listed in box 36, "direct payments under production limiting programmes" are also exempt from reduction commitments provided that:

❑ Such payments are based on fixed areas or yields;

❑ Such payments are made on 85% or less of the base level of production;

❑ Livestock payments are made on a fixed number of head.

These subsidy practices are often referred to as blue box measures.

Amber subsidies

Domestic support

Amber subsidies mainly cover domestic support subsidies that are considered trade distorting. The Agreement establishes a ceiling on the total domestic support (calculated as the Aggregate Measurement of Support, AMS) that governments may provide to domestic producers. In addition, it requires that AMS should be reduced by agreed percentages.

Box 36

Illustrative list of green subsidies granted to producers that are exempt from reduction commitments

(Agreement on Agriculture, Annex 2)

The following are a few examples from Annex 2 of the Agreement on Agriculture which lists subsidy practices that are exempt from reduction commitments, if the specific conditions prescribed by the Agreement are met:

❑ *Government expenditure on agricultural research, pest control, inspection and grading of particular products, marketing and promotion services.*

❑ *Financial participation by governments in income insurance and income safety-net programmes.*

❑ *Payments for natural disaster.*

❑ *Structural adjustment assistance provided through:*

   – *Producer retirement programmes designed to facilitate the retirement of persons engaged in marketable agricultural production;*

   – *Resource retirement programmes designed to remove land and other resources, including livestock, from agricultural production;*

   – *Investment aids designed to assist the financial or physical restructuring of a producer's operations.*

❑ *Payments under environmental programmes.*

❑ *Payments under regional assistance programmes.*

AMS is calculated on a product-by-product basis by using the difference between the average external reference price for a product and its applied administered price multiplied by the quantity produced. To arrive at AMS, non-product-specific domestic subsidies are added to the total subsidies calculated on a product-by-product basis.

The green and blue box subsidies described above are exempt from inclusion in AMS. Further, where support granted to a particular product is less than 5%, expenditure on subsidization of that product is excluded from the reduction commitment. Similarly, a non-product-specific domestic subsidy is excluded from the calculation if it does not exceed 5% of the value of agricultural production. For developing countries, these *de minimis* percentages are 10%.

Developing countries are further permitted, in order to encourage their agricultural and rural development, to exclude from the AMS calculation and thus from reduction commitments the following:

❑ Investment subsidies generally available to agriculture;

❑ Input subsidies generally available to low-income resource-poor producers; and

❑ Subsidies to encourage diversification from narcotic crops.

Countries are required to reduce the AMS calculated on the above basis by specific percentages. Table 2 in the annex indicates the reductions that must be made in domestic support by the countries which have made the related commitments. Developed countries have agreed to reduce AMS by 20% over a period of six years (from 1 January 1995) from the average level reached in the base period 1986-1988. Developing countries are required to reduce AMS by 13 1/3% over a period of 10 years. Because of these commitments, the total amount of AMS granted by countries which have undertaken commitments is expected to fall from US$ 197,721 million in the base period 1986-1988 to US$ 162,497 million by the end of the implementation period. (*See* table 2 in the annex to this chapter.)

Peace clause

Under the provisions of the Agreement on SCM, imports of both subsidized industrial and agricultural products can be subjected by importing countries to countervailing duties if they cause material injury to the domestic industry producing such products. In addition, it is open to a country, which considers that its interests are being adversely affected by the subsidy practices of another country, to challenge the practice by raising the matter under WTO's dispute settlement procedures.

Agreement on Agriculture, Article 13

One of the features of the Agreement on Agriculture is the "peace clause". The clause shields certain types of domestic support policies and export subsidies from remedial actions by other countries at the national and multilateral level.

Broadly, the Agreement provides that products benefiting from green box subsidies which are in full conformance with its provisions shall be non-actionable for the purpose of countervailing actions as well as for challenges in WTO through the invocation of dispute settlement procedures.

Other domestic support measures and export subsidies which are in conformity with the provisions of the Agreement may be the subject of countervailing duty actions, but due restraint is to be exercised by Members in initiating such investigations. This provision on "due restraint" does not apply to domestic support or export subsidy programmes that exceed reduction commitments; governments may investigate such subsidies for countervailing actions.

Net food-importing countries

Agreement on Agriculture, Article 16; Ministerial Decision on Measures concerning the Possible Negative Effects of the Reform Programme on Least-Developed and Net Food-Importing Developing Countries

Before concluding this broad overview of the provisions of the Agreement, it is important to note one provision of special interest to developing countries that are net importers of food.

The Agreement recognizes that the implementation of liberalization commitments (particularly the reduction of subsidies) may, by lowering surplus production, adversely affect the overall availability of basic foodstuffs. This may have a negative effect on least developed countries and on developing countries that are net importers of food.

In order to offset these negative effects, it has been agreed that:

❑ Action should be initiated to ensure that an increasing proportion of basic food aid is provided to these countries in a fully grant form;

❑ Technical and financial assistance should be provided to these countries to improve their agricultural productivity and infrastructure; and

❑ Appropriate steps should be taken to encourage financial institutions (e.g. IMF, World Bank) to consider the scope for establishing new facilities or enhancing existing facilities for providing assistance to these countries to help them face difficulties in financing commercial imports as a result of the liberalization measures taken in the Uruguay Round.

Business implications and future negotiations

From the point of business the major achievement of the reform programme has been that a beginning has been made in applying the GATT/WTO discipline to trade in this sector.

Agreement on Agriculture, Article 18

The Agreement on Agriculture provides that negotiations for the further liberalization of trade in this sector and for improving its rules should commence before the end of 1999. In order to prepare for such negotiations, the Committee on Agriculture has already begun a process of analysis and information exchange. In these discussions, a number of suggestions have been made on steps to be taken during the negotiations, including the following:

❑ To carry forward the process of liberalization;

❑ To find solutions to the problems faced by exporting enterprises as a result of the widely differing systems adopted by countries for administering the tariff quotas fixed for the implementation of their current and minimum access commitments;

❑ To bring the practices of State trading organizations engaged in trade in agricultural products under GATT discipline; and

❑ To ensure that the rules applicable to trade in agriculture recognize the need of countries to have a sufficient domestic output to provide for food security.

ANNEX

Table 1 — Export subsidy reduction commitments, by participant (in millions of United States dollars)

Participant	Export subsidies			Product composition of export subsidies
	Base	Final	Change	
European Union	13 274	8 496	-36	Bovine meat (19%), wheat (17%), coarse grains (13%), butter (13%), other milk products (10%)
Austria	1 235	790	-36	Live animals (45%), wheat (14%), bovine meat (13%), cheese (12%)
United States	929	594	-36	Wheat (61%), skim milk powder (14%)
Poland	774	493	-36	Meat preparations (39%), fruits and vegetables (21%)
Mexico	748	553	-26	Sugar (76%), cereal preparations (21%)
Finland	708	453	-36	Butter (25%), coarse grains (22%), other milk products (13%)
Sweden	572	366	-36	Pigmeat (21%), wheat (21%), coarse grains (17%)
Canada	567	363	-36	Wheat (47%), coarse grains (18%)
Switzerland	487	312	-36	Other dairy products (65%)
Colombia	371	287	-23	Rice (32%), cotton (20%), fruits and vegetables (23%)
South Africa	319	204	-36	Fruits and vegetables (24%), cereal preparations (14%), wheat (13%), sugar (10%)
Hungary	312	200	-36	Poultry meat (30%), pigmeat (26%), wheat (11%), fruits and vegetables (19%)
Czech Republic	164	105	-36	Other milk products (38%), fruits and vegetables (10%)
Turkey	157	98	-37	Fruits and vegetables (36%), wheat (23%)
New Zealand	133	0	-100	Not available
Norway	112	72	-36	Cheese (54%), pigmeat (19%), butter (12%)
Australia	107	69	-36	Other milk products (32%), skim milk powder (27%), cheese (25%), butter (16%)
Brazil	96	73	-24	Sugar (56%), fruits and vegetables (30%)
Slovak Republic	76	49	-36	Other dairy products (19%), cereal preparations (13%), bovine meat (13%)
Israel	56	43	-24	Fruits and vegetables (59%), plants (22%), cotton (17%)
Indonesia	28	22	-24	Rice (100%)
Iceland	25	16	-36	Sheep meat (78%), other dairy products (22%)
Cyprus	19	14	-24	Fruits and vegetables (67%), alcohol (16%)
Uruguay	2	1	-23	Rice (83%), butter (12%)

Source: WTO.

Notes:

1.   Commitments converted to US dollars using 1990/91 average exchange rates. Reduction commitments apply to individual product categories as defined in this table.

2.   The participants that have submitted schedules and do not maintain export subsidies include: Algeria, Antigua and Barbuda, Argentina, Bahrain, Barbados, Belize, Bolivia, Brunei Darussalam, Cameroon, Chile, Congo, Costa Rica, Côte d'Ivoire, Cuba, Dominica, Dominican Republic, Egypt, El Salvador, Fiji, Gabon, Grenada, Gambia, Ghana, Guatemala, Guyana, Honduras, Hong Kong (China), India, Jamaica, Japan, Kenya, Republic of Korea, Kuwait, Macau, Malaysia, Malta, Mauritius, Morocco, Namibia, Nicaragua, Nigeria, Pakistan, Paraguay, Peru, Philippines, Saint Kitts and Nevis, Saint Lucia, Saint Vincent and the Grenadines, Senegal, Singapore, Sri Lanka, Suriname, Swaziland, Thailand, Trinidad and Tobago, Tunisia, Zambia and Zimbabwe. Least developed countries are exempt from export subsidy reduction commitments.

Table 2   Reductions in domestic support to agricultural producers, by participant (in millions of United States dollars)

Participant	Base*	Final	Reduction (%)
Total	**197 721**	**162 497**	**18**
European Union	92 390	76 903	17
Japan	35 472	28 378	20
United States	23 879	19 103	20
Mexico	9 669	8 387	13
Canada	4 650	3 720	20
Finland	4 186	3 349	20
Poland	4 160	3 329	20
Republic of Korea	4 086	3 543	13
Switzerland	3 769	3 016	20
Sweden	3 429	2 743	20
Austria	2 534	2 027	20
Norway	2 247	1 797	20
Venezuela	1 305	1 131	13
Brazil	1 053	912	13
Thailand	866	745	13
Czech Republic	717	574	20
Israel	654	569	13
New Zealand	210	268	20
Hungary	613	490	20
Australia	460	368	20
Slovak Republic	435	348	20
Colombia	398	345	13
Iceland	222	177	20
Cyprus	127	110	13
Morocco	93	81	13
Tunisia	76	66	13
Costa Rica	18	16	13
South Africa	3	2	20

Source: WTO.

* Subsidies granted in 1986 to 1988.

CHAPTER 16

Results of market access negotiations

Summary

The preceding chapters describe the main features of the strengthened legal system that is now applicable under GATT 1994 to trade in goods. One of the important aims of this system is to assist countries to promote their economic development through increased trade by removing tariffs and other barriers to trade in negotiations among Members.

The seven rounds of negotiations held prior to the Uruguay Round had considerably reduced the tariffs applied by developed countries to industrial products. However, as the preceding chapters note, they made very little progress in removing the quantitative restrictions and other non-tariff measures applicable to imports. For instance, in the industrial sector, the developed countries' discriminatory quantitative restrictions on imports of textile products and clothing continued to be applied under the legal cover provided by the Multi-Fibre Arrangement. The rounds had also failed to modify the highly protectionist agricultural policies pursued by some developed countries which had almost closed their markets to competitive imports. Furthermore, no changes were made in their policies of subsidizing exports of agricultural products, which distorted conditions of competition in international trade.

The market access negotiations in the Uruguay Round greatly improved the situation. The main features of the Round's results can be summarized as follows:

❑ The tariff cuts countries have pledged to make on industrial products are much higher than those of the earlier Tokyo Round.

❑ By adopting the Agreement on Textiles and Clothing, countries have agreed to phase out the restrictions maintained under the Multi-Fibre Arrangement within a period of 10 years, i.e. by 1 January 2005.

❑ The Agreement on Agriculture has created a framework for gradually bringing the trade in agricultural products under GATT discipline and for liberalizing trade in the sector.

❑ Developing countries and economies in transition, which participated actively in the negotiations, have reduced their tariffs on both industrial and agricultural products.

❑ Almost all tariffs of developed countries have been bound against further increases; in developing and transitional economies, the proportion of tariffs that have been bound has risen significantly.

This process of liberalization was carried further after the conclusion of the Uruguay Round through negotiations on the Information Technology Agreement, which provides for the gradual elimination of tariffs on some 400 information technology products.

The 50 years that have elapsed since the GATT/WTO system came into existence have witnessed a gradual improvement in access to importing markets through removal or elimination by member countries of barriers to trade in eight rounds of multilateral trade negotiations. This chapter first describes the progress that took place in the last of these rounds – the Uruguay Round of trade negotiations. Then it gives an account of the trade negotiations which took place in certain sectors of the trade in goods since the conclusion of the Uruguay Round. The chapter concludes by outlining the steps that business persons will have to take to take full advantage of these liberalization measures.

Uruguay Round of trade negotiations

Industrial products

Reduction in tariffs

As a result of the rounds of negotiations held prior to the Uruguay Round, the average levels of tariffs in developed countries had come down from high levels of around 40% to about 10%. This average level was further reduced in the Uruguay Round by 40% overall. Developing and transitional economies also cut their tariffs, but by a lower figure of 30%. Least developed countries were not required to make reductions in their tariffs on a percentage basis but were encouraged to make token concessions by reducing tariffs on selected products. All these tariff cuts, with a few exceptions, were to be made in five equal stages so as to reach the final agreed rates applicable at the tariff line level by 1 January 1999.

In addition, developed countries and certain developing countries also agreed in the Uruguay Round to eliminate all tariffs in certain sectors, the so-called zero-for-zero sectors. These included pharmaceuticals, agricultural equipment, construction equipment, medical equipment, furniture, paper, steel and toys. As a result of these and other concessions, the proportion of industrial products entering developed country markets on an MFN duty-free basis was expected to more than double from 22% to 44%. The weighted average level of tariffs applicable to industrial products would fall from:

❑ 6.3% to 3.8% in developed countries;

❑ 15.3% to 12.3% in developing countries; and

❑ 8.6% to 6% in transition economies

when the process of staged reductions in tariffs agreed in the Uruguay Round was completed.

Binding of tariffs

Another important aspect of the negotiations was the progress made in binding tariffs. Virtually all imports into developed countries of both industrial and agricultural products now enter under bound rates; the proportions for developing and transition economies are 73% and 98% respectively. One of the major advantages of binding is the security of access it provides to foreign markets. Enterprises can plan the development of their trade without fear of duties being increased or access being restricted by quantitative restrictions.

Removal of quantitative restrictions

Equally important from the point of creating improved opportunities for trade are the provisions for phasing out quantitative restrictions on industrial products. As has been noted in chapter 14, the Agreement on Textiles and Clothing provides a four-stage programme for the elimination of restrictions on textiles and clothing by 1 January 2005. The Agreement on Safeguards requires countries applying voluntary export restraints and other grey area measures to eliminate them by 1 January 2000.

Agricultural products

In the agricultural sector, as has been described in chapter 15, considerable progress has been made in securing the liberalization of trade by:

❑ Eliminating non-tariff measures through the tariffication process.

❑ Binding tariffs and tariffs arrived at by tariffication against further increases.

❑ Reducing bound tariffs by 36% in developed countries and by 24% in developing countries.

❑ Current access and minimum access commitments in certain cases.

❑ Commitments to cut both the value and the volume of export subsidies by an agreed percentage.

❑ Commitment to reduce by an agreed percentage domestic support on the basis of an Aggregate Measurement of Support.

Post-Uruguay Round negotiations

Negotiations in two sectors of the trade in goods have taken place since the conclusion of the Uruguay Round.

Under the Ministerial Declaration on Trade in Information Technology Products (also known as the Information Technology Agreement or ITA), adopted at the 1996 Singapore Ministerial Conference, a number of WTO member countries agreed to reduce to zero the tariffs on such products as computers, telecommunications equipment, semiconductors, semiconductor manufacturing equipment, software and scientific instruments. As of April 1999, ITA had 31 participants (covering 46 Members and States or customs territories in the process of acceding to WTO). Member countries are at present considering the possibility of broadening the coverage to other information technology products.

Countries interested in the trade in pharmaceutical products have also agreed to add 450 products to the list of products on which they had in the Uruguay Round decided to remove tariffs on a zero-for-zero basis.

It is important to note that although the negotiations to eliminate tariffs on information technology products and pharmaceuticals took place among a limited number of countries, the concessions made will be extended on an MFN basis to all countries.

Assessment of liberalization gains from the Uruguay Round

From the point of view of business enterprises deciding on marketing strategies, it is important to be aware of the gains – in income and trade – that could flow from these liberalization measures.

WTO, other international organizations and research institutions have carried out macroeconomic studies to assess the impact which the implementation of the Uruguay Round commitments could have on world trade and world income.

Income and trade gains: estimates and reality

Estimates

Broadly speaking, these studies estimated that, when fully implemented, the liberalization measures agreed by governments would boost world income by 1% a year or by between US$ 200 billion and US$ 500 billion annually. World trade volumes would rise by 6% to 20% yearly depending on the assumptions made in the studies. These growth rates would be over and above the annual increase of 4% in world trade that was expected to take place even if the Uruguay Round results were not implemented.

More than one-third of the benefits were expected to flow from the removal of restrictions on imports of textiles and clothing products, and one-third from the liberalization of regimes on other industrial products. Agriculture was expected to contribute between 10% to 30%.

These gains would not, however, be shared equally among all countries. The major beneficiaries were expected to be developed countries and developing countries which had reached higher stages of development and whose exports of textiles were subject to restrictions. Countries in Africa and the least developed countries would benefit only marginally, if at all, from the liberalization measures.

The reality

Most analysts now consider that actual income and trade gains may be much smaller than foreseen. Problems posed by measurement methodologies and by the numerous factors which in practice cannot be easily assessed may be one reason. The other equally important reason is the failure of two basic assumptions to materialize.

First, in making the estimates, the analysts assumed that countries would implement their commitments fully, i.e. not merely in the letter but also in the spirit in which these commitments were made. This assumption has not been borne out by the facts and there has been significant backsliding in the implementation of commitments in the two sectors – textiles and agriculture – in which major gains were expected following liberalization.

As regards textiles, as has been noted in chapter 14, the developed countries maintaining restrictions were able to implement the first two phases without a significant reduction in restrictions on imports. They did this by taking advantage of the flexibility available under the relevant provisions of the Agreement on Textiles and Clothing. As a result, it is now clear that the bulk of the restrictions will be withdrawn only during the last stage or on the day (1 January 2005) the Agreement is terminated. The expected dramatic increase in the trade in textiles may therefore remain illusory during most of the transition period of 10 years.

In agriculture, a large number of tropical products in which developing (and particularly least developed) countries had an export interest were entering the markets of developed countries duty free or at low duty rates on either an MFN or a preferential basis even prior to the launching of the Uruguay Round. Consequently, further reductions may not by themselves have a perceptible influence on the trade in these products. As regards temperate zone agricultural products like cereals and meat, it now appears that the calculations of tariff equivalents sometimes over-estimated the incidence of non-tariff measures (this is often referred to as 'dirty tariffication'). The result is that, for a number of products, the level of protection provided by the new tariff rates even after reductions are made may be considerably higher than that existing previously.

The second assumption the analysts made was that the world economy would continue to grow at an even pace and that there would not be any downturn in growth and trade. These expectations have been belied by the Asian financial crisis which began in mid-1997, Japan's poor economic performance and the failure of the Russian economy to revive in 1998. It is now clear that with the consequential substantial reduction in economic growth, there will be an overall slowdown in the value of world trade for at least a year and even longer as a result of the lack of demand in Asian markets and the general decline in oil and other commodity prices.

Business implications

Varying impact on exports from different countries

It is thus clear that income and trade benefits may be much less than estimated in the macroeconomic studies, and some gains may even be negated by the recent downturn in the world economy. In addition, at least for some products, the implementation of commitments could have a varying impact on the export trade of individual countries. Thus, developing countries which enjoy preferential access in their major developed import markets may find that the preferential margin on their export products has been reduced as a result of reductions in MFN tariffs. The extent of this possible adverse impact will depend on how far the preferential access was meaningful in trade terms, taking into account such factors as the product's quality and price. For textiles, where restrictions are applied on a discriminatory basis, the impact of the removal of restrictions could vary for different supplying countries. Box 37 looks at the impact of the removal of MFA restrictions on textile products.

Studies at the micro-level (product or product sector level) will have to be undertaken to identify the impact of the Uruguay Round commitments on different products. These studies will have to be supplemented by research on, and analysis of, potential demand in liberalizing markets. Such analyses of demand should enable enterprises to formulate a strategy for taking advantage of new opportunities and, where necessary, to adapt to the competitive situation as it changes with the gradual implementation of the Uruguay Round commitments.

Undertaking such studies may be beyond the technical and financial resources of individual enterprises, particularly SMEs. In such instances, the initiative for carrying out the studies may have to be taken by national foreign trade research institutes or by associations of industries and chambers of commerce. In doing so, they may need financial assistance from their governments. International organizations could carry out studies on selected products or assist the relevant institutions and associations in different countries in undertaking them.

Marginalization of developing and least developed countries

As noted earlier, macroeconomic studies expected the majority of developing countries and most least developed countries to obtain only minor benefits, if any, from the liberalization measures taken during the Uruguay Round. The

> **Box 37**
>
> ***The impact of the removal of MFA restrictions on textile products***
>
> *In comparison to rates on other manufactured products, tariff rates on textile imports will continue to be high, even when the reductions agreed during the Uruguay Round are fully implemented. The main gains for trade are therefore expected to result from the removal of restrictions in some developed countries.*
>
> *Restrictions on imports lead to a rise in the prices of imports, as supplies tend to be insufficient to meet demand. Import restrictions thus penalize consumers, who have to pay higher prices. As to whether the importer or the exporter benefits from the premium resulting from the high price depends on where the licensing system is administered. If it is at the importing end, the importer is able to capture part of the difference between the normal import price and the wholesale price in the importing country. On the other hand, if the licences are issued by the exporting countries, exporters can appropriate part of the premium by charging higher export prices.*
>
> *Under the Agreement on Textiles and Clothing, the licences required for administering restrictions are issued by exporting countries. When quota restrictions are removed, exporting enterprises will not be able to claim the premium and will have to charge lower export prices. The decline in the value per unit of exports is expected to be offset by a rise in earnings as export volumes grow following the removal of restrictions. However, the growth of trade will in practice depend on the elasticity of demand (i.e. whether demand will increase with the fall in prices). Demand for textiles in most restraining markets is generally assumed to be elastic. But, at the enterprise level, the main issue is whether it is elastic for the particular category of textiles – say, shirts and children's clothes – which the enterprise is exporting and on which restrictions have been removed. If it is not, the enterprise may not benefit from the removal of restrictions and may even lose unless it is able to diversify its production and exports into lines for which demand is elastic.*
>
> *The removal of restrictions will lead to increased competition among supplying countries in the restraining importing market. As restrictions under ATC are applied on a discriminatory basis, the impact of such competition on different supplying countries could vary. For instance, exporting firms in country A, whose exports of shirts and children's clothing are restricted, may have to develop strategies to take advantage of the removal of restrictions. On the other hand, suppliers in other countries whose exports of such textile products were not restricted will have to prepare themselves to meet increased competition from the suppliers in country A. (See also chapter 14 on the Agreement on Textiles and Clothing.)*

decline in commodity prices and the difficulties that have occurred in the implementation of the Agreements have brought about the further marginalization of these countries in international trade.

In order to prevent any further deterioration of this situation, a number of developed countries have, in pursuance of decisions taken at the High-Level Meeting on Integrated Initiatives for LDCs' Trade Development, broadened the coverage of their generalized systems of preferences, with a view to allowing the import of all products of export interest to these countries on a duty-free basis. A few developing countries have also decided to adopt systems for importing selected products from these countries on a preferential basis, while proposals for introducing such systems are under consideration in some other countries. These actions are being complemented by integrated technical assistance to these countries at the enterprise level from WTO, UNCTAD, ITC and other international organizations; the ultimate objective is to build up national capacities for production and supply.

Potential for expanding trade with developing countries

In this context, it is necessary to bear in mind an important aspect of the Uruguay Round. This is the further stimulus it has provided to the liberalization process in both developing and transitional economies. The launching of the Uruguay Round almost coincided with a change-over to more open and liberal trade policies, even in developing countries which until then had followed more restrictive trade policies. By about the same time, the transition economies were taking initial steps towards market reform, privatization and the reorientation of economic and trade policies. Both groups of countries consolidated in the Uruguay Round their earlier unilateral tariff reductions either by binding them at reduced rates or by giving ceiling bindings. These tariffs are expected to fall further, in some cases even below the reductions agreed in the Uruguay Round. This will result from the additional liberalization measures that a number of countries are taking or propose to take on a unilateral basis in pursuance of their policies of promoting export-oriented growth.

The reductions in tariffs on an MFN basis could, in certain cases, lead to a decline in the preferential margins on products that are covered by regional preferential arrangements[19] or by interregional arrangements among developing countries[20]. The MFN tariff rates of most developing countries participating in such preferential systems will, however, continue to be relatively high even after reductions, with the result that the preferential margins, though narrower, may still provide meaningful trade benefits.

But more important than tariff reductions are the steps taken by developing countries to liberalize their non-tariff measures. These reduce or remove quota restrictions on, and licensing requirements for, imports and provide for the liberal allocation of foreign exchange to the import trade. In the past, non-tariff restrictions blocked the development of trade in products on which preferential concessions were exchanged under regional or interregional preferential arrangements. The liberalization of import regimes could provide a new stimulus to the expansion of this trade on both MFN and preferential terms.

Traditionally, many enterprises (particularly in some developing countries) have concentrated on markets in developed countries. The new market opportunities that have been created by liberalization measures in developing, least developed and transition countries (taken unilaterally or under structural adjustment programmes supported by the International Monetary Fund and the World Bank) should now encourage enterprises in these countries to give equal, if not greater importance, to trade development among themselves.

---

19 Such as the Common Market for Eastern and Southern Africa (COMESA) and the Economic Community of West African States (ECOWAS) in Africa, the Association of South-East Asian Nations (ASEAN) in Asia, and the Asociación Latinoamericana de Integración (ALADI) in Latin America.

20 Such as the Global System of Trade Preferences (GSTP).

PART THREE

International rules governing trade in services

CHAPTER 17

General Agreement on Trade in Services

Summary

Trade in services is growing and currently accounts for over 20% of all international trade. The General Agreement on Trade in Services (GATS),which was negotiated in the Uruguay Round, applies the basic rules for trade in goods to trade in services. However, the rules have been suitably modified to take into account the differences between goods and services and the four modes in which international trade in services takes place.

GATS consists of:

❑ *A framework of general rules and disciplines;*

❑ *Annexes addressing special conditions relating to individual sectors; and*

❑ *Liberalization commitments specific to the service sectors and subsectors listed in each country's schedule.*

The framework of rules requires countries not to discriminate between the service products and service providers of different countries in accordance with the MFN principle. However, it may be possible for a country to maintain for a transition period of 10 years measures that are not consistent with this principle. Under the national treatment principle embodied in the framework, countries should not treat foreign services and service providers less favourably than their own service products and service providers. While the framework does not impose a binding obligation, it requires countries to indicate in their schedules of concessions the sectors in which and the conditions subject to which such national treatment is to be extended.

Among the other important provisions of the framework of rules are those which:

❑ *Require member countries to ensure transparency in the regulations applicable to service industries and activities,*

❑ *Aim at ensuring the increasing participation of developing countries in the trade in services.*

The Agreement visualizes a continuous process of negotiations in WTO for the liberalization of trade in specific sectors. In addition, it provides that a new round of negotiations for the further liberalization of trade in all service sectors should begin in the year 2000.

The term 'services' covers a wide range of economic activities. The WTO Secretariat has divided these divergent activities into the following 12 sectors:

❑ Business (including professional and computer) services;

❑ Communication services;

❑ Construction and engineering services;

❑ Distribution services;

❑ Educational services;

❑ Environmental services;

❑ Financial (insurance and banking) services;

❑ Health services;

❑ Tourism and travel services;

❑ Recreational, cultural and sporting services;

❑ Transport services;

❑ Other services not included elsewhere.

These 12 sectors have been further divided into 155 subsectors; these are listed in annex I to this chapter.

Modes in which the service trade takes place

Difference between goods and services

How do services differ from goods? One of the main characteristics of services is that they are intangible and invisible; goods by contrast are tangible and visible. Furthermore, services, unlike goods, cannot be stored.[21] These differences between services and goods were vividly highlighted by *The Economist* when it asserted that "anything sold in trade that could not be dropped on your foot" is a service.[22]

Four modes of international service transactions

The different characteristics of goods and services also influence the modes in which international transactions take place. While international trade in goods involves the physical movement of goods from one country to another, only a few service transactions traditionally entailed cross-border movements. Examples of cross-border transactions are services that can be transmitted by telecommunications (e.g. transfer of money through banks) or services embodied in goods (e.g. a consultant's technical report or software on a diskette).

In the bulk of service transactions, however, the time and place of consumption cannot be separated, and proximity between the service supplier and the consumer is required. Such proximity can be established through a commercial presence in the importing country (for instance by setting up a branch or subsidiary company) or the movement of natural persons for temporary periods (e.g. lawyers or architects moving to another country to provide their services). The nature of a few service transactions requires consumers to move to the country where the services are available (e.g. tourists visiting countries of tourist interest or students going to another country for higher education).

---

21   The above description is not without limitations. Some services are visible (for example, a consultant's report on diskette). Some services are stored (for example, the telephone answering system).

22   As quoted in: *Liberalizing International Transactions in Services, A Handbook* (United Nations publication, Sales No. E.94.II.A.11), page 1.

Thus, unlike international transactions in goods which require a physical transit across a country's borders, services are supplied internationally according to one or a combination of four modes of supply, namely:

❑ Cross-border movement of service products;

❑ Movement of consumers to the country of importation;

❑ The establishment of a commercial presence in the country where the service is to be provided; and

❑ Temporary movement of natural persons to another country, in order to provide the service there.

While the lack of statistics makes any concrete estimate difficult to make, the total value of services traded through the last two modes is probably much greater than that of the trade taking place through the first two modes. However, the rapid changes in communication technology and the development of electronic commerce are increasingly making it possible for service companies to provide services through cross-border movements without having to establish a commercial presence in the importing countries.

Protection in the service sectors

Another major difference between goods and services lies in the way protection is granted by governments to domestic industries. Industries producing goods are generally protected by the imposition of tariffs or other border measures such as quantitative restrictions. As noted in chapter 2, GATT rules require countries to give such protection through tariffs and discourage them from using quantitative restrictions or other similar restrictive measures. Because of the intangible nature of services and as many service transactions do not involve cross-border movements, protection to service industries cannot be granted through measures applicable at the border. Service industries are protected mainly by national domestic regulations on foreign direct investment and the participation of foreign service suppliers in domestic industries. Such regulations may, for instance, prohibit foreign service suppliers (e.g. banks or insurance companies) from investing in or establishing a branch that is necessary for the supply of services. Regulations may be applied on a discriminatory basis to natural persons providing services, thus treating them less favourably than domestic producers (non-application of the national treatment principle). They may also provide for dissimilar treatment of service suppliers from different countries (non-application of the MFN principle).

The growing importance of international trade in services

Exports of services currently account for about US$ 1 trillion or 20% of world exports. Although the share of developing countries in total exports of services is relatively small, a few of them are already among the world's 25 leading exporters. The export trade in services is rising in importance not only in the more advanced developing countries, but also in some low-income and least developed countries.

A large number of developing countries are currently heavily dependent on imports of services. The import of services is steadily on the increase as the productivity of industries is today closely linked with the ready availability, at reasonable costs, of financial, computer and information services. Enterprises looking for markets in foreign countries have also to spend far more than they did in the past on market research and development, advertising and after-sales support.

The rapid technological progress that is taking place in communications is making it possible for suppliers, heretofore confined to domestic markets, to operate internationally. Banks and insurance companies can operate far more quickly and efficiently because of the development of fax, electronic mail and other facilities. Architects can provide their architectural designs and supervise work from thousands of miles away with the aid of up-to-date information technology. Likewise, consulting engineers can transmit computer-aided designs to customers in distant countries. The international trade in services is therefore expected to expand rapidly and, according to some, it may overtake trade in goods within the next 10 years.

General Agreement on Trade in Services

Prior to the Uruguay Round, trade in services was not subject to any discipline at the international level. The General Agreement on Trade in Services (GATS), which was negotiated in the Round, takes a first major step towards bringing the trade gradually under international discipline.

Objectives

GATS, Preamble

The objectives of GATS are similar to those of GATT. It aims at "promoting the economic growth of all trading partners and the development of developing countries" through the expansion of trade in services. It seeks to achieve this by applying to the service trade the rules of GATT, with the modifications necessary to take into account its special features.

Structure

GATS consists of:

❑ A framework text which sets out the general concepts, principles and rules that apply to measures affecting the trade in services.

❑ The annexes to the Agreement, which establish principles and rules for specific sectors and complement the text.

❑ Specific commitments liberalizing trade within the service sectors and subsectors listed in the national schedules of member countries.

Framework text

Scope and main obligation

GATS applies to government measures affecting services provided on a commercial basis. It thus covers both private-sector enterprises and companies owned (or controlled) by governments if they supply services on a commercial basis. Services obtained by government departments and agencies for their own use are excluded from the purview of the Agreement. The Agreement, however, provides that multilateral negotiations should be held to bring under international discipline such purchases, taking into account the relevant provisions of the Agreement on Government Procurement described in chapter 18.

GATS, Article I:3

The term 'services' covers any service in any service sector,[23] including their production, distribution, marketing, sales and delivery according to the four modes described earlier in this chapter.

---

23   According to the Annex on Air Transport, traffic and related rights are excluded from GATS coverage.

GATS, Part II	The obligations which the framework imposes can be broadly divided into two categories. These are:

❑ General obligations, which apply to all service sectors,

❑ Conditional obligations applicable to sectors covered by commitments specified in the national schedules.

General obligations

Among the important general obligations imposed by the framework text are those relating to:

GATS, Article III	❑ Transparency of regulations;
GATS, Article VII	❑ Mutual recognition of the qualifications required for the supply of services;
GATS, Articles VIII and IX	❑ Rules governing monopolies and exclusive service suppliers, and other business practices restraining competition;
GATS, Article II	❑ The extension of MFN treatment;
GATS, Article IV	❑ Measures to be taken to liberalize trade, including those securing the greater participation of developing countries.

These obligations are discussed below.

GATS, Article III:4	### *Transparency: establishment of enquiry and contact points*

Foreign suppliers often find it difficult to do business with firms in outside countries because of the rules and regulations applicable there. The lack of transparency of such rules poses even more serious problems in the service sectors where domestic regulations are the main means used to protect domestic producers from foreign competition. The Agreement therefore requires each member country to establish one or more enquiry points from which other member countries can obtain information on laws and regulations affecting trade in the service sectors of interest to their industries. In addition,

GATS, Article IV	in order to assist service suppliers in developing countries, the Agreement calls on developed country members to establish contact points. To obtain information from enquiry points, service enterprises will have to channel their requests through their national governments; requests for information from contact points can be made direct. A list of enquiry and contact points is given in annex II to this chapter.

The contact points are to be geared to providing information at the business level. In particular, the Agreement requires contact points to provide on request to service suppliers in developing countries information on:

❑ The availability of service technology;

❑ Commercial and technical aspects of the supply of services;

❑ Registering, recognizing and obtaining professional qualifications.

GATS, Article VII	### *Mutual recognition of qualifications required for the supply of services*

Companies or persons providing services have to obtain certificates, licences or other authorization entitling them to do business. Foreign suppliers often find it difficult to obtain such authorization because of differing regulatory requirements on educational qualifications and working experience. To overcome such difficulties, the Agreement urges its member countries to enter into bilateral or plurilateral arrangements for the mutual recognition of the qualifications required for obtaining authorization. It further provides that such mutual recognition systems should be open for accession by other member countries, if they can demonstrate that their domestic standards and requirements are comparable with those of the systems concerned.

GATS, Article VIII:1 and 2

Rules governing monopolies, exclusive service suppliers and other business practices restraining competition

Service industries often exercise monopoly powers in the domestic market; exclusive rights to supply services are sometimes given by governments to a small number of suppliers. In all such cases, members are under obligation to ensure that such suppliers do not abuse their monopoly or exclusive rights or act in a manner inconsistent with their general and specific obligations under the Agreement.

GATS, Article IX

GATS, Article XIX

The Agreement further recognizes that service suppliers could adopt practices that may distort competition and thereby restrain trade. Whenever a problem of this nature occurs, the affected member country has a right to request the member where the service supplier is situated for consultations with a view to eliminating such practices.

Other obligations of the framework text

A detailed explanation of the rules governing the extension of MFN treatment and those applicable to negotiations on liberalization measures is given further below. At this point it is appropriate to note the remaining important provisions of the framework text and of the annexes.

Conditional obligations and other provisions

As noted earlier, the Agreement imposes, in addition to the general obligations described above,[24] certain conditional obligations that aim at ensuring fuller implementation of the commitments assumed by countries. In relation to sectors where specific commitments are undertaken, these include the following obligations:

GATS, Article VI:1

❑ To ensure that all domestic regulations of general application affecting trade in services are administered in a reasonable and objective way;

GATS, Article VI:2

❑ To maintain or institute tribunals or procedures providing for the review of administrative decisions affecting trade in services;

GATS, Article VI:3

❑ To issue to foreign suppliers the authorization required for the provision of services within a reasonable period;

GATS, Articles IX, XII

❑ Not to apply restrictions on international transfers and payments, except when the country is in serious balance-of-payments difficulties.

Other provisions

Box 38 summarizes the remaining provisions.

Annexes to the Agreement

When the Uruguay Round was being concluded, it was thought that it might not be possible to complete the negotiations on trade liberalization in a number of sectors. It was therefore decided to complement the framework text with annexes, which lay down additional rules on sectoral specifications and provide guidelines for the continuation of negotiations on further liberalization. In pursuance of these guidelines, negotiations were held after the conclusion of the Round to improve commitments relating to the movement of natural persons and in such sectors as financial services and telecommunications.

---

24   The obligations which the rules on monopolies (GATS, Article VIII) and on increasing the participation of developing countries (GATS, Article IV) lay down can be considered conditional obligations even though they are listed under Part II of GATS (*General Obligations and Disciplines*).

Box 38

Other provisions in the GATS framework text

The remaining provisions in the framework text can be broadly divided into two groups. In the first group are the areas for which the text provides that negotiations should take place. In the second group are provisions granting exceptions to the general rules.

PROVISIONS ON FURTHER NEGOTIATIONS

The framework text provides that member countries should undertake further negotiations to develop rules governing the use of subsidies and the application of safeguard measures to trade in services.

PROVISIONS PROVIDING FOR EXCEPTIONS

Economic integration*. The Agreement permits countries to enter into arrangements for liberalizing trade among a limited number of countries, provided substantial service sectors are covered and the other conditions prescribed are met.*

Balance-of-payments restrictions*. Member countries are permitted to impose restrictions on transfer of payments, even in sectors in which they have undertaken specific commitments, when they are in balance-of-payments difficulties.*

Labour market integration*. The Agreement does not prevent a member country from entering into an arrangement with another country for the full integration of their labour markets by exempting each other's citizens from work permit requirements.*

General and security exceptions*. As with trade in goods, the Agreement does not prevent countries from taking measures which they consider necessary for the protection, inter alia, of public morals; human, animal and plant life; or their essential security interests.*

Rules on liberalization of services

GATS, Article XIX:1

GATS stipulates that negotiations to "achieve a progressively higher level of liberalization ... shall take place ... on a mutually advantageous basis" and aim "at securing an overall balance of rights and obligations" among participating countries.

GATS, Article IV;
Article XIX

Principles governing the participation of developing countries

In the determination of the nature and extent of the commitments that can be assumed by countries, the rules provide that due account should be taken of:

GATS, Article XIX:2

❑ National objectives, and

❑ The level of development of individual countries, both overall and in individual sectors.

GATS, Article XIX:2

Toward this end, they provide that developing countries participating in the negotiations should be accorded "appropriate flexibility" to enable them in assuming commitments:

❑ To open fewer sectors.

❑ To liberalize fewer transactions.

❑ To attach such access conditions as are necessary for the attainment of their development objectives. These could include the imposition on foreign suppliers wishing to invest in the service industry of conditions such as the establishment of a subsidiary (or other types of commercial presence) in the country, setting up a joint venture, or providing the local company access to their technology, information and distribution channels.

GATS, Article IV:3

The rules further require that in negotiations, particular account shall be taken of the "serious difficulty" of least developed countries in accepting "negotiated specific commitments in view of their special economic situation and their development, trade and financial needs."

In addition to these special provisions for developing countries, the principles and rules governing trade in goods are also applicable, with some modifications, to the exchange of concessions in the trade in services. These include:

❑ The most-favoured-nation (MFN) principle;

❑ National treatment principle; and

❑ Rules governing the binding of negotiated concessions.

MFN treatment

In trade in goods, the MFN principle requires a country to extend any "advantage, favour or privileges" it grants to another country (for instance, in lowering tariffs or in applying the rules and formalities for importation and exportation) to all other member countries. This obligation to extend MFN treatment is unconditional.

GATS, Article II:1; Annex on Article II Exemptions

GATS, Article II:2

GATS also imposes an obligation on countries to apply the MFN principle by according to other countries, in respect of the measures covered by the Agreement, "treatment no less favourable than that it accords to like services and service suppliers of any other country." The obligation to extend such treatment applies on both *de jure* and *de facto* basis. GATS, however, recognizes that not all countries may be able to assume such an obligation immediately. It therefore provides that a country could, if it so wishes, maintain measures that are inconsistent with the rule for a maximum transition period of 10 years.

GATS, Annex on Article II Exemptions

Box 39 explains the reasons that have prompted some countries to list exemptions. The exemptions are temporary and the need for maintaining them is to be reviewed periodically after five years; they are to be abolished after 10 years (i.e. by 1 January 2005).

National treatment principle

Closely related to the MFN principle is the principle of national treatment. The GATT national treatment rule prohibits member countries from imposing higher internal taxes on, or applying more rigorous domestic regulations to, an imported product than those imposed on a similar domestic product, after the imported product has entered the country on payment of tariffs and other charges payable at the border. The rule is intended to ensure that, in practice, the domestically produced product does not obtain protection higher than that resulting from the levy of tariffs.

GATS, Article XVII

Since countries do not impose tariffs on imports of services, the imposition of the national treatment principle, by requiring countries to apply their national regulations equally to both domestic and foreign suppliers, would have resulted in the sudden loss by domestic service industries of their entire protection. In the event, the GATS rules provide that the extension of the national treatment principle by countries would be based on the outcome of negotiations during which they would indicate the sectors or subsectors in which, and the conditions under which, they would be prepared to extend such treatment to foreign services and suppliers.

Box 39

GATS: exceptions to the MFN rule

One objective of countries in making exceptions to the MFN principle is to maintain the preferential treatment they extend to some countries in the service sector under regional cooperation or other arrangements. Thus the Nordic countries have excluded from the MFN obligation measures promoting Nordic cooperation. These measures include guarantees and loans to Nordic investment projects and financial assistance to companies of Nordic origin for the utilization of environmental technology. The European Union has, by making an exception to the MFN rule, ensured that the benefits of special arrangements which its member States have with certain countries* would not be automatically extended to nationals of other countries. The arrangements provide for the grant of temporary work permits to these countries' nationals on the basis of contracts between a company in an EU State and service providers in these countries in service sectors such as construction, hotels and catering.

Some countries with liberal import regimes have made exceptions to the MFN rule in such sectors as financial and maritime services. Their aim is to maintain their bargaining leverage when negotiating for liberalization with countries that have more restrictive regimes. In the financial sector, a number of these countries have removed some of these exceptions in the negotiation that took place after the conclusion of the Uruguay Round.

It is important to note that WTO member countries were required to exercise their right to obtain an exemption from the MFN rule before GATS came into force. However, in the sectors on which negotiations continued after the Uruguay Round (e.g financial services and telecommunications), it was possible for countries to claim an exemption from the MFN principle during the period of negotiations.

* In central, eastern and south-eastern Europe (including the Russian Federation, Ukraine and Georgia) and in the Mediterranean basin.

Type and nature of commitments

In the trade in services, no tariffs or fiscal duties are applicable when service products or suppliers enter the territory of another country. Protection to a domestic service industry is given through domestic regulations. A country wishing to liberalize has, therefore, to decide which measures to keep in place and which to modify or remove to bring them in conformity with GATS rules. The measures on which such decisions have to be made are those affecting the entry of a service product or service supplier into its market, and those affecting the post-establishment activity of service suppliers. They may include the following:

❑ Those that restrict the access of foreign service suppliers or products, and

❑ Those that discriminate between domestic and foreign suppliers or products.

In regard to market access measures which a country entering into negotiated commitments does not want to remove completely, it could stipulate that its commitments are subject to specified conditions. The forms such conditions can take are listed in Article XVI (*see* box 40). No other conditions may be imposed.

Likewise it is possible for a country, while making commitments to extend national treatment, to stipulate that it will continue to maintain certain practices that discriminate between foreign and domestic service suppliers or service products (e.g. higher rates of taxes on premiums collected by foreign insurance companies).

> **Box 40**
>
> *Type of conditions that countries may impose when assuming market access commitments*
> (General Agreement on Trade in Services, Article XVI)
>
> ❑ *Limitations on the number of service suppliers (e.g. foreign banks or insurance companies may establish only a specified number of branches or subsidiaries);*
>
> ❑ *Limitations on the total value of service transactions or assets (e.g. only 10% of the reinsurance value may be placed with foreign companies);*
>
> ❑ *Limitations on the total number of service operations or the total quantity of service output;*
>
> ❑ *Limitations on the total number of natural persons that may be employed in a particular sector or that a service supplier may employ (e.g. the majority of the board of directors must be citizens of the country);*
>
> ❑ *Measures which require specific types of legal entity through which a service can be supplied (e.g. in the banking or insurance business, subsidiaries must be incorporated);*
>
> ❑ *Limitations on foreign equity participation (e.g. maximum equity participation limited to 49%).*

Nature of the obligations which commitments impose

The commitments assumed by a country are recorded in its GATS schedule of commitments. Each schedule is divided into two parts: horizontal and sectoral. Horizontal commitments apply across the board to all service sectors; sectoral commitments are applicable to a specified service sector or subsector.

Entries in the schedule show the extent of the commitments which the country has agreed to give. These are listed separately for each of the four modes in which the international service trade takes place. The nature of the commitments that can be assumed under each mode are shown in box 41.

> **Box 41**
>
> *Nature of the commitments that can be assumed under each of the four modes of the international trade in services*
>
> ❑ *Full commitment. "None" or "No limitations", which implies that the country does not seek in any way to limit market access or national treatment through measures inconsistent with Articles XVI or XVII.*
>
> ❑ *Commitment with limitations. The country describes in detail the measures maintained which are inconsistent with the rules on market access or national treatment, and commits itself to take no other inconsistent measures.*
>
> ❑ *No commitment. "Unbound" indicates that the country remains free to maintain or introduce measures inconsistent with the rules governing market access or national treatment.*
>
> ❑ *No commitments technically feasible. The country indicates that in the sector in question, a particular mode of supply cannot be used (e.g. cross-border supply of hairdressing services).*

Liberalization commitments under GATS

The sections that follow describe in general the liberalization commitments that have been made during and after the Uruguay Round in the services sector. As has been said earlier, GATS provides for a continuous process of negotiations in WTO for the liberalization of the trade in services. In accordance with these provisions, negotiations for improving the liberalization commitments assumed in the Uruguay Round have been held in certain sectors and areas.

Schedules of commitments

The liberalization commitments assumed by countries are listed in each country's schedule of commitments. The extent and conditions to which and under which the basic principles of GATS (market access, national treatment and MFN treatment) apply to individual service sectors in any country can be assessed only by referring to that country's schedule, the character of the existing regulatory regime and the nature of the limitations, if any, to which the commitments are subject.

The schedules are complex as they cover 12 sectors and 155 subsectors. For each subsector, the commitments are further listed according to the four modes in which the service trade takes place.

As stated earlier, commitments under each mode may be either horizontal (covering the entire range of services) or specific to the sector or activity in question.

Box 42 presents an example of a schedule of horizontal and specific commitments. Where no limitations are indicated against any mode of supply (i.e. the entry 'None' in the schedule), the country enters into a binding commitment not to take any new measures to restrict entry into the market or the operation of the service. Where limitations have been indicated against a particular mode of supply (such as when incorporation of a company is made a condition for carrying out a service activity), the country is obliged not to impose any other limitations that would further restrict the entry of foreign suppliers. Where, however, the entry 'Unbound' appears under either horizontal or specific commitments, the country indicates that at least at that stage it maintains its freedom to modify its regulations and possibly to change the conditions of entry for foreign suppliers.

Horizontal commitments

Almost all limitations under horizontal commitments assumed in negotiations apply to services for which a commercial presence in the importing country is necessary, and to the movement of natural persons.

Broadly speaking, developed countries have not specified many horizontal limitations on the establishment of a commercial presence by foreign suppliers. The creation of a subsidiary company or a branch by a foreign supplier to carry out a service activity or to make an investment in the domestic service industry will therefore continue to be permitted under their existing legislation. These, as a rule, provide for the grant of authorization on liberal terms.

However, in the majority of the Uruguay Round schedules, horizontal commitments relating to the movement of natural persons were largely limited to:

❑ Intra-company transfers covering essential personnel, i.e. managers and technical staff linked with commercial presence in the host country, and

❑ Business visitors who are short-term visitors not gainfully employed in the host country.

Box 42

Format and example of a schedule of horizontal and specific commitments

Commitments	Mode of supply	Conditions and limitations on market access	Conditions and qualifications on national treatment
Horizontal commitments (i.e. across all sectors)	Cross-border supply	None	None, other than tax measures that result in difference in treatment of R & D* services.
	Consumption abroad	None	Unbound for subsidies, tax incentives, and tax credits.
	Commercial presence (FDI**)	Maximum foreign equity stake is 49%.	Unbound for subsidies. Under Law *x*, approval is required for equity stakes over 25% and for new investment exceeding *y* million.
	Temporary entry of natural persons	Unbound except for the following: intra-corporate transfers of executives and senior managers; specialist personnel for stays of up to one year; specialist personnel subject to economic needs test for stays longer than one year; service sellers (sales people) for stays of up to three months.	Unbound, except for categories of natural persons referred to in the market access column.
Specific commitment: Architectural services	Cross-border supply	Commercial presence required.	Unbound
	Consumption abroad	None	None
	Commercial presence (FDI**)	25% of senior management should be nationals.	Unbound
	Temporary entry of natural persons	Unbound, except as indicated under horizontal commitments.	Unbound, except as indicated under horizontal commitments.

* R & D: Research and development   ** Foreign direct investment

One of the key demands of developing countries was that member countries should assume firm and legally binding commitments to permit independent professionals to work abroad without being required to establish a company or other form of commercial presence. In the Uruguay Round negotiations these demands were met in only a very few instances. As a result of further negotiations held after the conclusion of the Round, six members have improved their commitments. The European Union and its member States have guaranteed to varying degrees opportunities for foreign professionals without commercial presence to perform temporary assignments in 14 Member States (excluding Portugal). The additional commitments of Switzerland and Norway are similar in nature but limited in scope. Canada has added a number of professions to its Uruguay Round commitments on the entry and temporary stay of foreign, contract-based professionals. Australia has introduced some flexibility to its existing offer on business visitors. India has improved some of its earlier commitments.

A number of developing countries have prescribed conditions which require foreign suppliers to establish joint ventures with domestic service industries. These conditions further limit in some cases the share in equity which foreign suppliers can hold. Some of these countries have taken advantage of the provisions of the Agreement on increasing participation of developing countries and have specified that approval of proposals to establish a commercial presence will be granted on the basis of such factors as economic need and the readiness of the foreign supplier to bring in the most up-to-date technology (*see* box 43 for details).

Box 43

Nature of limitations imposed by developing countries in their horizontal commitments permitting the establishment of a commercial presence

A number of developing countries have taken advantage of the provisions for increasing the participation of developing countries and have specified that permission to establish a commercial presence will be granted on the basis of economic need criteria to strengthen domestic service capacities. The conditions imposed for the attainment of this objective include the following:

❑ *The establishment of commercial presence will be allowed on the basis of a joint venture;*

❑ *The foreign supplier will be permitted to have less than a majority share in the equity of such a joint venture;*

❑ *A specific number of board members must be nationals of the country;*

❑ *The foreign service supplier should use appropriate and advanced technology and managerial experience;*

❑ *It should train and pass on the benefit of technology to local employees;*

❑ *It should employ, wherever possible, domestic subcontractors;*

❑ *It must furnish accurate and prompt reports on its operations, including technological, accounting, economic and administrative data.*

Sectoral commitments

Commitments undertaken by countries in their sectoral schedules complement their horizontal commitments. While developed countries have included in their schedules all service sectors, developing countries have exercised a certain degree of flexibility and have covered a limited number of sectors, taking into account such factors as the stage of their development.

The type of limitation specified in the sectoral schedules relates to the characteristics of the service activity and the modes in which service transactions primarily take place. The paragraphs that follow explain the nature and content of the commitments undertaken and the limitations imposed in six sectors in negotiations during and after the Uruguay Round:

❑ Financial services;

❑ Telecommunications services;

❑ Professional services;

❑ Construction and related engineering services;

❑ Health-related and social services; and

❑ Management consultancy services.

These sectors have been drawn, for the purpose of this Guide, from among the sectors in which developing countries are considered to have a potential for developing an export trade or for benefiting from import liberalization.

Financial services

Financial services fall into two broad categories: insurance and banking, both of which cover a range of activities. Insurance includes both life and non-life insurance, reinsurance, insurance intermediation, and auxiliary insurance services. Banking comprises all the traditional services such as acceptance of deposits, lending of all types, and payment and money transmission services. It also covers trading in foreign exchange, derivatives, securities underwriting, money brokering, asset management, settlement and clearing services, provision and transfer of financial information, and advisory and other auxiliary financial services.

Negotiations in this sector continued after the completion of the Uruguay Round as it was considered that the progress achieved in the Round was far from satisfactory. The renewed negotiations were held in two stages and were completed in December 1997.

In this sector most countries had made since the mid-1980s considerable progress in removing barriers to, or restrictions on, the establishment of branches or other types of commercial presence by foreign institutions or their business operations. Developed countries had taken such liberalization measures under agreements reached under the auspices of the Organisation for Economic Co-operation and Development (OECD). A large number of developing countries, which had been following highly protectionist policies, had also unilaterally begun the process of liberalization through the gradual removal of prohibitions or severe restrictions on the types of business which foreign banks could operate.

The post Uruguay Round negotiations have resulted in further improvements in the liberalization measures taken earlier in the insurance and banking subsectors and consolidation into binding commitments of those already undertaken. These commitments relate to the commercial presence of foreign service suppliers (branches, subsidiaries, agencies, representative offices) and eliminate or relax limitations on:

❑ Foreign ownership of local financial institutions;

❑ The juridical form of commercial presence; and

❑ Expansion of existing operations.

A number of developing countries have ensured that their domestic insurance and banking industries are exposed to foreign competition gradually by imposing limitations on foreign equity participation (not to exceed 49%) and on the number of foreign service suppliers (the number of branches to be established shall not exceed 15 during the specified period).

It is important to note in this context that GATS recognizes that governments find it necessary to exercise considerable regulatory control over the activities of banks, insurance companies and other financial institutions. Its Annex on Financial Services therefore provides that the liberalization commitments undertaken should not prevent them from taking "measures for prudential reasons, including the protection of investors, depositors, policyholders ... or to ensure the integrity and stability of the financial system." Although the Annex does not give details as to what constitutes prudential measures, licensing requirements intended to ensure business competence and financial integrity, minimum capital requirements and regular accounting requirements would

GATS, Annex on Financial Services, §20

ordinarily be considered prudential measures. Such measures do not have to be non-discriminatory, but they can be applied on a discriminatory basis if warranted by circumstances.

Telecommunications

Telecommunications play a dual role in the economies of countries: they provide the communication infrastructure, and they act as a channel for trade. In the past, because of its importance to infrastructural development and its strategic and political significance to a number of countries, the industry was developed as a State monopoly. However, the revolutionary technological changes in communications and information technology have made the ability of business enterprises to offer their goods and service products in international markets at competitive prices dependent on the availability of up-to-date and cheaper communication services. The recognition that a well-developed technology sector will improve competitiveness gradually led to the privatization of State monopolies and the removal of restrictions on the entry of foreign suppliers and their products.

Telecommunications services can be broadly divided into two categories: basic telecommunications and value-added services.

Basic telecommunications services cover "any telecommunication transport service". They include voice telephony, data transmission, telex, telegraph, facsimile, private leased circuit services (i.e. the sale or lease of transmission capacity), and network services (i.e. telecommunications infrastructure which permits telecommunication between and among defined network termination points).

Value-added services are those services through which suppliers 'add value' to the customer's information by enhancing its form or content or by providing for its storage and retrieval. They include: electronic mail; voice mail; on-line information and database retrieval; electronic data interchange; enhanced/value-added facsimile services, including store and forward, store and retrieval; code and protocol conversion; and on-line information and/or data processing (including transaction processing).

Negotiations in this sector continued after the Uruguay Round because of the very limited progress made in the Round in liberalizing trade in basic telecommunications. The renewed negotiations were completed in February 1997. They aimed primarily at liberalizing trade in basic telecommunications, even though a few countries improved the commitments they made in the Uruguay Round on value-added services.

The commitments made cover the entire range of basic telecommunications services. On voice telephone services, countries committed themselves to allowing competition from foreign suppliers in providing local services, domestic long distance services, and international services. About 40% of the governments making offers on public voice telephone services have, however, indicated that these offers would be implemented by the date specified in their schedules. Other service areas in which commitments were made to allow some degree of foreign competition include cellular/mobile telephone operations, leased circuit services (such as mobile data and paging) and mobile satellite services.

An important aspect of the negotiations on the telecommunications sector was the recognition, given the structures of the industry, that even after privatization and liberalization, the monopolistic control which private firms providing basic telecommunication facilities would be able to exercise may not always lead to efficiency and lower costs to the users of the services.

It was therefore necessary for countries taking liberalizing measures to establish regulatory frameworks to ensure that users are able to access basic telecommunication facilities on fair terms. This recognition has resulted in the adoption of a 'reference paper' which lays down the principles and rules to be followed to guarantee that existing firms do not adopt anti-competition practices to prevent the entry of new firms, and charge users and consumers higher prices than are justified by costs. These principles and rules apply to:

❑ The establishment of independent regulatory authorities;

❑ The adoption of competitive safeguards;

❑ Measures to ensure interconnection;

❑ Transparent and non-discriminatory licensing practices;

❑ Universal service obligations.

Professional services: accountancy services

Professional services cover a wide range of services such as legal, architectural, engineering, medical and accountancy services. The post Uruguay Round negotiations in this sector focused mainly on accountancy services.

Accountancy is important to the production of both physical goods and services. The range of activities undertaken by accountancy firms is wide and expanding. This is due to the fact that the skills developed by accountancy professionals in order to produce, process, analyse and audit financial information can be used for other purposes. As a result, in addition to their traditional role in implementing and enforcing prudential requirements and financial regulatory measures, these firms are increasingly providing taxation and investment services, merger audits, and management consultancy services.

Demand for accountancy services flows from both mandatory requirements under national company laws and clients seeking advice on various issues. Although individuals are also consumers of accountancy services, much of the services are provided to enterprises.

Professional services, including accountancy, are regulated in different ways by different countries (and sometimes even within countries). The regulations cover both the service provider and the service itself. Differences among countries in regulatory measures on professional qualifications, technical standards and licensing, could make it difficult for professionals from one country to supply their services to another country. These considerations resulted in a Ministerial Decision on Professional Services (adopted by the WTO Council for Trade in Services in March 1995) for the commencement of work on the elaboration of disciplines for the trade in professional services. Such disciplines would supplement the specific commitments assumed by countries in the Uruguay Round and ensure that the regulatory measures adopted by countries do not constitute unnecessary barriers to the supply of professional services.

The work resulted in the adoption in 1998 of *Disciplines on Domestic Regulation in the Accountancy Sector* by the Council for Trade in Services. The disciplines include rules in the following areas:

❑ *Transparency*. Members should make available, either directly or through enquiry and contact points established by them, the names and addresses of competent authorities responsible for formulating accountancy regulations and for the licensing of professionals or firms.

❑ *Licensing requirements and procedures*. "Licensing requirements (i.e. the substantive requirements, other than qualification requirements, to be satisfied in order to obtain or renew an authorization to practice)" and "Licensing procedures (i.e. the procedures to be followed for the submission and processing of an application for authorization to practise)" "shall be pre-established, publicly available and objective." Further, "licensing procedures shall not in themselves constitute a restriction on the supply of the service."

❑ *Qualification requirements*. Members should ensure that its competent authorities take account of qualifications acquired in the territory of another Member, on the basis of equivalency of education, experience and/or examination requirements.

❑ *Technical standards*. "Members shall ensure that measures relating to technical standards are prepared, adopted and applied only to fulfil legitimate objectives."

The *Disciplines* are binding on Members which have given commitments in the accountancy sector but will not have immediate legal effect. WTO Members will continue their work on domestic regulation in the context of the Working Party on Professional Services (WPPS). WPPS aims to develop general disciplines for professional services while retaining the possibility to develop additional sectoral disciplines.

Before the end of the forthcoming round of service negotiations, which commence in January 2000, all the disciplines developed by WPPS are to be integrated into GATS and will then become legally binding. The *Disciplines* on the accountancy sector includes a "stand-still provision", effective immediately, under which all WTO Members, including those without GATS commitments in the accountancy sector, agree, to the fullest extent consistent with their existing legislation, not to take measures which would be inconsistent with the accountancy disciplines.

Construction and related engineering services

This sector covers:

❑ General construction work for buildings;
❑ General construction work for civil engineering;
❑ Installation and assembly work; and
❑ Building completion and other work.

The national schedules of 48 countries contain commitments in this sector.

Trade in the sector does not take place through cross-border movements or through the movement of consumers to places abroad. However, suppliers of construction engineering services are required to establish an office in the country where the services are to be provided. The competitiveness of most construction engineering companies in developing countries in regard to work in outside countries is greatly dependent on how far the latter countries permit technicians like masons and plumbers and other workers to stay for temporary periods.

As regards the right to establish a commercial presence in order to engage in construction engineering activities, all developed countries and a large number of developing countries have indicated in their schedules that they impose no limitations. In other words, they will apply to foreign companies the rules applicable to domestic suppliers on the establishment of companies for the conduct of such activities. A few developing countries have, however, indicated that foreign suppliers wishing to engage in the construction business must set up a joint venture with domestic companies providing such services.

The countries which require foreign suppliers to establish joint ventures or some other type of operation involving domestic suppliers include India, Malaysia, Morocco, Pakistan, Thailand and Turkey.

As regards the movement of natural persons, all countries have specified that this mode of providing service is unbound. In other words, the countries have not undertaken any commitment to allow persons below managerial level to enter the country to work on the basis of temporary contracts in the construction industry.

Health-related and social services

Only a limited number of countries have made commitments in this sector. This is partly due to the fact that, in many countries, such services are provided not by the private sector but by government or public hospitals. The sector covers the following:

❑ Hospital services,

❑ Other human health services, and

❑ Social services.

As regards the right of foreigners to establish hospitals, both the European Union and the United States have indicated that such requests will be subject to need-based quantitative limits taking into account such factors as the number of beds in relation to the population of each region. Some developing countries have specified that the establishment of hospitals with foreign participation will be possible only on the basis of joint ventures with local participation.

Most countries have, however, specified that the movement of natural persons to provide such services is unbound. This means that they will continue to apply their existing regulations, which do not generally recognize as equivalent degrees and other professional qualifications obtained in other countries and thus do not permit foreigners holding such qualifications to work in hospitals as doctors, nurses or midwives, or to provide other health or social services.

Management consultancy services

Management consultancy services cover a wide range of activities such as general, financial, production, marketing and human resource consultancy services.

It is possible to provide such services across borders through communications facilities. However, for more effective servicing, a commercial presence in the country where the service is to be provided is essential. Of the 45 countries that have included management consultancy services in their schedules, a large majority have bound the supply of such services without limiting it on a cross-border basis or requiring the establishment of a commercial presence. A few developing countries have, however, not bound the supply of service on a cross-border basis and have indicated that the establishment of a branch or office will be possible only on the basis of joint ventures with local consultancy firms. None of these countries have agreed to bind the supply of services through the movement of natural persons. This means that the existing regulations which prohibit foreign suppliers from providing such services unless they have established a commercial presence in the country will continue to apply.

Business implications

Assessment of benefits

In the Uruguay Round and the negotiations held after it, countries have taken the first steps towards liberalizing the international trade in services. Unlike trade in goods, it is however not possible to quantify the potential trade effects of liberalization in the sector for two reasons. There is nothing equivalent to customs duties in the service sector. As protection is granted through domestic regulations which discriminate against foreign suppliers, the effect of such measures or their removal cannot easily be quantified.

It is however generally believed that, by and large, most countries have in the negotiations tried to consolidate their earlier liberalization measures by undertaking commitments not to withdraw or modify them. The immediate advantage to exporting service enterprises flows mainly from the security of access to foreign markets these commitments provide.

Benefits for service industries in developing countries

For service industries in developing countries, the main advantage of the liberalization measures taken by these countries – whether unilaterally or in the context of the Uruguay Round – are expected to flow from the efficiency gains from increased competition in their domestic markets. The entry of foreign service providers in service sectors like telecommunications, banking and insurance will force domestic industries in countries where they were highly protected to improve their competitive position by adopting more efficient methods of providing services. The resulting better performance of the service industry will benefit not only the general public but also manufacturing enterprises in their export trade. The ability of such enterprises to compete in foreign markets depends heavily on how efficiently communications, banking and insurance services are available to them.

New opportunities for collaboration with foreign suppliers

The commitments assumed by governments also provide service industries in developing countries a new opportunity to collaborate with foreign service industries and to benefit from their technology. In negotiating collaborative arrangements, the industry can use as bargaining leverage the limitations imposed by their governments in their schedules of commitments. These, *inter alia*, specify that approval will be granted only if foreign service suppliers agree to bring in the most up-to-date technologies and to train local employees in their use.

Benefits of contact points

One of the major handicaps which service industries in developing countries suffer when entering into collaborative arrangements is their lack of knowledge of the commercial and technical aspects of the services and technologies they want to obtain. GATS therefore provides for the establishment by developed countries of contact points from which such information can be obtained by interested service industries in developing countries.

New export opportunities

On the export side, developing countries are generally considered to have a comparative advantage in service sectors that are either labour intensive or require highly skilled technical personnel. The sectors or subsectors in which it may be possible for these countries to develop trade, taking into account the above two factors, are listed below:

❑ Business services, including management consultancy services, computer services, professional services, rental services;

❑ Construction and engineering;

❑ Educational services;

❑ Environmental services;

❑ Health services;

❑ Tourism and travel services; and

❑ Recreational, cultural and sporting services;

Already some developing countries have become importers or exporters of services that can be provided through the movement of technically qualified natural persons. These services include computer software and health services (nursing).

The link of commitments with domestic legislation

The description earlier in this chapter of commitments in several sectors provides a broad idea of the nature and content of the commitments that countries have assumed in regard to services. However, the commitments relate only to certain aspects of domestic regulations. In order to assess their beneficial impact, it is necessary to examine them against the full background of the domestic regulations and rules applicable to the service sector in the countries making the commitments. In some cases, the commitment may simply reaffirm or bind an existing practice, for instance, of giving approval to the establishment of a branch or a subsidiary company. In other cases, it may amount to accepting a new obligation.

For service suppliers interested in developing trade, the information contained in the national schedules will therefore be of practical value only if they have all the relevant information on the domestic legislation, rules, regulations and practices forming the backdrop to such commitments. To assist service and other industries in obtaining such information, GATS requires member countries to establish enquiry points. These should provide information on the laws and regulations applicable to the service sector.

Increased opportunities for natural persons to provide services

In some sectors, the competitive advantage of a number of developing countries, particularly the more advanced among them, arises from the existence of a vast pool of technically qualified people. Many skills-intensive services are provided through the temporary movement of natural persons to the countries where the service is provided. The horizontal commitments which countries have assumed in recently concluded negotiations on the movement of natural persons will now provide new opportunities for technically and professionally qualified persons to provide such services, without having to establish an office or other form of commercial presence.

Importance of adopting a juridical personality

It is important to note that, in their horizontal and sectoral commitments, a number of countries have indicated the conditions they currently apply when permitting their companies to employ for temporary periods the services of foreign technicians and specialists. While these commitments open up only limited opportunities, knowledge of the conditions imposed should enable foreign companies to take full advantage of them. The commitments often indicate that approval will be granted if the local company enters into a contract with a legally constituted foreign business enterprise to obtain the services of a specialist. It will therefore be desirable for persons interested in providing such services to organize themselves into a company or partnership rather than to act as individuals or loosely formed groups.

Opportunities for the expansion of trade among developing countries

Lastly, the commitments assumed by developing countries have opened up new opportunities for the expansion of South-South trade in services through the establishment of joint ventures and other collaborative arrangements especially on a regional basis. Apart from promoting South-South trade, regional consortia have a larger potential to compete with industrialized countries in bidding for service contracts. Such consortia can offer an impressive range of skills and experience, thus enhancing their image and underlining their competence, particularly in relation to work in their own region.

WTO classification of service sectors

SECTORS AND SUB-SECTORS	CORRESPONDING CPC [a] Section B

1. **BUSINESS SERVICES**

   A. **Professional services**

a.	Legal services	861
b.	Accounting, auditing and bookkeeping services	862
c.	Taxation services	863
d.	Architectural services	8671
e.	Engineering services	8672
f.	Integrated engineering services	8673
g.	Urban planning and landscape architectural services	8674
h.	Medical and dental services	9312
I.	Veterinary services	932
j.	Services provided by midwives, nurses, physiotherapists and paramedical personnel	93191
k.	Other	

   B. **Computer and related services**

a.	Consultancy services related to the installation of computer hardware	841
b.	Software implementation services	842
c.	Data processing services	843
d.	Database services	844
e.	Other	845+849

   C. **Research and development services**

a.	R & D services on natural sciences	851
b.	R & D services on social sciences and humanities	852
c.	Interdisciplinary R & D services	853

   D. **Real estate services**

a.	Involving own or leased property	821
b.	On a fee or contract basis	822

   E. **Rental/leasing services without operators**

a.	Relating to ships	83103
b.	Relating to aircraft	83104
c.	Relating to other transport equipment	83101+83102+ 83105
d.	Relating to other machinery and equipment	83106-83109
e.	Other	832

---

a/ Central Product Classification (United Nations).

SECTORS AND SUB-SECTORS	CORRESPONDING CPC Section B
F. **Other business services**	
a. Advertising services	871
b. Market research and public opinion polling services	864
c. Management consulting service	865
d. Services related to management consulting	866
e. Technical testing and analysis services	8676
f. Services incidental to agriculture, hunting and forestry	881
g. Services incidental to fishing	882
h. Services incidental to mining	883+5115
i. Services incidental to manufacturing	884+885 (except for 88442)
j. Services incidental to energy distribution	887
k. Placement and supply services of personnel	872
l. Investigation and security	873
m. Related scientific and technical consulting services	8675
n. Maintenance and repair of equipment (not including maritime vessels, aircraft or other transport equipment)	633+ 8861-8866
o. Building-cleaning services	874
p. Photographic services	875
q. Packaging services	876
r. Printing, publishing	88442
s. Convention services	87909*
t. Other	8790
2. **COMMUNICATION SERVICES**	
A. Postal services	7511
B. Courier services	7512
C. Telecommunication services	
a. Voice telephone services	7521
b. Packet-switched data transmission services	7523**
c. Circuit-switched data transmission services	7523**
d. Telex services	7523**
e. Telegraph services	7522
f. Facsimile services	7521**+7529**
g. Private leased circuit services	7522**+7523**
h. Electronic mail	7523**
i. Voice mail	7523**
j. On-line information and database retrieval	7523**
k. Electronic data interchange (EDI)	7523**
l. Enhanced/value-added facsimile services including store and forward, store and retrieve	7523**
m. Code and protocol conversion	n.a.
n. On-line information and/or data processing (including transaction processing)	843**
o. Other	
D. **Audiovisual services**	
a. Motion picture and video tape production and distribution services	9611
b. Motion picture projection service	9612
c. Radio and television services	9613
d. Radio and television transmission services	7524
e. Sound recording	n.a.
f. Other	
E. **Other**	

SECTORS AND SUB-SECTORS	**CORRESPONDING CPC** Section B

3. CONSTRUCTION AND RELATED ENGINEERING SERVICES

A.	General construction work for buildings	512
B.	General construction work for civil engineering	513
C.	Installation and assembly work	514+516
D.	Building completion and finishing work	517
E.	Other	511+515+518

4. DISTRIBUTION SERVICES

A.	Commission agents' services	621
B.	Wholesale trade services	622
C.	Retailing services	631+632
		6111+6113+6121
D.	Franchising	8929
E.	Other	

5. EDUCATIONAL SERVICES

A.	Primary education services	921
B.	Secondary education services	922
C.	Higher education services	923
D.	Adult education	924
E.	Other education services	929

6. ENVIRONMENTAL SERVICES

A.	Sewage services	9401
B.	Refuse disposal services	9402
C.	Sanitation and similar services	9403
D.	Other	

7. FINANCIAL SERVICES

A.		**All insurance and insurance-related services**	812**
	a.	Life, accident and health insurance services	8121
	b.	Non-life insurance services	8129
	c.	Reinsurance and retrocession	81299
	d.	Services auxiliary to insurance (including broking and agency services)	8140
B.		**Banking and other financial services (excluding insurance)**	
	a.	Acceptance of deposits and other repayable funds from the public	81115-81119
	b.	Lending of all types, including consumer credit, mortgage credit, factoring and financing of commercial transaction	8113
	c.	Financial leasing	8112
	d.	All payment and money transmission services	81339**
	e.	Guarantees and commitments	81199**
	f.	Trading for own account or for account of customers, whether on an exchange, in an over-the-counter market or otherwise, the following:	
		- money market instruments (cheques, bills, certificates of deposits, etc.)	81339**
		- foreign exchange	81333
		- derivative products including, but not limited to, futures and options	81339**
		- exchange rate and interest rate instruments, including products such as swaps, forward rate agreements, etc.	81339**
		- transferable securities	81321*
		- other negotiable instruments and financial assets, including bullion	81339**
	g.	Participation in issues of all kinds of securities, including underwriting and placement as agent (whether publicly or privately) and provision of service related to such issues	8132
	h.	Money broking	81339**
	i.	Asset management, such as cash or portfolio management, all forms of collective investment management, pension fund management, custodial depository and trust services	8119+** 81323*

SECTORS AND SUB-SECTORS	CORRESPONDING CPC Section B
j. Settlement and clearing services for financial assets, including securities, derivative products, and other negotiable instruments	81339** or 81319**
k. Advisory and other auxiliary financial services on all the activities listed in Article 1B of MTN.TNC/W/50, including credit reference and analysis, investment and portfolio research and advice, advice on acquisitions and on corporate restructuring and strategy	8131 or 8133
l. Provision and transfer of financial information, and financial data processing and related software by providers of other financial services	8131

    C.   Other

8. HEALTH-RELATED AND SOCIAL SERVICES (other than those listed under 1.A.h-j.)

A. Hospital services	9311
B. Other human health services	9319 (other than 93191)
C. Social services	933
D. Other	

9. TOURISM AND TRAVEL-RELATED SERVICES

A. Hotels and restaurants (including catering)	641-643
B. Travel agencies and tour operators services	7471
C. Tourist guides services	7472
D. Other	

10. RECREATIONAL, CULTURAL AND SPORTING SERVICES (other than audiovisual services)

A. Entertainment services (including theatre, live bands and circus services)	9619
B. News agency services	962
C. Libraries, archives, museums and other cultural services	963
D. Sporting and other recreational services	964
E. Other	

11. TRANSPORT SERVICES

    A. Maritime transport services

a. Passenger transportation	7211
b. Freight transportation	7212
c. Rental of vessels with crew	7213
d. Maintenance and repair of vessels	8868**
e. Pushing and towing services	7214
f. Supporting services for maritime transport	745**

    B. Internal waterways transport

a. Passenger transportation	7221
b. Freight transportation	7222
c. Rental of vessels with crew	7223
d. Maintenance and repair of vessels	8868**
e. Pushing and towing services	7224
f. Supporting services for internal waterway transport	745**

    C. Air transport services

a. Passenger transportation	731
b. Freight transportation	732
c. Rental of aircraft with crew	734
d. Maintenance and repair of aircraft	8868**
e. Supporting services for air transport	746

    D. Space transport   733

SECTORS AND SUB-SECTORS	CORRESPONDING CPC Section B
E. Rail transport services	
a. Passenger transportation	7111
b. Freight transportation	7112
c. Pushing and towing services	7113
d. Maintenance and repair of rail transport equipment	8868**
e. Supporting services for rail transport services	743
F. Road transport services	
a. Passenger transportation	7121+7122
b. Freight transportation	7123
c. Rental of commercial vehicles with operator	7124
d. Maintenance and repair of road transport equipment	6112+8867
e. Supporting services for road transport services	744
G. Pipeline transport	
a. Transportation of fuels	7131
b. Transportation of other goods	7139
H. Services auxiliary to all modes of transport	
a. Cargo-handling services	741
b. Storage and warehouse services	742
c. Freight transport agency services	748
d. Other	749
I. Other transport services	
12. OTHER SERVICES NOT INCLUDED ELSEWHERE	95+97+98+99

The (*) indicates that the service specified is a component of a more aggregated CPC item specified elsewhere in this classification list.

The (**) indicates that the service specified constitutes only a part of the total range of activities covered by the CPC concordance (e.g. voice mail is only a component of CPC item 7523).

National enquiry and contact points[a/] General Agreement on Trade in Services

AUSTRALIA
The Director
Services Trade Section
Trade Negotiations and Organisations Division
Department of Foreign Affairs and Trade
Parkes ACT 2600
Tel: +(61 6) 261 3156
Fax: +(61 6) 261 3514

BAHRAIN
Directorate of Foreign Trade Relations
Ministry of Commerce
P.O. Box 5479
Manama
Tel: (+973) 531 063
Fax: (+973) 536 145

BRAZIL
Ministério das Ralações Exteriores
Bloco H, Anexo I, Sala 508
70 170-900 Brasília DF
Tel: +(55 61) 211 6374, +(55 61) 211 6375,
        +(55 61) 211 6376, +(5561) 211 6377
Fax: +(55 61) 223 7362

BRUNEI DARUSSALAM*
International Relations and Trade and Development
Division
Ministry of Industry and Primary Resources
Bandar Seri Begawan 1220
Tel: (+673 2) 382 822, (+673 2) 382 850
Fax: (+673 2) 382 846, (+673 2) 383 811

CANADA*
Services Trade Policy Division
Department of Foreign Affairs and International Trade
125 Sussex Drive
Ottawa, Ontario
K1A OG2
Tel: +(1 613) 944 2046
Fax: +(1 613) 944 0058

CHILE
Departamento de Servicios e Inversiones
Dirección General de Relaciones Económicas
Internacionales
Avenida Libertador Bernardo O'Higgins 1325

2° piso
Santiago
Tel: +(56 2) 696 0043
Fax: +(56 2) 696 0639

COLOMBIA
Ministerio de Comercio Exterior
Dirección de Negociaciones
Calle 28, Número 13 A 15, Piso 6
Santafé de Bogotá, D.C.
Tel: +(571) 336 2495
Fax: +(571) 336 2482

CUBA
Ministerio de Justicia
Calle O No. 216 entre 23 y 25, Vedado
Código Postal 10400
La Habana
Tel: +(53 7) 324 536, +(53 7) 322 931
Fax: +(53 7) 333 088

CZECH REPUBLIC*
Ministry of Industry and Trade
Department of International Trade Organizations
Politických vezn 20
Praha 1
Tel: +(420 2) 2406 2569
Fax: +(420 2) 2422 1560

DOMINICAN REPUBLIC
Secretariado Técnico de la Presidencia
Ave. México, esq. Dr. Delgado (Palacio Nacional)
Santo Domingo
Tel: +(809) 685 7701, +(809) 682 5430
Fax: +(809) 686 7040

EGYPT
The Department of International Economic Organizations
Trade Representation Department (TAMSEEL)
Ministry of Trade and Supply
Cairo
Tel: (+20 2) 346 8830, 347 1890
Fax: (+20 2) 344 4398, 345 1840

ECUADOR
Subsecretaría Económica
Ministerio de Relaciones Exteriores
Avenida 10-de-Agosto y Carrión

---

a/ Unless otherwise stated, the addresses given are enquiry points. An asterisk (*) indicates that the address given is both
    an enquiry and a contact point.

Quito
Tel: +(593 2) 561 032
Fax: +(593 2) 569 805

EL SALVADOR
Ministerio de Economía
Dirección de Política Comercial
Edificio C-2, Tercera Planta Centro de Gobierno
Plan Maestro
Calle Guadalupe y Alameda Juan Pablo II
San Salvador, C.A.
Tel/Fax: +(503) 221 4771

EUROPEAN COMMUNITIES*

EUROPEAN COMMISSION*
DGI - External Relations
Services and External Dimension of the Union
Unit I/M/1
Rue de la Loi 200
1049 Brussels, Belgium
Tel: +(32 2) 296 5649
Fax: + (32 2) 299 2435

AUSTRIA*
Federal Ministry for Economic Affairs
Directorate II/11a
Stubenring 1
1011 Vienna
Tel: +(43 1) 711 00 (ext. 6915/5516)
Fax: +(43 1) 718 0508, +(43 1) 715 9651
Telex: 111145 regeb a

BELGIUM*
Ministère des affaires économiques
Administration des relations économiques
Rue du Cornet 43
1040 Bruxelles
Tel: +(32 2) 206 5811
Fax: +(32 2) 230 0050

DENMARK*
Ministry of Foreign Affairs
The North Group N.4
Asiatisk Plads 2
1448 Copenhagen K
Tel: +(45) 3392 0000
Fax: +(45) 3392 0433

FINLAND*
Ministry for Foreign Affairs
Department for External Economic Relations
Unit for International Economic Organisations
P.O. Box 176
00161 Helsinki
Tel: +(358 9) 1341 5531
Fax: +(358 9) 1341 5599

FRANCE*
Ministère de l'économie et des finances
Direction des relations économiques extérieures
Sous Direction des affaires multilatérales
Bureau des échanges internationaux de services
139 rue de Bercy
75772 Paris Cedex 12
Tel: +(33 1) 5318 8252
Fax: +(33 1) 5318 9655

GERMANY*
Federal Office for Foreign Trade Information - BFAI

Scharnhorststr. 36
10115 Berlin
Tel: +(49 30) 2014 5200
Fax: +(49 30) 2014 5204

GREECE*
Ministry of National Economy
General Secretariat for International Economic
Relations
General Directorate for External Economic and
Commercial Relations
Directorate for External Trade Policy
1 Kornarou Street
10563 Athens
Tel: +(30 1) 328 6308
Fax: +(30 1) 328 6179

IRELAND*
Department of Tourism and Trade
WTO Section
Kildare Street
Dublin 2
Tel: +(353 1) 662 1444
Fax: +(353 1) 676 6154

ITALY*
Ministero degli Affari Esteri
Dirizione Generale degli Affari Economici
Piazzale della Farnesina 1
000194 Rome
Tel: +(39 6) 3691 3874
Fax: +(39 6) 3691 5280
E-mail: Econ.Quinto@agora.stm.it

LUXEMBOURG*
Ministère des affaires étrangères
Direction des relations économiques internationales et
de la coopération
2911 Luxembourg
Tel: +(352) 478 2355
Fax: +(352) 22 2048

NETHERLANDS*
Ministry of Economic Affairs
Directorate-General for Foreign Economic Relations
Trade and Investment Policy Department (ALP: B227)
P.O. Box 20101
2500 EC Den Haag
Tel: +(31 70) 379 6331, +(31 70) 379 6250
Fax: +(31 70) 379 7221
E-mail: M.F.T.RiemslagBaas@MinEZ.nl

PORTUGAL
Enquiry point:
Ministry of Foreign Affairs
General Directorate for Community Affairs
R Cova da Moura 1
1300 Lisbon
Tel: +(351 1) 395 4588, +(351 1) 395 4589
Fax: +(351 1) 395 4540

Contact point:
Ministry of Economy
ICEP - Investment, Trade and Tourism of Portugal
Av. 5 de Outubro 101
1050 Lisbon
Tel: +(351 1) 793 0103
Fax: +(351 1) 795 2329

SPAIN*
Ministerio de Economía y Hacienda
Secretaria de Estado de Comercio, Turismo y de la
Pequeña y Mediana Empresa
Dirección General de Comercio Exterior
Subdirección General de Comercio Internacional de
Servicios
Paseo de la Castellana 162, 5a Planta
28046 Madrid
Tel: +(34 1) 349 3781
Fax: +(34 1) 349 5226

SWEDEN*
Kommerskollegium (National Board of Trade)
First Division
Första Utrikeshandelsbyrán
Box 6803
S-113 86 Stockholm
Tel: +(46 8) 690 4800
Fax: +(46 8) 306 759

UNITED KINGDOM*
Department of Trade and Industry
Trade Policy and Europe Directorate 2
Room 347
Kingsgate House
66-74 Victoria Street
London SW1E 6SW
Tel: +(44 171) 215 4248
Fax: +(44 171) 215 4252

GHANA
The Director (Multilaterals)
Ministry of Trade and Industry
P.O. Box M.47
Accra
Tel: +(233 21) 667 382
Fax: +(233 21) 662 428
E-mail: moti@ighmail.com

GUATEMALA
Ministerio de Economía
Dirección de Negociaciones Comerciales Internacionales
8a Av. 10-43 Zona 1
3° Piso
Guatemala C.A.
Tel: (502) 238 3331 ext. 3301
Fax: (502) 238 3331 3xt. 3375

HAITI
Directeur du commerce extérieur
Ministère du commerce et de l'industrie
Champ-de-Mars
Port-au-Prince (W.I.)
Tél: (509) 228 167
Fax: (509) 238 402, 235 950

HONG KONG
The Assistant Director General
Multilateral Division
Trade Department
Hong Kong Government
Trade Department Tower
Nathan Road 700
Kowloon
Fax: +(852) 2789 2491

HONDURAS
Secretaria de Economía y Comercio
Dirección General de Política Comercial

Edificio Salamé 3° piso
Calle Peatonal
Tegucigalpa
Tel: +(504) 226 055, +(504) 221 819
Fax: +(504) 381 336

HUNGARY
Ministry of Industry and Trade
Department of International Organisations and Tariff
Policy
Honvéd. u. 13-15
1880 - Budapest
Tel/Fax: +(36 1) 331 2167

ICELAND
Ministry for Foreign Affairs
External Trade Department
Raudararstig 25
150 - Reykjavík
Tel: +(354) 560 9930
Fax: +(354) 562 4878

INDIA
Trade Policy Division
Ministry of Commerce
Udyog Bhawan
New Delhi 110011
Tel: +(91 11) 301 3691, +(91 11) 301 6461
Fax: +(91 11) 301 4418, +(91 11) 301 3583

ISRAEL*
Ministry of Finance
The International Division
P.O. Box 13195
Jerusalem 91131
Tel: +(972 2) 670 5296
Fax: +(972 2) 651 3207

Ministry of Industry and Trade
Foreign Trade Administration
30 Agrron Street
Jerusalem 94190
Tel: +(972 2) 622 0289
Fax: +(972 2) 624 3005

JAMAICA
The Director
International Trade and Negotiations Division
Planning Institute of Jamaica
8 Ocean Boulevard
Kingston Mall
Tel: (1876) 967 3690-2
Fax: (1876) 967 4871, (1876) 967 3688

JAPAN
Ministry of Foreign Affairs
Services Trade Division
Kasumigaseki 2-2-1, Chiyoda-ku
Tokyo
Tel: +(81 3) 3580 3311 ext. 2751 or 2752
Fax: +(81 3) 3592 6296

Ministry of Foreign Affairs
Services Trade Division
Kasumigaseki 2-2-1
Chiyoda-ku
Tokyo
Tel: +(81 3) 3580 3311 ext. 2751 or 2752
Fax: +(81 3) 3592 6296

KENYA*
Services:
Department of External Trade
P.O Box 43137
Nairobi
Tel: +(254 2) 333 555
Fax: +(254 2) 226 036

Movement of natural persons:
(a) Ministry of Labour & Manpower Development
Social Security House
P.O. Box 40326
Nairobi
Tel: +(254 2) 729 700, +(254 2) 729 800
Fax: +(254 2) 726 497

(b) Immigration Department
Office of the President
Nyayo House
P.O. Box 90284
Nairobi
Tel: +(254 2) 333 551
Fax: +(254 2) 220 731

Air transport services:
Ministry of Transport & Communication
P.O. Box 52692
Nairobi
Tel: +(254 2) 729 200
Fax: +(254 2) 726 362

Financial services:
Ministry of Finance
Treasury Building
P.O. Box 30007
Nairobi
Tel: +(254 2) 338 111
Fax: +(254 2) 330 426

LIECHTENSTEIN
Office for Foreign Affairs
Heiligkreuz 14
9490 Vaduz
Tel: +(41 75) 236 6057
Fax: +(41 75) 236 6059

MADAGASCAR
Ministère chargé du commerce
B.P. 454
Antananarivo 101
Tel: +(261 2) 261 40, +(261 2) 207 58
Fax: +(261 2) 264 26, +(261 2) 312 80

MALDIVES
Ministry of Trade and Industries
Government of Maldives
Ghaazee Building
Ameeru Ahmed Magu
Male 20-05
Tel: (960) 323 668, (960) 325 205
Fax: (960) 323 840
E-mail: trademin@dhivehnet.net.mv

MEXICO
Secretaría de Comercio y Fomento Industrial
Dirección General de Negociaciones de
Servicios y Coordinación con Europa
(Ministry of Trade and Industrial Development
Directorate General for Negotiations on Services and
Coordination with Europe)

Alfonso Reyes 30, Colonia Condesa
06140 Mexico DF
Tel: + (52 5) 729 9140, + (52 5) 729 9141
Fax: + (52 5) 729 9381

MOROCCO
Ministère du commerce extérieur
Boulevard Moulay Youssef
10000 Rabat
Tel: + (212 7) 751 532
Fax: + (212 7) 735 023

NEW ZEALAND
The Trade Negotiations Division
Ministry of Foreign Affairs and Trade
Private Bag 18-901
Wellington
Tel: +(64 4) 494 8500
Fax: +(64 4) 472 9596

NORWAY
Royal Ministry of Foreign Affairs
Department of External Economic Affairs
Section IV (Services, investment)
PO Box 8114 Dep
0032 - Oslo
Tel: +(47) 2224 3907, +(47) 2224 3921,
        +(47) 2224 3600
Fax: +(47) 2224 3600

PAKISTAN
Assistant Chief
ITO Wing
Ministry of Commerce
State Life Building No 5, 7th Floor
Blue Area
Islamabad

PANAMA
Ministerio de Comercio e Industrias
Viceministerio de Comercio Exterior
Dirección Nacional de Servicios al Comercio Exterior
Apartado postal 552359
Paitilla
Tel: +(507) 236 0122, 236 0347
Fax: +(507) 236 0495
E-mail: secomex@mici.gob.pa

PARAGUAY*
Ministerio de Industria y Comercio
Subsecretaría de Estado de Comercio
Avenida España 323 c/EE.UU
Asunción
Tel/Fax: +(59 521) 227 140
E-mail: ssccmic@oka.net.py

PERU
Dirección de Relaciones Económicas Internacionales
Ministerio de Relaciones Exteriores
Jirón Lampa No. 535
Lima
Fax: +(51 1) 426 0128

PHILIPPINES
National Economic Development Authority (NEDA)
NEDA sa Pasig
Amber Avenue, Pasay City
1600 Metro Manila

POLAND*
Ministry of Economy
Trade and Services Department
GATS Enquiry Point
Plac Trzech Krzyzy 3/5
00-507 Warsaw
Tel: (48 22) 693 5148, (48 22) 621 8828
Fax: (48 22) 693 5096

QATAR
Department of Commerce
Ministry of Finance, Economy and Commerce
P.O. Box
22355 Doha
Tel: (0974) 432 103
Fax: (0974) 431 412

REPUBLIC OF KOREA*
World Trade Organization Team
Ministry of Foreign Affairs and Trade
Government Complex Sejongro
Seoul
Tel: +(82 2) 720 2188, +(82 2) 739 9142
Fax: +(82 2) 738 9726
E-mail: wto@mofat.go kr

ROMANIA
Directorate for Multilateral Relations
Ministry of Industry and Commerce
17, Apolodor Street
Bucharest 7000
Tel: (401) 411 1190, 410 2186
Fax: (410) 411 2342

SINGAPORE
Singapore Trade Development Board
230 Victoria Street # 09-00
Bugis Junction Office Tower
Singapore 188024
Tel: +(65) 337 6628
Fax: +(65) 337 6898

SLOVAK REPUBLIC*
Ministry of Economy
Trade Policy Division
Department of International Organizations
Mierová 19
82715 - Bratislava
Tel: +(42 7) 574 2515
Fax: +(42 7) 574 3579

SLOVENIA
Ministry of Economic Relations and Development
State Secretary for Trade Policy
Kotnikova 5
1000 Ljubljana
Tel: +(386 61) 178 3542
Fax: +(386 61) 178 3611

SOUTH AFRICA
The Director
Foreign Trade Relations
Department of Trade and Industry
Private Bag X84
Pretoria 0001
Tel: +(2712) 310 9413, +(2712) 310 9380
Fax: +(2712) 320 7905

SRI LANKA
Director of Commerce

Department of Commerce
4th Floor, Rakshana Mandiraya
Vauxall Street 21
Colombo 2
Tel: +(94 1) 329 733, +(94 1) 430 068
Fax: +(94 1) 430 233
Telex: 21908 Commerce

SURINAME
Mrs. M. Tilborg
Ministry of Finance/Economic Affairs Department
Section of International Economic Affairs
Gravenstraat
Paramaribo
Tel: (597) 471 069, (597) 475 614
Fax: (597) 476 314, (597) 476 309

SWITZERLAND*
Federal Office for Foreign Economics Affairs
3003 Berne
Tel: +(41 31) 324 0867
Fax: +(41 31) 324 0967

THAILAND*
Division of Trade in Services
Department of Business Economics
Ministry of Commerce
Ratchadamnoen Klang Road
Bangkok 10200
Tel: +(66 2) 282 6171, +(66 2) 282 6172,
          +(66 2) 282 6173, +(66 2) 282 6174,
          +(66 2) 282 6175, +(66 2) 282 6176,
          +(66 2) 282 6177, +(66 2) 282 6178,
          +(66 2) 282 6179
Fax: +(66 2) 629 1792, +(66 2) 280 0775,
          +(66 2) 280 0826
Telex: 84361 DEPBUSE TH

TRINIDAD AND TOBAGO
Mr Bernard Sylvester
Ministry of Trade and Industry
Level 12, Riverside Plaza
Besson Street
Port of Spain
Tel: (868) 627 0057, (868) 627 1913
Fax: (868) 627 8488
E-mail: mini@trinidad.net

TURKEY
The Under-Secretariat of Treasury
General Directorate of Banking and Exchange
Inönü Bulvari
06510 Emek-Ankara
Fax: +(312) 212 8775

UGANDA
(a) National enquiry point
The Ministry of Trade and Industry
Directorate of Foreign Trade
Farmers House, Parliament Avenue
P.O. Box 7103
Kampala
Tel: (256 41) 254 091 / 2, (256 41) 230 933
Fax: (256 41) 252 578

(b) Sectoral enquiry points
Labour
The Ministry of Labour and Social Services
17/19 Hannington Road
Crested Towers Building

P.O. Box 5261
Kampala
Tel: (256 41) 258 334

Financial and banking services
The Bank of Uganda
Research Department
P.O. Box 7120
Kampala
Tel: (256 41) 259 866
Fax: (256 41) 230 878

Transport services
The Ministry of Transport and Communications
Airport Road
P.O. Box 10
Entebbe
Tel: (256 42) 201 01 / 9
Fax: (256 42) 201 35

Tourism
The Uganda Tourist Board
IPS Building, Parliament Avenue
P.O. Box 7211
Kampala
Tel: (256 41) 342 196 / 7
Fax: (256 41) 342 188

Telecommunications
The Uganda Post & Telecommunications Corporation
P.O. Box 7171
Kampala
Tel: (256 41) 256 151
Fax: (256 41) 345 505
E-mail: uptccp@imul.com

Energy
The Ministry of Natural Resources
Amber House
29/53 Kampala Road
P.O. Box 7172
Kampala
Tel: (256 41) 230 243, (256 41) 254 732

Insurance
The National Insurance Corporation
NIC Building
Pilkinton Road
P.O. Box 7134
Kampala
Tel: (256 41) 258 001/ 3
Fax: (256 41) 259 925

UNITED ARAB EMIRATES
WTO Division
Ministry of Economy and Commerce
P.O. Box 901
Abu Dhabi
Tel: (+971 2) 265 000
Fax: (+971 2) 260 000
E-mail: economy@emirates.net.ae

UNITED STATES OF AMERICA*
Chair, Trade Policy Sub-Committee on Services
Office of the United States Trade Representative
Washington, D.C. 20508
Tel: +(1 202) 395 7271
Fax: +(1 202) 395 3891

URUGUAY*
Ministerio de Relaciones Exteriores
Dirrección General para Asuntos Económicos Internacionales
Colonia 1206
Montevideo
Tel: +(598 2) 920 618
Fax: +(598 2) 917 413

VENEZUELA
Instituto de Comercio Exterior
Dirección General de Negociaciones Comerciales
Internacionales
Dirección para Asuntos de la OMC
División sobre Comercio de Servicios
Avenida Libertador
Centro Comercial "Los Cedros", Piso 5
Caracas 1050
Tel: +(58 2) 731 1676, +(58 2) 731 1955,
           +(58 2) 761 0419, +(58 2) 761 6555
Fax: +(58 2) 762 2961

ZAMBIA
The Chief Economist
(Commerce & Trade)
Ministry of Commerce
Trade and Industry
P.O. Box 31968
Lusaka
Tel: +(260) 122 1475, 122 6673
Fax: +(260) 122 3273
E-mail: comtrade@zamnet.zm

PART FOUR

Government procurement and State trading

CHAPTER 18

Government procurement

Summary

The rules of GATT specifically exempt purchases made by governments and the agencies controlled by them from the national treatment rule. Government agencies importing their requirements are also not obliged to extend MFN treatment to external suppliers of such products but only to give them fair and equitable treatment. These provisions permit purchasing agencies to buy their requirements, if they so wish, from domestic producers, even though products of comparable quality are offered for sale by foreign suppliers at lower prices.

The Agreement on Government Procurement, which was extensively revised in the Uruguay Round, requires its member countries to accord national and MFN treatment to government purchases. The obligation to extend such treatment applies to purchases made by the government agencies listed by each member country in the annexes to the Agreement. These annexes form an integral part of the Agreement. The Agreement further requires the listed agencies to make their purchases by inviting tenders, in which foreign suppliers should have a fair and equitable opportunity to participate.

The new Agreement on Government Procurement is, however, plurilateral and, unlike the multilateral Agreements described in the preceding chapters of this Guide, WTO member countries are not obliged to join it. The Agreement's current members are predominantly developed countries. Only three developing countries/areas – Hong Kong (China), the Republic of Korea and Singapore – have so far acceded to it. Developing countries that are not members are not bound by the obligation it imposes to extend MFN and national treatment to foreign products and suppliers.

It is important to note, that in order to prepare developing countries to accede to the Agreement, work is currently being carried out to develop an interim agreement on transparency in government procurement. The agreement, which will be multilateral in character, will not impose obligations on member countries to extend MFN and national treatment. It will only carry procedural provisions leading to improved transparency in the methods adopted by government purchasing agencies for procuring goods. (See chapter 11.)

In almost all countries, governments and the agencies controlled by them are significant buyers of goods and services. Such purchases often represent 10% to 15% of a country's gross national product. The international trade in government-purchased products and services is steadily on the increase and currently amounts to several billion dollars annually.

Historical background to the evolution of rules

The international rules governing this trade are evolving. When GATT 1947 was being negotiated, almost all countries required their government departments and agencies to accord price preferences to domestic producers and to buy foreign goods only if the domestic prices were higher (by, say, 10% to 15%) than the prices of imported products. In addition, where goods were imported, purchasing agencies were often obliged to buy from suppliers in countries with which their governments had close trade relations or political ties.

The practice of giving price preferences was not consistent with the national treatment principle which, as has been noted, does not permit imported products to be treated less favourably than products of domestic origin. Likewise, obliging purchasing agencies to obtain their imports only from a limited number of designated countries was not in conformity with the principle of non-discrimination embodied in the MFN rule.

GATT 1994, Article III:8(a)

As countries were not prepared at that time to change these practices, the GATT rules specifically exclude procurement by government agencies of goods for their own use and not intended for commercial sale from the application of the national treatment rule. The rules also do not require countries to extend MFN treatment to sources of products imported by government agencies for their own use. They are merely asked to extend fair and equitable treatment to such suppliers.

GATT 1994, Article XVII:2

Agreement on Government Procurement

Policies which require government purchasing agencies to buy locally, even though foreign goods are available at lower prices, increase government expenditure and add to the burden on tax payers. These considerations, among others, led GATT member countries to negotiate in the Tokyo Round an Agreement on Government Procurement. This Agreement, which applied only to goods, was extensively revised and broadened to cover purchases by governments of services during the parallel negotiations that took place during the Uruguay Round.

Aim

Agreement on Government Procurement, Preamble

The main aim of the Agreement on Government Procurement is to require governments to apply commercial considerations when procuring goods and services for their own use by not discriminating between domestic and foreign supplies and thus to utilize tax revenues and other public funds more effectively. It is, however, a plurilateral agreement and, unlike the multilateral Agreements discussed earlier, does not oblige WTO members to accede to it. Its current membership is dominated by developed countries, with only three developing countries/areas – Hong Kong (China), the Republic of Korea and Singapore – on the roster.

Coverage

Agreement on Government Procurement, Article I and Appendix I

The obligations which the Agreement imposes apply only to purchases made by the procurement entities that have been listed by each member country in its annexes. These annexes are an integral part of the Agreement. The entities listed include:

❑ Ministries, departments and other central government offices;

❑ Sub-central organizations such as municipalities, corporations and other local bodies;

❑ In the case of federal States, government departments and agencies at provincial and State level;

❑ Public utilities supplying electricity and drinking water, and running airports, ports and urban transport.

It is open to member countries to specify in the annexes the products and services to be covered by the Agreement. In regard to goods, member countries have broadly indicated that the Agreement will apply to all purchases by the listed entities. The only exceptions are purchases by departments of defence of defence requirements; purchases made by such departments of non-defence requirements are, however, covered.

While the Agreement therefore applies to almost all contracts awarded by the government agencies concerned for the procurement of goods, only a beginning has been made in relation to purchases of services. All member countries have included construction services in the Agreement's coverage. Thus this service segment, on which governments spend a high proportion of their budgetary resources, has come under the Agreement's discipline. As regards other services, the rules of the Agreement apply only to those specified in each member country's annex. Among these are:

❑ Management consultancy and related services;
❑ Market research services;
❑ Computer and related services;
❑ Accounting and auditing services;
❑ Advertising services;
❑ Building cleaning services; and
❑ Publishing and printing services.

Substantive provisions

Agreement on Government
Procurement, Article III

The Agreement's most important obligation requires purchasing entities to extend to imported products, services and suppliers national and MFN treatment. The first prevents them from giving price or other preferences to domestic suppliers; the second prohibits them from discriminating among outside supplying countries.

Operational provisions

Agreement on Government
Procurement, Articles VII
to XVI

In order to ensure the implementation of these substantive obligations and to provide fair and equitable opportunities for trade to interested domestic and foreign suppliers, the Agreement lays down a number of procedural rules. In particular, it requires entities making purchases above specified threshold limits:

❑ To do so only by inviting tenders;

❑ To ensure that foreign suppliers have a fair and equitable opportunity to participate in the tendering process; and

❑ To award the contract to the tenderer who has been determined to be fully capable of undertaking the contract and whose tender "is either the lowest tender or which in terms of the specific evaluation criteria set forth in the notice is determined to be most advantageous".

Box 44 explains the various methods that can be used in inviting tenders and the conditions for their use.

> ## Box 44
> ### *Rules on government tendering procedures*
>
> *The Agreement requires that, in order to provide fair and equal commercial opportunities to domestic and foreign suppliers and at the same time ensure efficient and expedient procurement, government purchasing entities should make their purchases by inviting tenders. These entities have an option to use one of the following three methods:*
>
> ❑ *Open tenders, under which all interested suppliers may submit a tender;*
>
> ❑ *Selective tendering procedures, under which only suppliers who have been identified as having the necessary qualifications are invited to tender; and*
>
> ❑ *Limited tendering procedures, under which in certain special circumstances purchases are made through direct negotiations with identified suppliers.*
>
> *For tenders under selective procedures, enterprises generally maintain a list of qualified suppliers. The Agreement stipulates that in qualifying suppliers, the purchasing entities:*
>
> ❑ *Should not discriminate between foreign and domestic suppliers;*
>
> ❑ *Should impose only such conditions in regard to technical qualifications, financial guarantees, and establishing the commercial capability of suppliers as are necessary to ensure the firm's competence to fulfil the contract; and*
>
> ❑ *Should allow suppliers to apply at any time for qualification.*
>
> *The Agreement provides that limited tendering systems should be used only in special situations such as:*
>
> ❑ *When no tenders are received in response to an open and selective tender;*
>
> ❑ *When the tenders submitted have been collusive;*
>
> ❑ *When additional deliveries of replacement parts are required from a supplier whose tender has been accepted.*
>
> *Further, in order to ensure adequate transparency in the invitations to tender, the Agreement requires member countries to notify WTO of the list of publications in which invitations to tender are publicized.*

Greater public scrutiny of award decisions

Agreement on Government Procurement, Article XVIII

In the area of government procurement, it is not uncommon to hear complaints that contracts involving huge amounts have been awarded to a tenderer with the right political connections. Allegations are also often heard that contracts have been awarded to domestic or foreign firms that have made clandestine payments to the persons responsible for making award decisions. The Agreement visualizes bringing such malpractices under control by providing for greater public scrutiny of decisions to award contracts. It therefore requires purchasing entities to publish:

❑ A post-award notice stating the nature and quantity of the product or services covered by the contract;

❑ The name and address of the winning tenderer;

❑ The value of the winning award; and

❑ The highest or lowest offer that was taken into account in the award of the contract.

In addition, if an unsuccessful bidder requests it, the purchasing entity is required to give the bidder its reasons for both the rejection and the selection.

Challenge procedures

Agreement on Government Procurement, Article XX

The Agreement also calls on its member countries to establish at the national level an independent review body to hear challenges or complaints and requests for redress from domestic or foreign suppliers against a purchasing entity which in their view has not adhered to the rules of the Agreement in awarding a contract. The procedure for investigating such challenges should, *inter alia*, provide for:

❑ Interim measures to correct breaches of the Agreement's rules, including measures which may result in the suspension of the procurement process, or

❑ Payment of compensation to the challenging tenderer, which may be limited to the costs of preparing the tender or the challenge.

In addition, when the government of the country where the foreign supplier is situated is satisfied that the rules of the Agreement have not been followed by the entity in awarding the contract, it can invoke WTO dispute settlement procedures.

Special provisions for developing countries

Agreement on Government Procurement, Article V

As noted earlier, only three developing countries/areas have so far acceded to the Agreement. The reasons for the reluctance of developing countries to join the Agreement can generally be attributed to the apprehension that, on becoming a member, they will have to change their existing policies. These policies currently require their purchasing agencies to buy locally whenever possible and, when they are allowed to invite tenders from foreign suppliers, to give price preferences to domestic producers. Further, in order to promote the development of SMEs, domestic rules often oblige purchasing agencies to prefer SME products to those of large firms.

However, the Agreement does provide for special and differential treatment. This permits developing countries to negotiate for accession without being obliged to bring all their practices in conformity with the Agreement immediately on joining. They can stipulate, for instance, that the discipline of the Agreement should apply only to a specified number of purchasing agencies.

Agreement on Government Procurement, Article V:5

Furthermore, they can negotiate for "exclusions from the rules on national treatment" certain products or services for which they wish to continue to extend price preferences to domestic producers by buying from them even though the prices quoted by foreign suppliers are lower.

Agreement on Government Procurement, Article V:12 - 13

The Agreement has specific provisions on special treatment to be accorded to least developed countries with respect to products or services originating from them. It imposes an obligation on developed countries to provide assistance, on request, to potential tenderers in these countries in submitting tenders, and in complying with technical regulations and standards relating to products or services subject to an intended procurement.

Agreement on Government Procurement, Article V:11

Furthermore, to enable suppliers in developing countries that have become members of the Agreement to benefit fully from the opening of the government procurement market, each developed country is required to establish information centres from which information can be obtained on:

❑ Laws, regulations and practices relating to government procurement;
❑ Addresses of entities covered by the Agreement;
❑ Nature and volume of products or services procured, including available information on future tenders.

From the strictly legal point of view, requests for such information can be made only by members of the Agreement. In practice however most, if not all, of these information centres may be willing to provide information to developing country members of WTO even though they may not have acceded to the Agreement itself. The Agreement further visualizes the establishment at an appropriate time in the future of an international information centre. As such a centre will provide information and assistance to interested suppliers in developing countries, the chances of its being set up will depend greatly on how many developing countries accede to the Agreement in the near future.

Negotiations for improvements in the Agreement

Agreement on Government Procurement, Article XXIV:7

The Agreement calls on member countries to undertake further negotiations, within a period of three years from its entry into force (1 January 1996) and periodically thereafter, to improve the Agreement. In pursuance of these provisions, the Committee on Government Procurement initiated in February 1997 negotiations covering following elements:

❑ Simplification and improvement of the Agreement, including, where appropriate, adaptation to advances in information technology;

❑ Elimination of discriminatory measures and practices that distort open procurement;

❑ Expansion of the product coverage of the Agreement; and

❑ Broadening membership of the Agreement.

The participating countries are planning on completing the negotiations at least on the first item (simplification and improvement of the Agreement) in 1999, well in advance of the Third Ministerial Conference.

Interim agreement on government procurement

As noted earlier, only three developing countries/areas have become members of the Agreement. One reason for this is the developing countries' apprehension that the Agreement's imposition of the MFN and national treatment principles will require them to do away with their existing practices, under which domestic suppliers benefit from price preferences. In order to encourage developing countries to prepare themselves for acceding to the Agreement, the 1996 Singapore Ministerial Conference decided to establish a Working Group on Transparency in Government Procurement to examine the desirability of negotiating in WTO an interim agreement on transparency in government procurement. The interim agreement, unlike the Agreement on Government Procurement, is to be a multilateral agreement binding on all member countries. It will, however, not impose substantive obligations for the extension of MFN and national treatment but will set out such procedural provisions as will result in greater transparency in the methods used by government purchasing agencies in procuring goods. Chapter 24 presents an overview of the discussions that are currently taking place in the Working Group.

Work on government procurement under the provisions of GATS

GATS, Article XIII:2

Article XIII:2 of GATS calls for multilateral negotiations on government procurement in services within two years from the date of entry into force of the WTO Agreement. In pursuance of this provision, a Working Party on GATS

Rules has been established by the Council for Trade in Services to undertake preparatory work for negotiations in the area of government procurement. (The Working Party is also responsible for the development of rules on emergency safeguard measures and subsidies.)

Business implications

A number of products purchased by government agencies in developed countries can be supplied by enterprises in developing countries. An indicative list of such products is given in box 45.

At present, suppliers from developing countries are not able to put in bids as they have no access to notices of tenders from purchasing agencies in developed countries. The adoption of electronic systems by purchasing agencies for the issue of tenders will make this information available on the Internet. This will greatly improve the access of business enterprises, particularly in developing countries that have been able to develop Internet facilities, to the government procurement market in other countries. There is also vast potential for regional trade development in the procurement sector among developing countries.

Box 45

Products purchased by government agencies that can be supplied by enterprises in developing countries

Textiles and clothing
Footwear
Office machines and data-processing equipment
Office furniture
Telecommunications equipment
Pharmaceuticals
Medical equipment
Food and food products
Sanitary, heating and lighting fittings
Motor vehicles
Electrical machinery
Paper, printing and publishing products
Rubber and plastic products
Cleaning materials and equipment

CHAPTER 19

State trading

Summary

The GATT rules impose two main obligations on member countries in regard to State trading enterprises. First, they require these enterprises to conduct their business on the basis of commercial considerations. Second, in order to ensure transparency in the products imported and exported by such enterprises, they require member countries to notify the WTO Secretariat on their activities.

Understanding on the Interpretation of Article XVII of GATT 1994, §1

Although with the increasing trend towards privatization, countries are reducing their reliance on State trading, it still continues to play an important role in at least some countries in the import and export of certain goods, particularly food and food products, and commodities traded in bulk. State trading enterprises are broadly defined as:

> Governmental and non-governmental enterprises, including marketing boards, which have been granted exclusive or special rights or privileges, including statutory or constitutional powers, in the exercise of which they influence through their purchases or sales the level or direction of imports or exports.

State trading needs to be distinguished from government procurement, which is discussed in the preceding chapter (chapter 18). Under government procurement, the domestically produced or imported product is purchased by a government agency for its own use or consumption or for the production of goods or services for sale. In the case of State trading, imports are obtained primarily for sale in the home market and domestic products are purchased for sale in the home market and for export to foreign markets.

The GATT rules on State trading basically apply to State trading enterprises engaged in the import and export of goods.

Main obligations

To conduct business in accordance with commercial considerations

GATT 1994, Article XVII:1

The basic obligation GATT imposes on State trading enterprises is to "act in a manner consistent with the general principles of non-discriminatory treatment". It states that, in practice, this can be achieved by:

❑ Making "purchases or sales solely in accordance with commercial considerations, including price, quality, availability and marketability, transportation and other conditions of purchase or sale"; and

❑ By providing enterprises in other countries an adequate opportunity "compete for participation in such purchases and sales."

Transparency

The other major obligation under the Agreement is transparency. The notification obligations that the GATT imposes for this purpose have been further strengthened by the adoption of the Understanding on the Interpretation of Article XVII of GATT 1994 (State trading) in the Uruguay Round. The Understanding requires member countries to notify the Council for Trade in Goods of:

❑ State enterprises engaged in foreign trade;

❑ The products imported or exported by them; and

❑ Other information (given in response to a questionnaire) so as to permit a clear appreciation of the manner in which the enterprises conduct their trade.

Understanding on Article XVII, §4

It is also open to a country to make a counter-notification to the Council for Trade in Goods when it considers that a State trading enterprise in another country has not met its notification obligation with respect to its State trading activities.

Understanding on Article XVII, §5

The responsibility for reviewing the notification and counter-notifications made by member countries rests with the Working Party on State Trading Enterprises which has been established in accordance with the provisions of the Understanding. In 1997 and 1998, the Working Party revised the questionnaire on State trading which is used by member countries to discharge their notification obligation and made considerable progress in the development of an illustrative list of the activities of State trading enterprises and the types of relationship that exist between these enterprises and their governments. The revised questionnaire has been approved by the Council for Trade in Goods and will provide a basis for the provision of information by member countries on their State trading practices.

Business implications

The information on products imported and exported by State trading organizations and on the practices they follow in making purchase decisions is expected to help private-sector business firms in entering into commercial transactions with these organizations.

Trade-related aspects of intellectual property rights

Agreement on Trade-Related Aspects of Intellectual Property Rights

Summary

The development of international trade can be adversely affected if the standards adopted by countries to protect intellectual property rights (IPRs) vary widely from country to country. Furthermore, the lax or ineffective enforcement of such rights can encourage trade in counterfeit and pirated goods, thereby damaging the legitimate commercial interests of manufacturers who hold or have acquired those rights. The Agreement on Trade-Related Aspects of Intellectual Property Rights (TRIPS), negotiated in the Uruguay Round, therefore lays down minimum standards for the protection of intellectual property rights as well as the procedures and remedies for their enforcement. It establishes a mechanism for consultations and surveillance at the international level to ensure compliance with these standards by member countries at the national level.

The structure of the Agreement is built on the existing international conventions dealing with IPRs. Its provisions apply to the following intellectual property rights:

❑ Patents;
❑ Copyright and related rights;
❑ Trademarks;
❑ Industrial designs;
❑ Layout-designs of integrated circuits;
❑ Undisclosed information; and
❑ Geographical indications.

In order to ensure that holders of intellectual property do not abuse the exclusive rights available to them, these rights are subject to a number of limitations and exceptions. These aim at ensuring a balance between the legitimate interests of right holders and users of intellectual property.

The Agreement also lays down procedures for consultations between governments when one party has reasons to believe that the licensing practices or conditions of an enterprise from another member country constitute an abuse of the Agreement or have adverse effects on competition.

The Agreement provides a transitional period of five years (i.e. up to 1 January 2000) for developing countries to bring their IPR legislation in conformity with the provisions of the Agreement. For least developed countries the transitional period is 11 years (up to 1 January 2006).

The provisions of the Agreement on plant inventions and varieties are currently being reviewed, in accordance with the relevant provisions. The Agreement further provides that all its provisions should be reviewed after a period of five years, i.e. in 2000.

Intellectual property rights and their implications for international trade

The objects of intellectual property are the creations of the human mind, the human intellect, thus the designation 'intellectual property'.

They include copyright, patents and industrial designs. Copyright relates to the rights of creators of literary, scientific and artistic works. Patents give exclusive rights to inventors; however, inventions can be patented only if they are new, non-obvious and are capable of industrial applications. Industrial designs are new or original aesthetic creations determining the appearance of industrial products. These three rights are available for limited durations.

Intellectual property also includes trademarks, service marks and appellations of origin (or geographical indications). In the case of these property rights, the aspect of intellectual creation – although existent – is less prominent. However, protection is granted to trademarks and other signs to enable manufacturers to distinguish their products or services from those of others. Trademarks help manufacturers build consumer loyalty. They also assist consumers in making informed choices on the basis of the information provided by manufacturers on the quality of their products.

Implications of IPRs for trade

Any unauthorized use of intellectual property constitutes an infringement of the right of the owner. Until about two decades ago, such infringements had implications largely for domestic trade. Furthermore, the problems they posed were considered to be mainly at the national level which – apart from affecting the interests of the owners of rights – impinged on scientific progress and cultural life.

In recent years, however, there has been increasing realization that the standards adopted by countries to protect their IPRs as well as the effectiveness with which they are enforced have implications for the development of international trade. There are many reasons for this, of which three are especially worth noting.

First, economic activity in most developed countries is increasingly becoming research- and technology-intensive. As a result, their export products – both traditional (such as chemicals, fertilizers and pharmaceuticals) and comparatively new (telecommunications equipment, computers, software) – now contain more technological and creative inputs that are subject to intellectual property rights. Manufacturers are therefore keen to ensure that wherever they market their products these rights are adequately protected, thus enabling them to recoup their R & D expenditure.

Second, with the removal of restrictions on foreign investment by a large number of developing countries, new opportunities are emerging for the manufacture in these countries of patented products under licence or within joint ventures. The willingness of industries in industrialized countries to enter into such arrangements and to make their technology available, however, depends on how far the IPR system of the host country provides them an assurance that their property rights to technology will be adequately protected and not usurped by local partners making use of reverse engineering.

Third, the technological improvements in products entering international trade have been matched by technological advances that have made reproduction and imitation simple and cheap. In countries where laws on IPRs are not strictly enforced, this has resulted, as box 46 shows, in increased production of counterfeit and pirated goods, not only for sale in domestic markets but also for export.

> **Box 46**
> **Trade in counterfeit and pirated goods**
>
> *Estimates of revenue foregone by industries as a result of counterfeiting, pirating and other infringement of intellectual property rights vary widely, but there is no doubt that the value involved is significant.*
>
> *Goods are treated as counterfeit when they are offered for sale particularly under well-known trademarks which the seller has no authority to use. These are generally labour-intensive products which, because of the reputation of the brand name, can be sold at high prices. They include clothing, shoes, watches, cosmetics, leather goods, and household and sporting goods.*
>
> *Pirated goods are those that infringe copyright and related rights. Book publishers, producers of records, discs, films, tapes and cassettes are often the victims of violation of copyright and related rights. Technological progress has greatly facilitated the art of copying. The computer software industry is the leading victim of the speed with which intellectual property can be illegally copied and distributed on an international scale.*

WIPO conventions on IPRs

Efforts to develop rules providing adequate protection to intellectual property rights at the international level have been made for over a century, mainly under the auspices of the World Intellectual Property Organization (WIPO) and its predecessor organizations. As a result, a number of conventions laying down international obligations to protect the rights of owners of IPRs have been adopted. Box 47 lists these conventions and indicates their coverage and main fields of application.

Background to the Uruguay Round negotiations on IPRs

Proposals that action should be taken in GATT to control the trade in counterfeit and pirated goods were made by developed countries as early as the Tokyo Round of negotiations. When the Uruguay Round was being launched, these countries proposed that the negotiations should not only cover trade in counterfeit goods but also aim at developing minimum standards of protection for adoption by member countries. While developing countries were in general not opposed to the proposals for action on counterfeit goods, they initially resisted discussion on minimum standards. They were apprehensive that such negotiations would require them to change their policies. For development and social reasons, these policies excluded certain products from patentability or provided shorter protection periods than the 20 years for which patent protection was generally granted by developed countries for inventions relating to such products as pharmaceuticals, chemicals, fertilizers, insecticides and pesticides. They were also fearful that the adoption of minimum standards would lead to increased royalty payments for the use of patented technology under licence and thus to higher prices for the products so manufactured.

These views, however, did not prevail and pressures from developed countries ultimately resulted in the negotiations focusing to a greater extent on the establishment of substantive and uniform standards providing a higher level of protection for intellectual property rights. It is important to note in this context that the attitude of both developed and developing countries evolved as the negotiations proceeded. It was thus possible to reach a consensus on the Agreement on TRIPS which, *inter alia*, lays down minimum standards for the protection of all the main categories of intellectual property rights.

Box 47

Intellectual property rights: instruments, subject matter, fields of application and related WIPO and other international agreements

Types of intellectual property rights		Subject matter	Main fields of application	Major international agreements
Types of instrument				
Industrial property	Patents	New, non-obvious, industrially applicable inventions	Manufacturing	Paris Convention; Patent Cooperation Treaty; Budapest Treaty
	Utility models	Functional designs	Manufacturing	Paris Convention
	Industrial designs	Ornamental designs	Clothing, motor cars, electronics, etc.	Hague Agreement; Paris Convention; Locarno Agreement
	Trademarks	Signs or symbols to distinguish the goods and services of one enterprise from those of others	All industries	Paris Convention; Madrid Agreement (international registration); Nice Agreement; Madrid Protocol (not yet in force); Trademark Law Treaty (not yet in force)
	Geographical indications	Identification of the place of origin of goods indicative of the quality or other characteristics associated with the area	Agricultural and food industries, notably the sectors for wine and spirits	Lisbon Agreement; Madrid Agreement (false indications)
Literary and artistic property	Copyrights and neighbouring rights	Original works of authorship and related contributions from performers, producers of sound recordings, and broadcasting organizations	Printing, entertainment (audio, video, motion pictures) software, broadcasting	Berne Convention; Rome Convention; Geneva Convention; Brussels Convention; Universal Copyright Convention
Sui generis protection	Breeders' rights	New, stable, homogenous, distinctive varieties	Agriculture and food industry	Union for the Protection of New Varieties of Plants (UPOV)
	Integrated circuits	Original layout designs	Micro-electronics industry	Washington Treaty (not yet in force)
Trade secrets		Secret business information	All industries	

Source: Carlos Braga, "Trade-Related Aspects of Intellectual Property Rights: The Uruguay Round Agreement and Its Economic Implications" (World Bank conference paper, 26-27 January 1995).

Note: With the exception of UPOV, all treaties identified above are administered by WIPO. The Washington Treaty, not yet in force, has also been negotiated under WIPO auspices. The Rome Convention is administered jointly by WIPO, ILO and UNESCO. The Universal Copyright Convention is administered by UNESCO.

Agreement on Trade-Related Aspects of Intellectual Property Rights

Structure

The TRIPS Agreement builds on the main international conventions on intellectual property rights by incorporating (by reference) most of their provisions. It further provides that countries may in pursuance of these conventions guarantee higher protection than is required by the TRIPS Agreement, as long as it does not contravene the Agreement's provisions.

The main provisions of the Agreement can be divided into the following five groups:

❑ Basic principles and general obligations.
❑ Minimum standards of protection covering:
 – The subject matter protected,
 – The rights conferred,
 – Permissible exceptions to those rights, and
 – The minimum duration of protection.
❑ Anti-competitive practices in contractual licences.
❑ Domestic procedures and remedies for the enforcement of intellectual property rights.
❑ Transitional arrangements for the implementation of the rules at the national level.

Basic principles and general obligations

Agreement on TRIPS, Articles 3 and 4
Agreement on TRIPS, Article 3:footnote

The Agreement reaffirms the basic principle of national treatment embodied in the various intellectual property right conventions. In particular, it states that in regard to the "availability, acquisition, scope, maintenance and enforcement" of intellectual property rights foreign nationals shall not be accorded treatment that is less favourable than that accorded by a country to its own nationals. In addition countries are required to extend MFN treatment to foreign nationals by not discriminating among them.

Minimum standards, including duration of protection

The Agreement breaks new ground by defining the main elements of protection, the rights to be conferred and the minimum term of protection for each of the following IPRs:

❑ Patents;
❑ Copyright and related rights;
❑ Trademarks;
❑ Industrial designs;
❑ Layout-designs of integrated circuits;
❑ Undisclosed information, including trade secrets.
❑ Geographical indications, including appellation of origin.

Agreement on TRIPS, Section 8 (Article 40)

The Agreement also has a section on the control of anti-competitive practices in contractual licences.

Patents

Agreement on TRIPS, Article 27

Definition and coverage. Patents provide property rights to inventions.[25] The Agreement provides that for an invention to be registered as a patent:

❑ It must be new;
❑ It must involve an inventive step; and
❑ It must be capable of industrial application.

The Agreement further stipulates that countries shall grant patents for inventions in *all fields of technology* and for both:

❑ Products, and
❑ Processes, including those used in manufacturing products.

---

25 An 'invention' may be defined as a novel idea which permits in practice the solution of a specific problem in a field of technology.

Furthermore, patents are to be granted without discrimination as to place of invention and whether products are imported or locally produced. The only products or processes which countries are permitted to exclude from patentability are:

❑ Diagnostic, therapeutic and surgical methods for the treatment of humans or animals;

❑ Plant and animal inventions other than micro-organisms;

❑ Essentially biological processes for the production of plants and animals other than non-biological and microbiological processes.

However, where a country excludes plant and animal inventions and plant varieties from patentability, it is expected to protect them under an effective *sui generis* system. (The Latin term *sui generis* means 'of its own kind'.) It is generally considered that this provision aims at encouraging countries to use the *sui generis* system provided by the UPOV[26] Convention on the Protection of New Varieties of Plants (described in box 48).

Box 48

Convention for the Protection of New Varieties of Plants

The objective of the UPOV Convention is to ensure that the member States acknowledge the achievements of breeders of plant varieties, by making available to them exclusive property rights on the basis of a set of uniform and clearly defined principles. To be eligible for protection, varieties have to be:

❑ *Distinct from existing commonly known varieties;*

❑ *Sufficiently homogenous;*

❑ *Stable; and*

❑ *New in the sense that they must not have been commercialized.*

Like all intellectual property rights, the rights of plant breeders are granted for a limited period of time, at the end of which the varieties protected by them pass into public domain. Authorization from the holder of the right is not required for the use of the protected variety in research, including its use in breeding other new varieties.

Note: The convention is administered by the International Union for the Protection of New Varieties of Plants (UPOV). The 1991 revision of the Convention entered into force on 24 April 1998.

Agreement on TRIPS, Article 27:3(b)

The Agreement provides for a review in 1999 of the option to exclude from patentability certain plant and animal inventions. Work related to the review process has been initiated by the Council for TRIPS.

Agreement on TRIPS, Article 28

Rights of patent holders. Patents give patent owners exclusive property rights; these allow them to prevent others from using the inventions covered. Manufacturers wishing to use patented inventions must obtain licences or authorizations from the patent owners, who normally will require them to pay royalties.

The Agreement clarifies these exclusive rights of patent owners. In particular, it states that where the subject of a patent is a product, third persons can make, sell or import that product only with the consent of the patent owner. Where a process is patented, third parties cannot use the process without the patent owner's consent; neither can they, without this consent, sell or import products directly obtained with the patented process.

---

26   International Union for the Protection of New Varieties of Plants.

Furthermore, the Agreement provides that in civil proceedings for infringement of the patent on a manufacturing process, an infringing product shall be presumed to have been produced by using the patented process if it is identical to that produced by the patented process. In such cases, as it is generally difficult for the patent owner to gather evidence to establish that the process has actually been used, the burden of proof shall be on the defendant, i.e. he or she will have to establish that the product has been manufactured with a process different from that covered by the patent.

Agreement on TRIPS, Article 31

Compulsory licensing. What happens if a patent owner refuses to license the use of the patented invention by demanding unreasonable terms? The law in many countries provides that where the patented product is not available or is available at exorbitant prices, the government may on grounds of public interest authorize an interested manufacturer to use the patent against payment to the patent holder of an adequate royalty. However, the Agreement lays down strict conditions for such licensing to ensure that compulsory licences are issued only in exceptional situations and on an objective basis. In particular, it provides that compulsory licences may be granted only when the interested manufacturer has failed in his or her efforts to obtain the authorization on reasonable terms and conditions. Box 49 lists some of the other conditions which must be fulfilled before governments can intervene and license a manufacturer to use patented technology.

Agreement on TRIPS, Article 29

Disclosure of information. Although patent owners have exclusive property rights over their inventions, they cannot withhold technical information on these inventions. The legislation of most countries require applicants for patents to disclose such information on the products or processes to be patented as will enable technically qualified persons to understand and use it for further research or for industrial application after the expiry of the terms of the patents. Such information can be obtained by any interested person from the patent office, after paying the necessary charges.

Box 49

Conditions prescribed in the Agreement on TRIPS for the compulsory licensing of patents
(Agreement on TRIPS, Article 31)

As a general rule, a compulsory licence for the use of a patented technology may be granted by the government of the country where the patent is registered if the interested user (which can be the government itself or a company or private individual) has been unsuccessful in obtaining the licence from the patent holder on reasonable commercial terms. In national emergencies, other circumstances of extreme urgency and in cases of public non-commercial use, this condition does not have to be met. However, the patent holder has to be informed about the use.

The grant of such compulsory licence shall further be subject to the following conditions:

❑ *Such licence shall be granted for supply predominantly to the domestic market.*

❑ *It shall be terminated if and when the circumstances which led to it cease to exist.*

❑ *In the case of semi-conductor technology, the licence shall only be for public non-commercial use or to remedy adjudicated anti-competitive practices.*

❑ *The grant of such a licence shall be for non-exclusive use.*

❑ *The patent owner shall be paid adequate remuneration, taking into account the economic value of the licence.*

❑ *The patent holder shall have a right to appeal against the decision to grant compulsory licence or any decision relating to the remuneration provided.*

These provisions for public disclosure of information balance two objectives of governments in giving patent rights. By giving exclusive rights, governments provide inventors an incentive for research and a reward for their inventive work. The exclusive rights also enable manufacturers to recoup, and profit from, their investment on research and development. At the same time, by requiring inventors to make a public disclosure of information on their inventions, governments seek to ensure that these inventions are used for the benefit of the community at large and for further technological R & D. While such information cannot be employed for commercial purposes by others until the expiry of the patent, it is open to any university, research or business organization to use it for further research. They may even apply for a secondary patent on the basis of the earlier patented invention. The Agreement clarifies this by stating that the legislation of member countries "shall require that an applicant for a patent shall disclose the invention in a manner sufficiently clear and complete for the invention to be carried out by a person skilled in the art".

Agreement on TRIPS,
Articles 9-14

Copyright and related rights

The subject matter of copyright protection includes works in the literary, scientific and artistic domain, whatever the mode or form of expression. For a work to enjoy copyright protection, however, it must be an original creation. The idea in the work does not need to be new but the form, be it literary, artistic or scientific, in which it is expressed must be the original creation of the author.

Rights comprised in copyright. Owners of copyright in a protected work have a right to exclude others from using it without their authorization. The rights of copyright owners are therefore often described as exclusive rights to authorize others to use the protected work. Authorization from copyright owners is usually required in the following situations:

❑ Reproduction rights: copying and reproducing the work;
❑ Performing rights: performing the work in public (e.g. play or concert);
❑ Recording rights: making a sound recording of the work (e.g. phonograms or sound recordings in the technical language of copyright law);
❑ Motion picture rights: making a motion picture (often called cinematographic work in technical language);
❑ Broadcasting rights: broadcasting the work by radio or television;
❑ Translation and adaptation rights: translating and adapting the work.

In addition to these exclusive rights of an economic character, copyright laws provide original authors moral rights. These rights enable authors, even after they have transferred their economic rights, to claim authorship of the work and to object to any distortion or other derogatory action in relation to the work which would be prejudicial to their reputation or honour.

Related rights. Literary and artistic works are created in order to be disseminated among the public. This cannot always be done by the authors themselves, for it often requires intermediaries who use their professional skills to give the works appropriate forms of presentation to make them accessible to a wide public.

In addition to protecting the rights of authors of works, it is therefore also necessary to protect the rights of:

❑ Performing artists in relation to their performance;
❑ Producers of phonograms in relation to their phonograms; and
❑ Broadcasting organizations in relation to their radio and television programmes.

These related rights of performing artists, record producers and broadcasters are also called neighbouring rights because they have developed in parallel to copyright and the exercise of these rights is often linked with the exercise of copyright. Copyright laws frequently deal also with neighbouring rights.

Provisions of the TRIPS Agreement. The main provisions on copyright and neighbouring rights are contained in the Berne Convention. The TRIPS Agreement clarifies and adds to the Convention's provisions on:

❑ Computer programmes and databases;

❑ Rental rights to computer programmes, sound recordings and films;

❑ Rights of performers and producers of phonograms; and

❑ Rights of broadcasting organizations.

Box 50 summarizes the Agreement's provisions.

Box 50

Copyright provisions in the Agreement on TRIPS

Computer programmes *(Article 10). The Agreement provides that computer programmes should be considered literary works and protected under national copyright laws.*

Rental rights *(Article 11). The Agreement requires countries to provide authors of computer programmes, sound recordings and cinematographic films "the right to authorize or to prohibit the commercial rental" of their copyright works. A member country "shall be excepted from this obligation in respect of cinematographic works unless such rental has led to widespread copying of such works ... materially impairing the exclusive right of reproduction conferred on ... authors".*

Protection of performers, producers of phonograms (sound recordings) and broadcasting organizations.

Performers (Article 14). The Agreement provides that performers shall have, "in respect of a fixation of their performance on a phonogram", the right to prevent the reproduction of such fixation. They shall also have a right to prevent "broadcasting by wireless means and the communication to the public of their live performance" without their authorization.

Producers. Phonogram producers shall have the right to authorize or prohibit the direct or indirect reproduction of their phonograms.

Broadcasting organizations. These organizations shall have the right to prohibit the following acts from being carried out without their authorization:

❑ *Fixation;*

❑ *Reproduction of fixations;*

❑ *Rebroadcasting by wireless or communication on television of their broadcasts.*

See box 52 for provisions on periods of duration.

Agreement on TRIPS,
Articles 15-21

Trademarks

A trademark is a sign which serves to distinguish the goods or services of an industrial or commercial enterprise from those of other enterprises. Such a sign may consist of one or more distinctive words, letters, names, numerals, figurative elements and combination of colours. Such a sign may combine any of the above-mentioned elements. As the basic purpose of a trademark is to distinguish, the laws of most countries provide that any mark to be protected must be distinctive.

Purpose served by trademarks. Trademarks serve a twofold purpose. They help their owners sell and promote their products by stimulating brand loyalty. They serve consumers by assisting them in making a choice among several possibilities and by encouraging trademark owners to maintain or improve the quality of the products sold under their trademarks.

Although in some countries and in some situations the right to the exclusive exploitation of a trademark may be obtained by its extended use in commerce and without registration, it is generally necessary for effective protection that a trademark is registered in a government office (usually the office which grants patents). Applicants wishing to register a trademark are required to state the nature of the goods in respect of which a mark is to be registered. The rationale for this rule is that registrants of trademarks should be able to use the signs in question only for the goods so stated. However, in practice, the prevention of the use of trademarks for other goods or services is contingent on the likelihood of the consumer confusing them with registered marks. This is tested on the basis of the similarity of the goods or the reputation of the mark.

International rules on the use of trademarks. International rules on trademarks are contained in the Paris Convention. The Agreement on TRIPS complements these rules in the following areas:

❑ Definition of 'trademark'.

❑ Exclusive rights of trademark owners.

❑ Prohibition of the imposition of special requirements for the use of trademarks.

❑ Licensing and assignment of trademarks.

❑ Cancellation of trademarks.

Agreement on TRIPS, Article 15

Definition of 'trademark'. The Agreement provides that signs or combinations of signs capable of distinguishing the goods or services of one undertaking from those of other undertakings can be registered as trademarks. These include names, letters, numbers, figurative elements or combinations of colours. A country may provide that a mark that has been in use for a period is eligible for registration.

Agreement on TRIPS, Article 16

Exclusive rights. The owners of registered trademarks have exclusive rights to prevent third parties from using on identical or similar goods signs that are similar to those in respect of which the trademark is registered where such use would cause confusion. When an identical trademark is used on goods and services that are identical, "a likelihood of confusion shall be presumed."

Agreement on TRIPS, Article 20

Special requirements. The Agreement urges countries not to impose on the use of trademarks special requirements which, for example, would be detrimental to their capacity "to distinguish the goods or services of one undertaking from those of other undertakings." It also obliges countries to discontinue the practice of permitting the use of foreign trademarks only if these are combined with another trademark, such as one of a national origin.

Agreement on TRIPS, Article 21

Licensing and assignment of trademarks. The Agreement leaves member countries free to determine the "conditions on the licensing and assignment of trademarks". However, it states that the owners should not be compelled to grant licences for the use of trademarks. Moreover, owners "shall have the right to assign a trademark with or without the transfer of the business to which the trademark belongs."

Agreement on TRIPS, Article 19

Cancellation of trademarks. The protection granted to the proprietor of a registered mark is based on the assumption that he or she will use it in commerce. The laws of most countries provide for cancellation of the mark if it is not used over a certain period. The laws of most countries provide for the cancellation of marks that are not being used as the number of marks being filed for registration every year is rising at spectacular rates. In fact, the proliferation of marks and their increasing use in commerce has led to a real dearth of symbols or trademarks available for adoption and use by new applicants. Human ingenuity in evolving new signs, by combining letters, numbers or pictures, is after all not without limits.

The TRIPS Agreement lays down certain guidelines which registration authorities are expected to follow in cancelling trademarks because of non-use. It provides that a registered trademark can be cancelled "only after an uninterrupted period of at least three years of non-use". In taking such decisions, adequate weight should be given to the circumstances beyond the control of the foreign trademark owner, such as import restrictions imposed by governments on the import of products carrying a trademark. Moreover, use, for example by licensees, should be recognized as use by the owner of the mark.

Agreement on TRIPS, Articles 25-26

Industrial designs

Not all countries currently protect industrial designs, which cover the ornamental features of products including shapes, lines, motifs and colours. Industrial designs are protected mainly in consumer articles, of which textiles, leather and leather products, and motor cars are examples.

Agreement on TRIPS, Article 25

The TRIPS Agreement imposes an obligation on its member countries to protect industrial designs that are:

❏ New, or
❏ Original.

The designs thus need to be either novel or original to qualify for protection.[27] The owner of the protected design has exclusive right to its use and can prevent third parties who have not obtained his or her consent from "making, selling or importing articles bearing or embodying a design which is a copy, or substantially a copy, of the protected design".

Agreement on TRIPS, Article 25

The Agreement has a special provision to take into account the short life cycle and the sheer number of new designs in the textile sector. It provides that "any cost, examination or publication" must not "unreasonably impair the opportunity to seek or obtain such protection."

Agreement on TRIPS, Articles 22-24
Agreement on TRIPS, Article 22

Geographical indications

Geographical indications aim at informing the consumer that a good has the quality, reputation or other characteristic "essentially attributable to its geographical origin". The Agreement provides that member countries should adopt "legal means" to prevent "the use of any means in the designation or presentation that indicates or suggests that the good in question originates in a geographical area other than the true place of origin in a manner which misleads the public as to the geographical origin of the good".

The most common example of how geographical indications can mislead the public is provided by 'Champagne' which is not a trademark but a region in France. In principle it is not permissible to call wine produced elsewhere (in Argentina or the United States, for example) 'Champagne' even though the producing country may regard the wine as comparable to French champagne.

---

27 In the Uruguay Round negotiations, some countries had proposed that property rights for industrial designs should be granted only if they were "new and original". The application of such a cumulative principle was not, however, favoured by a number of countries, which felt that the application of the principle would make it difficult to obtain protection for industrial designs.

Since the Agreement does not lay down the method by which these indications should be protected, there are wide variations in the way laws deal with them. While some countries have specific geographical indication laws, others use trademark law, consumer protection law, marketing law, common law or a combination of these.

The products to which these laws apply in developed countries are predominantly wines and spirits. There are however a few exceptions. United States law for instance prevents the application of the geographical indication 'Idaho' to potatoes and onions, and 'Real California cheese' to cheese not produced in the region.

The Agreement has special provisions aiming at acceptance of greater discipline by countries in the use of geographical indications on wine and spirits. In particular, it provides that interested parties must adopt legal means to prevent the incorrect use of a geographical indication on products not originating in the place so indicated. This applies even when the public is not being misled.

Other intellectual property rights

The provisions of the Agreement on layout-designs of integrated circuits and undisclosed information are briefly noted in box 51.

Box 51

Other intellectual property rights
(Agreement on TRIPS, Articles 35-39)

Layout-designs of integrated circuits (Articles 35 to 38). Except when it provides otherwise, the Agreement requires countries to protect the layout-designs of integrated circuits in accordance with the Treaty on Intellectual Property in Respect of Integrated Circuits, adopted in Washington in 1989. Additional provisions stipulate, inter alia, that importing or selling articles incorporating a protected integrated circuit without authorization from the right holder shall be considered unlawful. However, acquisition of an article by persons who do not know that it incorporates an unlawfully reproduced layout-design does not constitute an unlawful act. "Innocent infringers" may sell or dispose of stock acquired before they became aware that the use of the layout-design is unlawful; however, they shall be liable to pay the right holder a reasonable royalty. Another provision of the Agreement prohibits compulsory licensing of the protected right except in cases of public non-commercial use or to remedy practices determined by a judicial or administrative process to be anti-competition.

Undisclosed information (Article 39). The TRIPS Agreement carries provisions which, for the first time in public international law, explicitly require undisclosed information – trade secrets or know-how – to benefit from protection. The protection applies to information that is secret, that has commercial value because it is secret, and that has been subject to reasonable steps to keep it secret. The Agreement does not demand that undisclosed information should be treated as a form of property, but it does stipulate that a person lawfully in control of such information must have the possibility of preventing it from being disclosed to, acquired by, or used by others without his or her consent in a manner contrary to honest commercial practices. Furthermore, the Agreement has provisions on undisclosed test data and other data whose submission is required by governments "as a condition of approving the marketing of pharmaceutical or of agricultural chemical products". Member governments must protect such data against unfair commercial use.

Duration of intellectual property rights

Intellectual property rights (other than trademarks, geographical indications and undisclosed information) are limited in duration. Currently, the minimum periods of protection vary from country to country. The Agreement establishes minimum regulatory periods for the different property rights. These are set out in box 52.

Box 52
Minimum periods of protection for intellectual property rights
(Agreement on TRIPS, various Articles)

Patents	*20 years from the date of filing of the application for a patent (Article 33).*
Copyright	*Life of the author plus 50 years.*
	Cinematographic work: 50 years after the work has been made available to the public or, if not made available, after the making of such work.
	Photographic work or works of applied art: 25 years after the making of the work.
	Performers and producers of phonograms: 50 years from the end of the calendar year in which the fixation (phonogram) was made or the performance took place (Article 14:5).
	Broadcasting: 20 years from the end of the calendar year in which the broadcast took place (Article 14:5).
Trademarks	*7 years from initial registration and each renewal of registration; registration is renewable indefinitely (Article 18).*
Industrial designs	*At least 10 years (Article 26:3).*
Layout-designs of integrated circuits	*10 years from the date of registration or, where registration is not required, 10 years from the date of first exploitation (Article 38:2 and 3).*

IPR owners lose their rights when the duration of protection expires. From then on patents, copyright, industrial designs and other property rights can be exploited by any member of the public without having to obtain authorization from any right holder.

Restrictive practices

To ensure that improved and increased protection of IPRs does not adversely affect the transfer of technology on reasonable commercial terms, the Agreement provides that countries may adopt appropriate measures, including legislation, to prevent intellectual property holders from:

❑ Abusing their rights,

❑ Adopting practices that unreasonably restrain trade or adversely affect the transfer of technology.

Enforcement provisions

One feature of the TRIPS Agreement which distinguishes it from the WIPO conventions is the emphasis it lays on enforcement by its member countries of its standards and rules. Towards this end, the Agreement prescribes the institutional mechanism, procedures and remedies that countries should adopt:

Agreement on TRIPS, Articles 42-61

❑ To enable IPR holders to obtain redress under civil law;

❑ For the prosecution of counterfeiters and pirates under criminal law;

❑ For providing provisional relief; and

❑ To prevent release by customs authorities of counterfeit, pirated and other goods that infringe IPRs.

Civil remedies

The Agreement states that national courts shall be able "to order prompt and effective provisional measures" to preserve evidence in regard to alleged infringement of intellectual property rights, and to prevent an infringement from occurring, *inter alia*, by preventing the entry of imported goods into the channels of commerce in their jurisdiction. Where infringement of IPRs has been established, the courts shall have the authority to order the infringer to pay to the right holder damages to compensate for the injury. In addition, in order to create an effective deterrent, the courts are authorized to order the destruction of the infringing goods so that they do not enter commercial channels.

Agreement on TRIPS,
Article 61

Criminal proceedings

The Agreement further calls on countries to see that, where there is "wilful trademark counterfeiting or copyright piracy on a commercial scale", the infringer is prosecuted under criminal law and imprisoned or fined to an extent sufficient to provide a deterrent.

Agreement on TRIPS,
Article 50

Provisional measures

Since in both civil and criminal proceedings, the judicial procedures may take a fair amount of time, the Agreement provides that judicial authorities must have the authority to order prompt and effective provisional measures. Such measures should be taken:

❑ To prevent infringement from occurring, and

❑ To prevent infringing goods from entering commercial channels.

Agreement on TRIPS,
Article 51

Prevention of release of infringing goods by customs authorities

Member countries are further required to adopt procedures under which holders of intellectual property who have grounds for suspecting that:

- Counterfeit goods infringing on their trademarks, or

- Pirated goods infringing on their copyright

are likely to be imported could request Customs not to release the goods. Countries have the option to prescribe procedures for the suspension of release from Customs of products that infringe on patents and other IPRs.

Agreement on TRIPS,
Articles 65-66

Transitional periods

The national legislation of a number of countries, particularly developing and least developed countries, do not at present conform to the provisions of the TRIPS Agreement described above. For instance, in the area of patents, while the Agreement requires that as a rule patents should be given for inventions in all fields of technology, some countries exclude from patentability chemicals, food and food products. The duration for which patents are granted for inventions relating to fertilizers, insecticides and pharmaceuticals is also much shorter in some countries than the 20 years provided for by the Agreement. Furthermore, in regard to pharmaceuticals, some countries grant protection only to processes and not to products. In the area of copyright, many countries do not treat computer programmes as eligible for protection. A number of countries do not provide protection for industrial designs.

To enable industry and trade in these countries to prepare themselves for the changes required by the Agreement on TRIPS, member countries have been given the following transitional periods within which to bring their national legislation and regulations in conformity with the provisions of the Agreement:

❑ Developed countries: one year, i.e. up to 1 January 1996. This period has already expired.

❑ Developing countries: five years, i.e. up to 1 January 2000.

❑ Transition economies: five years, i.e. up to 1 January 2000, if they are facing problems in reforming their intellectual property law.

❑ Least developed countries: 11 years, i.e. up to 1 January 2006.

'Mail-box' obligations

Agreement on TRIPS,
Article 65.4

In addition, developing countries that at present provide patent protection to processes and not to products in a given area of technology, for example in the pharmaceutical and agricultural chemical sectors, can delay up to 1 January 2005 the application of the obligation to protect products.

Agreement on TRIPS,
Article 70.8

This flexibility available to developing countries is subject to an important condition. The country concerned must have established from the date the Agreement came into force (i.e. on 1 January 1995) a mechanism (the 'mail-box') for receiving applications for patents from domestic and foreign inventors. These applications need not be examined for patentability until the country starts applying product patent protection in the pharmaceutical and agricultural chemical sectors, i.e. at the end of the 10-year transition period (1 January 2005).

Most new pharmaceutical and agricultural chemical products may, however, be sold only after the producing company has been able to obtain authorization from the regulatory authorities to market them. Such authorization is generally granted after the regulatory authorities have satisfied themselves, on the basis of results of tests carried out by the company requesting authorization, that the product will not have harmful effects on human and animal health, plant life and the environment. The Agreement provides that if the regulatory authorities grant marketing authorization to the producers which have filed applications for patenting a pharmaceutical or agricultural chemical product under the 'mail-box' arrangement, they must give these producers the exclusive right to market that product for a period of five years, or until the patent is granted, whichever is shorter.

Agreement on TRIPS,
Article 70.9

Agreement on TRIPS,
Article 65.5

Stand-still provision

During the transition periods, member countries are required not to take any measures that will result in a lower level of protection to IPRs than that already existing in their territories. This is referred to as the 'stand-still' or the 'non-backsliding' clause. All countries are under an obligation to apply MFN and national treatment rules from 1 January 1996.

Business implications

The TRIPS Agreement will, to a large extent, have a harmonizing effect on standards for the protection of intellectual property rights throughout the world. With the exception of obligations in regard to pharmaceutical and agricultural chemical products, harmonization can be expected by 2000 when the transition period for the implementation of the Agreement by both developing and transition economies comes to an end. The emphasis of the Agreement on enforcement will result in stricter application at the national level of intellectual property rights both in domestic markets and at the border.

Challenges

For the business person from developing and transition economies, the Agreement offers both challenges and advantages. The challenges arise from the three factors discussed below.

Obligations to change IPR systems

First, the Agreement will require significant changes in the IPR regimes of many developing countries. Modifications will be required in the large number of countries which provide terms of patent protection that are shorter than the 20 years set out in the Agreement, allow exceptions to the 20-year term or stipulate another duration. Computer programs must be protected under copyright as literary works. A large number of developing Members (and two developed Members) did not have any type of protection for computer software in April 1994 and a few countries provided protection through legal instruments other than copyright law.

Despite these difficulties, it is expected that a large number of developing countries will have modified their laws to bring them in conformity with the provisions of the Agreement by 1 January 2000, when the transition period provided to them for the implementation of the Agreement comes to an end.

They have, however, up to 1 January 2005 to implement provisions on the patenting of pharmaceuticals and agricultural chemical products. Most developing countries have by now established, as required by the Agreement, a 'mail box' for receiving applications for patents in these product sectors.

It will be necessary for the business community to prepare itself for these changes.

Difficulties in using reverse engineering

Second, stronger protection will make it more difficult for industries in developing countries to use through reverse engineering and other means the technology developed by foreign companies and for which the latter hold patent rights. In the past, reverse engineering had been an important source of technology particularly for SMEs. With the implementation of the Agreement, companies with registered patent rights can be expected to be more vigilant about ensuring that their patented technology is not used without payment of royalty.

Issues relating to 'traditional knowledge'

Third, recent years have witnessed phenomenal progress in research in biotechnology and genetic engineering. In some cases, the resulting inventions are based on the generic resources available only in the tropics, i.e. mainly in developing countries.

Some environmental groups have complained that although company research into genetic resources has drawn on the traditional knowledge of indigenous or local communities, these communities do not benefit from the patents on the resulting inventions. For centuries, parts of plants (roots, barks, leaves, flowers and fruits) have been used in developing countries to relieve pain and treat infections and other complaints. They have also been used as insecticides and herbicides. Local knowledge of these varied uses, while it is not recorded in any book or document, is part of the communal heritage. This knowledge of the food-giving capacities of plants as well as their life-support qualities is passed on from mouth to mouth and from one generation to another.

The issue of acknowledging and rewarding the contribution of indigenous and local communities whose traditional knowledge is used in patented inventions is being discussed at the international level. The Food and Agriculture Organization of the United Nations (FAO), for instance, has developed the concept of farmers' rights, i.e. "rights arising from the past, present and future contribution of farmers in conserving, improving and making available plant genetic resources." The Convention on Biological Diversity addresses the question of how countries where genetic resources are located can participate in biotechnological research activities and share, on mutually agreed terms, in the fruit of such research.

It is important to note that although the TRIPS Agreement is silent on the question of the participation of countries and communities in the benefits arising from research into the genetic resources originating in their territories, there is nothing in the Agreement that blocks such countries from entering into contractual arrangements requiring companies to pay them fees for research and royalties from any resulting patented invention.

The advantages

The challenges which the factors and developments described above pose to the business community have to be weighed against the favourable impact which IPR rules could have on:

❑ The encouragement of creativity and innovation;

❑ The transfer of technology on commercial terms to business enterprises in developing countries;

❑ The protection of consumers by controlling the trade in counterfeit goods; and

❑ Both the export and the import trade.

These aspects are taken up in greater detail in the paragraphs that follow.

Encouraging creative and innovative work

More effective protection of IPRs such as copyright, patents and industrial designs will, by rewarding intellectual work, encourage innovative and creative work in developing countries. As has been noted, the rules on patents, for instance, seek to maintain a balance between the need to protect the rights of patent holders and the need of industries and society as a whole to benefit from new and improved knowledge. The Agreement calls on its member countries to enforce strictly the provisions requiring patent applicants to disclose the technical information that will enable technically qualified persons to reconstruct the inventions. Access to such information will make it possible for the industrial sector, particularly in the more advanced and other countries with a sufficient number of technically qualified persons, to utilize it for further research and to develop processes or products that differ from those patented. This stimulation of the inventive process will certainly benefit the country as a whole.[28]

---

28   *The Outcome of the Uruguay Round: An Initial Assessment* (United Nations publication, Sales No. E.94.II.D.28), pp. 196 - 203.

Transfer of technology on commercial terms

Increased protection of IPRs will greatly facilitate attempts by companies in developing countries to enter into joint ventures and other collaboration arrangements for the transfer of technology on commercial terms. There is increasing evidence to show that IPR protection in host countries is an important factor in decisions of companies in developed countries to invest in developing countries. It certainly plays a major role in investment decisions in the chemical and pharmaceutical industries. Recent studies indicate that it is also a significant variable in other industries,[29] particularly those manufacturing products that are imitation prone (e.g. electronic and computer products).

Increased protection to IPRs will encourage foreign partners in joint ventures to undertake greater research and development work in the host developing country. At present most research work is undertaken in their own countries. Such a development will enable local partners to influence to a greater extent both the content and the priorities of research work.

On balance, therefore, it can be argued that, over the medium and long term, IP protection as envisaged in the Agreement will have positive effects on the growth of the inventive process in developing countries. In the short term, however, as some studies show, improved protection may force industries in certain sectors such as pharmaceuticals and chemicals to pay higher prices for acquiring patented technology.[30]

Impact on the trade in counterfeit goods

The emphasis of the Agreement on the enforcement of its provisions is also expected to help bring under control production of, and trade in, counterfeit and pirated goods. In the coming years the WTO consultation and dispute settlement mechanism will put increasing pressure to bear on countries with a significant output of such goods to improve the enforcement of their trademark and copyright laws. It is also in the long-term interest of domestic industries and consumers to see that these laws are enforced.

The occurrence of counterfeiting is frequently due to the fact that small enterprises are not fully aware of the legal implications of using trademarks without authorization from their owners. There is some evidence to show that pirates and counterfeiters are often able to switch to legitimate activities once the legal environment changes.[31]

Counterfeiting also adversely affects the export interests of small domestic producers who produce under licence for manufacturers in outside countries. In recent years, a number of manufacturers marketing products under their brand names have had either the product itself or parts of it produced by SMEs in developing countries to take advantage of lower production costs. These manufacturers are more willing, as the case cited in box 53 indicates, to enter into such arrangements with countries where IPRs are effectively protected.

Relevance to the export and import trade

Business enterprises will have to bear in mind the provisions of the TRIPS Agreement in planning their sales strategies for foreign markets. In particular, it will be necessary for them to examine whether the processes they use in manufacturing the product or any of its inputs are subject to a patent or other

29   Carlos Braga, "Trade-Related Aspects of Intellectual Property Rights: The Uruguay Round Agreement and Its Economic Implications" (World Bank conference paper, 26-27 January 1995).
30   *The Outcome of the Uruguay Round...*, pp. 196 - 203.
31   *Ibid*, p. 48.

Box 53

Importance of the enforcement of IPRs to production under licence: a cautionary tale

A large importer of carpets in a developed country (country A) was importing carpets from small manufacturers in a least developed country (country B) which had long traditions of such artisanal work. The ornamental design and motifs were provided by the importer. In order to prevent use of the design by other producers, the importing firm had registered the industrial design as an intellectual property both in its country and in the country of production. After having spent a considerable amount on advertisement and publicity, the importing firm was able in a few years to develop a market for carpets manufactured according to its design.

This led other small manufacturers in country B to produce carpets with an identical design for export to country A. The importer in country A tried to get the IPR authorities in country B to stop production and export by these manufacturers in view of its exclusive right to the use of the protected industrial design. However, because of the lax enforcement of IPRs in country B, no action was taken. The importer therefore decided to terminate the arrangement and shift production to another country which had a reputation for enforcing its intellectual property law.

IPR in the target export market. Likewise, where the product offered for sale in a foreign market bears a trademark, it will be necessary to ensure that a similar mark is not in use or registered in that market. If their trademarks are considered 'confusingly similar' to other trademarks, exporting enterprises may expose themselves to legal suits for infringement of property rights.

These considerations should also be kept in mind by enterprises in placing their import orders. It will be necessary, particularly in regard to products that are widely counterfeited or pirated, for importers to satisfy those concerned that, where the foreign supplier claims that the product to be imported is produced under a licence, it has the necessary authorization to do so. Otherwise, the importer will risk facing a suit for damages from the trademark owner and the possibility of the goods being confiscated by Customs on arrival.

Summing up

In sum, if trade-related IPR friction is to be avoided, it is necessary for all business enterprises engaged in foreign trade not only to familiarize themselves with the system set up by the Agreement but to be fully aware of the obligations it imposes and the rights it creates in their favour. They should also undertake through their associations studies of the practical problems of selling in foreign markets and those arising from the application of the TRIPS Agreement. Briefing governments on the findings of such studies will enable government representatives to negotiate, during the reviews provided for by the Agreement, modifications to its provisions to meet some of the concerns of the business community.

PART SIX

Subjects added to the WTO work programme for study and analysis

CHAPTER 21

Trade and environment

Evolving global trends

During the last two decades, the interlinkage between trade and environment has become an increasingly important issue in international trade relations. Growing awareness of the need to protect the environment and to promote the sustainable development of available resources has led to a rise in environmental policy measures. Such measures are normally implemented by governments through regulatory or economic instruments. In some cases, both types of instruments are used.

The main regulatory measures, also known as 'command and control measures,' are as follows:

❑ Product standards setting out the characteristics with which a product sold in a particular market must conform;

❑ Regulations imposing process and production methods (PPM) and pollution standards;

❑ Import and export bans on products that are hazardous or harmful to health;

❑ Import and export restrictions decreed for the conservation and sustainable development of natural resources; and

❑ Packaging and labelling requirements.

Economic instruments include taxes on products that are hazardous or harmful to health; emission charges and other price-based measures; and environmental subsidies.

In comparison to regulatory instruments, economic instruments offer, in theory at least, a number of inherent advantages: greater cost-effectiveness, permanent incentives to reduce pollution, and revenue sources for the government. In practice, however, for both economic and administrative reasons, governments may consider direct regulation and control more appropriate and effective in certain situations. For instance, regulatory measures may be adopted where it is imperative that the emission of certain toxic pollutants or the use of hazardous products or substances should be completely prohibited. In other circumstances, regulatory measures may be supplemented by economic instruments to strengthen enforcement.

A country's choice of instrument – whether regulatory or economic – depends on the strengths and weaknesses of its political and administrative structures, and should be determined on a case-by-case basis. Such choices should take into account factors such as the measure's environmental effectiveness, economic efficiency, administrative feasibility and costs, equity and acceptability to the public.

The environmental policy measures taken by governments can affect trade in several different ways. It is worth noting three of these.

First, there are apprehensions that environmental standards may change conditions of competition. Producers in countries with stricter environmental standards worry about the impact of such standards on their costs and their ability to compete in world markets.

Second, producers in countries with less stringent standards (mainly developing countries and economies in transition) fear that their products may be subjected to trade measures on the ground that they have been produced by industries which do not meet the higher pollution or emission standards of importing countries. Any such measure, whether in the form of a compensatory tax or outright prohibition of, or a restriction on, imports, would amount to a unilateral assertion of jurisdiction over the environmental practices and priorities of other nations.

Third, there has been growing public concern with the global commons (for example, ozone depletion and climate change), species diversity and the treatment of animals. From the viewpoint of trade policy, this has raised an important question as to whether international environmental agreements dealing with global environmental issues should contain provisions that require members to restrict trade with non-parties, with a view to forcing them to join such agreements.

WTO provisions

The Agreement Establishing the World Trade Organization brought "trade-related aspects of environmental policies" clearly within the WTO mandate. The preamble to the Agreement states that its objective of "raising standards of living and ensuring full employment" by "expanding the production of and trade in goods and services" is to be achieved by making "optimal use of the world's resources in accordance with the objective of sustainable development, seeking both to protect and preserve the environment ... in a manner consistent with ... needs and concerns at different levels of economic development."

The main operational provisions governing trade measures taken by governments for environmental reasons are contained in GATT 1994. However, GATT does not carry direct references to environmental matters, mainly because the full implications of environmental and ecological degradation resulting from pollution or over-exploitation of natural resources were not known when the GATT text was first negotiated.

The general exceptions provided for by Article XX of GATT 1994 can be used by countries to adopt trade measures for the attainment of environmental objectives, if the conditions laid down are met. The Article permits countries to impose prohibitions or other restrictions not otherwise allowed under the provisions of GATT 1994, if they:

❑ Are necessary to protect human, animal or plant life and health [Article XX(a)], and

❑ Relate to the conservation of exhaustible natural resources if such measures are made effective in conjunction with restrictions on domestic production and consumption [Article XX(g)].

In a recent dispute brought before WTO (on imports of certain shrimp and shrimp products and their effects on sea turtles), the Appellate Body ruled that the term 'exhaustible natural resources' for the purposes of GATT Article XX(g) should be interpreted to mean not only 'mineral' or 'non-living' natural resources but also 'renewable' and 'living' natural resources like sea turtles.

Any trade restrictive measures taken in accordance with the above provisions of Article XX must, however, meet the following conditions:

❏ That they do not constitute means of unjustifiable discrimination where the same conditions prevail (the GATT principle of non-discrimination),

❏ That they are not a disguised restriction on trade.

In addition to the provisions of GATT 1994, certain provisions of some of the associated WTO Agreements are relevant to the interrelationship between trade and environment. These include provisions on standards in the Agreements on SPS and TBT, and the provisions on subsidies in the Agreements on SCM and Agriculture.

Trade-related issues

The main responsibility for WTO's work on trade and environment has been assigned to the permanent Committee on Trade and Environment (CTE). Discussions on the implications for trade of measures taken by countries for environmental purposes therefore take place in this Committee; they also take place in the Committees established under the individual WTO Agreements mentioned above.

The sections that follow briefly describe the trade issues that are being addressed in the light of the provisions of WTO law. The issues covered are listed below:

❏ Environmental measures with significant effects on trade, and the provisions of WTO law

– Use of process and production methods in environmental regulations;

– Packaging requirements;

– Environmental labelling;

– Consumption and other taxes imposed for environmental purposes.

❏ Trade provisions in multilateral environmental agreements.

❏ Environmental benefits of trade liberalization.

Environmental measures with significant effects on trade, and the provisions of WTO law

Use of process and production methods in environmental regulations

Standards can broadly be divided into two categories: product standards, and process and production methods (PPM). Product standards lay down specifications for product characteristics (such as performance, product safety, dimensions) and requirements for packaging or labelling. They need to be distinguished from PPM standards which stipulate how goods are to be produced. PPM standards apply to the production stage, i.e. before products are placed on the market for sale.

It is only logical that each country should have a sovereign right to insist that imported products should meet the product standards applicable to goods produced domestically with a view to protecting the environment, or the health and safety of its people, or its animal life. The SPS and TBT Agreements require countries to use international standards in formulating such standards. Where international standards are not available or are considered inappropriate, countries must ensure that standards are not adopted or applied in a way as to create unnecessary barriers to trade.

The rules of the SPS and TBT Agreements do not allow countries to prohibit or restrict imports on the grounds that the imported product has not been produced according to the PPM standard imposed on domestic industries. The Agreement on TBT makes a single exception to this rule: a country may prohibit imports of a product when the PPM used affects its characteristics or quality.

However, an importing country may not restrict imports solely because a product has been produced in a plant which does not meet its national standards for water or air pollution, or because the product has not been made according to the methods of production the country prescribes. Any such requirement would be tantamount to obliging an exporting country to adopt the PPM of the importing country, which the exporting country may have good reasons not to use because of its environmental and ecological conditions.

Despite WTO law, pressures from environmental lobbies are forcing governments to introduce laws which have an impact on trade because imports are then restricted on the ground that they have not been produced according to the methods of production imposed by these laws. Such methods include the following:

❑ Management practices for forest resources;
❑ Norms for catching fish;
❑ Methods for fattening animals or for enhancing the milking capacities of cows; and
❑ Methods for killing animals.

For instance, there are moves in the Netherlands to allow imports of wood and wood products only if they are accompanied by a certificate issued by competent authorities stating that the wood raw material has been obtained from forests that are managed sustainably. The European Union bans imports of furs from animals caught with leg-hold traps. The United States has laws which restrict imports of tuna from countries which do not require their fishermen to prevent dolphins from being killed unnecessarily when tuna fishing, an obligation imposed on United States fishermen. Likewise, the United States prohibits imports of shrimp from countries which do not adhere to national standards for preventing the taking of sea turtles in the course of shrimp trawling.

The standards used for the imposition of such trade measures are generally not based on scientific principles, but reflect value preferences in importing countries. In some instances, the standards may, in the case of the proposed import restrictions on tropical timber, be based partly on scientific considerations and partly on the value preferences of the importing country. Such measures amount to the imposition of values by importing countries on exporting countries.

The United States measures prohibiting imports of tuna and shrimp were brought to the attention of GATT/WTO under dispute settlement procedures by countries which considered that their export trade was being adversely affected. In both cases the rulings have gone against the United States. The Panels and the Appellate Body have taken the view that these measures are not justifiable under the general exceptions allowed by Article XX, as they were applied on a discriminatory basis and constituted unjustifiable barriers to trade. They have further suggested that, as such measures constitute extraterritorial application on other countries of one country's PPM standards, importing countries contemplating such measures should explore the possibility of negotiating international cooperation arrangements among all interested exporting and importing countries, in order to ensure that such measures are consistent with the provisions of Article XX.

The difficulties inherent in negotiating international cooperation agreements should, however, not be minimized. Such negotiations are time consuming, and the environmentalists pressing for immediate action may not approve of their governments postponing action until consensus is reached at an international level. Moreover, such negotiations tend to be complex, as in most cases the PPMs proposed are not based on scientific considerations but on values to which certain countries or groups in these countries attach importance. Values that may be significant to affluent and well-off societies are not necessarily shared by those with low incomes and differing priorities.

Packaging requirements

Objectives of packaging regulations

'Package' or 'packaging' can be defined as a material or item that is used to protect or contain a commodity or a product.

The main environmental objective for which new packaging requirements are being adopted is to reduce the amount of packaging that enters the waste stream, particularly packaging that has to be disposed of through incineration or landfills. It is estimated that 25% to 30% by weight of the waste generated by a typical household in European countries is packaging waste. As most of these countries are running out of landfill space, the new regulations aim at encouraging domestic manufacturers, importers and foreign companies to reduce the packaging waste that has to be disposed of, *inter alia*, by requiring them to reuse the packaging material several times and to recycle the material which cannot be used more than once.

In addition, packaging requirements may be adopted to reduce the resource intensity of packaging (e.g. by discouraging the use of materials requiring energy-, water- or air-intensive processes) or to control the risks associated with certain types of packages.

Types of requirements

The policy measures taken by governments to achieve the above objectives could include command and control instruments (such as outright bans or mandatory collection or recycling requirements) or economic instruments, which primarily aim at internalizing the externalities of packaging production, use or disposal and at influencing behaviour through the price mechanism. Box 54 highlights the main features of the measures used.

While most of these requirements are imposed uniformly throughout a country under national legislation, it is not uncommon for provincial or local government bodies to adopt a deposit refund or other schemes for the collection of packaging waste, where they consider such schemes necessary for the efficient disposal of packaging waste.

Trade effects of packaging requirements

Even when packaging requirements are applied on a non-discriminatory basis to domestically produced and imported products, they may pose special problems or difficulties to foreign suppliers, particularly in the following situations:

Box 54

Examples of packaging requirements introduced for environmental reasons

Regulatory measures

These include measures prohibiting the use of:

❑ *Packaging materials containing lead, mercury, cadmium;*

❑ *Containers that are not refillable or recyclable; and*

❑ *Packaging material that does not contain or has less than a specified proportion of recycled material.*

Deposit refund systems (DRS). A number of countries have adopted mandatory deposit refund systems for beer and soft-drink containers. Some countries have extended the system to cover containers for detergents and paints. As the consumer can claim the deposit only by returning the containers, the system creates an incentive for them to do this.

Mandatory recycling or recovery laws. In order to facilitate the recycling of packaging waste, the laws of a few countries require households to sort packaging waste (e.g. cans, bottles and paper containers) for separate collection.

Economic instruments

Virgin material tax. This tax can be levied on raw materials used for the production of packaging material. The aim of such an input tax is to reduce the use of virgin materials in favour of recycled materials.

Product charges. These charges are levied on packaging materials. They may be designed to encourage the use of packaging materials that are considered environmentally friendly. For instance, packaging products made entirely from recycled materials may be tax exempt, while those made partly from recycled material may face lower charges. Higher charges would be payable on containers that are not recyclable or refillable.

Cooperative arrangements

In addition, the industry may agree to abide by a voluntary code of conduct negotiated by private-sector associations with a view to reducing the generation of new packaging waste and to increasing the use of refillable or recyclable packaging material.

❑ Where packaging requirements vary from country to country, foreign suppliers may have to incur higher costs to ensure that their exports meet the differing requirements.

❑ Packaging requirements are often formulated on the basis of the packaging materials in common use in an importing country and its waste facilities or priorities; such requirements may discourage overseas suppliers from continuing to use indigenous packaging materials.

❑ Foreign suppliers, particularly in developing countries, may find it difficult to comply with legislation in importing countries which imposes obligations related to the collection and reuse, recycling or final disposal of the packaging waste, if:

   – They find that the costs of joining obligatory programmes (membership and subscription fees, as well as the costs of making their packaging acceptable under the programmes) are high in relation to their total sales in the import market; and

– The facilities do not cater to the packaging materials they use. For instance, the programme may provide for the collection of plastics, corrugated paper or paperboard but not for the collection of wooden packaging materials, jute or the other materials widely used in developing countries.

Some difficulties can be greatly reduced by harmonizing packaging and disposal requirements internationally. There are, however, doubts as to whether international harmonization is feasible; and if feasible, whether it is necessarily desirable, because of the wide differences in national supplies of packaging materials, waste disposal facilities, and the preferences of industries and consumers.

Legal provisions

The TBT Agreement carries specific provisions on packaging. As noted earlier, the Agreement applies primarily to technical regulations specifying product characteristics. It clarifies that such characteristics may include "packaging ... or labelling requirements as they apply to a product, process or production method."

Environmental labelling

Types of environmental labels

Recent years have seen a marked increase in the use of environmental labels on products or their packages to highlight their environmental attributes or features. Most of these labels are voluntary, in that the decision to use a label is taken by manufacturers or by retailers marketing the products under their trade names. In some cases, however, the labels may be enforced by mandatory regulations. Such regulations are intended to warn consumers against the hazardous environmental qualities of products, for instance, on their chlorofluorocarbon (CFC) content.

Voluntary environmental labels are used as a marketing technique to promote sales of products on the basis of their environmental attributes. They can be broadly divided into two categories. In the first category would fall environmental marketing labels which declare the claims of manufacturers and retailers that the product bearing the label has certain specified environmental attributes or qualities. In some cases, in order to assure consumers of the accuracy of the environmental claims, the claims may be certified by independent research laboratories and inspection agencies.

These environmental labels need to be distinguished from the labels falling into the second category, where authorization to use the label is granted by a government-sponsored or a private independent body when it is satisfied that the applicant producer or supplier has met the criteria and conditions it has laid down for the award of the label. The labels in this second category are generally termed 'eco-labels'.

Eco-labelling systems

One of the important features of the eco-labelling system is that the criteria used for awarding the right to use the label are developed by an eco-labelling body. Such criteria are almost invariably determined on the basis of a life-cycle analysis, a process also referred to as the cradle-to-grave approach. Under this approach, an assessment is made of the impact on the environment of the product in various stages of its life cycle. These stages include pre-production (i.e. processing of raw materials), production, distribution (including packaging), utilization or consumption, and disposal after use.

The methodologies for life-cycle analysis vary from system to system. In some systems, detailed analysis of a product's environmental impact is made on the basis of data collected on input and output for each component of a product at every stage of its life cycle. Other systems analyse environmental impact only in relation to certain stages in a product's life cycle. The criteria developed by technical experts on the basis of a life-cycle analysis are approved by a jury consisting of representatives of the industry concerned, environmental, consumer and other groups, and the government. In most cases, even though the environmental impact of the product in all stages of production may have been taken into account, the final criteria may be based on only one or two environmental attributes (e.g. energy consumption in use, recyclability).

The extent of government involvement in the decision-making process, in relation to both the selection of products and the criteria used for the award of the label, varies from country to country. The eco-labelling bodies have to rely, at least initially, on governments for financial support, particularly as the research and technical work for the development of criteria based on the cradle-to-grave approach call for considerable expenditure.

Regulations on the establishment of autonomous eco-labelling bodies often require juries to submit their decisions to governments for approval. In most cases, however, governments are not expected to overrule the juries. For instance, for the Austrian and Nordic labels, the recommendations of the jury are generally accepted. For the German Blue Angel label, the jury has absolute authority to determine product categories and criteria. In contrast, the French Government may substantially change the product criteria which the standardization body (the Association française de normalisation or AFNOR) proposes. In India, representatives of Ministries such as the Environment and Industry are members of the Steering Committee which selects products and determines criteria.

Government involvement in labelling programmes is, on the whole, considered desirable as it is in a better position to ensure that the criteria adopted are based on objective considerations and that they reflect the balanced views of industry, environmental groups and other interest groups.

Eco-labelling programmes aim to protect the environment by raising consumer awareness of the environmental effects of products and hence to modify buying behaviour, and by bringing about a change in product specifications in favour of more environmentally friendly materials and technologies. Under such programmes, labelling is conceived of as a market-oriented instrument which does not establish any binding requirements or restrictions.

Trade effects of eco-labelling systems

Box 55 contains an illustrative list of eco-labelling systems in both developed and developing countries. It can be seen that many eco-labelling systems are sponsored by governments. As the products for which eco-labels have been developed are comparatively few, there is little evidence of their adverse impact on trade.

There are, however, apprehensions that such labelling programmes may put developing countries in a position of competitive disadvantage when a number of schemes now under preparation become operational. These fears are heightened by the fact that foreign suppliers are not able to participate in the negotiations on product selection and eco-labelling criteria.

The problems of foreign producers, particularly those in developing countries, may be exacerbated if the criteria (especially those related to PPMs) are influenced almost entirely by the domestic industry and the environmental values of groups in the country adopting the system. Furthermore, these producers may find it almost impossible to obtain the right to use eco-labels if the criteria differ from country to country.

Box 55
Illustrative list of eco-labelling systems

Government-sponsored eco-labelling systems

❑ *Developed countries*

- Blue Angel: Germany
- Eco Mark: Japan
- Environmental Choice: Canada
- NF Environment: France
- White Swan: Nordic countries
- European Union label

Australia, Austria, the Netherlands and New Zealand have also started eco-labelling programmes.

❑ *Developing countries*

- Eco-logo: Republic of Korea
- Eco-Mark: India
- Green Label: Singapore

Efforts to develop eco-labelling systems in some other developing countries are at various stages of development.

Private labelling schemes (non-government)

❑ *Scientific Certification System, earlier known as the Green Cross: United States*
❑ *Green Seal: United States*
❑ *Good Environmental Choice: Sweden*

Two private initiatives in Germany, one for textiles and another for tropical timber, are developing criteria for labelling these products.

GATT provisions on environmental labelling

The main provisions of GATT law applicable to environmental labelling are contained in the TBT Agreement.

Consumption and other taxes imposed for environmental purposes

Internal taxes and charges – such as consumption taxes, product charges, emission charges and administrative charges – are being increasingly used for the attainment of environmental objectives. Box 56 cites some of the environmental purposes for which such taxes are levied.

GATT rules

GATT rules permit countries to levy on imported products (in addition to customs duties) internal taxes that are payable on like domestic products. To ensure that such taxes do not result in a higher level of protection for domestic production, Article III.2 of GATT reiterates the national treatment rule in regard to internal taxation and states that imported products should not be subjected "directly or indirectly, to internal taxes or other internal charges of any kind in excess of those applied ... to like domestic products." Product and administrative charges would thus be consistent with GATT rules so long as they are not levied on imported products at a rate higher than that applicable to products of domestic origin.

Box 56
Taxes levied for the attainment of environmental objectives

Product charges

These are applied to products that are polluting or because some of their components create disposal problems. Among these products are toxic chemicals, detergents containing phosphates, batteries containing heavy metals and non-returnable packaging. Such charges may also be levied at a lower rate to encourage consumption of less-polluting products such as lead-free petrol.

Emission charges

These are applied on pollutants released into the air, water or soil, or on the generation of noise. They may be levied at the point of consumption (in which case they are similar to product charges and would have similar trade effects) or they may take the form of user charges to cover the cost of public treatment of effluents and waste.

Administrative charges

These are generally applied in conjunction with regulatory instruments to cover the costs of government services, and can take the form of license, registration, testing and control fees.

The use of revenues raised by the application of internal taxes on imports

Can internal taxes on polluting products applicable to both domestically produced and imported products be levied to raise revenue for financing environmental programmes of solely domestic benefit?

This issue was considered in 1987 by a GATT Dispute Settlement Panel on the basis of a complaint made by the European Community, Canada and Mexico in relation to the United States Superfund Amendment and Reauthorization Act. The Act authorized a tax on imported and domestically produced chemicals used in the manufacture of derivatives to fund the Superfund programme for cleaning up hazardous wastes resulting from industrial production in the country. The United States claimed that the measures were consistent with GATT Article III – the Article which permits countries to make border tax adjustments by levying internal taxes on imported products provided the national treatment rule was strictly adhered to. The European Community argued that the tax should not have been levied on imported products.

The Panel concluded that the tax was consistent with the national treatment principle of Article III and thus eligible for a border tax adjustment. As regards the above point made by EC, the Panel observed that:

> ...the tax adjustment rules of the General Agreement distinguish between taxes on products [direct taxes] and taxes not directly levied on products [indirect taxes]; they do not distinguish between taxes with different policy reasons. Whether a sales tax on a product is levied for general revenue purposes or to encourage the rational use of environmental resources is therefore not relevant for the determination of the eligibility of a tax for border tax adjustment.

As regards the contention that, in accordance with the polluter-pays principle, only domestic production should have been taxed, the Panel observed that the principle, although accepted by OECD countries on a voluntary basis, was not part of GATT law. In particular, it stated that: "The General Agreement's rules on border tax adjustment" give a GATT member country "the possibility to follow the Polluter-Pays Principle, but they do not oblige it to do so."

The Panel, however, observed that if a GATT member country

> ...wishes to tax the sale of certain domestic products (because their production pollutes the domestic environment) and to impose a lower tax or no tax at all on the imported products (because their consumption or use causes fewer environmental problems) it is, in principle, free to do so.

The Panel Report appears to suggest that it considered it inequitable that the tax, which was intended solely to finance the importing country's domestic environmental programme, should have been levied also on imported products. However, as its mandate required it to examine the case on the basis of the existing law, the Panel, while holding that the United States measures were consistent with GATT, suggested that the GATT Group on Environmental Measures and International Trade should examine whether the polluter-pays principle should be included in GATT law and whether any changes in GATT rules relating to border tax adjustment were necessary. The annex to this chapter describes the main features of this principle.

Trade provisions in multilateral environmental agreements

There are over 140 international agreements and instruments in the environmental field. About 20 of these multilateral environmental agreements (MEAs) contain trade provisions. These can be grouped into three categories:

❑ Agreements to control transborder pollution or to protect the global commons. Examples of such agreements are the Vienna Convention for the Protection of the Ozone Layer and its Montreal Protocol on Substances That Deplete the Ozone Layer, and the Agreement on Climate Change.

❑ Agreements to protect endangered species, migratory birds, and animals, fish and sea animals. Examples are the Convention on International Trade in Endangered Species of Wild Fauna and Flora (CITES) and the International Convention for the Regulation of Whaling. Among the provisions of these Agreements are guidelines on methods for catching or killing wild animals or fish.

❑ Agreements to control production and trade in hazardous products and substances. Examples are the Basel Convention on the Control of Transboundary Movements of Hazardous Wastes and their Disposal, and the London Guidelines for the Exchange of Information on Chemicals in International Trade.

Broadly speaking, the obligations imposed by these agreements on participating countries in order to control trade take the form of a prohibition on imports and exports.

From the viewpoint of GATT law, the imposition of restrictions on trade with the other countries participating in an MEA may not present any problem, as all the MEA participants have agreed to the imposition of restrictions. Each member country would be able to justify the restriction as being necessary under Article XX for the protection of health or the conservation of resources in its territory.

The situation would be different where the MEA also imposes a prohibition on trade with countries that are not parties to the agreement. An illustration often cited in this context is the Montreal Protocol. It calls on countries that are parties to it to eliminate production and consumption of substances that deplete the ozone layer (listed as 'controlled substances') by the year 2000. As regards trade with parties, the Protocol leaves it to each country to decide how it should restrict its exports and imports of such substances, taking into account its overall commitment to eliminating production and consumption of such substances by the target date. The parties to the Protocol, however, were required to prohibit trade with non-parties in substances that deplete the ozone layer immediately after the Protocol became operational. Similar provisions which require parties to apply more trade-restrictive measures to non-parties than to parties are incorporated in the Basel Convention and in CITES.

These provisions raise two sets of questions. First, are the trade provisions requiring member countries to prohibit or restrict their trade with countries that are not parties to the environmental agreements really necessary and desirable from the economic point of view? The second question is whether these provisions, which apply on a discriminatory basis to imports or exports from non-parties, are consistent with the obligations of parties under the general principles of international law and, more particularly, GATT law.

These issues are being discussed in the bodies concerned with the environment such as UNEP and in the WTO Committee on Trade and Environment (CTE). However, as CTE noted in its 1996 report, the WTO rules provide broad scope for such measures and there was as yet no agreement among member countries to change the related WTO provisions.

Environmental benefits of trade liberalization

One of the broader and important issues receiving the attention of CTE is the relationship between trade liberalization, and environmental protection and sustainable development. To provide a basis for discussion on the subject, the WTO Secretariat has prepared a background paper covering a number of sectors (agriculture, energy, fisheries, forestry, non-ferrous metals, textiles and clothing, leather, and environmental services), outlining the most prevalent trade restrictions and distortions in each sector and the environmental benefits associated with their elimination.

The paper notes that, to a great extent, trade liberalization is not the primary cause of environmental degradation, nor are trade instruments the first-best policy for addressing environmental problems. The most significant part of the relationship between trade liberalization and the environment is reflected in its indirect effects on levels and patterns of production and consumption. Therefore, the environmental benefits of removing trade restrictions and distortions are also likely to be indirect and not readily identifiable in general terms.

The basic premise of the Secretariat's paper is that in well-functioning market-based economies, prices register the relative scarcity of resources and consumer preferences; their role is, *inter alia*, to allocate resources efficiently. The welfare of society can be undermined, however, when market prices fail to capture the effects of environmentally damaging activities and therefore send misleading signals on the optimal use of environmental resources. Resource misallocation undermines effective environmental management. Distorted prices obscure the abundance of under-utilized environmental resources, contribute to the excessive depletion of exhaustible resources, generate new environmental problems, and increase the excessive use of environmentally damaging inputs.

The background paper, however, points to a positive relationship between the removal of trade restrictions and distortions and improved environmental quality. Such a relationship results in:

❑ More efficient factor-use and consumption patterns through enhanced competition;

❑ Poverty reduction through trade expansion and the encouragement of a sustainable rate of natural resource exploitation;

❑ An increase in the availability of environment-related goods and services through market liberalization; and

❑ Better conditions for international cooperation through a continuing process of multilateral negotiations.

For developing countries, trade is the main means available to secure the resources needed for environmental protection. The political promises made at the United Nations Conference on Environment and Development (UNCED) of large financial and technology transfers to developing countries to help them meet their economic development and environmental protection needs have not been fulfilled. As a result, trade liberalization in favour of products of export interest to developing countries has become a fundamental requirement to help them achieve sustainable development. In addition, to address some of the most pressing global environmental problems (e.g. climate change), liberalizing trade in environmental goods and services can make a significant contribution.

Future work

CTE continues to carry out analytical work on these and other related issues. The decision on whether there should be negotiations leading to the development of new rules in this area will be taken at the third Ministerial Conference to be held in November 1999.

References

Trade and environment. (WTO, background paper submitted to the Trade and Environment Seminar, Cairo, 1998).

Rege, Vinod. GATT Law and environment-related issues affecting trade of developing countries. *Journal of World Trade*, 28:3, 1994.

ANNEX

Polluter-pays and user-pays principles

According to the polluter-pays principle (PPP) the polluter should be made to bear the expenses incurred by public authorities for the abatement of pollution and its prevention and for the maintenance of the environment in an acceptable state. It complements the user-pays principle (UPP) which was developed by OECD subsequently. While PPP is concerned with pollution, UPP deals with the pricing of exhaustible natural resources. It states that the price of a natural resource should reflect the full range of costs involved in using it, including the costs of the external effects associated with exploiting, transforming and using the resource, together with the costs of future uses forgone.

The economic rationale on which both these principles are based is that when environmental costs are fully internalized, and are thus reflected in prices, the market mechanism can be expected to encourage the adoption of techniques for pollution abatement and for the conservation of exhaustible resources to levels consistent with sustainable development, and to help prevent distortions in investment allocation and trade patterns. The implementation of the two principles by all countries could thus facilitate the sustainable development of the world's resources.

It is visualized that the internalization of costs in accordance with these two principles can be achieved through command and control measures (ranging from process and product standards to individual regulations and prohibitions) and/or through economic instruments (providing for the levy of various kinds of pollution charges).

CHAPTER 22

Trade and investment

Background: discussions in GATT/WTO on trade and investment

The General Agreement on Tariffs and Trade (GATT) came into existence some 50 years ago. It is important to recall that it was negotiated on the basis of the trade provisions of the Havana Charter, which contained chapters on foreign direct investment and restrictive business practices. These, however, were not included in GATT. The Havana Charter did not become operational because of the failure of the United States to ratify it.

The question of including in the text of GATT investment provisions was raised soon after GATT became operational. In the 1955 Review, a Resolution on International Investment for Economic Development was adopted, which recognized that an increased flow of capital into countries in need of investment from abroad, particularly into developing countries, would facilitate the attainment of the objectives of the General Agreement. It recommended that countries in a position to provide capital for international investment, and those which desired to obtain such capital, should use their best endeavours to create conditions to stimulate the international flow of capital. These included providing security for existing and future investment, the avoidance of double taxation, and facilitating the transfer of earnings of foreign investments. It urged GATT member countries to enter into consultations or participate in negotiations directed to the conclusion of bilateral and multilateral agreements on these matters.

In the years that followed, GATT extended the scope of its rules, initially confined to measures applied by governments at the border, to internal policy measures. Even though the new rules adopted in the 1970s during the Tokyo Round of negotiations in such areas as subsidies, technical specifications and government procurement aimed primarily at the removal of barriers to trade, some of them are also relevant to the competitive conditions which foreign investors face. For instance, as is explained in detail later in this chapter, the rules developed in the area of subsidies are applicable to some aspects of the incentives provided by governments to attract foreign investment.

Another important development in the work of GATT has been the gradual evolution of international rules governing the treatment of foreign companies. Originally, GATT rules imposed obligations on governments only in respect of foreign goods. They were not concerned with the treatment of foreign persons, legal or natural, operating in their territories, the issue at the heart of investment policy. The General Agreement on Trade in Services and the Agreement on Trade-Related Aspects of Intellectual Property Rights, negotiated in the Uruguay Round, impose important obligations on governments regarding the treatment of foreign nationals or companies within their territories. In addition the Agreement on Trade-Related Investment Measures, also negotiated in the Uruguay Round, requires governments not to place conditions on investors, such as local content requirements, that are inconsistent with the provisions of GATT.

Taking into account these developments, as well as the important role which foreign direct investment (FDI) now plays in the globalizing world economy, it was decided at the 1996 Singapore Ministerial Conference to establish a Working Group on the Relationship between Trade and Investment. Its mandate is to examine the relationship between trade and investment, it being understood that the creation of the Working Group is without prejudice to the issue of whether multilateral disciplines on investment should be established within the framework of WTO. The Singapore Ministerial Declaration provides that any decision to launch negotiations on investment disciplines in WTO would require explicit consensus. Thus, the work taking place in the Group is intended to be an educational process and not a negotiation.

FDI: its importance and impact; existing agreements and WTO provisions

Growing importance of FDI

Foreign direct investment (FDI) is an important driving force in globalization, which characterizes the modern world economy. The escalating flow of FDI, which has been accompanied by rising foreign portfolio equity investment, underscores the increasingly major role played by transnational corporations (TNCs) in the economies of both developed and developing countries. The liberalization of FDI regimes particularly by developing and transition economies, which in the past restricted FDI flows, and the steps they have taken to promote it have more than doubled annual global flows over the past decade; the flows to developing countries have increased more than fivefold (see table below).

Foreign direct investment inflows, 1986-1997
(in billions of United States dollars)

Economies	1986-1991 (Annual average)	1992	1993	1994	1995	1996	1997
World	159.3	175.9	217.6	24	3331.1	337.6	401
Developed countries	129.6	120.3	138.9	141.5	211.5	195.4	233
Developing countries	29.1	51.1	72.5	95.6	105.5	129.8	149
Africa	2.9	3.1	3.6	5.7	5.1	4.8	4.7
Latin America	9.5	17.6	17.2	28.7	31.9	43.8	56.1
Asia	16.4	29.6	51.2	60.7	67.3	80	86.9
Central and Eastern Europe	0.65	4.4	6.1	5.9	14.2	12.3	18.4
Least developed countries	0.8	1.5	1.7	0.8	1	1.9	1.8

Source: UNCTAD, *World Investment Report 1998 Trends and Determinants* (United Nations Publication, Sales No. E.98.II.D.5).

Origin and direction of FDI flows to developing countries

Origin

Investment in most host regions of the developing world is dominated by three developed countries/areas. The European Union is the source of most investments in Africa and Europe, Japan in Asia, and the United States dominates investment in Latin America.

A few developing countries (such as China, India, the Republic of Korea and Singapore in Asia, and Argentina, Brazil and Chile in Latin America) have in recent years also become FDI sources, particularly for developing countries in their respective regions.

Direction

FDI flows are directed mainly to a few developing countries. For instance, taking the four-year period 1993 to 1997, of the total FDI flows to developing countries, about a third went to China. The next largest recipients were Mexico, Singapore, Brazil, Malaysia and Indonesia. Overall, 20 developing countries, mostly the more advanced among them, received about 90% of the total FDI flow to developing countries. All the remaining developing and least developed countries received barely 10% of the total. The 48 least developed countries received 1.4% of the total flow to the developing world.

Forms of FDI

Foreign direct investment generally takes two forms: greenfield, or investment in new production facilities, and mergers and acquisitions (M&As).

Cross-border M&As have been on the rise in recent years; they accounted for about half of the total flow of FDI in 1997. Though most M&As are taking place among companies in the United States and Europe, the phenomenon is also noticeable in some developing countries and in transition economies, particularly where State enterprises are being privatized.

Beneficial impact of FDI on host countries: transfer of technology

Among the reasons for the change in the attitude of many developing and transition countries to FDI is the belief that it can be an important channel for technology transfer, with technology broadly defined as including not only scientific processes, but also organizational, managerial and marketing skills.

FDI is often associated with secondary benefits through the diffusion of technology to firms in the host country. This diffusion may be deliberate, such as when technology is licensed by the affiliate to a domestic firm, or it may take the form of a technological spillover which occurs when the activities of the multinational firm yield benefits for local economic agents beyond those intended by the multinational.

FDI may also produce other unintended efficiency-enhancing effects, such as when local rivals are forced to upgrade their own technological capabilities as a consequence of competitive pressure from the local affiliate of the TNC. In the United States, for example, the entry of Japanese automobile manufacturers into the local market via FDI caused the major domestic automobile producers (themselves multinational firms) to upgrade their own products and to increase the efficiency of their domestic production facilities. This has benefited all consumers in the United States, whether they purchased Japanese or American automobiles. There is considerable evidence that similar benefits occur in developing countries. FDI from the Republic of Korea, for example, contributed to the development of a locally owned garment-exporting industry in Bangladesh.

In many circumstances, FDI may result in a greater diffusion of know-how than other ways of serving the market. While imports of high-technology products, as well as the purchase or licensing of foreign technology, are important channels for the international diffusion of technology, FDI provides more scope for spillovers. For example, the technology and productivity of local firms may improve as foreign firms enter the market and demonstrate new technologies and new modes of organization and distribution, provide technical assistance to their local suppliers and customers, and train workers and managers who may later be employed by local firms. Foreign subsidiaries may themselves conduct research and development activities aimed at adapting the parent firm's innovation to local conditions. Clearly FDI leads to more extensive personal interaction with foreigners and exposure to new ways of doing things than does trade.

FDI and anti-competitive practices

FDI, by increasing the 'contestability' of markets (i.e. flexibility for entry or exit by firms) generally results in increased competition. In certain situations however consumers and users in the host countries may not benefit from such investment through lower prices and better quality goods and services, if the TNC investing in the country is able to charge monopoly prices by securing a dominant position. (*See* also chapter 23.)

FDI and foreign portfolio equity investment

FDI involves decisions to invest in another country by establishing subsidiaries, affiliates or joint ventures. Recent years have also witnessed a rise in the flow of funds for foreign portfolio equity investment (FPEI). By contributing to, or participating in, the equity capital of firms, both FDI and FPEI can enhance the development of the enterprise sector in host countries. There are however important differences in regard to both the motivation for the two types of investments and the short- and long-term impact which they could have on the economies of the host countries.

In principle, FPEI is distinguished from FDI by the degree of management control that the foreign investor exercises on a venture. An investment is normally considered FDI when it involves an equity capital stake of 10% or more[32] of the ordinary share of the incorporated enterprise or its equivalent for an unincorporated enterprise. Portfolio equity investors usually provide financial capital by purchasing shares of a company without any involvement in the company's management. The type of investors is also different. While FDI investors are firms engaged in the production of goods and services, portfolio equity investors are more often either financial institutions, institutional investors (such as pension funds, insurance companies or investment trusts) or individuals who are mainly interested in the financial returns on their investments.

These differences highlight the major contrast between the motivations for FDI and FPEI. In making FDI, TNCs are interested in ensuring that the inputs they need or the final products which they manufacture are produced in the most efficient way and at the lowest cost. They are therefore more influenced in their decisions by the long-term effects the investment can have on the competitiveness of the corporation as a whole and the returns from the capital invested and the technology provided. The overriding motivation for investment by portfolio equity investors on the other hand is their participation in local earnings through capital gains and dividends. Their interest in the long-term fortune of the enterprises is limited.

---

32   The IMF *Balance-of-Payments Manual* states that FDI is investment that reflects the objective of a resident entity in one economy to obtain a lasting interest in an enterprise resident in another economy, and that the lasting interest implies the existence of a long-term relationship between the direct investor and the enterprise and a significant degree of influence by the investor on the management of the enterprise. The concept of lasting interest was not defined by IMF in terms of a specific time-frame, and the more pertinent criterion adopted was that of the degree of ownership in an enterprise. A percentage of 10 or above of ownership was often deemed to reflect a lasting interest.

FPEI flows therefore tend to be volatile. Investors try to liquidate investments by selling their equity positions in secondary markets if their profits are declining or the prices of their equity holdings are falling. TNCs on the other hand tend to take a more long-term view of their investments; even in a crisis situation, they may be reluctant to liquidate their share in the equity of their affiliates, where 'sunk' costs are high and the production of the affiliate is interlinked with their international production.

In practice, the difference in the degree of volatility between FPEI and FDI may not be as marked as described above and depends on the mechanism used for channelling the portfolio investment. The portfolio funds are often invested by venture capital companies, which provide equity capital for new companies at the start-up stage; they are often closely involved in managing them, either directly or indirectly, by providing advisory services. Although their overriding motive is to achieve capital gain, venture capital investors often wait several years before selling their equity stakes.

Government measures to promote investment

Relaxation of regulatory regimes

The last two decades have witnessed the widespread liberalization of laws and regulations on foreign investment, especially in developing countries and transition economies. In most cases, this liberalization of foreign investment policies has been part of a market-oriented reform of economic policies involving trade liberalization, deregulation and privatization. The measures taken include:

❏ Simplification of screening requirements for approving inward FDI;

❏ Opening up industries to foreign investment;

❏ Minimizing restrictions on foreign equity participation;

❏ Encouraging foreign investors to take interest in the privatization process and in infrastructure development (two areas which need heavy capital and technological investments).

Grant of investment incentives

In addition, almost all countries provide incentives to attract FDI. These take the following three forms:

❏ Financial incentives, involving the provision of funds directly to the foreign investor by the host government, for example, in the form of investment grants and subsidized credits.

❏ Fiscal incentives, designed to reduce the overall tax burden for a foreign investor. To this category belong such items as tax holidays and exemptions from import duties on raw materials, intermediate inputs and capital goods.

❏ Indirect incentives, designed to enhance profitability for the investor in various indirect ways. For example, the government may provide land and designated infrastructure at less-than-commercial prices. Or it may grant the foreign firm a privileged market position, in the form of preferential access to government contracts, a monopoly position, a closing of the market for further entry, protection from import competition or special regulatory treatment.

Imposition of performance requirements

A number of countries, particularly the developing ones, impose performance requirements in order to ensure that the investment made conforms to their national objectives and priorities. These, *inter alia*, require foreign investors:

❑ To produce a certain percentage of the inputs used in the final product in the host country (local content requirement);

❑ To export a given level of goods or services; and

❑ To achieve a given level of research and development in the country.

Bilateral, regional and multilateral investment instruments

Bilateral investment treaties

The desire of governments to facilitate FDI flows is also reflected in the dramatic increase in bilateral investment treaties for the protection and promotion of investment during the 1990s. As of 1 January 1997, there were 1,330 such treaties involving 162 countries as compared to 440 treaties in the beginning of the decade.

Nearly 62% of these treaties are between developed countries and developing countries. The developed countries that have been active in negotiating such treaties with developing countries include France, Germany, the Netherlands, the United Kingdom and the United States. The treaties focus on protecting the interests of investing companies from expropriation, compensation for losses due to armed conflict or internal disorder, and the transfer of payments. The definition of investment used broadly covers both FDI and foreign equity portfolio investment. Some treaties provide for the extension of national treatment. Such provisions, requiring parties not to extend less favourable treatment to foreign investors than that accorded to domestic investors, apply only after local production or commercial presence in the host country has been established as a result of investment. Only a very limited number of agreements provide for the extension of national treatment at entry of investment.

Developing countries have also begun to conclude bilateral investment treaties with one another. In 1997, 11% of all such treaties were among developing countries. The countries which are active in concluding such treaties, mainly with other developing countries in their respective regions, are Algeria, Chile, China and the Republic of Korea. This development reflects the emergence of firms from developing countries as outward investors.

Regional arrangements dealing with investment issues

In addition to these bilateral investment treaties, arrangements have been adopted to promote foreign investment on a regional basis under regional cooperation arrangements. The regional agreements containing provisions for the non-discriminatory treatment of foreign investors include the Treaty of Rome establishing the European Economic Community, the Agreement on the European Economic Area and the Agreements establishing ASEAN, MERCOSUR and NAFTA. Many of these Agreements provide for the extension of national treatment to foreign investment at both the pre-entry and post-entry stages.

Multilateral agreement on investment

Although several efforts were made in the past to develop a binding multilateral instrument containing comprehensive substantive rules on foreign investment, none were successful. More recently, negotiations were held among OECD countries on developing a comprehensive multilateral agreement on investment (MAI). Although these negotiations were held among OECD member countries, they had declared that the resulting agreement would be open for accession by other countries. The draft agreement aimed at imposing obligations on member countries to extend non-discriminatory treatment to foreign and domestic investors in both the pre-establishment and post-establishment phase by applying the national treatment principle; to abolish performance requirements; and to discipline the use of investment incentives by the application of the three basic principles – MFN, national treatment and transparency.

The negotiations have however ended without accord being reached on the draft text of the agreement because of the serious differences among participating countries on the inclusion of special provisions on labour, environment and cultural industries.

Box 57 lists some multilateral investment instruments that are now in force. Of these, the instruments that impose binding obligations are narrow in scope and do not establish substantive norms, while the instruments that set forth substantive norms are non-binding.

Box 57
Existing multilateral foreign investment instruments

Within the World Bank Group, two multilateral instruments of a legally binding nature specifically relating to foreign investment have been concluded. One is the Convention on the Settlement of Investment Disputes between States and Nationals of Other States, which was concluded in 1965 and entered into force in October 1966. It establishes facilities for the resolution of disputes between investors and States through conciliation and arbitration in the International Centre for the Settlement of Investment Disputes (ICSID).

The other agreement concluded under the auspices of the World Bank Group is the Convention Establishing the Multilateral Investment Guarantee Agency, which was concluded in 1985 and which entered into force in April 1988. Based on a belief that the flow of foreign investment to developing countries can be facilitated and promoted by alleviating concerns related to non-commercial risks, the principal aim of the Multilateral Investment Guarantee Agency is to provide a multilateral investment insurance mechanism as a complement to national, regional and private investment insurance schemes. The Convention also contemplates a role for the Agency with regard to substantive standards for the treatment of investment. Under Article 12(d) of the Convention, the Agency must, in guaranteeing an investment, satisfy itself, inter alia, as to "the investment conditions in the host country, including the availability of fair and equitable treatment and legal protection for the investment". Article 23 of the Convention deals with investment promotion and stipulates that, in addition to research and technical assistance activities, the Agency is to facilitate the conclusion of agreements among members of the Convention on the promotion and protection of foreign investment.

Substantive multilateral norms for the treatment of foreign investment are contained in the non-binding Guidelines on the Treatment of Foreign Direct Investment, developed in the World Bank Group following an April 1991 request by the IMF-World Bank Development Committee for the preparation of a report on "an overall legal framework which would embody the essential legal principles so as to promote foreign direct investment". The Guidelines were "called to the attention" of the members of the World Bank Group by the Development Committee in September 1992 "as useful parameters in the admission and treatment of private foreign investment in their territories, without prejudice to the binding rules of international law". They differ in two main respects from the work initiated in 1977 in the United Nations on a Code of Conduct for Transnational Corporations. First, they cover only general principles to guide governmental behaviour toward foreign investors; rules of good conduct for foreign investors are not included. Second, they do not purport to represent a codification of customary international law in regard to the treatment of foreign investment, but rather to formulate generally acceptable international standards which support the objective of promoting foreign investment. The five sections of the Guidelines address the scope of application, the admission of foreign investment, standards of treatment of foreign investment, expropriation and unilateral alterations or termination of contracts, and settlement of disputes.

Mention should also be made of other multilateral instruments that are somewhat different in scope but are nevertheless relevant in this context. Several United Nations General Assembly Resolutions adopted in the 1960s and 1970s include provisions on foreign investment mainly with a view to affirming certain rights of host States. Matters relating to social policy have been dealt with in the (non-binding) ILO Tripartite Declaration of Principles concerning Multinational Enterprises and Social Policy which was adopted in 1977 and took effect in 1978. The Declaration contains principles commended to governments, employers' and workers' organizations of home and host countries and to multinational enterprises.

Source: WTO, *Annual Report 1996*, vol. 1, *Special Topic: Trade and Foreign Direct Investment.*

WTO provisions

As noted earlier, a number of provisions in WTO law deal with trade-related investment issues. Some of these are listed below.

Agreement on Subsidies and Countervailing Measures

The Agreement on SCM defines the concept of 'subsidy' and establishes disciplines on the provision of subsidies. In the three categories of investment incentives described earlier, viz. fiscal incentives, financial incentives and indirect incentives, a few types of measures would constitute subsidies as defined in the Agreement on SCM. That is, they can involve a financial contribution by a government or public body, and confer a benefit. (*See* chapter 8.)

Agreement on Trade-Related Investment Measures

The Agreement on TRIMs prohibits countries from using five types of trade-related investment measures (such as local content requirements) which are considered inconsistent with the provisions of GATT 1994 on national treatment (Article III) and those prohibiting the use of quantitative restrictions (Article XI).

All countries maintaining trade-related investment measures that were inconsistent with the provisions of the Agreement were required to notify them within 90 days of the coming into operation of the Agreement. In regard to such notified measures, developing countries are given a transition period of five years (i.e. up to 1 January 2000) to eliminate them. A longer period of seven years (i.e. up to 1 January 2002) is provided to least developed countries for this purpose.

The limited coverage of the Agreement on TRIMS led countries to stipulate that its operation should be reviewed in five years. The Agreement provides that any such review should also consider complementing its provisions with provisions on investment and on competition policy. (*See* chapter 13.)

General Agreement on Trade in Services

The other important provisions on investment are contained in GATS. The Agreement recognizes that, unlike international trade in goods which takes place through cross-border movement, trade in services takes place through three other modes. One mode is the establishment of a commercial presence in the country where the service is to be provided. GATS further visualizes that countries may agree in trade negotiations to give commitments permitting foreign suppliers on a selective sector-by-sector basis to establish such commercial presence (e.g. by setting up a subsidiary or a branch). In making such commitments, it is open to a country to impose certain permitted conditions limiting market access or the extension of national treatment to foreign suppliers (e.g. limits on foreign equity participation).

There is a basic difference in the approach to providing rights to foreign investors under some regional and multilateral agreements and that adopted under GATS. The regional and multilateral agreements provide for what has come to be known as a 'top down' or 'negative list' approach. Countries are expected to agree to open up for FDI all sectors of industries – whether producing goods or service products – subject to a limited number of exceptions. GATS on the other hand, has adopted a 'bottom up' or 'positive list' approach. Countries are allowed to liberalize gradually and to specify during trade negotiations the service sectors in which they would be willing to grant foreign suppliers the right to establish a commercial presence and to invest. (*See* chapter 17.)

Agreement on Trade-Related Aspects of Intellectual Property Rights

Although the TRIPS Agreement does not directly address foreign investment, its provisions on minimum standards for the protection of intellectual property, domestic enforcement procedures and international dispute settlement are relevant to the legal environment affecting foreign investment (the definition of 'investment' in many intergovernmental investment agreements expressly includes intellectual property). (*See* chapter 20.)

Description of the main issues and points raised in the discussions in the WTO Working Group

Main issues raised

Against the background information provided in the preceding section on trends in FDI and on bilateral and multilateral agreements on investment, this section describes the main points made and the differing views expressed in the Working Group on the Relationship between Trade and Investment.[33] The basis for discussions in the Group is provided by the submissions of delegations and the analytical papers prepared by the Secretariats of WTO, UNCTAD and OECD. In order to provide a structure for its discussions, the Working Group drew up a work programme in its first meeting in June 1997 in the form of a "Checklist of Issues Suggested for Study". The checklist has four main themes:

❑ The implications of the relationship between trade and investment for development and growth;

❑ Economic relationship between trade and investment;

❑ Stocktaking and analysis of existing international agreements on investments; and

---

[33] The Working Group was established in accordance with the Singapore Ministerial Declaration of December 1996.

❑ A number of questions relevant to assessing the advantages of a possible initiative in WTO to establish a set of multilateral rules on investment.

The paragraphs that follow attempt to give an overview of the points made and views expressed in the discussions under each theme. It is important to note that the overview is not comprehensive and may not reflect fully the emphases and nuances attached by the various delegations to the points they made.

Implications of the relationship between trade and investment for development and growth

The Group noted that the experience of a number of countries had demonstrated that FDI brought to the host country a package of tangible and intangible assets. The intangible benefits included technological innovations, managerial skills and human resource development. FDI also helped domestic industries to increase their efficiency by stimulating competition. These intangible benefits were considered far more important than FDI's contribution to capital formation, tax revenue and balance of payments.

Some delegations however pointed out that while FDI played an important positive role in transferring intangible assets to the recipient developing countries, these countries sometimes had to confront the negative effects of such investment. Examples of these negative effects were: restrictions on the activities of foreign affiliates imposed by parents in the context of technology transfer agreements; the risk facing some developing countries of becoming locations for simple assembly operations; instability of the trade balance and of the balance of payments on account of FDI, as illustrated by the recent experience of some countries in South-East Asia; the exercise of undue political influence by foreign firms; and the negative impact of foreign affiliates on domestically available financing and competition in the domestic market, including small and medium-sized enterprises.

Economic relationship between trade and investment

The degree of correlation between trade and investment

In the discussion on this issue, the Group noted that the empirical research on the relationship between foreign trade and investment flows had established that there was an overall positive relationship between the outward flow of investment and the exports of the home country. This was also true of the relationship between the inward flow of investment and the exports of the host country. The studies thus showed that trade effects were positive for both home and host countries. In the case of host countries, the trade impact was more pronounced in countries that followed open and liberal trade policies in order to encourage export-oriented growth, than in countries which still relied on import substitution for promoting economic growth.

However, the view was expressed that it would not be appropriate to place too much emphasis on complementarity between trade and FDI; it was also necessary to look at the effects of such investment on efficiency, employment and economic development. Furthermore, it was pointed out that there was a need to supplement studies of a general nature with more disaggregated analysis of the relationship between trade and investment in specific industries and service sectors.

The impact of investment policies and measures on trade

Under this item the Group discussed the possible impact which investment policies, particularly those relating to investment incentives and performance requirements, could have on trade and investment.

On *investment incentives*, it was stated that studies by international organizations had demonstrated that investment incentives were not a major determinant in location decisions by transnational corporations. In the last decade the use of incentives had increased and the types of incentives used had become more diversified. This had resulted in harmful competition among countries to attract FDI. The indiscriminate use of incentives could distort investment flows in favour of countries that could afford to finance incentives, but in the long run the use of incentives implied losses for all countries involved in such competition, ultimately leading to a transfer of resources to foreign investors. Moreover, incentives could distort international trade flows by artificially favouring production in certain countries to the detriment of countries that were not able to grant incentives, especially when production was destined for export. Empirical studies had also shown that investment incentives could distort the productive structure in host countries by favouring production in certain sectors. In addition, investment incentives entailed high administrative costs, were difficult to administer, and were often granted in a non-transparent manner.

Some delegations however pointed out that, notwithstanding arguments advanced in recent academic literature, investment incentives remained a useful policy instrument in the pursuit of development strategies. The argument that incentives were nothing more than a transfer of income from countries to firms and that the more intense the competition among host countries the greater the proportion of potential gains transferred to multinational enterprises failed to give due recognition to the fact that incentives were not intended to support enterprises that were not viable. Rather, they were geared towards attracting growth, income and employment-creating investment.

On *performance requirements*, it was argued that these requirements deprived enterprises of the flexibility needed to adapt to changing economic circumstances. Performance requirements and incentives created distortions not only in international markets but also in the domestic markets of host countries in so far as competition between different investors was distorted when investments made at different times were subject to different performance requirements and incentives.

However, a point was made that, while trade-related performance requirements, such as local content measures, had been demonstrated not to have positive effects, performance requirements relating to transfer of technology, the promotion of research and development, and the promotion of alliances between foreign and domestic firms generally had been shown to have positive effects. If applied in a market-friendly manner, performance requirements in regard to the transfer of technology and the conduct of research and development could also be viewed as indirectly contributing to the attainment of the objectives of competition policy, in so far as they facilitated access to technology by firms (including small and medium-sized firms), and to economic diversification.

On the *relationship between foreign investment and competition policy*, the point was made that an open and liberal FDI regime increased the prospects for new entry and thus for competition in specific markets. By facilitating the entry of new competitors, liberal investment rules prevented domestic oligopolies, eliminated local distribution bottlenecks and reduced the likelihood of cartels and monopolies.

But it was recognized that highly competitive foreign companies might, by displacing local competitors, acquire dominant positions in the domestic market and abuse these positions. The application of competition law and policy to mergers, acquisitions and joint ventures was therefore an important aspect of the interface between investment and competition policy.

The view was, however, expressed that, though competition would generally lead to greater economic efficiency and ultimately to economic growth and development, some developing countries could have reasons for limiting the pursuit of efficiency as an immediate objective. This arose from the need to take into account competing objectives, including development objectives and the promotion of small and medium-sized enterprises.

Stocktaking and analysis of existing bilateral, regional and international agreements

It was stated that bilateral investment treaties had an important advantage in that they could be tailored to the specific circumstances of the parties involved and could address specific concerns, such as development issues. They could also be concluded more quickly than regional or multilateral agreements and could improve bilateral economic and diplomatic relations. Like bilateral investment treaties, regional agreements on investment were also more politically feasible than multilateral agreements as they involved fewer participants and could be more precisely customized to address individual concerns.

Some delegations were however of the view that experience with bilateral investment treaties did not demonstrate that they were a major determinant of investment decisions. There was therefore little evidence to show that a multilateral framework based on such treaties would have a significant impact on investment flows. It was also argued that, more generally, there was little empirical evidence to suggest that location decisions were greatly influenced by the existence of investment agreements.

The other view was that there was no reason to expect an automatic correlation between the existence of bilateral investment treaties and the size of investment flows, given that such treaties were concluded by governments and not by private parties. Governments presumably negotiated such treaties for a variety of reasons, and it was possible to conceive of situations in which governments entered into negotiations on such treaties for long-term benefits without necessarily expecting short-term results.

It was further argued that the development of a comprehensive set of consistent multilateral rules binding on all WTO member countries would allow for a stable, transparent and consistent environment for firms operating in the global market, whatever their ownership structure or place of incorporation. The global application of broadly the same investment disciplines would remove for investors the complexity arising from the existing framework of bilateral and regional investment agreements and thus facilitate compliance. The adoption of such multilateral rules would provide the following additional advantages over bilateral agreements:

❑ While the negotiation of a bilateral investment agreement, especially an agreement between a developing country and a developed country might be affected by the unbalanced political and economic power relations between the countries in question, this risk was reduced in a multilateral negotiation.

❑ A multilateral approach could enable countries to take a progressive approach to liberalization.

❑ A multilateral agreement could resolve the problem of inconsistencies between bilateral investment agreements. Furthermore, a multilateral agreement on investment negotiated in WTO would ensure consistency of multilateral investment rules with GATS, the TRIMs Agreement and other WTO provisions.

❑ A multilateral agreement would also provide more scope for harmonizing rules and, since changes to the rules would need to be agreed by all parties, it would result in the greater predictability of rules.

Questions relevant to assessing the advantages of a possible initiative in WTO to establish a set of multilateral rules on investment

From among the questions discussed in the Working Group on the advantages of adopting in WTO a set of multilateral rules on investment, the issues raised on the definition of investment and the development implications of possible multilateral rules on investment are briefly noted below.

Definition of investment

In the discussion on the definition of the term 'investment' in a possible international agreement on investment, a number of delegations favoured an "asset-based definition" covering both direct and portfolio investment. It was suggested that the problems that could arise from the inclusion of portfolio investment could be addressed through exceptions and qualifications. Thus, including portfolio investment in a definition of investment in an agreement did not necessarily imply that all obligations of the agreement would apply to such investment.

Some delegations were of the view that the Working Group was established on the clear understanding that its work would be limited to FDI as such. The inclusion of portfolio investment in a definition might have certain policy implications that required further study, including the causes and direction of the volatility of portfolio investment flows and its impact on host economies.

Development implications of possible multilateral rules on investment

Another prominent theme in the discussions in the Working Group was how to reflect the development dimension in any multilateral set of investment rules.

It was argued that one way of doing this was to ensure, in drafting each element of any multilateral set of rules, that consideration was given to development implications.

Some delegations doubted whether the development orientation of a multilateral investment agreement could be ensured simply by adding the development dimension to each of its elements. One also had to look at the structure and design of the proposed instrument and the guiding objectives which determined its contents. In addition, it was necessary to deal with the basic issue of whether the very notion of a multilateral framework for investment *per se* was compatible with the need to preserve the ability of governments to pursue development strategies suited to the special problems of individual countries.

A view was expressed that it must be acknowledged that development was greatly dependent on investment. In the absence of an international discipline that would encourage the flow of investment, countries would find it difficult to attain development objectives.

References

UNCTAD, *World Investment Report 1998 Trends and Determinants* (United Nations Publication, Sales No. E.98.II.D.5).

WTO, *Annual Report 1996*, vol. 1, *Special Topic: Trade and Foreign Direct Investment*

WTO, *Annual Report 1998*, vol. 1, *Special Topic: Globalization and Trade*

CHAPTER 23

Trade and competition policy

The subject of the interaction between trade and competition policy was added to the work programme of WTO as a result of decisions taken at the 1996 Singapore Ministerial Conference. The Working Group which has been established is expected to study and analyse "issues raised by Members relating the interaction between trade and competition policy, including anti-competitive practices," and to "identify areas that merit further consideration in the WTO framework."[34] In carrying out analytical work, the Group is expected to take into account the provisions of the Agreement on Trade-Related Investment Measures, provisions in WTO law on investment and competition policy, and discussions in the Working Group on Trade and Investment.

Competition policy issues in international trade

Defining competition policy

The term 'competition policy' is used in different ways in different countries and in different contexts. At its broadest, it includes all policies relevant to competition in the market, including trade policy, regulatory policy and policies adopted by governments to address the anti-competitive policies of enterprises, whether private or public. In the narrow sense, the term is used to cover the last-mentioned aspect, i.e. laws or policies governing the anti-competitive behaviour of enterprises.

Reasons for including trade and competition in the WTO work programme

Concern at the possible adverse effects of anti-competitive business practices (often referred to as 'restrictive business practices') was expressed as far back as 50 years ago when GATT was being established. The 1947 draft of the Havana Charter contained, in addition to provisions on trade policy, provisions on restrictive business practices and the establishment of an International Trade Organization. The Havana Charter could not be implemented because of the failure of the United States Congress to ratify it. Although the trade policy provisions of the Charter were used to establish GATT, efforts to incorporate provisions on competition policy were frustrated by the divergence of views among negotiating countries on the need for their inclusion. Since then, some countries proposed international rules in this area in GATT discussions, but these proposals were not vigorously pursued.

Increasing interest in recent years in discussions on competition policy can be attributed to many factors. Four of these are noted below.

---

34 Singapore Ministerial Declaration, §20.

❑ There is a growing perception that as governmental barriers are peeled back through successive rounds of trade negotiations, trade restrictions and distortions resulting from the practices of enterprises may be increasing in importance.

❑ Associated with this is the increasing integration of the world economy, spurred not only by trade liberalization but also by the vast expansion of foreign direct investment (FDI). Thus, the anti-competitive practices of enterprises acquire an increasingly transborder dimension, affecting several countries and, in some cases, the whole world.

❑ A further influence has been the growth of international rules, at the bilateral, regional and multilateral levels, that protect the interests of foreign companies operating within a country's territory. For example, in the WTO, as a result of the Uruguay Round, there are now international trade rules of this nature in the area of services and intellectual property and a Working Group is studying the relationship between trade and investment. Some countries feel that such international rules should be accompanied by enhanced international cooperation to control anti-competitive business practices by the companies in question.

❑ Lastly, an important development has been the growing convergence of views, apparently with less of the old North/South and East/West differences, that competition law is often the appropriate legal means for addressing the anti-competitive practices of enterprises even if agreement on specific details still has a considerable way to go.

Forms of anti-competitive business practices

There are four main types of business practices that can have anti-competitive effects and affect international trade. These are:

❑ Horizontal restraints (arrangements between competing firms producing identical or similar products to restrain competition);

❑ Vertical restraints (anti-competitive arrangements between firms along the production-distribution chain);

❑ Abuse of a dominant position;

❑ Mergers.

Horizontal restraints

Horizontal restraint arrangements could take three forms:

❑ Import cartels and related arrangements;
❑ Export cartels and related arrangements;
❑ International cartels.

Import cartels and related arrangements

Import cartels formed by domestic importers or buyers and similar measures (such as boycotts of, or collective refusals to deal with, foreign competitors) are of obvious concern from a market access perspective. Related issues are exclusions of foreign competitors from, or discriminatory terms of membership of trade associations and, in particular, the exclusionary use of standard-setting by such associations. 'Hard core' cartels such as price fixing, output restraints, market division and customer allocation are normally prohibited outright under competition law, although not always unambiguously (in some jurisdictions, they may be permitted if importers are faced with dominating foreign suppliers and competition on domestic markets is not held to be substantially restrained). Other cooperative arrangements among competitors, such as in standard-setting and joint purchasing, are often subject to a rule-of-reason analysis.

Export cartels and related arrangements

Export cartels can be divided into two groups. 'Pure' export cartels direct their efforts exclusively at foreign markets. 'Mixed' export cartels restrain competition in the exporting country's home market as well as in foreign markets.

Pure export cartels are treated as being outside the scope of most countries' competition laws for two reasons. One is that these cartels are considered to be beyond the jurisdiction of domestic competition laws, and the other is that they are explicitly exempted from the application of the laws. Mixed export cartels are generally subject to essentially the same requirements or outright prohibitions as cartels that affect the domestic market alone, although some countries provide special exemptions for such cartels where the domestic restraint or effect is ancillary to the restraint on export trade.

International cartels

International cartels and market sharing agreements between firms in two or more countries are generally recognized as being akin to horizontal price-fixing and other collusive agreements within a single country. In both cases, competition is limited, prices are raised, output is restricted, and markets are allocated for the private benefit of firms. To the extent that their effects in a jurisdiction are similar to those of national cartels, the enforcement of existing competition law should go far in providing a remedy. For example, in the 1940s and 1950s, the United States anti-trust authorities prosecuted a large number of cartel cases involving international markets for primary products and manufactured goods. These cases involved price fixing and the direct allocation of national markets among firms that would otherwise be in competition, reinforced by prohibitions against importing and exporting by the participating firms. In many of these cases, the cartels were built around patent cross-licensing schemes. In the 1990s, there has been a new wave of prosecution of international price-fixing cartels among producers of such products as lysine, citric acid and fax paper.

Another important category of horizontal arrangements about which concerns have been expressed in relation to their possible implications for the exercise of market power in international markets is that of cooperative arrangements for research and development, particularly where the design of legislative provisions for R & D joint ventures make them susceptible to strategic use. Most jurisdictions with modern competition statutes make some form of special provision for inter-firm cooperation (joint ventures and consortia) in R & D programmes that otherwise might not be carried out. It has been noted, however, that provision for such arrangements should not take the form of blanket exemptions from competition law, since competition also has an important role to play in providing incentives for timely innovation and adoption of new technology.

Vertical market restraint arrangements

Vertical market restraint arrangements could cause trade concerns where they prevent foreign firms from having access to distribution networks controlled by domestic suppliers. The practices used include:

❑ Exclusive dealing requirements that prevent distributors from marketing products;

❑ Tied selling that makes purchase of one product of a given brand conditional on purchasing another product of the same brand;

❏ Loyalty or sales rebates that provide financial incentives not to distribute the products of competitors; and

❏ Exclusive territories that prevent distributors from selling outside certain geographical areas.

Abuses of dominant position

The classification of restrictive business practices into horizontal and vertical restraints follows an economic logic. Most competition laws, however, also distinguish between agreements among firms and the 'abuse of dominant position' or 'monopolization'. The latter is defined as a practice employed by dominant firms to maintain, enhance or exploit a dominant position in a market. The practices that can be dealt with under this rubric include:

❏ Exclusive dealing;

❏ Market foreclosure through vertical integration;

❏ Tied selling;

❏ The control of scarce facilities and vital inputs or distribution channels;

❏ Price and non-price predation;

❏ Price discrimination;

❏ Exclusionary contractual arrangements; and

❏ In some jurisdictions, even the simple charging of higher than competitive prices, or the imposition of other 'exploitative' abuses.

Mergers

One can distinguish between three fundamentally different types of mergers: horizontal, vertical and conglomerate mergers.

Horizontal mergers bring together two or more firms in the same line of business and in the same geographic market, which in itself tends to push prices upward, exactly as with a cartel. However, the competition policy decision with regard to horizontal mergers is complicated by the fact that, since a merger allows former rivals to integrate their production facilities, it may also affect the costs of production. If a merger lowers variable costs, it may actually lead to lower market prices than before the merger, and such a merger may then be desirable from a social point of view.

Vertical mergers involve firms that are engaged in different stages of production and marketing within an industry. This type of merger activity is often undertaken to achieve efficiencies by reducing transaction and other costs through the internalization of different stages of production and distribution, but may also be employed to foreclose sources of inputs or distribution channels to competitors.

Conglomerate mergers integrate firms operating in unrelated lines of business. Such mergers normally do not raise concerns from a competition policy point of view, since typically they do not increase the degree of market power that can be exercised by the firms in the relevant product markets.

Main elements of competition law

Before turning to the description of the points made in discussions in the Working Group on the problems resulting from anti-competitive business behaviour, it may be desirable to note briefly the main features of national competition laws that aim at bringing under control such behaviour.

The main objective of national competition laws in countries where they exist is to preserve and promote competition as a means to ensure the efficient allocation of resources in an economy, resulting in the best possible choice of quality, the lowest prices and adequate supplies for consumers. In addition to promoting efficiency, many competition laws make reference to other objectives, such as the control of concentration of economic power, promoting the competitiveness of domestic industries, encouraging innovation, supporting small and medium-sized enterprises, and encouraging regional integration. Some of these additional objectives may sometimes be in conflict with the efficiency objective.

Most competition laws deal with enterprise behaviour by prohibiting such anti-competitive business practices as competition-restricting horizontal agreements, acquisitions and abuses of dominant positions, as well as substantially restrictive vertical distribution agreements. In addition, an increasing number of competition laws deal with alterations to the structure of markets, through the control of mergers and acquisitions as well as joint ventures aimed at avoiding the creation of dominant firms, monopolies, or even oligopolies. In some laws, the divestment of parts of monopolies is also authorized to change the structure of markets.

These laws also contain exceptions and exemptions to the application of their provisions. These can cover, among others, labour, regulated industries (e.g. telecommunications, defence, agriculture), small and medium-sized enterprises, and certain types of cooperative arrangements, including R & D joint ventures.

A number of countries, however, are reviewing the soundness and validity of those across-the-board exemptions. The emphasis is increasingly on applying competition law to all business practices. It is then the task of the competition authority or courts to consider business practices, and focus on those that have the highest probability of anti-competitive effects and the least justification based on efficiency.

Overview of the main issues under discussion in the WTO Working Group[35]

Main issues under discussion

The main focus of discussions in the WTO Working Group on the Interaction between Trade and Competition Policy has been on the interaction between trade policy and development on the one hand and competition policy on the other. The following provides some highlights of the discussions that have been held in the Group, *inter alia*, under the following main headings:

❑ Relationship of trade and competition policy to development and economic growth;

❑ Impact of anti-competitive practices of enterprises and associations on international trade;

❑ State monopolies and regulations;

❑ Relationship between investment and competition policy;

❑ Relationship between trade-related aspects of intellectual property rights and competition policy;

❑ Impact of trade policy on competition.

---

35   This overview has been taken largely from the report of the Working Group on its activities in 1997 and 1998. For fuller details, the reader should consult the report itself ["Report (1998) of the Working Group on the Interaction between Trade and Competition Policy to the General Council" (WTO, WT/WGTCP/2, 8 December 1998)].

Relationship of trade and competition policy to development and economic growth

The Group paid particular attention to the analysis of the relationship of trade and competition policy to development. In this context, it was pointed out that in a number of countries competition law and policy had been implemented or strengthened not in isolation, but rather as one element of a package of interrelated reforms of policies aimed at promoting economic and social development. A central feature of these reforms had been greater reliance on market forces as an engine of development and adjustment and on the creation of a framework aimed at ensuring that such forces operate in the public interest, notably by promoting or maintaining competition in markets. The related reforms included external market-opening measures (including liberalization of trade and foreign investment regimes), privatization and sector-specific regulatory reforms/deregulation. The various elements of the package were considered to be mutually reinforcing.

A related point made in the discussions concerned the heightened importance of competition policy as a tool for development in the current globalizing economic environment, as compared to previous eras. The argument was made that, whereas in the past, countries could hope to achieve development through other (possibly more interventionist) tools and approaches, these approaches were no longer workable because of the extent to which trade liberalization and globalization of business activities had taken place and the increased importance of foreign direct investment as an engine of growth in the present economic environment. As a result of these developments, anti-competitive practices of enterprises were increasingly international in scope, and appeared to be more significant than in the past. Consequently, according to this view, a vigorous competition policy was necessary to respond appropriately to these concerns and to establish a climate conducive to investment and economic growth.

While the view that competition had a role to play in economic development received broad support in the Group, a view was also expressed that a comprehensive competition law might not be strictly necessary to ensure the desired degree of competition. This reflected several underlying considerations.

Of the 134 Members of WTO, only between 70 and 80 have competition laws. Even in countries where such laws exist, enforcement may in some cases be lax because of the lack of financial resources and of persons with expertise in competition law. Given the extremely complex nature of the law, its adoption by countries which do not have such legislation at present is going to be time consuming.

Moreover, if competition laws are to meet the objective of promoting economic growth by improving economic efficiency and making markets competitive, many Members believe that they must take into account the particular characteristics of developing countries such as low income levels, skewed distribution of wealth, low levels of education and asymmetric information. These may require them to adopt a more flexible approach and selective government intervention in the market. For instance, the competition legislation of most developed countries provide for special treatment of small and medium-sized industries. In developing countries the need to extend to these industries special treatment – by providing them tax and other incentives, and access to finance on concessional terms – may be even greater. The governments of these countries may also find it necessary to play a more active role in markets to safeguard national security (by maintaining production capacities in industries considered essential), protect labour rights, and preserve national culture (by regulating cultural industries).

Impact of the anti-competitive practices of enterprises and associations on international trade

The discussion on the impact of anti-competitive practices of enterprises on international trade focused broadly on the following three categories:

❑ Practices affecting market access for imports;

❑ Practices affecting international markets, where different countries were affected in largely the same way; and

❑ Practices with a differential impact on the national markets of countries.

Practices affecting market access for imports

The specific examples of practices affecting market access for imports cited by Members in the discussion included actual cases of:

❑ Domestic import cartels;

❑ International cartels that allocated national markets among participating firms;

❑ The unreasonable obstruction of parallel imports;

❑ Control over importation facilities;

❑ Exclusionary abuses of a dominant position and vertical market restraints that foreclosed markets to competitors, certain private standard-setting activities and other anti-competitive practices involving industry associations.

The point was made that anti-competitive practices of these types could have the effect of reducing or eliminating the potential gains from trade liberalization. As an illustration of this point, the Group was informed of a number of case studies of sectors in which conventional external trade barriers had been removed. The presumption underlying these studies was that, in general, when a country implemented far-reaching trade liberalization, there was an expectation that domestic prices should tend towards import parity levels. The case studies had however identified several situations where this response had not been forthcoming, owing to the anti-competitive practices of enterprises. Factors that tended to facilitate or underlie such anti-competitive practices included high market concentration levels, inelastic demand (reflecting a lack of substitutes), the prior existence of a cartel, and control by a dominant enterprise of scarce facilities that were necessary for imports to occur.

In reflecting on the effects of these practices and their implications for international trade, the point was made that the nature and severity of these effects would vary depending on the type of practice, the market power of incumbent firms and other circumstances.

Practices affecting international markets where different countries were affected in largely the same way

The foremost example of anti-competitive practices in this category was the problem of international cartels that affected price and output across multiple country markets. A large number of cases in which competition authorities in various countries had uncovered such cartels were brought to the attention of the Group. Cartels operating in certain service sectors such as international maritime shipping or financial services were said by some Members to be particularly harmful to trade, since they not only restrained trade within the relevant service but also raised the price of that service to exporters, introducing another level of distortion.

The point was however made that, notwithstanding the general condemnation of cartels and similar arrangements, a flexible approach to the application of competition law in regard to certain types of inter-firm practices could often be warranted. These practices might include, first, non-conventional horizontal arrangements, such as strategic alliances, joint ventures and R & D consortia, whose effects were not necessarily the same as more conventional arrangements such as mergers and cartels, and tended to be very fact-specific, and, second, certain arrangements involving small and medium-sized enterprises.

Practices with a differential impact on international markets

An example of a widely cited anti-competitive practice in this category was that of export cartels. It was said that the victims of export cartels would often include developing countries which were importing machinery or consumer products. Furthermore, it was suggested that the extent of such cartels and their deleterious effects on international trade and development might well be greater than was widely known, since most countries did not insist on registration of such cartels; they simply turned a blind eye to them. The matter of mergers which were judged to be benign or even beneficial in one market, but were not necessarily so in other markets, was also discussed. The point was made that the incidence of such cases might well be less frequent where countries employed a consumer welfare standard, rather than a total welfare standard, to evaluate mergers. The reason was that, under the latter approach, mergers that yielded significant efficiency gains in the home market might be deemed acceptable even where they entailed substantial anti-competitive effects, including effects which might be felt in foreign markets.

Factors facilitating anti-competitive practices that affect trade

The Group had an extensive discussion of factors, including government policies and measures, that could facilitate harmful anti-competitive practices by enterprises and thereby undermine the potential benefits of trade liberalization. Factors referred to in this context included:

❑ The existence or non-existence of a well-constituted competition law and policy;

❑ Statutory exemptions or protective regulatory regimes covering the conduct in question;

❑ A failure to adequately enforce existing laws and policies relating to anti-competitive practices;

❑ The existence of other government policies that implicitly or explicitly sanctioned or encouraged anti-competitive conduct; and

❑ The lack of effective rules governing access to essential facilities, in the context of deregulation.

Furthermore, it was noted that the problem of eradicating anti-competitive enterprise practices could be particularly challenging in circumstances where former State enterprises that had exercised self-regulatory power were privatized without steps being taken to limit their market power.

State monopolies and regulations

State monopolies and exclusive rights

In the discussion on this subject, the harm that State monopolies and exclusive rights could have on both competition and market access was widely commented on. It was noted that the WTO recognized that, in their operations, enterprises enjoying such privileges might create serious obstacles to trade. These effects could arise in the market where the exclusive rights were being exercised, upstream markets, and downstream markets. Particular reference was made to the impact that monopoly buyers and sellers could have in restricting competition and trade, including by creating a lack of transparency and serving as a tool for the implementation of national trade policies. As a result, they could have the effect of limiting imports and introducing market distortions. Some Members referred to the positive role that State monopolies and exclusive rights had played, particularly in developing countries where market forces were sometimes still in their infancy.

Regulatory policies

Some delegations shared with the Working Group their national experience with deregulation and the benefits which had flowed from it. It was said that this experience had shown that a commitment to competitive markets, rather than regulatory approaches, as the primary instruments of economic governance yielded major benefits for competition, trade and consumer welfare, created efficiencies and promoted innovation. Results in terms of reduced consumer prices had in many cases exceeded expectations. The importance of a rigorous competition law and policy to complement market-liberalizing regulatory reforms, in order to prevent the continuation or emergence of anti-competitive practices in a deregulated market, was emphasized. The Group was informed of the results of work in OECD which had shown that there was ample evidence that regulatory reform, properly carried out and with an adequate understanding of policy linkages, could improve significantly sectoral and economy-wide economic performance, and at the same time enhance the capacity of governments to protect important public interests such as environmental and consumer protection. The Group was also informed of a recent study presented to the UNCTAD Intergovernmental Group of Experts on Competition Law and Policy which had examined empirical evidence concerning the benefits for development of applying competition legislation. Evidence summarized in the study indicated that the replacement of administered pricing by liberal market pricing could provide importance gains in efficiency and consumer welfare.

Relationship between investment and competition policy

In the discussions in the Group, the point was made that a liberal FDI regime could increase competition in the market. A well-functioning competition policy could also help in removing obstacles to inward FDI resulting from the behaviour of incumbents and contribute towards providing an attractive legal framework for foreign investors. In this context, it was pointed out that in developing and transition economy countries in particular, FDI liberalization often constituted part of a broader policy package spanning also such areas as trade liberalization, regulatory reform and privatization as well as competition policy. It was also pointed out that a sound competition policy and law could contribute to providing an attractive environment for FDI by providing a stable and transparent legal framework of the kind familiar to many foreign investors and signalling a commitment to market institutions and mechanisms.

In the consideration of the relationship between investment and competition policy, the inconsistencies or contradictions that could arise between these policies were also discussed. It was suggested that excessive regulation of investment, for example through screening regulations or performance requirements, could harm both investment and competition. The view was expressed that not only could such measures deter beneficial flows of capital and technology with the attendant stimulation of competition in local markets, but also often proved an inferior and possibly counterproductive policy instrument when dealing with competition policy concerns. Others noted, however, that the application of a screening process for investment was not, in itself, a form of excessive regulation; rather, it was the manner in which it was applied (more liberally vs. more restrictively) which would determine whether it constituted excessive regulation. The point was also made that competition policies that were not implemented in a transparent, stable, neutral and non-discriminatory (with regard to nationality) way could constitute a deterrent to inward investment.

The point was made that the interlinkage between trade, investment and competition was already recognized in a number of WTO instruments, such as the GATS, TRIMs and TRIPS Agreements. Reference was also made to regional arrangements where the same interlinkage was evident. The view was expressed that, apart from providing for cooperation and consultation procedures and paving the way for possibly more detailed rules, the existing WTO instruments fell short of preventing restrictive business practices or limiting regulatory abuses in the field of competition policy; the challenge was to remove the inadequacies of existing WTO rules and to increase the synergies between investment and competition policies in a more systemic manner.

Relationship between the trade-related aspects of intellectual property rights and competition policy

The relationship between intellectual property rights and competition policy raises complex issues. The aim of the exclusive property rights granted under intellectual property regimes is adequate remuneration for the assets resulting from intellectual work. The aim of competition law on the other hand is to ensure that the monopoly rights of rights holders are not exploited by them to obtain unreasonably high remuneration and that the market assigned to the property is fair and equitable.

In this context, the Group noted the change in the attitude of some competition authorities on the question of the market power of holders of intellectual property rights. There has been a reduction in the tendency of courts and competition authorities to presume that intellectual property rights such as patents necessarily give the holder market power. There is now much greater readiness to examine this issue on a case-by-case basis, recognizing, for example, that of the thousands of patents granted each year, only a relatively small minority provide significant market power.

Moreover, in the application of competition law to intellectual property issues, there is now also a much greater appreciation of efficiency benefits from the licensing of intellectual property rights, in addition to the potential anti-competitive effects that licensing arrangements can have in some cases. The national competition authorities of some countries have issued guidelines on licensing practices that would be presumed acceptable and those that might require examination by them. Where an individual licensing practice needs to be examined, this is generally done on a case-by-case basis according to a 'rule of reason' standard, by which pro-competitive benefits are weighed against anti-competitive effects.

Impact of trade policy on competition

Under this heading the Group attempted to identify aspects of trade policy and provisions in WTO law which had an impact on competition. Some delegations referred in this context to the difference in the approach to dealing with predatory pricing under competition and anti-dumping laws. 'Predatory pricing' may be defined as the practice followed by an enterprise to monopolize the market by driving competitors out of business through sales below production costs so that subsequently they can be raised above the cost level. Under competition law, complaints about anti-competitive behaviour can be made only where predatory intent on the part of the monopoly producer is established. Under the anti-dumping law, on the other hand, anti-dumping duties can be levied on imported products which are alleged to be dumped without requiring the complaining industry to establish predatory intent on the part of exporting enterprises. However, certain other delegations felt that the purposes of anti-dumping and competition laws were fundamentally different, and that it was misguided to compare the two or to suggest that anti-dumping would benefit from the incorporation of competition policy principles.

Bilateral, regional and international agreements dealing with competition policy issues

With the liberalization of trade and investment flows on a worldwide basis, most cases raised under competition law involve the investigation of anti-competitive practices in more than one country. This has brought about the development of bilateral, regional and international cooperation agreements which aim at fostering cooperation in, and harmonized approaches to, the enforcement of competition law.

A number of regional arrangements carry provisions on cooperative arrangements for the enforcement of competition law (*see* box 58 for details).

Box 58

Regional arrangements: provisions on cooperation in the enforcement of competition law and the treatment of anti-dumping cases

Cooperation in the enforcement of competition law

The Agreement on the European Economic Area (EEA) establishes competition rules applicable to undertakings in EEA which correspond to Article 85 (general prohibition against anti-competitive practices), Article 86 (abuse of dominant position) and Article 90 (public undertakings) of the EC Treaty and to the relevant secondary legislation. The regime for merger control under the Treaty is also applied under the EEA Agreement.

The EFTA States that are contracting parties to the EEA Agreement have established a separate institutional system for the administration of these provisions. The EEA Agreement also contains provisions on the attribution of cases between the responsible EFTA authority and the EC Commission in the field of competition.

Several cooperation agreements have been set up between the competition agencies of the countries that form MERCOSUR, establishing procedures for reciprocal consultations and reciprocal technical assistance. Especially close links have been forged between the competition agencies of Argentina and Brazil; this has had a positive impact in unifying the standards used by the two agencies.

In NAFTA, the Working Group on Competition has been mandated to study the relationship between competition policy and trade in the context of the free trade area created by NAFTA. Issues so far studied by this Group on a comparative basis have included horizontal restraints, export cartels, merger control, abuse of dominance, national treatment and private rights of action. More recently, the Group has turned to studying competition cases with a transborder dimension, for instance monopolistic practices impeding market access.

Treatment of anti-dumping

Competition rules in the Closer Economic Relations Agreement between Australia and New Zealand, inter alia, provide for the non-application of anti-dumping measures on their bilateral trade. All complaints involving sales at prices below cost of production are dealt with under the competition laws of the two countries.

In the case of MERCOSUR, the Protocol for the Defence of Competition, calls on member countries to discuss from the beginning of the year 2000 how anti-dumping complaints against imports from member countries should be handled.

Among the important cooperation agreements at the international level are:

❑ The UNCTAD set of Multilaterally Agreed Equitable Principles and Rules for the Control of Restrictive Business Practices, adopted in 1980, and

❑ OECD recommendations concerning Cooperation between Member Countries on Anti-competitive Practices Affecting International Trade, revised in 1995.

Both these arrangements are recommendatory and are not legally binding. In the case of UNCTAD, implementation of the set is encouraged through regular annual meetings of a Group of Experts and related activities of the Secretariat. The OECD recommendations, on the other hand, encourage countries to establish cooperation arrangements among competition authorities in different countries. The means that have been adopted by member countries to foster such cooperation include:

❑ Providing notice of applicable time periods and schedules for decision-making in anti-competitive cases;

❑ Sharing factual and analytical information, subject to national laws governing confidentiality of information; and

❑ Coordinating discussions or negotiations on remedies in situations where the interests of more than one country could be affected.

Issues relating to the development of cooperation at the international level among competition authorities

Against this background, the Working Group considered the potential benefits of, and considerations that might militate against, a strengthening of international cooperation in the field of competition law and policy, to counteract the harmful effects of the anti-competitive practices of enterprises and associations on international trade.

It was recognized that cooperation already existed at a number of levels, and had been an important factor in the prosecution of a number of arrangements that had been discussed in the Group. Moreover, to be of genuine value, cooperation had to develop over time, and had to be founded on a mutuality of interest, trust and commonality of purpose. Nonetheless, the view was expressed that an expansion of cooperative approaches, including possibly at the multilateral level, was warranted. In particular, it was said that work was needed to address gaps in the remedies available to the international community in all three of the categories of anti-competitive practices of enterprises and associations that had been discussed in the Group:

❑ Practices affecting market access for imports;

❑ Practices affecting international markets, where different countries were affected in largely the same way; and

❑ Practices having a differential impact on the national markets of countries.

With regard to the first category, gaps could arise for the following reasons: the non-existence of a law; statutory exemptions or protective regulatory regimes covering the conduct in question; or a failure to adequately enforce a law which was applicable.

Regarding the second category, the issue was how to enhance cooperation to provide appropriate remedies for such practices, while minimizing conflicts of jurisdiction.

With regard to the third category, the question was that new arrangements for international cooperation were needed to better address these practices.

In addition, the proposals outlined below have been made for work to be done on specific anti-competitive practices, based on the degree of consensus which already appeared to exist with respect to each practice, and their clear importance for international trade.

First, regarding hard core cartels, where it was said that there was strong international consensus, there was a good prospect for adopting common enforcement efforts in this area.

Second, on export cartels, consideration needed to be given to means to strengthen the application of competition law in this area.

Third, concerning vertical agreements, it was generally recognized that a balancing of pro- and anti- competitive effects was appropriate in this area. It would be useful if the Group could identify an illustrative list of factors that might be considered by enforcement authorities in undertaking the required balancing in particular cases.

Fourth, in the area of abuse of a dominant position, the Group might usefully develop a list of abusive practices that could have the effect of foreclosing markets, and a set of criteria to be used in identifying a dominant position in a market.

Fifth, with regard to mergers, the Group might examine the scope for convergence in procedural requirements, and the feasibility of enhanced inter-agency cooperation, in order that different jurisdictions' concerns could be addressed at minimal costs.

There was, however, a divergence of views in the Group regarding the desirability and practicality of these proposals. In response to the suggestions made regarding the three specific categories of practices that had been discussed, other views expressed were as follows.

With regard to the first category of practices, in most cases, domestic competition laws should be adequate to handle this. The implication was that all countries should have, and should enforce, a well-constituted competition law. With regard to the second category of practices, it was clear that inter-agency cooperation could be helpful in addressing practices such as international cartels. At an appropriate stage, it would be helpful if agencies could deepen cooperation to the extent of sharing confidential information with each other. However, a process of mutual confidence-building and, in some cases, institution-building was needed if this was to take place. With regard to the third category, all that could reasonably be expected was that countries with overlapping interests in particular cases would consult with each other. For a variety of reasons, including different effects in different national markets as well as differing legal standards, it was inevitable that, from time to time, different jurisdictions would reach different conclusions regarding the acceptability of particular arrangements and transactions.

Focus of the Group's future work

The Group is expected to continue discussions on these and other issues raised by member countries during the deliberations it proposes to undertake in 1999. In doing such work, the General Council, has requested it to focus on:

❑ Approaches to promoting cooperation (on anti-competition practices) among member countries, including in the field of economic cooperation;

❏ The relevance of fundamental WTO principles of national treatment, transparency and most-favoured-nation treatment to competition policy and *vice versa*; and

❏ The contribution of competition policy to achieving the objectives of WTO, including the promotion of international trade.

References

UNCTAD, *World Investment Report 1998 Trends and Determinants* (United Nations Publication, Sales No. E.98.II.D.5).

WTO, *Annual Report 1997*, vol. 1, *Special Topic: Trade and Competition Policy*

WTO, *Annual Report 1998*.

WTO. Report (1998) of the Working Group on the Interaction between Trade and Competition Policy to the General Council. WT/WGTCP/2.

CHAPTER 24

Transparency in government procurement practices

As noted in chapter 18, the Agreement on Government Procurement negotiated in the Uruguay Round is a plurilateral Agreement. In other words, unlike the other associated Agreements, which are binding on all WTO Members, the Agreement is binding only on the countries that have acceded to it.

While most developed countries are members, only three developing countries/areas, all at a higher stage of development, have acceded to it. These are Hong Kong (China), the Republic of Korea and Singapore. Most developing and transition countries are therefore not bound by the substantive and procedural obligations the Agreement imposes, but they are bound by GATT 1994.

GATT excludes "procurement by government agencies of goods for their own use and not intended for commercial sale" from the application of the MFN and national treatment rules. However, it stipulates that while countries are not expected to abide fully by the MFN principle, they should, when purchasing from other countries, extend to suppliers from different countries "treatment that is fair and equitable".

In order to bring the practices of all countries under international rule, the Singapore Ministerial Conference decided, as a result of an initiative taken by the United States and the European Communities, to establish in WTO a Working Group on Transparency in Government Procurement "to conduct a study on transparency in government procurement practices ... to develop elements for inclusion in an appropriate agreement". Membership of such an agreement would be obligatory for all WTO Members. It would not, however, require purchasing agencies to accept the substantive obligations to extend MFN and national treatment which the Agreement on Government Procurement imposes. According to the proponents of the proposal, the main advantage of such an agreement would be improved transparency in government procurement practices.

This chapter is divided into two sections. The first provides a brief description of the main provisions of the Agreement on Government Procurement and outlines the reasons for the reluctance of developing countries to accede to it. The second focuses on the discussions that took place in the Working Group in 1997-1998.

Agreement on Government Procurement

Coverage and obligations

The Agreement applies to trade in both goods and services. However, its coverage is limited to the procurement of the goods and services and by the procuring entities each Member has specified in its schedule in the Annexes to Appendix I of the Agreement. These Annexes form an integral part of the Agreement.

The obligations which the Agreement imposes can be broadly divided into two categories: substantive and procedural.

Among the important substantive obligations are those which require purchasing agencies to apply MFN and national treatment to goods and to services contracts above the value thresholds specified in Annexes 1 to 3 of Appendix I of the Agreement. By requiring purchasing agencies to extend national treatment to foreign suppliers, the Agreement prevents them from extending to domestic suppliers price or other types of preferences.

Agreement on Government Procurement, Article I.4

The procedural obligations aim at ensuring that:

Agreement on Government Procurement, Article VII-XVI

❏ Tendering procedures (open, selective and limited) remain open and transparent and provide an opportunity to all interested foreign suppliers to participate;

❏ There is transparency in post-award information; and

Agreement on Government Procurement, Article XVIII.1
Agreement on Government Procurement, Article XX

❏ Challenge procedures providing remedies are available to unsuccessful domestic and foreign suppliers as well as to foreign suppliers which consider that the contract has been awarded in violation of the Agreement.

Reasons for the reluctance of developing countries to accede to the Agreement

Three of the many reasons for the reluctance of developing countries to accede to the Agreement are noted below.

First, in their view, membership of the Agreement will bring about only marginal export gains for them. The major gains will accrue to the developed countries' manufacturing and service industries able to take advantage of the improved access to developing country markets under the Agreement.

Second, there is a potential for the development of regional trade among developing countries in the procurement sector. But for the development of this trade, membership of the Agreement is not necessary as liberalization measures can be taken at the regional level.

Third, for most developing countries, the efficiency gains to procurement agencies from the application of the Agreement may not be significant in view of the following:

❏ The purchase of goods through tenders is widely prevalent.

❏ In low-income and least developed countries, where a high proportion of government expenditure is financed by international financial institutions and donor countries, purchases are made according to World Bank guidelines, which are similar in many respects to the provisions of the Agreement on Government Procurement. Furthermore, the Agreement is not applicable to tied purchases from donor countries. The share of tied aid in total bilateral assistance is high.

In addition, while membership of the Agreement will not necessarily result in higher exports or efficiency gains, it will oblige developing countries to eliminate policies requiring purchasing agencies to give price preferences to domestic suppliers. Such policies aim, *inter alia*, to encourage the development of small-scale industries and backward regions.

Working Group on Transparency in Government Procurement

In 1997-1998, the Working Group identified the possible main elements of an agreement on transparency in government procurement. In addition to the relevant provisions of the Agreement on Government Procurement, the Group took into account the World Bank Guidelines on Government Procurement, the UNCITRAL Model Law on Procurement of Goods, Construction and Services, and national laws.

Possible main elements of an agreement on transparency in government procurement

An attempt is made here to present the main points made during the Group's discussions in 1997-1998 on the possible elements of an agreement to ensure transparency before and after a procurement contract is awarded.

It needs to be emphasized that the overall picture given in this section does not go into the detail of the widely differing views expressed on both the desirability of including a particular element and its scope and content.

Elements for ensuring transparency before a contract is awarded

Scope and coverage

Coverage of entities. Entities at all levels of government, including subcentral levels of government and enterprises owned or influenced by government, might be covered by a transparency agreement.

Coverage of products. The scope of a transparency agreement might extend to all goods and services and any combination of goods and services.

Threshold values. In principle, the coverage of a transparency agreement should not be limited to contracts above a certain threshold level, but certain provisions might be more flexibly applied to smaller contracts.

Coverage of transactions. Acquisition by any contractual means, including, for example, lease or rental, might be covered.

Procurement methods

Any provisions on procurement methods should be flexible enough to accommodate the differing procurement methods used in national practices, and should allow for the possibility of using methods not based on tendering. While the methods employed by member countries of the Agreement on Government Procurement were generally based on tendering for high-value contracts (open, selective, limited), they also used other methods (e.g. purchase cards, electronic catalogues) for low-value contracts.

According to one view on the main procurement methods, open or international bidding with no limitations on the number of potential bidders was the most transparent method. Selective procedures were justifiable where it was not feasible or efficient to consider and evaluate a large number of potential bids, as long as all potentially interested suppliers were given the same opportunity to access information on procurement and to seek to be invited to bid.

Another view held that open and selective tendering should be considered equally transparent, provided selective tendering was conducted in accordance with appropriate principles. Open tendering was not always the most cost-effective method, particularly for complex procurements.

On the third main procurement method, limited tendering (e.g. individual, sole-source, single-source or direct tendering), it was suggested that, since information and selection criteria were not made publicly available, this method should be used only in justified and exceptional circumstances.

International instruments and national practice accepted a common range of circumstances and conditions under which the use of limited tendering was warranted.

Decisions on qualifications of suppliers

Registration and qualification systems had a useful role in the procurement process provided they were fully transparent. The key principle of transparency as regards this issue was that decisions on registration and qualification of suppliers should be taken only on the basis of criteria that had been identified early in the process and predisclosed to suppliers sufficiently in advance. Any changes in qualification requirements should be made known to all interested suppliers.

Publication of laws and procedures

The publication of national legislation provided not only a clear road map for potential suppliers but also a check against arbitrary practices within procurement regimes. The resulting procedural certainty reduced the costs of the procurement cycle.

Notice of invitation to tender

Information on procurement opportunities in notices of invitations to tender should be sufficient to allow potential suppliers to assess their interest in participating in the proposed procurement procedure and to seek tender documents. National practices on the amount of detail to be included in initial tender notices and in the subsequent tender documentation varied considerably, and it might not be necessary to have precise minimum requirements on their specific contents or to seek harmonization on this point. It would be sufficient for a transparency agreement to develop elements in the form of general principles.

Information on tender opportunities

On advance information on tender opportunities, there were two issues: where the information could be found and its content.

Publications. With regard to where the information could be found by potential suppliers, the following points were made:

❑ Procurement opportunities and the related procedural requirements should be made known and be generally available to interested parties through an accessible source;

❑ Information on tender opportunities should be published in the printed and/or electronic media. The printed media could be an official gazette or a national newspaper of wide circulation;

❑ Electronic publications should be used where feasible, taking into account the level of development of individual WTO Members. The Internet addresses of electronic publications could be made available. As electronic publication offered significant benefits in terms of both time and costs, it would be increasingly used in the coming years.

Information content. While national practices diverged on the extent of information provided, information on procurement opportunities in notices of invitation to tender and notices of tender documents should be sufficient to allow potential suppliers to assess their interest in participating in the proposed procurement or qualification system and enable them to prepare adequate bids or proposals for qualification. Members should be able to decide whether information on procurement opportunities should be disseminated solely by means of tender notices, or whether the bulk of the information should be contained in the tender documentation or be made available by other means.

Information on preferences accorded to domestic suppliers. Transparency on the existence of preferences or other discriminatory requirements would enable potential foreign tenderers to determine whether they had an interest in entering a specific procurement process in spite of discriminatory national policies. Interested suppliers would be able to distinguish between procurement opportunities reserved for domestic suppliers and those open to international competition only if information on any discriminatory policies was made available to them in advance. The provision of information on price preferences or qualification requirements favouring domestic suppliers would enable suppliers to gauge their interest and assess their real chances of winning a contract.

Language. The language requirement for the publication of notices of invitation to tender should be limited to an official national language. Translation into a WTO language could become too burdensome.

Time limits

On the minimum time limits made available to potential suppliers for fulfilling requirements at different stages of the procurement process, a suggestion was made that, rather than establishing specific minimum time periods in a transparency agreement, the Group might agree on a general principle, as in the UNCITRAL Model Law or in Article XI:1 of the Agreement on Government Procurement.

Elements for ensuring transparency after the procurement contract is awarded

Transparency of decisions on contract awards

For transparency in decision-making on the award of procurement contracts, it was essential that decisions should be taken strictly on the basis of the evaluation criteria (including criteria on technical specifications) set out in advance in the tender documents, and on the basis of the information provided on how the criteria were to be applied. Furthermore, in order to ensure that decisions were seen to be taken in this way, the criteria should be set out so as to ensure that they could be applied objectively.

While it might not be necessary to require the public opening of tenders to ensure transparency, procuring entities should have procedures in place to ensure the impartiality of the procurement process.

Ex post information to be sent to unsuccessful bidders

As to the purpose and operation of *ex post* information, the following points were made:

❑ This type of information was made available to tenderers who had failed to win a bid to provide them with an opportunity to ascertain that they had been treated equitably according to the requirements and the criteria set out in the tender documentation, and that applicable rules and practices had been followed during the procurement process.

❑ The means by which such information was to be given should be a matter of choice for Members, but it should be known to interested parties. In this connection, the view was expressed that it would be time-consuming and burdensome to inform unsuccessful bidders individually of the outcome of their bids.

Domestic review procedures

The imposition of rules was not enough to obtain transparency in government procurement. There must also be a domestic review mechanism to introduce accountability into the process and to ensure that the rules were respected by everyone involved in a procurement process. The availability of an avenue for reviewing procurement processes was a key element of transparency. A mechanism for reviewing complaints from suppliers or a bid challenge system guaranteed due process and public accountability throughout a procurement process, and established the transparency of the process. The existence of a review mechanism might make public procurement authorities more aware of the need to make sure that the procedures used in particular procurements were in conformity with applicable laws and regulations.

Such review or appeal mechanisms could be based on the review procedures of the WTO Agreements, for example the Agreements on Anti-dumping Practices, Customs Valuation, Preshipment Inspection and TRIPS.

The other view was that the issue of review went beyond that of transparency and was therefore not within the mandate of the Working Group. It was also premature to take up the question. Furthermore, review provisions in a transparency agreement could bring about an increase in the number of challenges on flimsy grounds, increasing costs and delaying the award of contracts.

Moreover, domestic procedures in many countries provided for a review to ascertain whether procurements had been made in accordance with domestic law and procedures. As they would have a wider scope than any obligations that might be agreed in a transparency agreement, it might not be feasible to limit the application of review procedures to specific transparency obligations in a WTO agreement on transparency.

Application of WTO dispute settlement procedures

With regard to dispute settlement between governments, the general view was that it would be premature to consider the applicability of provisions on dispute settlement before the elements of a transparency agreement had been more clearly identified. Furthermore, the Group's mandate was to discuss the elements of an appropriate agreement on transparency which could take the form of a binding agreement or a code urging countries to use their best endeavours to abide by its guidelines; only an agreement with binding obligations could be subject to WTO dispute settlement procedures.

Technical cooperation, and special and differential treatment of developing countries

Technical cooperation would be important in ensuring the successful implementation of a future transparency agreement. It could also help Members in developing domestic procurement regimes and in taking practical steps to enhance the transparency of their procurement policies and practices. Specific suggestions on the types of assistance that could be provided are listed in box 59.

Ongoing work

The Working Group is continuing its work on developing elements for inclusion in an agreement on transparency in government procurement. It has scheduled three meetings for 1999. Decisions on how further work on the development of the agreement should be carried out – including whether it should be fully binding or whether it should take the form of a code requiring Members only to undertake 'best endeavours' to implement it – are expected to be taken at the third Ministerial Conference, scheduled for November 1999.

Box 59

Types of assistance that could be provided to developing countries under an agreement on transparency in government procurement

Development of national legislation and procedures

❑ *Legal advice on, and assistance in, drawing up national legislation;*

❑ *Analysis of, and guidance on, administrative and policy options;*

❑ *Drawing up procedures for publication;*

❑ *Establishment and implementation of bid challenge systems;*

❑ *Practical steps to make procurement more user-friendly, such as developing standard forms for tender notices and fill-in bid forms, as well as developing a common procurement vocabulary.*

Training

❑ *Training for those who have to implement, use or enforce new legislation, procedures and/or practices;*

❑ *Training the judiciary;*

❑ *Training trainers to enable them to run training programmes in, for example, business schools or colleges of public administration in beneficiary countries;*

❑ *Training purchasers and suppliers;*

❑ *Exchange of officers.*

Institution building

❑ *Administrative cooperation to enhance institution building and the exchange of information.*

Access to information by suppliers

❑ *Workshops, seminars and the production of user guides, including the development of Internet Web sites, search engines and databases, to provide information on opportunities for doing business with governments at home and abroad, and to facilitate access to that information. Such assistance could benefit small and medium-sized enterprises, by increasing their confidence and effectiveness in entering procurement markets at home and abroad.*

Use of information technology

❑ *The development of information technology tools for the dissemination of information on procurement opportunities and practices, and/or the establishment of full electronic tendering, as well as to facilitate the collection of relevant economic data and statistics.*

❑ *The provision of office, information technology and other equipment necessary for the implementation and enforcement of legislation, procedures and practices.*

CHAPTER 25

Trade facilitation

Trade facilitation is one of the new subjects added to the WTO work programme at the 1996 Singapore Ministerial Conference. The Ministerial Declaration of that Conference directed the Council for Trade in Goods to undertake exploratory and analytical work in this area. The relevant paragraph in the Declaration reads as follows:

> [The Ministers] direct the Council for Trade in Goods to undertake exploratory and analytical work, drawing on the work of other relevant international organizations, on the simplification of trade procedures, in order to assess the scope for WTO rules in this area.

The discussion in this chapter is organized as follows:

❑ The international and regional governmental and other organizations that have been doing work in this area, the work done so far, and work underway in the main organizations.

❑ The concept of trade facilitation and the provisions of the WTO Agreements aiming specifically at promoting trade facilitation.

❑ The main reasons behind the proposals for involving WTO in the work on trade facilitation and the subject areas suggested for inclusion in the work programme.

❑ Ongoing discussions in WTO.

Work by international organizations other than WTO

The recognition that methods for doing business and governmental procedures for clearing internationally traded goods could lead to delays and add to costs has prompted a number of organizations to adopt conventions and other legal instruments that lay down rules, recommendations or standards to facilitate trade. Box 60 lists the various international inter-governmental and non-governmental organizations that are currently engaged in work on trade facilitation.

Most of the organizations listed in the box cover the limited subject areas falling within their mandates.

WTO law on trade facilitation

Defining trade facilitation

There is no agreed definition of trade facilitation and the term is used in different organizations to cover different ranges of activities. At the broadest

---

Box 60

Organizations engaged in work on trade facilitation

International inter-governmental organizations

International Civil Aviation Organization (ICAO)
International Monetary Fund (IMF)
International Maritime Organization (IMO)
International Trade Centre UNCTAD/WTO (ITC)
Organisation for Economic Co-operation and Development (OECD)
United Nations Conference on Trade and Development (UNCTAD)
United Nations Economic Commission for Europe (ECE)
United Nations Commission on International Trade Law (UNCITRAL)
United Nations Economic and Social Commission for Asia and the Pacific
   (ESCAP)
World Customs Organization (WCO)
World Bank

International non-governmental organizations

International Chamber of Commerce (ICC)
International Chamber of Shipping (ICS)
International Air Transport Association (IATA)
International Organization for Standardization (ISO)
International Road Transport Union (IRU)
International Federation of Freight Forwarders Associations (FIATA)

Regional organizations, free trade areas and customs unions

Asia-Pacific Economic Cooperation forum (APEC)
European Union (EU)
North American Free Trade Agreement (NAFTA)

---

level, the term is applied to include the work done by UNCTAD to encourage countries to establish national Trade Points which group together, either physically or electronically, the various agencies participating in foreign trade transactions so that they can provide the services required to complete such transactions efficiently and promptly. In the narrower sense, however, the term is applied to work on improving the documentary requirements and procedures imposed by countries to secure compliance with the rules applicable to traded goods at the time of importation, exportation and during transit. Such measures include:

❑ Customs control measures to obtain compliance with customs laws and regulations;

❑ Technical regulations to ensure that goods meet the mandatory standards specified in national laws and regulations;

❑ Veterinary inspections of animals and animal products to protect animal and human life from the pests and diseases that they may carry;

❑ Phytosanitary inspections of plants and plant products to prevent the introduction and the spread of pests;

❑ Quality control inspections (other than those mentioned above) to ensure that the goods correspond to the minimum international or national standards specified in relevant laws and regulations.

WTO Agreements: provisions on trade facilitation

In some of the areas covered by the narrower definition, the WTO Agreements carry provisions which facilitate trade, as can be seen in box 61.

Box 61
WTO provisions to facilitate trade

Subject areas	*WTO Agreements*
Customs control measures	❑ *Agreement on Customs Valuation. This delineates the rules for determining the value of imported goods for the purpose of levying ad valorem customs duties. (See chapter 3.)*
	❑ *Agreement on Rules of Origin. The agreement on this subject is being developed in WTO on the basis of the technical work currently being undertaken by WCO on the harmonization of rules of origin. The agreement will set out the rules for determining the origin of goods imported on an MFN basis for such purposes as the application of safeguard measures or the levy of anti-dumping duties. (See chapter 12.)*
	❑ *Agreement on Preshipment Inspection. The Agreement specifies the rules on how prices recommended by PSI companies, after verification before importation in the importing country, can be used to determine value for Customs purposes. (See chapter 4.)*
	❑ *Agreement on Import Licensing Procedures. The Agreement lays down rules on the issuance of import licences covering products to which licensing systems are applicable. (See chapter 6.)*
Compliance with technical, sanitary and phytosanitary regulations	*The Agreements on Technical Barriers to Trade and on the Application of Sanitary and Phytosanitary Measures set out principles and rules which seek to ensure that rules and procedures adopted at the national level in the areas covered by the Agreements do not constitute barriers to trade. (See chapter 5.)*
	In addition, GATT 1994 contains provisions which, by adding transparency to rules and regulations adopted at the national level and by ensuring that they do not constitute barriers to trade, aim at facilitating trade.
	❑ *Article V: Freedom of transit.*
	❑ *Article VIII: Fees and formalities connected with importation and exportation.*
	❑ *Article X: Publication and administration of trade regulations.*

Proposals calling for WTO involvement in trade facilitation

Reasons for the proposals

It is important to note that the main thrust of the WTO provisions cited above is the removal of the non-tariff barriers resulting from the rules applied by countries at the border to imported and exported goods.

Over the years, international organizations have been developing guidelines for countries to follow in adopting procedures at the practical level in relation, for instance, to the customs clearance of import and export goods. In the process they have gained considerable expertise on trade facilitation. The proposals calling for the involvement of WTO in addition have three broad reasons behind them.

Improving the enforceability of the rules

The first has to do with the difference in the legal nature and the enforceability of obligations within the WTO framework and those developed by other organizations.

The bulk of the rules of the WTO Agreements are legally binding on member countries. By contrast, only a small number of the legal instruments adopted by other organizations like ECE and WCO impose binding obligations. Most of them take the form of guidelines, of which the United Nations Layout Key for Trade Documents, the United Nations EDIFACT (Electronic Data Interchange for Administration, Commerce and Transport) standards for data transmission through computers, and the ISO standards are examples. They may also be issued as models or as recommended procedures or practices (e.g. the Annexes to the International Convention on the Simplification and Harmonization of Customs Procedures, also known as the Kyoto Convention).

These guidelines or recommended practices do not impose binding obligations but simply call on countries to use their 'best endeavours' to abide by them. Most of them do not need to be formally accepted and ratified by governments.

Enforceability, even in the case of the small number of instruments that are binding (for instance, the main text of the Kyoto Convention but not its Annexes), differs considerably from that imposed by the WTO legal instruments.

These differences emanate from the nature of the sanctions available in the event of breach. Countries whose interests are adversely affected by another country's failure to comply with a WTO rule can invoke dispute settlement procedures. Failure to carry out the decisions of the Dispute Settlement Body can lead to the imposition of retaliatory countermeasures by aggrieved countries. Such countermeasures can take the form of increased tariffs on imports from the country in default or the payment of compensation by this country.

No such sanctions are available under the instruments developed by other organizations. While some instruments do carry provisions for the consideration of complaints against non-compliance by management committees and for the settlement of disputes, the only sanction they provide is moral pressure and, if that fails, censure.

By adopting rules in some of these areas in WTO or by bringing some of the instruments negotiated in other organizations within the ambit of WTO law, the proponents of the proposal hope to make the rules more enforceable. Such rules would generally be binding and would carry with them the threat of the imposition of trade sanctions in the event of non-compliance.

In this context, it is important to note that while the WTO Agreements impose binding obligations on Members, in a few cases member countries are merely required to use their best endeavours to implement some of their provisions. For instance, most of the provisions on special and differential treatment of developing countries impose best-endeavour obligations on developed countries.

Improving political willingness to abide by rules

The second reason for suggesting that WTO should develop rules in new subject areas is in the domain of political economy. The proponents believe that, given the importance being attached to the WTO legal system in the globalizing world economy, countries will be more willing to apply the standards or recommendations of other organizations if they are brought within the ambit of the WTO system.

This can be done in two ways. One is to impose binding obligations that in certain areas member countries will abide by the rules developed by other international organizations. The Agreements on TBT and SPS stipulate, for instance, that standards adopted by ISO, the Codex Alimentarius Commission, the International Plant Protection Convention and the International Office of Epizootics should be treated as international standards and impose binding obligations on countries to use them as a basis for their mandatory regulations unless they can justify the need for deviations under the specific exceptions provided by the Agreements.

The other approach is to make certain conventions or agreements part of the WTO legal system. The Agreement on TRIPS, for instance, by reference to the Berne Convention, makes it part of the Agreement and imposes additional obligations on Members. It is argued that, in a similar way, it may be possible to make compliance with the "the Kyoto Convention and its Annexes as well as the other standards and recommendations developed by other organizations" mandatory by integrating them into the WTO system.

Necessity for adopting international standards on electronic data transmission

The third reason for suggesting WTO's greater involvement in trade facilitation arises from the technological progress in transmitting data through electronic devices, making it increasingly necessary for all countries to adopt international standards. The development of the UN/ECE EDIFACT standard for data transmission, for instance, was stimulated by the difficulties being caused by the differing standards for data transmission in the United States and the European Union. Countries which fail to encourage the electronic transmission of the data required by banks, importers, other trade operators and Customs will find themselves at an increasing disadvantage in international markets. The involvement of WTO will further encourage work at the technical level to develop data transmission standards and ensure that such standards are adopted by all countries.

Subject areas suggested for inclusion in a WTO work programme on trade facilitation

The specific subjects to be included in a WTO work programme on trade facilitation have not yet been identified and the question of whether WTO should play a direct role in the subject area has not yet been decided. However, the submissions made by some countries provide some indications of a possible WTO role. Broadly speaking, they say that it may be desirable to adopt binding rules in the following areas:

❑ Adoption of continuous or non-stop procedures for the clearance of goods by electronic means.

❑ Adoption of binding uniform standards for the transmission of information through electronic means by using standards developed by UN/ECE, ISO and UNCTAD.

❑ Adoption of audit-based systems for customs control. Under these systems consignments are not checked individually; they use risk assessment and management procedures and allow authorized traders to certify origin and clear goods through Customs.

❑ Simplification and standardization of documents used in import and export procedures.

❑ Adoption, as part of the WTO legal system, of the revised standards and recommendations that may be agreed in the framework of the WCO Kyoto and Istanbul Conventions.

❑ Adoption of guidelines to combat customs-related corruption and other malpractices on the basis of the WCO's Arusha Declaration.

Work in progress

Informal exploratory and analytical meetings of interested member countries are currently being held under the auspices of the Council for Trade in Goods. The discussions in these meetings have so far focused on:

❑ Import and export procedures and requirements (including customs and border-crossing problems);

❑ Physical movement of consignments (transport and transit) as well as payments, insurance and other financial requirements that affect the cross-border movement of goods;

❑ Electronic facilities and their importance in facilitating international trade;

❑ Technical cooperation and development in relation to the simplification of trade procedures; and

❑ The relationship between the WTO Agreements and facilitation.

Decisions on how further work is to be pursued are expected to be taken at the Third Ministerial Conference in 1999 on the basis of the recommendations on the Council for Trade in Goods which will take into account the results of the informal consultations.

CHAPTER 26

Electronic commerce

What is electronic commerce

There is no universally accepted definition of the term 'electronic commerce'. However, it is generally used to cover the "distribution, marketing, sale or delivery of goods and services by electronic means". The rapid growth in electronic commerce during the last decade has been due to the increasing use of the Internet for commercial purposes.

A commercial transaction can be divided into three main stages:

❑ The advertising and searching stage;

❑ The ordering and payment stage; and

❑ The delivery stage.

Any or all of these stages can be carried out on the Internet (or by other electronic means such as the fax or the telephone) and may therefore be covered by the concept of electronic commerce.

Electronic means are being increasingly used aggressively by commercial firms to advertise and market both goods and services all over the world. Virtually all products can be sold on the basis of the information available on the Internet. Information on prices, quality, delivery and payment conditions enables manufacturing companies, retailers or consumers in far-off countries to order their requirements from the most competitive suppliers. Physical goods are then delivered by other means of transport.

It is becoming increasingly possible to deliver certain types of products electronically; in fact any product that can be reduced to a digital format can be delivered in this way. The potential product range is vast: financial and insurance services, audio-visual products (films, games and music), travel services (airline tickets, hotel reservations), news and information services (on-line wire services and data bank retrievals), telecommunications services, and information technology services and software. This list is not exhaustive and additional products are likely to be found suitable for electronic trade in the future. Today, computer software is the leading product sold via the Internet.

Benefits of electronic commerce

Electronic commerce provides consumers and business enterprises with information on the availability worldwide of products or services, prices and conditions of sale, enabling them to obtain their supplies on the best terms possible. It provides suppliers with an on-line marketing service, and enables them to do business without having to open an establishment or to hire an agent abroad. Virtual shops and contact points on the Internet, by facilitating

> **Box 62**
>
> **Main instruments of electronic commerce**
>
> *There are six main instruments of electronic commerce: the telephone, fax, television, electronic payment and money transfer systems, electronic data interchange and the Internet. While the term 'electronic commerce' is used in many discussions to refer exclusively to the Internet and other network-based commerce, the telephone, fax and television are in common use as media for commercial transactions, particularly in industrialized countries. Orders, for example, are regularly placed over the telephone and paid for by credit card. The emergence of instruments like the Internet did not therefore mean the invention of electronic commerce.*
>
> *But the Internet does open up many new possibilities: with the Internet most elements of a commercial transaction can be conducted on an interactive basis with one or several persons, unconstrained by time and space, in a multimedia environment with sound, image and text transmission, and at relatively low (and still declining) costs. This makes the Internet much more versatile than other instruments of electronic commerce. The latter typically need to be used in combination with each other or with more traditional instruments such as mail or physical shopping, for a transaction to be concluded. The Internet will therefore reduce the barriers to communications and trade to a greater degree than established electronic and traditional means of commerce.*
>
> **Source**: WTO, *Electronic Commerce and the Role of the WTO* (1998).

communications, eliminate some of the delays in the flow of supplies. The quick and assured availability of supplies may also enable industries, wholesalers and retailers to reduce the levels of inventories and stocks they hold. This will help companies, particularly the small and medium-sized, to reduce their costs.

Internet-based international trade

The United States accounts for the bulk of the trade conducted through the Internet. Its Internet-based sales are expected to reach US$ 200 billion - US$ 300 billion in 2001, attributable mainly to sales in the domestic market. This will be equivalent to 2%-3% of the country's economy-wide sales. The use of electronic means to sell products and services is also on the increase in Europe, though it is much smaller in magnitude than trade in the United States.

Reliable estimates of Internet-based international trade do not exist. Rough estimates, however, indicate that it could reach US$ 40 billion - US$ 60 billion by 2001.

Internet commerce and developing countries

In general, developing countries lag far behind developed markets in the availability of the technical requirements for conducting electronic commerce. This can partly be attributed to the inadequate development of their telecommunications infrastructures and to the cost of using the Internet. In addition to the cost of basic computer equipment, the cost of using the Internet depends on several factors, including the costs of routers and other computing facilities and, to a lesser degree, the wages of operators.

Internet charges can be significantly higher in developing than in developed countries. Thus, the average cost of a subscription to a dial-up Internet connection in Africa is quoted by ITU as US$ 75 per month compared to US$ 10 in the United States and US$ 15 in the United Kingdom. Considering the low levels of income in Africa,[36] these subscription charges are almost prohibitive and beyond the reach of the common man. Further, the cost of local or long-distance telephone calls giving access to the Internet can be significantly higher in developing countries.

Many of the human skills needed for electronic commerce are distinct from those required for other forms of trade. The more stages of a commercial exchange are carried out electronically, the more specific are the skills required. Basic computer knowledge and knowledge of the Internet are needed even if only to search for a product on the Net. Extensive language skills may be required to browse foreign Internet sites. If a product is to be advertised through the Internet, skills in designing an Internet site are necessary and, if electronic payments are to be accepted, there is a need for people with skills in electronic money transfer. While some developing countries are well advanced in developing these human resource capacities, most of them do not yet have a widely skilled workforce in these areas.

Problems and issues

Revenue implications of electronic commerce

Physical products that are ordered from other countries electronically are delivered by air, rail, road or sea. Customs duties on such products are collected at the border, much like the duties collected on products ordered through non-electronic means.

However, products like books, films and music may be digitized and transmitted to consumers directly. This may lead to an anomalous situation as Internet trade grows. A book or a CD record may have to pay customs duty when crossing a border, while their digitized versions delivered direct to consumers through the Internet would escape such duties. It may also be difficult to collect Internet taxes (e.g. value-added or sales tax) on such products.

Recent research, however, shows that non-collection of customs duties on digitized products may not have serious implications for a country's revenue. Only a limited number of countries have high duties on products that can be rendered digital, and customs duties collected on such products contribute only a small share to government revenue even in these countries. Moreover, it is not impossible to tax electronic transmission, if a country wants to do so. Different methods that can be adopted for this purpose are being studied at present.

Protection of intellectual property rights

Increasing Internet trade may pose problems in the enforcement of intellectual property rights. Similar trademarks can exist in different territories; in the borderless world of electronic commerce, this may lead to conflict. A related issue is the allocation of domain names and the resolution of conflicts arising from the use of the same or similar domain names. In one initiative, WIPO has been asked

---

36   NUA Internet Surveys, "Constraints on the Development of 'Wired' Economy in Africa" (15 May 1998).

to develop recommendations for the resolution of trademark and domain name disputes and to report its findings to the United States Department of Commerce in 1999.

Other legal issues

Trade and business communications through electronic means give rise to a number of questions of a legal nature. Among those are: What is the origin of electronically traded products? When is an electronically delivered product 'domestic' and when is it 'imported'? How do traders who use electronic means of communication deal with situations in which national laws or international conventions applicable to international trade transactions require 'written' agreements, 'original' documents or 'manual' signatures? How can the authenticity of a message be secured, so that parties will know with certainty the identity of a sender of an electronic message or enable them to verify that an electronic message has not been altered in transmission? Uncertainty over the enforcement and potential for redress of electronically concluded contracts may create obstacles to the development of electronic commerce across borders. The use of electronic means of communication, for instance in preparing and concluding a contract and in delivering products, requires not only technological solutions but an appropriate legal framework.

A number of initiatives at the international level have been taken to assist governments to deal with inadequacies in applicable laws. For example, UNCITRAL, the United Nations body responsible for promoting the harmonization and unification of international trade law, has undertaken work which led to the adoption of a Model Law on Electronic Commerce in 1996. The Model Law establishes rules and norms for the validation and recognition of contracts formed through electronic means, sets default rules for contract formation and performance, defines the characteristics of valid electronic writing and an original document, provides for the acceptability of electronic signatures for legal and commercial purposes, and supports the admission of computer evidence in courts and arbitration proceedings. The Model Law can be used by States to enact legislation that will help remove legal obstacles to, and uncertainties arising from, electronic commerce. Both the United States and OECD are encouraging the development of an international convention on electric transactions based on the Model Law. The convention will have two aims: eliminate paper-based legal barriers to electronic transactions, and provide an effective approach to authentication.

Some initiatives have also been taken by individual countries, the European Communities and international organizations to deal with the legal issues arising from electronic commerce. These include contractual interchange and trading partner agreements which address issues related to EDI (electronic data interchange). EDI is an order-management system which is defined as a set of data definitions that permit business forms to be exchanged electronically. It has been around since computers came into existence, but as it is complex and expensive to implement, typically requiring dedicated and proprietary value-added networks (VANs), it has never really caught on except among large companies with long-term and high-value supply partnerships. However, there are now numerous software companies seeking to deliver EDI across the Internet, which should put it within the reach of smaller business enterprises and effect savings for the larger ones. However, for this to be workable on an international level, there must be a universal standard for sending EDI information over the Net. Several national trade facilitation bodies as well as regional and international organizations have been working on this aspect.

Finally, almost all countries, developed and developing, are concerned about the content of the Internet. This is natural, as the Internet contains a wide range of more or less desirable 'information'. There are many differing views on what may constitute risks to public morals, security or other types of offensive material. To police all the content available on the Internet is next to impossible. However, possibilities exist to prevent access to undesirable content, either through individual filtering software installed on the personal computer or, on a broader level, by Internet service providers.

WTO work programme

The increasing use of the Internet and other electronic means in international trade in goods and services led WTO Members, at the Geneva Ministerial Conference (held in May 1998), to adopt a *Declaration on Global Electronic Commerce* directing the General Council "to establish a comprehensive work programme to examine all trade-related issues relating to global electronic commerce". In accordance with this mandate, work on examining whether any modifications or improvements are necessary in the rules on trade in goods and services and in the area of intellectual property is ongoing in the relevant WTO forums. In addition, the General Council has asked the Committee on Trade and Development to examine, *inter alia*, the effects of electronic commerce on the trade of developing countries and particularly that of small and medium-sized enterprises in these countries, and the means for maximizing benefits accruing to them. The General Council is expected to submit its report on work done and its recommendations for action to the Third Session of the Ministerial Conference, to be held in November 1999.

Customs duties on electronic transactions

In the same Declaration, the Members agreed to continue (until the next Ministerial Conference) "the current practice" of most of them of "not imposing customs duties on electronic transmissions" (digitized products). A decision on whether the Declaration should be extended and made binding is to be taken at the third Ministerial Conference, taking into account the progress of the General Council's work programme.

Summing up

The value of electronic commerce, an increasingly significant feature of international trade, is expected to increase dramatically in the new century. In order to participate in this trade, countries will have to build their capacities to engage in this trade as a priority. The difficulties, however, of doing this should not be underestimated. Countries need to invest in both physical and human infrastructures, specialized education and training, and provide an appropriate legal framework for conducting commerce electronically.

Index

INTERNATIONAL TRADE CENTRE

UNCTAD CNUCED

WTO OMC

The International Trade Centre UNCTAD/WTO (ITC) is the focal point in the United Nations system for technical cooperation with developing countries in trade promotion. ITC was created by the General Agreement on Tariffs and Trade (GATT) in 1964 and since 1968 has been operated jointly by GATT (now the World Trade Organization, or WTO) and the UN, the latter acting through the United Nations Conference on Trade and Development (UNCTAD). As an executing agency of the United Nations Development Programme (UNDP), ITC is directly responsible for implementing UNDP-financed projects in developing countries and economies in transition related to trade promotion.

ITC works with developing countries and economies in transition to set up trade promotion programmes for expanding their exports and improving their import operations. This covers six areas:

■ Product and market development: Direct export marketing support to the business community through advice on product deve- lopment, product adaptation and international marketing for commodities, manufactures and services.

■ Development of trade support services: Creation and enhancement of foreign trade support services for the business community provided by public and private institutions at the national and regional levels.

■ Trade information: Establishment of sustainable national trade information services and dissemination of information on products, services, markets and functions to enterprises and trade organizations.

■ Human resource development: Strengthening of national institutional capacities for foreign trade training and organization of direct training for enterprises in importing and exporting.

■ International purchasing and supply management: Application of cost-effective import systems and practices in enterprises and public trading entities by strengthening the advisory services provided by national purchasing organizations, both public and private.

■ Needs assessment and programme design for trade promotion: Conception of effective national and regional trade promotion programmes based on an analysis of supply potential and constraints, and identification of related technical cooperation requirements.

In addition to specific technical cooperation projects with individual developing countries and economies in transition, or groups of these countries, ITC provides services from its headquarters in Geneva that are available to all such countries. These include publications on trade promotion, export development, international marketing, international purchasing, supply management and foreign trade training, as well as trade information and trade statistics services of various types.

The broad policy guidelines for ITC's technical cooperation work are determined by the governing organs of ITC's parent bodies. Recommendations on ITC's future work programme are made to these organs by ITC's annual intergovernmental meeting, the Joint Advisory Group on the International Trade Centre UNCTAD/WTO (JAG).

ITC is headed by an Executive Director. Several hundred staff work at ITC's headquarters and in the field. In addition a number of consultants are assigned to ITC projects in developing countries and economies in transition.

For more information contact:

International Trade Centre UNCTAD/WTO
Palais des Nations   Tel.: (41-22) 730 01 11
1211 Geneva 10   Fax: (41-22) 733 44 39
Switzerland   E-mail: itcreg@intracen.org
                      Web site: http://www.intracen.org

COMMONWEALTH SECRETARIAT

The Commonwealth Secretariat is the principal international organisation of the Commonwealth. It was established in 1965 and forms the Commonwealth's own civil service based in London, effectively carrying out the priorities of its 54 member governments.

The Secretariat works towards advancing the Commonwealth's fundamental values including good governance and democracy; sustainable economic and social development; and the rule of law, human rights and gender equality. Its primary duties include promoting consultation and exchanges among members, preparing and circulating information on issues of concern, particularly in international and economic affairs, assisting in advancing the development of member countries, acting as a focal point for specialised Commonwealth institutions and organising and servicing intergovernmental meetings.

Fifty Commonwealth members are developing countries and the Commonwealth Fund for Technical Co-operation (CFTC) is the principal means by which the Commonwealth promotes economic and social development in these countries. Administered by the Commonwealth Secretariat, the CFTC is the development wing of the Commonwealth. The CFTC operates on the principle of mutual assistance, with governments contributing financial and technical skills on a voluntary basis and obtaining technical assistance as needed.

Within the operational framework of the CFTC, the Commonwealth Secretariat has been helping its developing member countries in implementing economic reform programmes. The Export and Industrial Development Division (EIDD) provides specialised technical assistance services to developing member countries to help them establish and strengthen appropriate export promotion structures, develop the necessary infrastructure, widen their export base, improve quality standards and enlarge market access for their products. Assistance to such member countries for understanding and benefiting from the new international trade agreements is a key component of the work undertaken by the Division.

In this respect, the Division offers technical assistance programmes specifically designed to assist developing countries to cope with preparing for, and participating in, the multilateral trading system. Several member states from across the Commonwealth have benefited from assistance in meeting WTO accession requirements. An important component of this programme is the technical advice provided to representatives of Commonwealth Developing Countries to the WTO, through a Geneva-based consultant. The Export and Industrial Development Division further seeks to support the trade and industry development goals of member states through its **Combinet** initiative, an electronic network which links businesses and trade-related organisations throughout the Commonwealth.

Contact:
The Export and Industrial Development Division
Commonwealth Secretariat
East Wing, Marlborough House
Pall Mall
London SW1Y 5HX
Telephone: (44) 020 7747 6300
Fax: (44) 020 7747 6307
Web site: http://www.thecommonwealth.org